THE WALLFLOWER

YAMATONADESHIKO SHICHIHENGE

3

Tomoko Hayakawa

TRANSLATED AND ADAPTED BY
David Ury

LETTERED BY
Dana Hayward

DEL
REY

BALLANTINE BOOKS • NEW YORK

The Wallflower 3 is a work of fiction. Names, characters, places, and incidents are the products of the author's imagination or are used fictitiously. Any resemblance to actual events, locales, or persons, living or dead, is entirely coincidental.

2005 Del Rey® Books Trade Paperback Edition

Published in the United States by Del Rey® Books, an imprint of Random House Publishing Group, a division of Random House Inc., New York.

Del Rey is a registered trademark and the Del Rey colophon is a trademark of Random House, Inc.

Originally published in Japan in 2001 by Kodansha Ltd., Tokyo as *Yamatonadeshiko Shichihenge*. This publication—rights arranged through Kodansha Ltd.

Library of Congress Control Number: 2004095918

ISBN 0-345-47999-8

Printed in the United States of America

Del Rey Books Manga website address: www.delreymanga.com

9 8 7 6 5 4 3 2 1

First Edition

Translator and adapter—David Ury

Lettering—Dana Hayward

Cover design—David Stevenson

Contents

A Note from the Author   iv

The Wallflower, Volume 3   2

Bonus Manga   204

About the Creator   206

Honorifics   207

Translation Notes   209

Preview of Volume 4   214

A Note from the Author

THE PRINTER BROKE, SO I DREW THE BEE BY HAND.

HER BELLY AND HER BUTT ARE SO FAT THAT SHE CAN'T EVEN FLY.

♥ Ever since my debut as an artist, people have told me, "your guy characters are too skinny, and their eyes are too small" or "they have weird taste in clothes." (What do you mean?) I was once asked to change them so they'd appeal to a broader audience. I thought about it, but I just couldn't do it. I follow my own path. Wanna come along?

—**Tomoko Hayakawa**

THE wallflower

YAMATONADESHIKO SHICHIHENGE

ヤマトナデシコ七変化♡

CONTENTS

Chapter 10
Blood-Splatteringly Steamy Love at the   5
Hot Springs (Part 2)

Chapter 11
Who's the Real Enemy ... Kyohei or the Test?   45

Chapter 12
The Girl in the Storm   85

Chapter 13
Beautiful Party People   125

Chapter 14
I Am Number One!   163

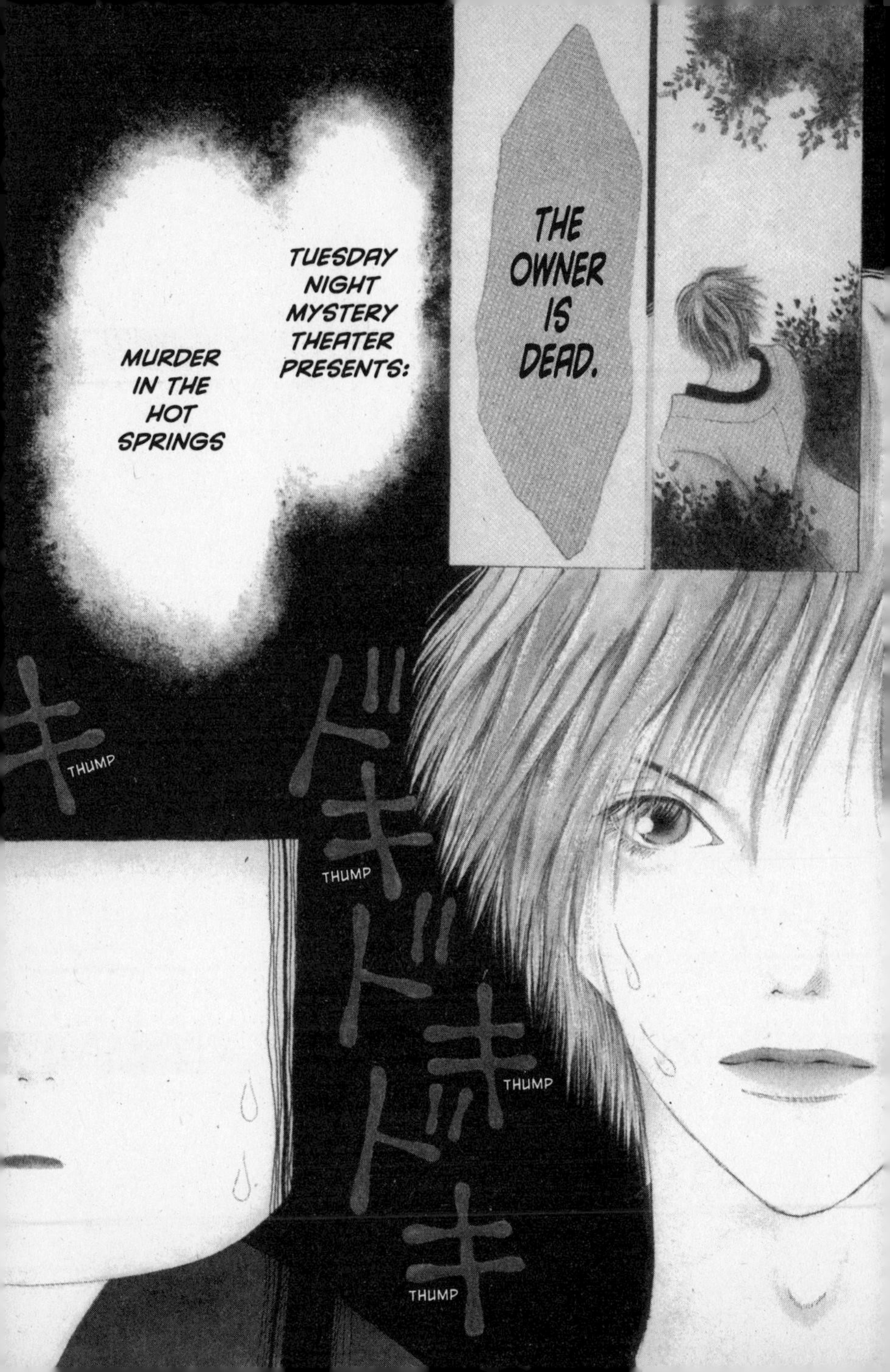

THE OWNER IS DEAD.
TUESDAY NIGHT MYSTERY THEATER PRESENTS:
MURDER IN THE HOT SPRINGS
キ
THUMP
ドキドキドキ
THUMP
THUMP
THUMP

THE wallflower

YAMATONADESHIKO SHICHIHENGE

♥ BOOK 3 ♥

ヤマトナデシコ七変化♡

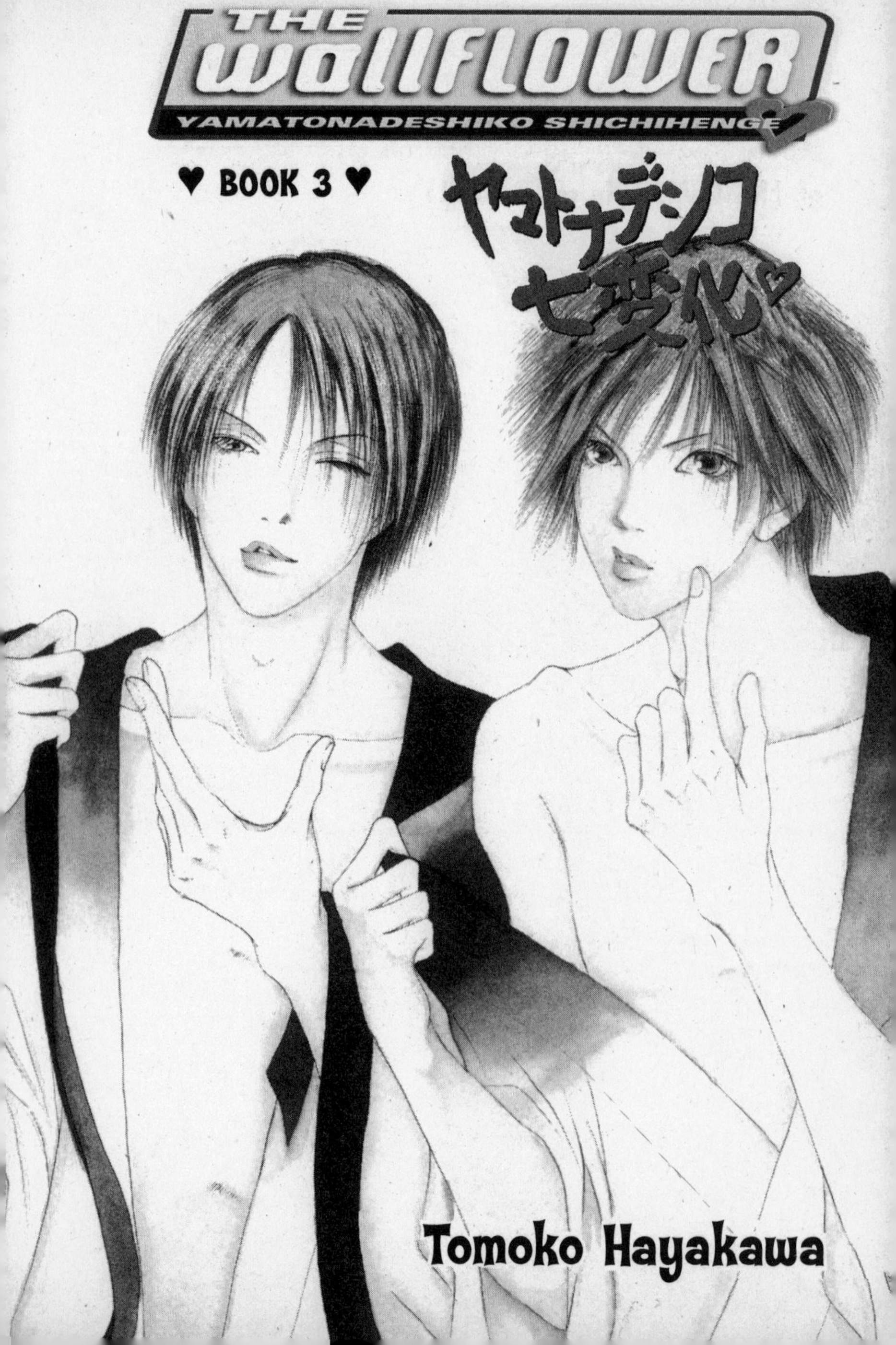

Tomoko Hayakawa

Chapter 10
Blood-Splatteringly Steamy Love at the Hot Springs (Part 2)

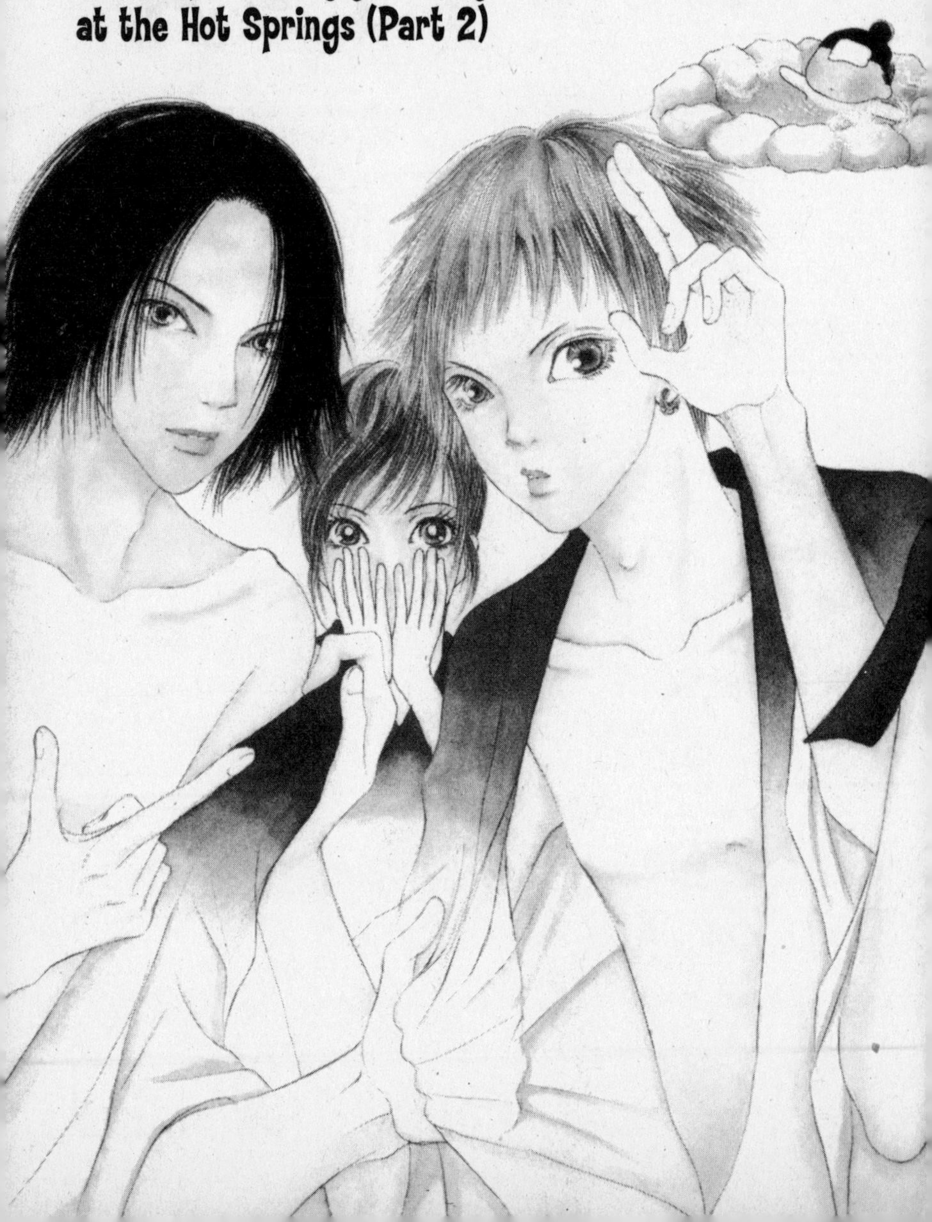

WALLFLOWER'S BEAUTIFUL CAST OF CHARACTERS (?)

SUNAKO IS A DARK LONER WHO LOVES HORROR MOVIES. WHEN HER AUNT, THE LANDLADY OF A BOARDING HOUSE, RUNS OFF WITH HER BOYFRIEND, SUNAKO IS FORCED TO LIVE WITH FOUR HANDSOME GUYS. SUNAKO'S AUNT MAKES A DEAL WITH THE BOYS, WHICH CAUSES NOTHING BUT TROUBLE FOR SUNAKO. "MAKE SUNAKO INTO A LADY, AND YOUR RENT WILL BE FREE." THE GUYS FORCE SUNAKO TO TAKE A TRIP TO A HOT SPRINGS RESORT, ALONG WITH TAKENAGA'S HOT LOVE INTEREST, NOI-CHAN. THERE, THEY STUMBLE ACROSS A MURDER. WHAT WILL HAPPEN TO SUNAKO AND THE GANG?

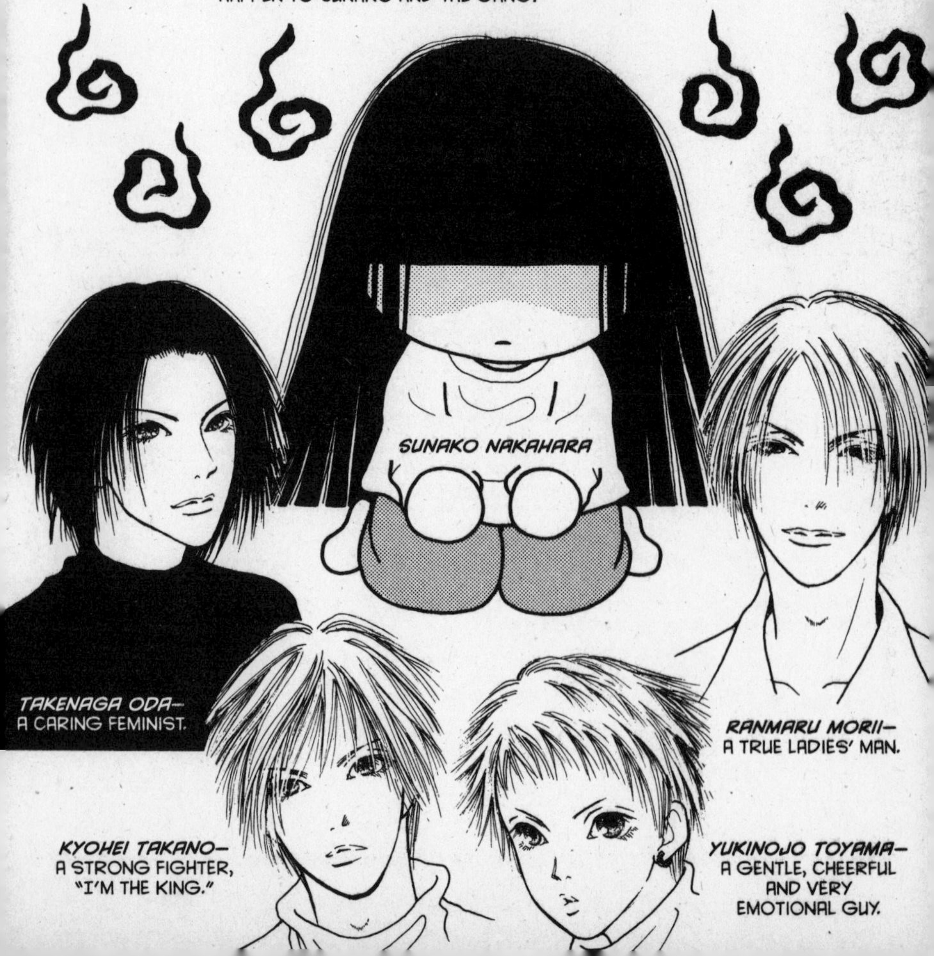
SUNAKO NAKAHARA
TAKENAGA ODA— A CARING FEMINIST.
RANMARU MORII— A TRUE LADIES' MAN.
KYOHEI TAKANO— A STRONG FIGHTER, "I'M THE KING."
YUKINOJO TOYAMA— A GENTLE, CHEERFUL AND VERY EMOTIONAL GUY.

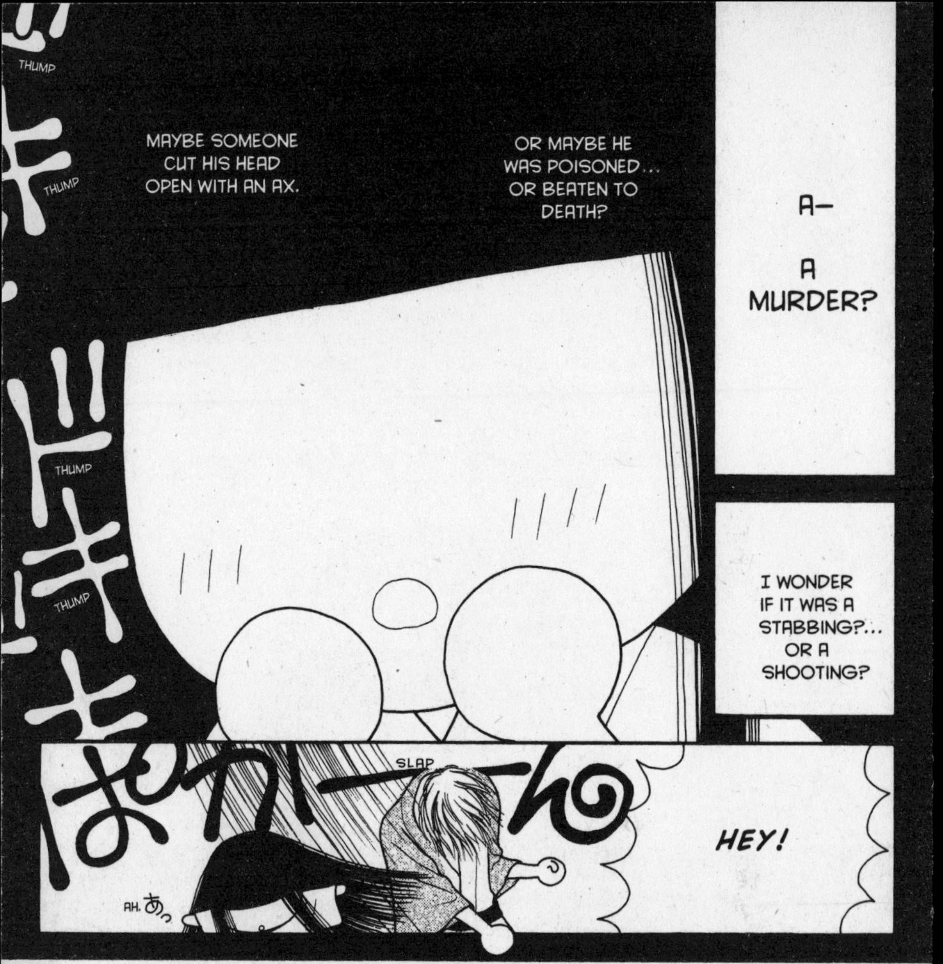
A—
A MURDER?
I WONDER IF IT WAS A STABBING?... OR A SHOOTING?
OR MAYBE HE WAS POISONED... OR BEATEN TO DEATH?
MAYBE SOMEONE CUT HIS HEAD OPEN WITH AN AX.
THUMP
THUMP
THUMP
THUMP
HEY!
SLAP
AH. あっ

BEHIND THE SCENES

THE STORYBOARDS FOR "BLOOD-SPLATTERINGLY STEAMY LOVE AT THE HOT SPRINGS" WERE REALLY TOUGH TO DRAW. I KEPT CHANGING THE STORY.

FIRST, RANMARU WAS BEING CHASED BY THE DETECTIVE, AND THE GUYS WERE TRYING TO PROTECT HIM... AND THEN... THE GUYS WERE ALL SEARCHING FOR THE REAL KILLER... AND THEN... THERE WAS RANMARU'S LOVE STORY TOO. ANYWAY, THIS IS WHAT I ENDED UP WITH. SIGH.

THANK GOODNESS. IT REALLY BROUGHT OUT MY LOVE FOR SUSPENSE THRILLERS. OH, GOD. WELL, AT LEAST I GOT TO DRAW "TAKENAGA" AND "NOI-CHAN" ENJOYING THEIR NANOSECOND-LONG KISS. THAT WAS ENOUGH TO SATISFY ME.

RYU IS SO COOL. THANK YOU, YOU GENIUS. ← HE'S MY ASSISTANT.

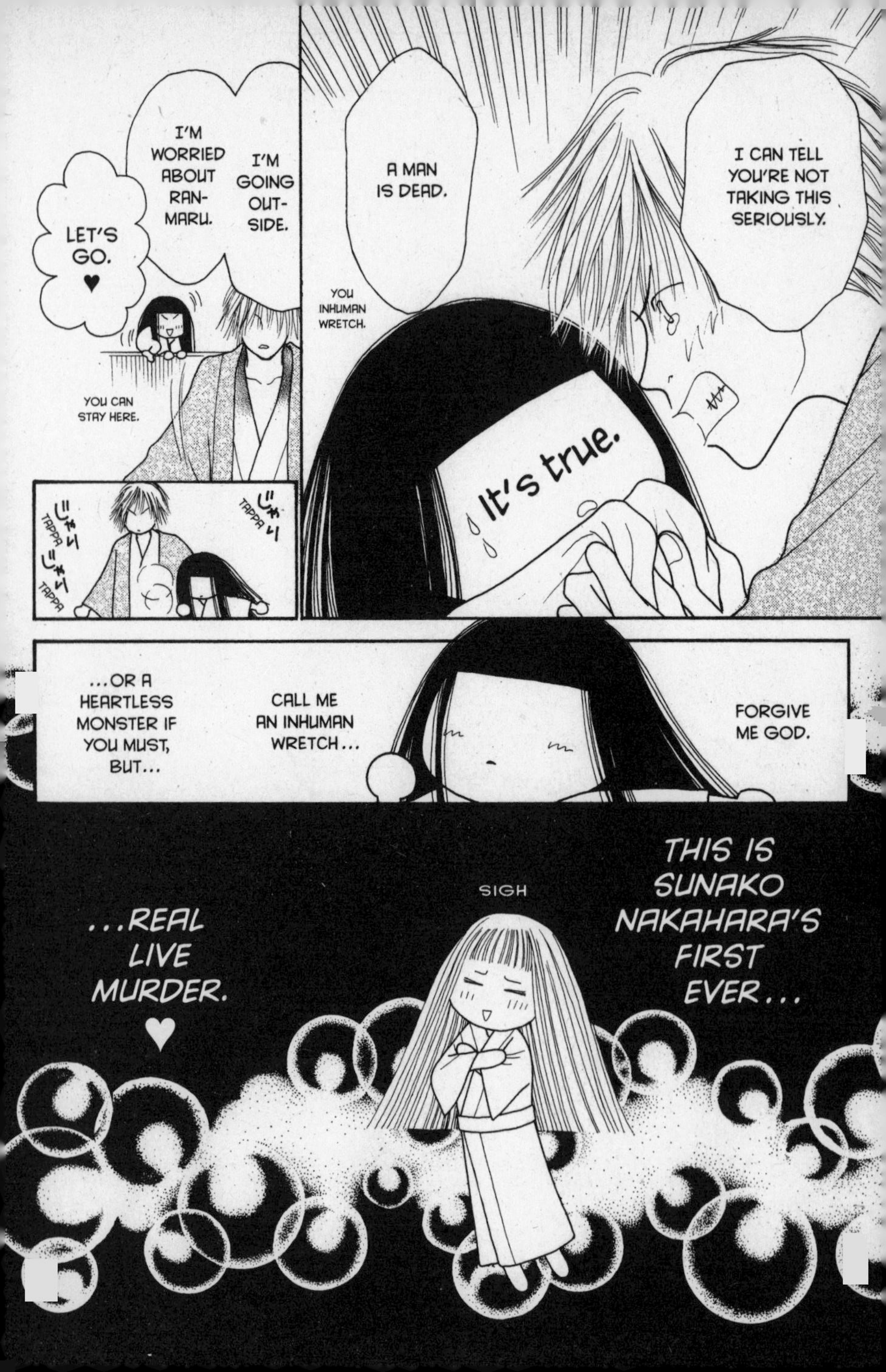
I CAN TELL YOU'RE NOT TAKING THIS SERIOUSLY.
A MAN IS DEAD.
YOU INHUMAN WRETCH.
It's true.
I'M WORRIED ABOUT RAN-MARU. I'M GOING OUT-SIDE.
LET'S GO. ♥
YOU CAN STAY HERE.
じゃり TAPPA
じゃり TAPPA
じゃり TAPPA
FORGIVE ME GOD.
CALL ME AN INHUMAN WRETCH...
...OR A HEARTLESS MONSTER IF YOU MUST, BUT...
THIS IS SUNAKO NAKAHARA'S FIRST EVER...
SIGH
...REAL LIVE MURDER. ♥

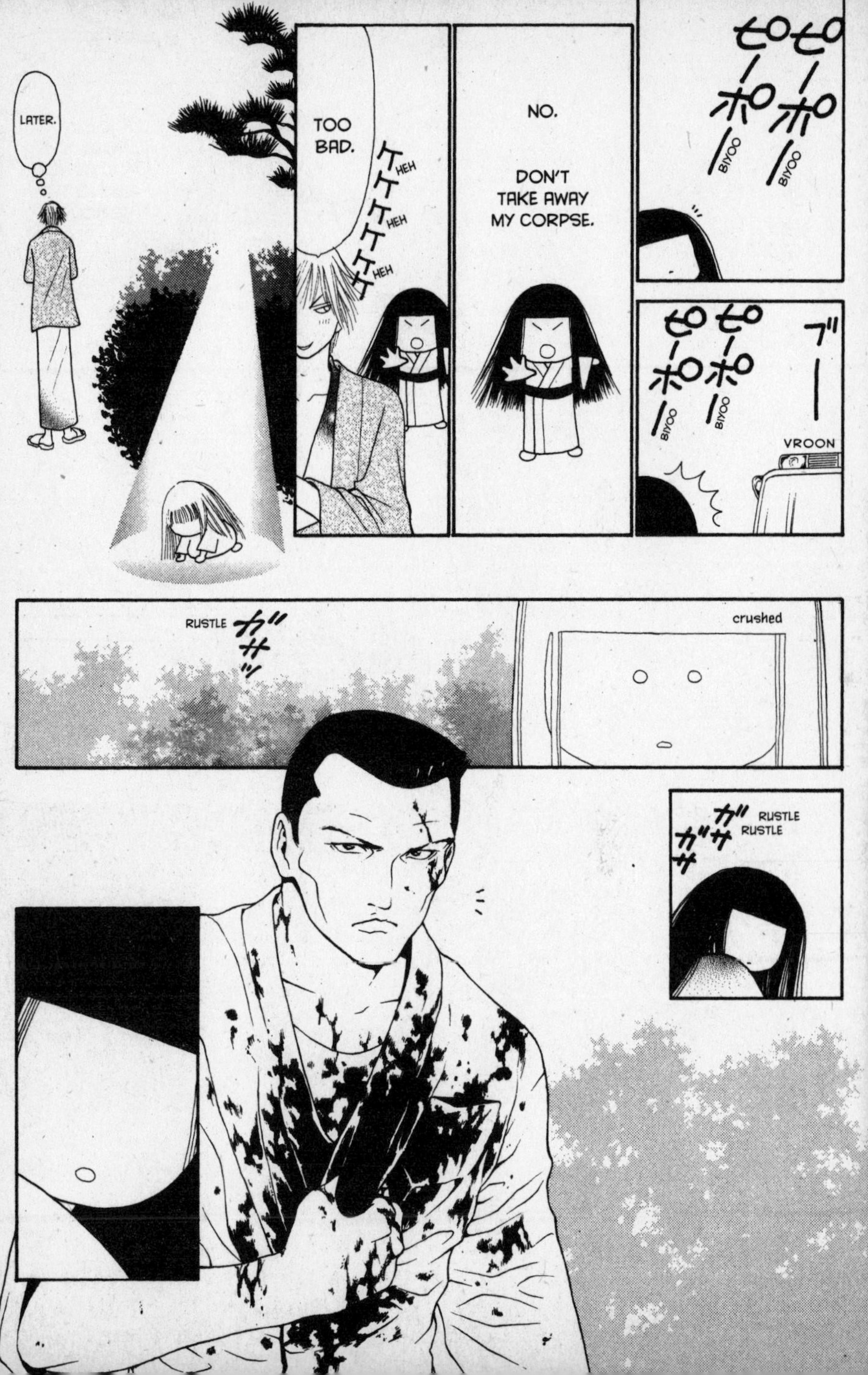
ピーポー ピーポー
BIYOO BIYOO
ブー
VROON
ピーポー ピーポー
BIYOO BIYOO
NO.
DON'T TAKE AWAY MY CORPSE.
TOO BAD.
ケケケケケ
HEH HEH HEH
LATER.
crushed
RUSTLE
ガサッ
RUSTLE RUSTLE
ガサ ガサ

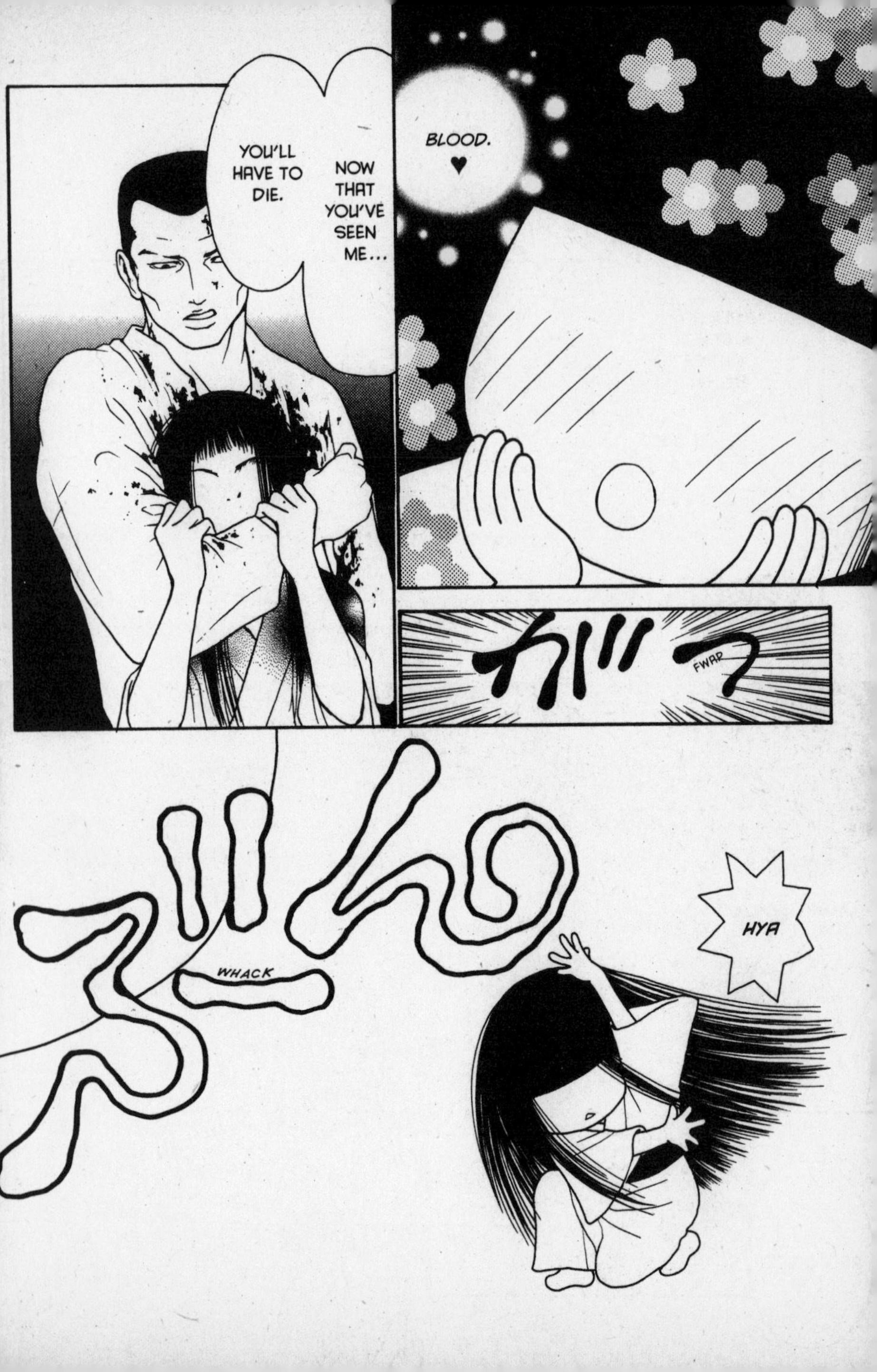
BLOOD. ♥
ガッ
FWAR
NOW THAT YOU'VE SEEN ME...
YOU'LL HAVE TO DIE.
WHACK
HYA

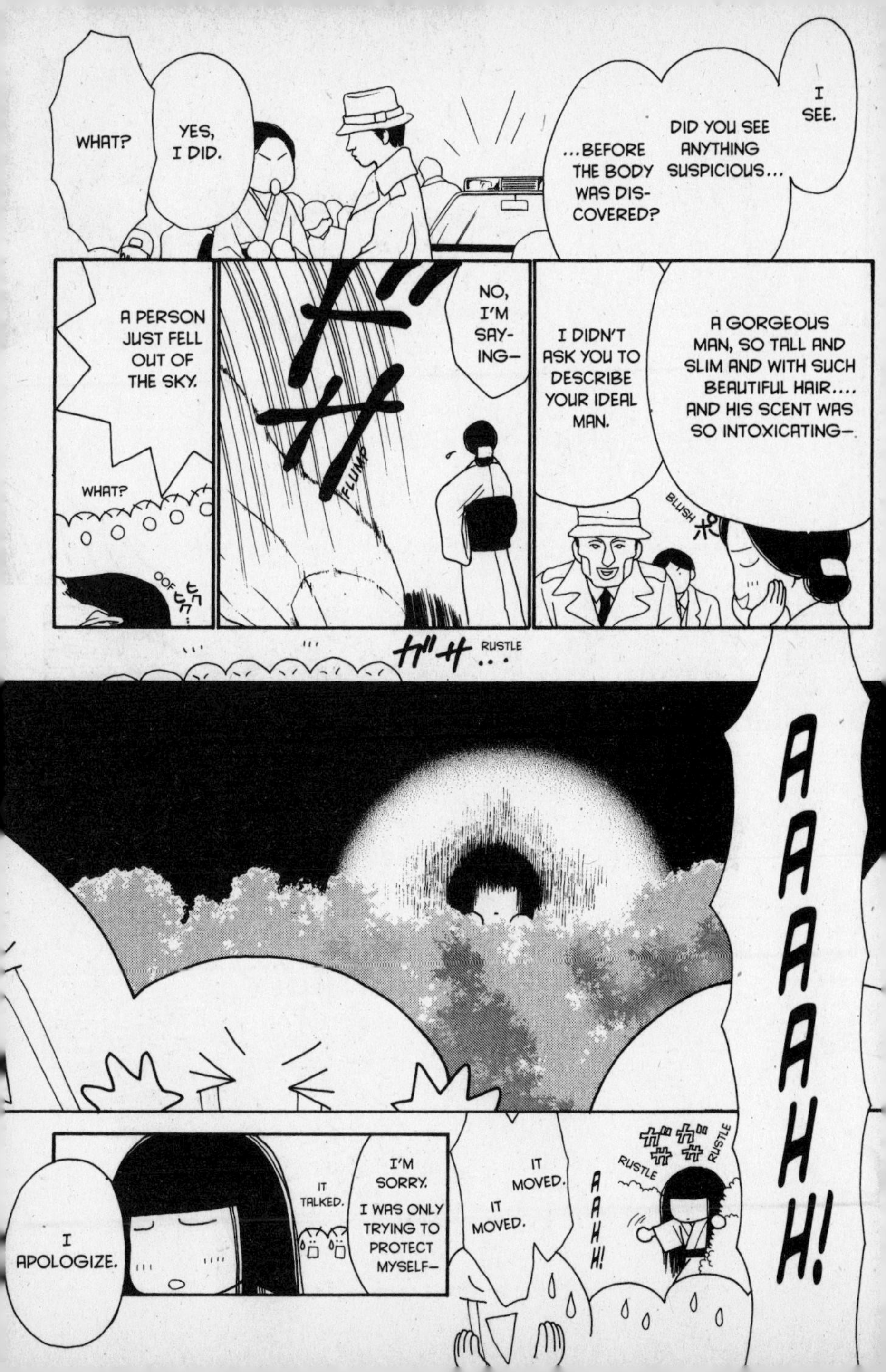
I SEE.
DID YOU SEE ANYTHING SUSPICIOUS...
...BEFORE THE BODY WAS DIS-COVERED?
YES, I DID.
WHAT?
A GORGEOUS MAN, SO TALL AND SLIM AND WITH SUCH BEAUTIFUL HAIR.... AND HIS SCENT WAS SO INTOXICATING—.
BLUSH
I DIDN'T ASK YOU TO DESCRIBE YOUR IDEAL MAN.
NO, I'M SAY-ING—
FLUMP
A PERSON JUST FELL OUT OF THE SKY.
WHAT?
OOF
RUSTLE...
AAAAAH!
RUSTLE
RUSTLE
AAHH!
IT MOVED.
IT MOVED.
I'M SORRY. I WAS ONLY TRYING TO PROTECT MYSELF—
IT TALKED.
I APOLOGIZE.

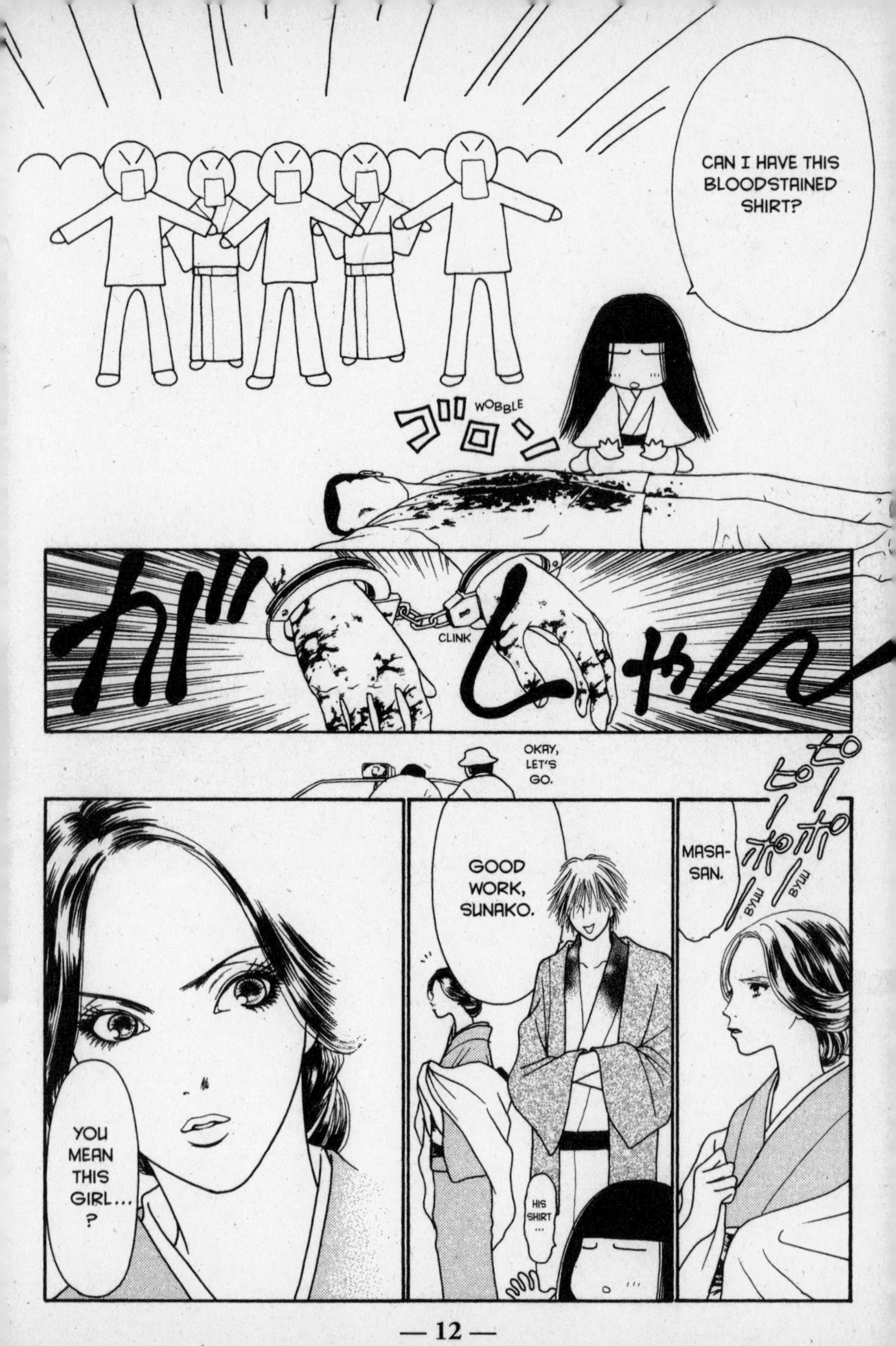
CAN I HAVE THIS BLOODSTAINED SHIRT?
WOBBLE
CLINK
OKAY, LET'S GO.
MASA-SAN.
BYUU
BYUU
GOOD WORK, SUNAKO.
HIS SHIRT ...
YOU MEAN THIS GIRL... ?

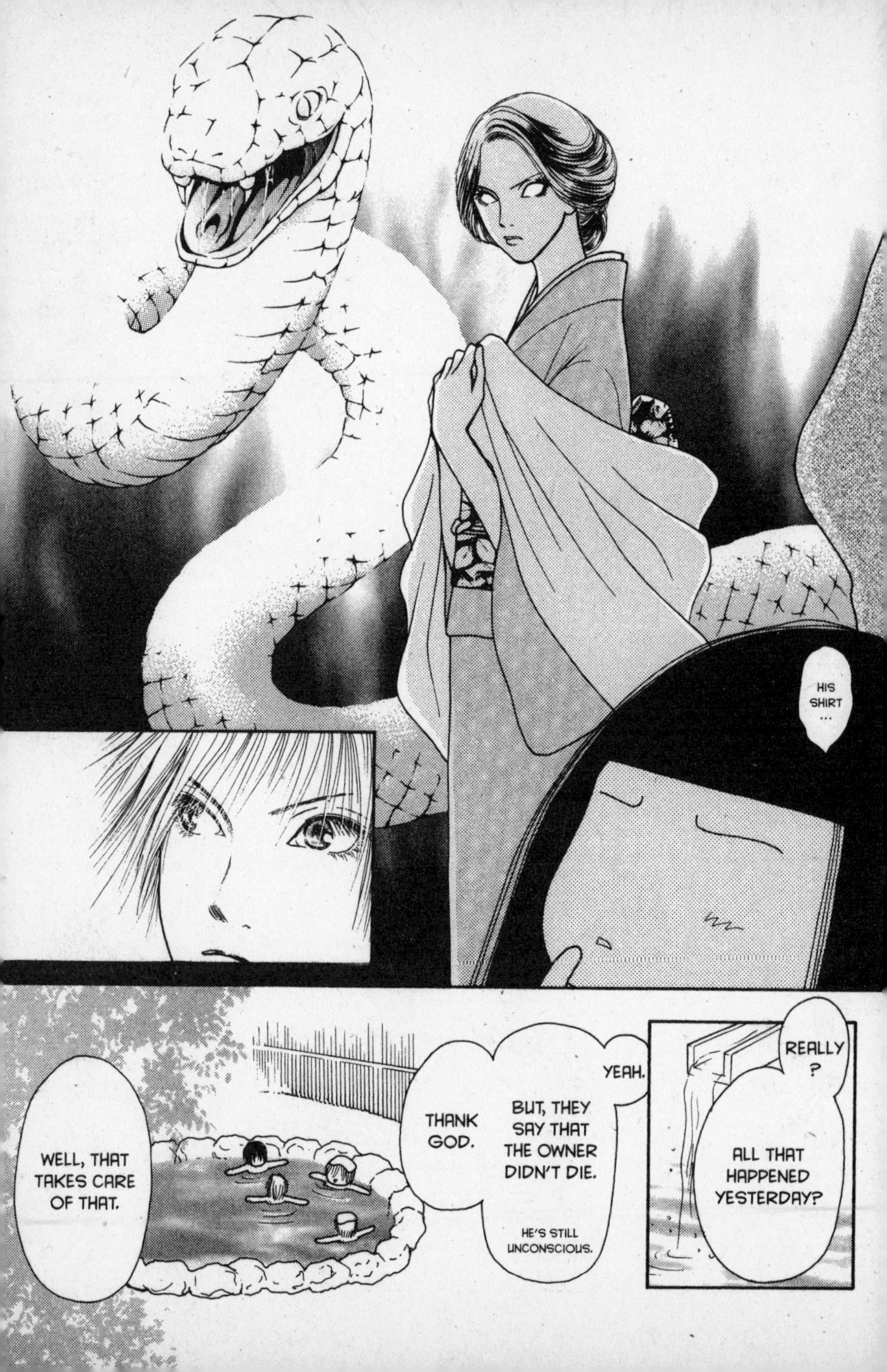
HIS SHIRT ...
REALLY?
ALL THAT HAPPENED YESTERDAY?
YEAH.
BUT, THEY SAY THAT THE OWNER DIDN'T DIE.
HE'S STILL UNCONSCIOUS.
THANK GOD.
WELL, THAT TAKES CARE OF THAT.

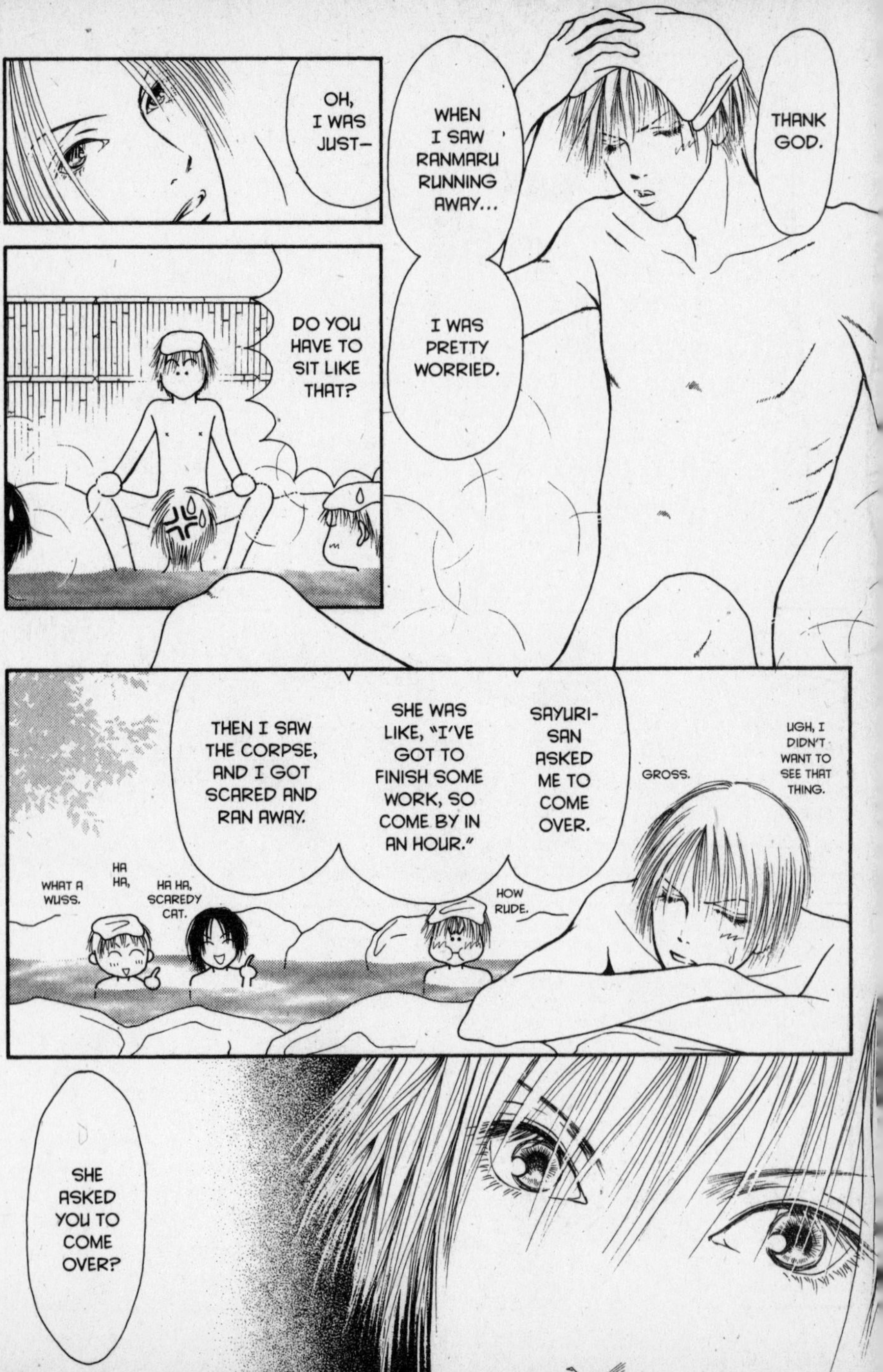

THANK GOD.
WHEN I SAW RANMARU RUNNING AWAY...
I WAS PRETTY WORRIED.
OH, I WAS JUST—
DO YOU HAVE TO SIT LIKE THAT?
UGH, I DIDN'T WANT TO SEE THAT THING.
GROSS.
SAYURI-SAN ASKED ME TO COME OVER.
SHE WAS LIKE, "I'VE GOT TO FINISH SOME WORK, SO COME BY IN AN HOUR."
THEN I SAW THE CORPSE, AND I GOT SCARED AND RAN AWAY.
HOW RUDE.
HA HA, SCAREDY CAT.
HA HA,
WHAT A WUSS.
SHE ASKED YOU TO COME OVER?

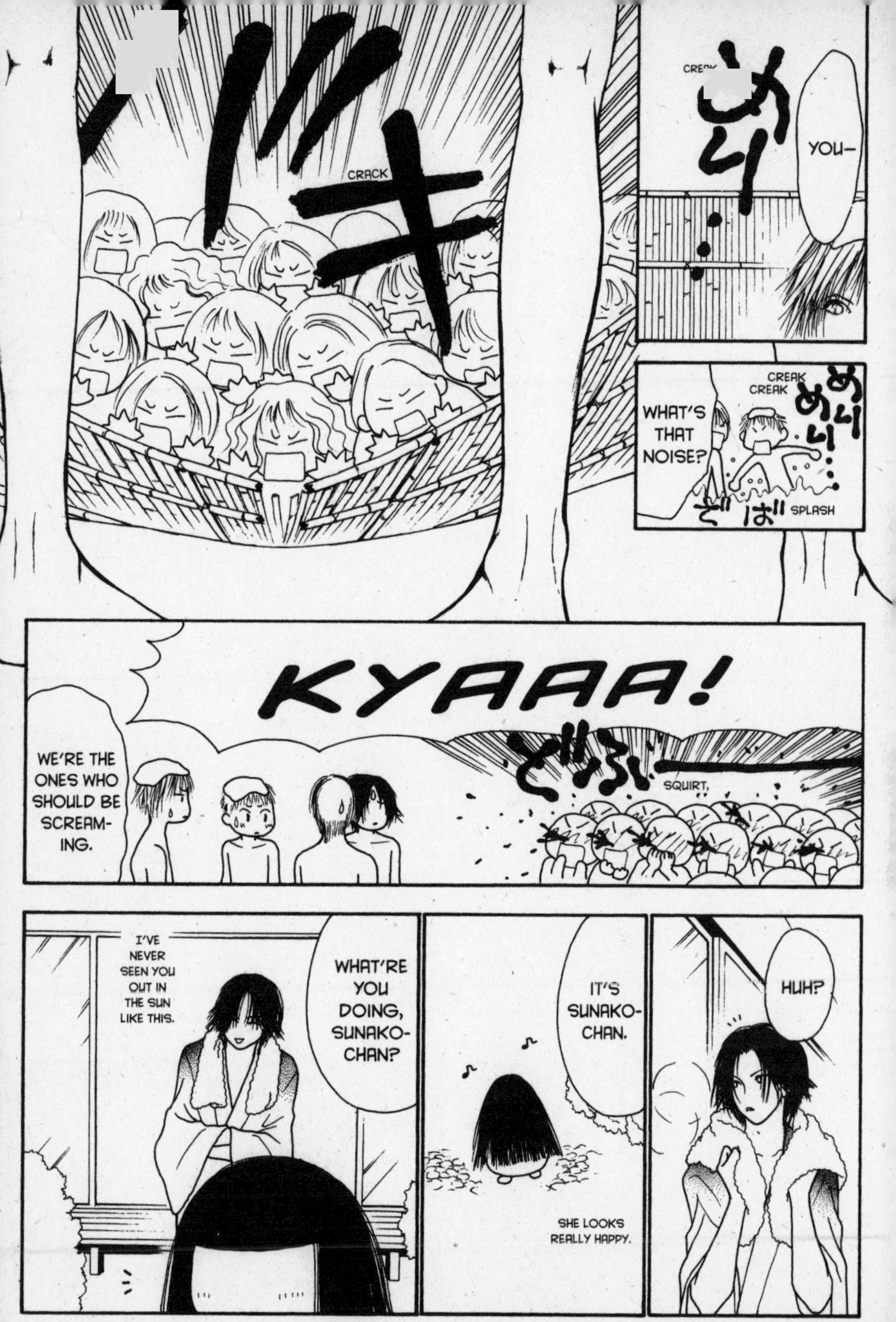

YOU—
WHAT'S THAT NOISE?
CREAK CREAK
めりめり
ざば
SPLASH
CRACK
KYAAA!
SQUIRT,
WE'RE THE ONES WHO SHOULD BE SCREAM-ING.
HUH?
IT'S SUNAKO-CHAN.
SHE LOOKS REALLY HAPPY.
WHAT'RE YOU DOING, SUNAKO-CHAN?
I'VE NEVER SEEN YOU OUT IN THE SUN LIKE THIS.

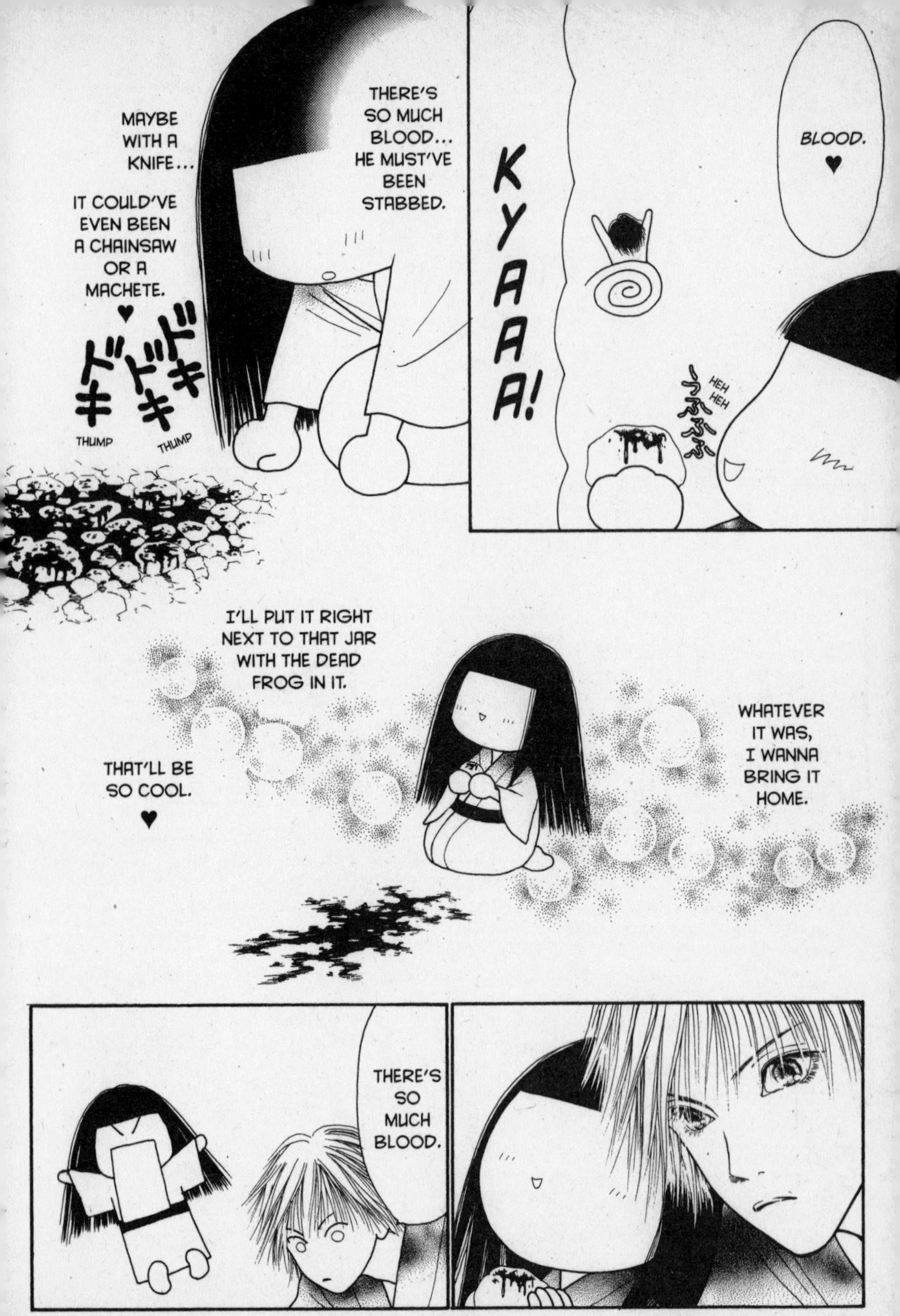
BLOOD. ♥
KYAAA!
うふふ
HEH HEH
THERE'S SO MUCH BLOOD... HE MUST'VE BEEN STABBED.
MAYBE WITH A KNIFE...
IT COULD'VE EVEN BEEN A CHAINSAW OR A MACHETE. ♥
ドキドキ
THUMP THUMP
WHATEVER IT WAS, I WANNA BRING IT HOME.
I'LL PUT IT RIGHT NEXT TO THAT JAR WITH THE DEAD FROG IN IT.
THAT'LL BE SO COOL. ♥
THERE'S SO MUCH BLOOD.

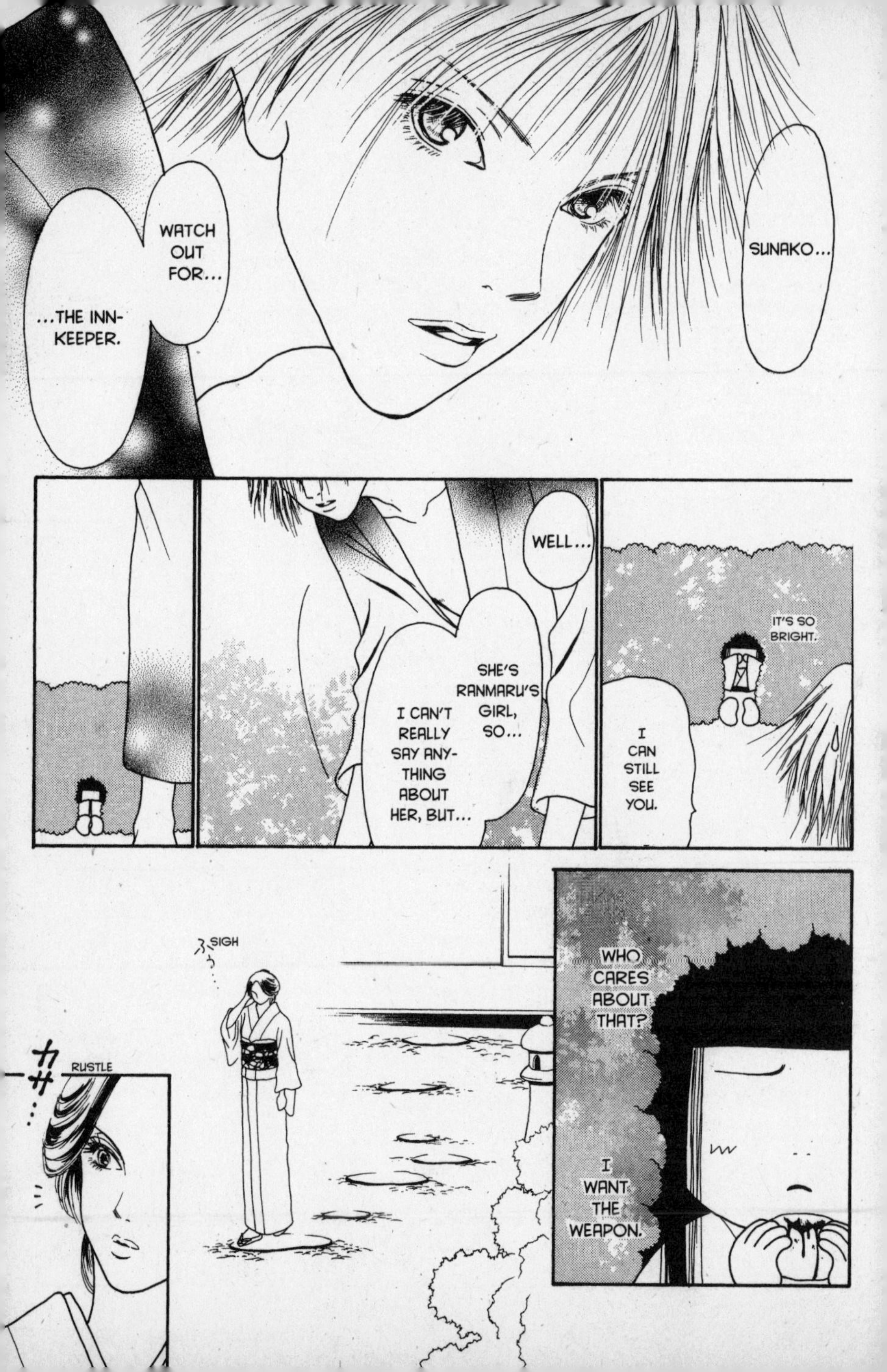
SUNAKO...
WATCH OUT FOR...
...THE INN-KEEPER.
IT'S SO BRIGHT.
I CAN STILL SEE YOU.
WELL...
SHE'S RANMARU'S GIRL, SO...
I CAN'T REALLY SAY ANY-THING ABOUT HER, BUT...
WHO CARES ABOUT THAT?
I WANT THE WEAPON.
SIGH
RUSTLE

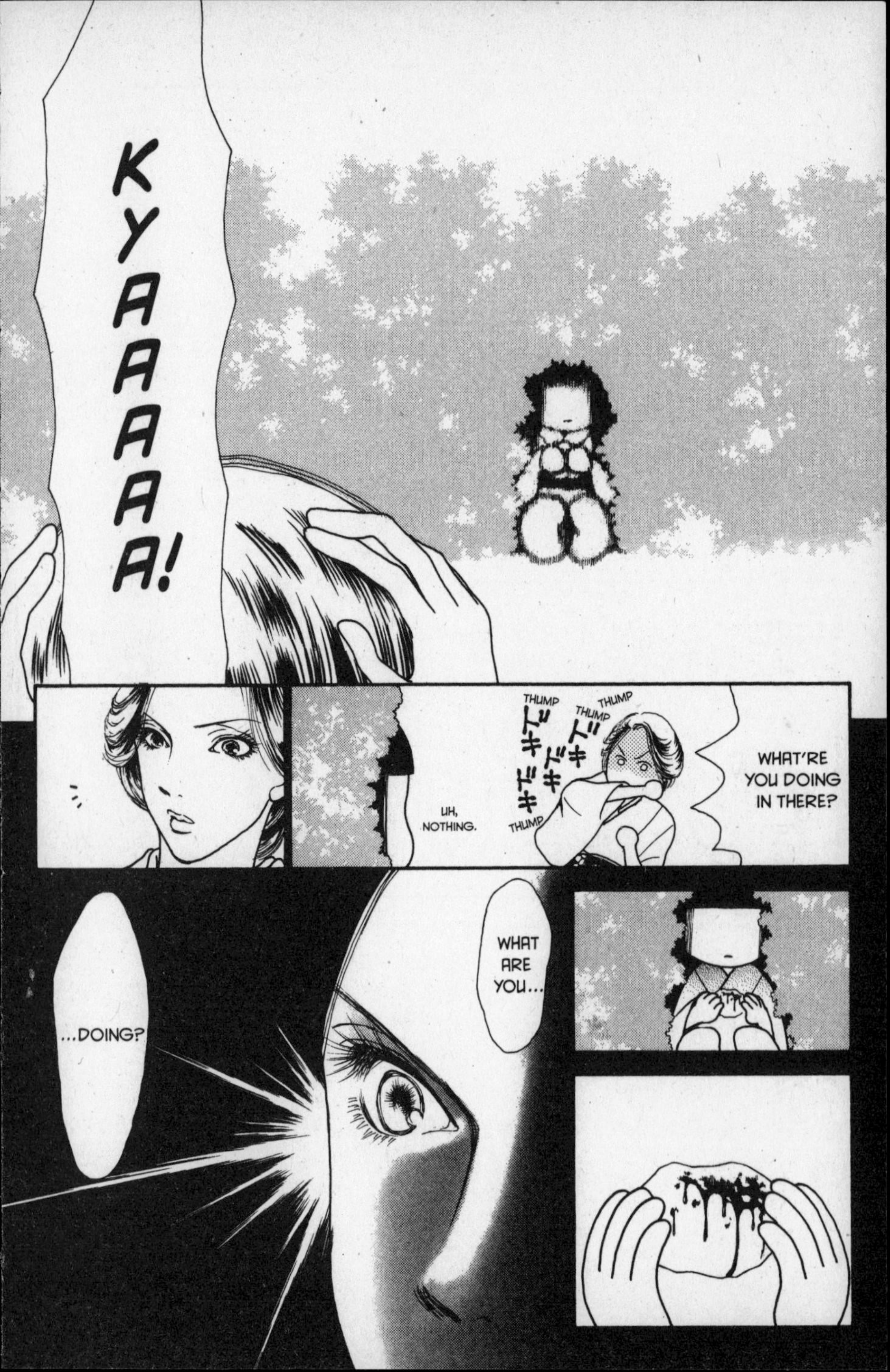
KYAAAAAA!
WHAT'RE YOU DOING IN THERE?
THUMP
THUMP
THUMP
THUMP
UH, NOTHING.
WHAT ARE YOU...
...DOING?

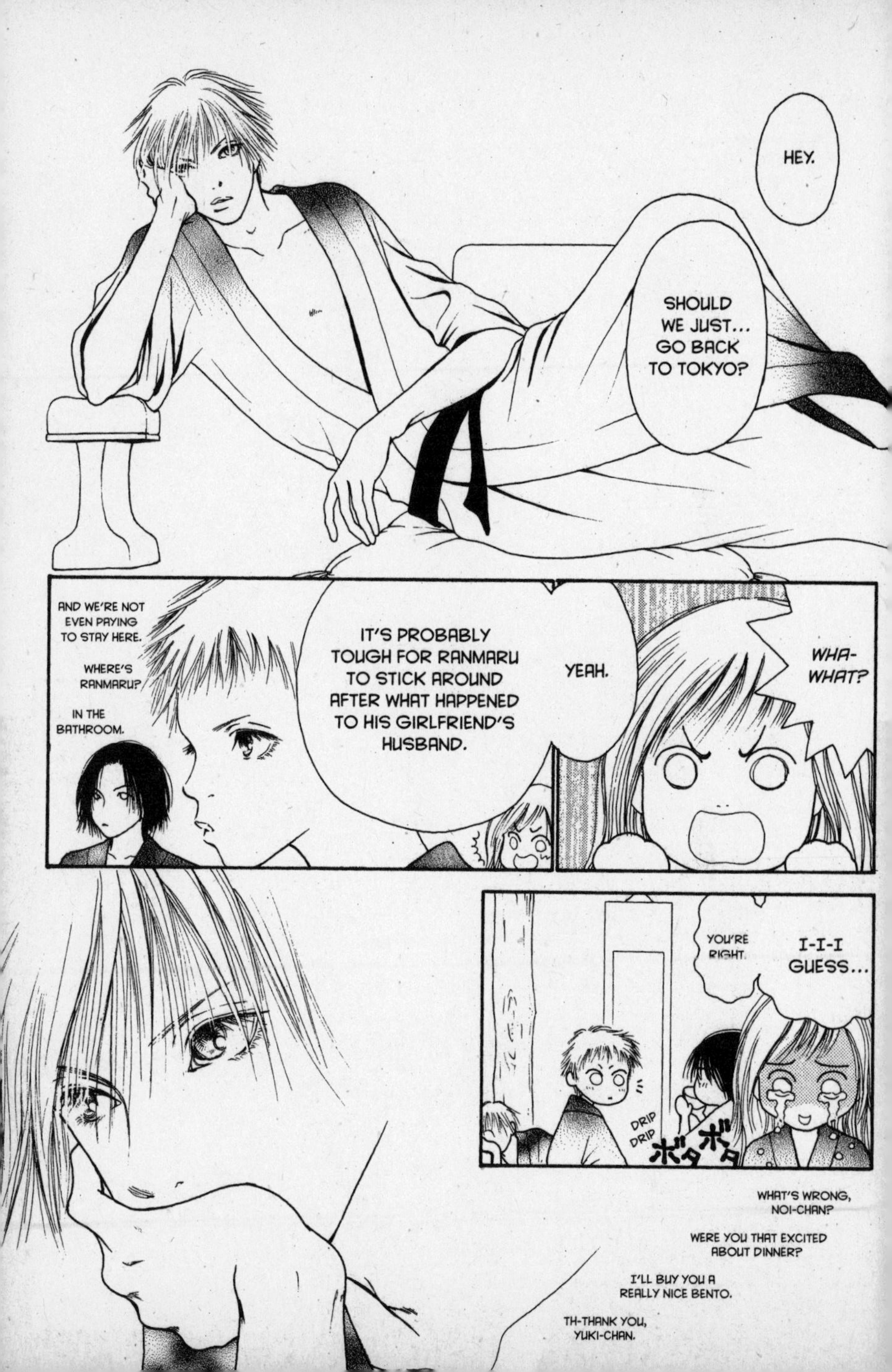
HEY.
SHOULD WE JUST... GO BACK TO TOKYO?
WHA- WHAT?
IT'S PROBABLY TOUGH FOR RANMARU TO STICK AROUND AFTER WHAT HAPPENED TO HIS GIRLFRIEND'S HUSBAND.
YEAH.
AND WE'RE NOT EVEN PAYING TO STAY HERE.
WHERE'S RANMARU?
IN THE BATHROOM.
I-I-I GUESS...
YOU'RE RIGHT.
DRIP DRIP
ボタボタ
WHAT'S WRONG, NOI-CHAN?
WERE YOU THAT EXCITED ABOUT DINNER?
I'LL BUY YOU A REALLY NICE BENTO.
TH-THANK YOU, YUKI-CHAN.

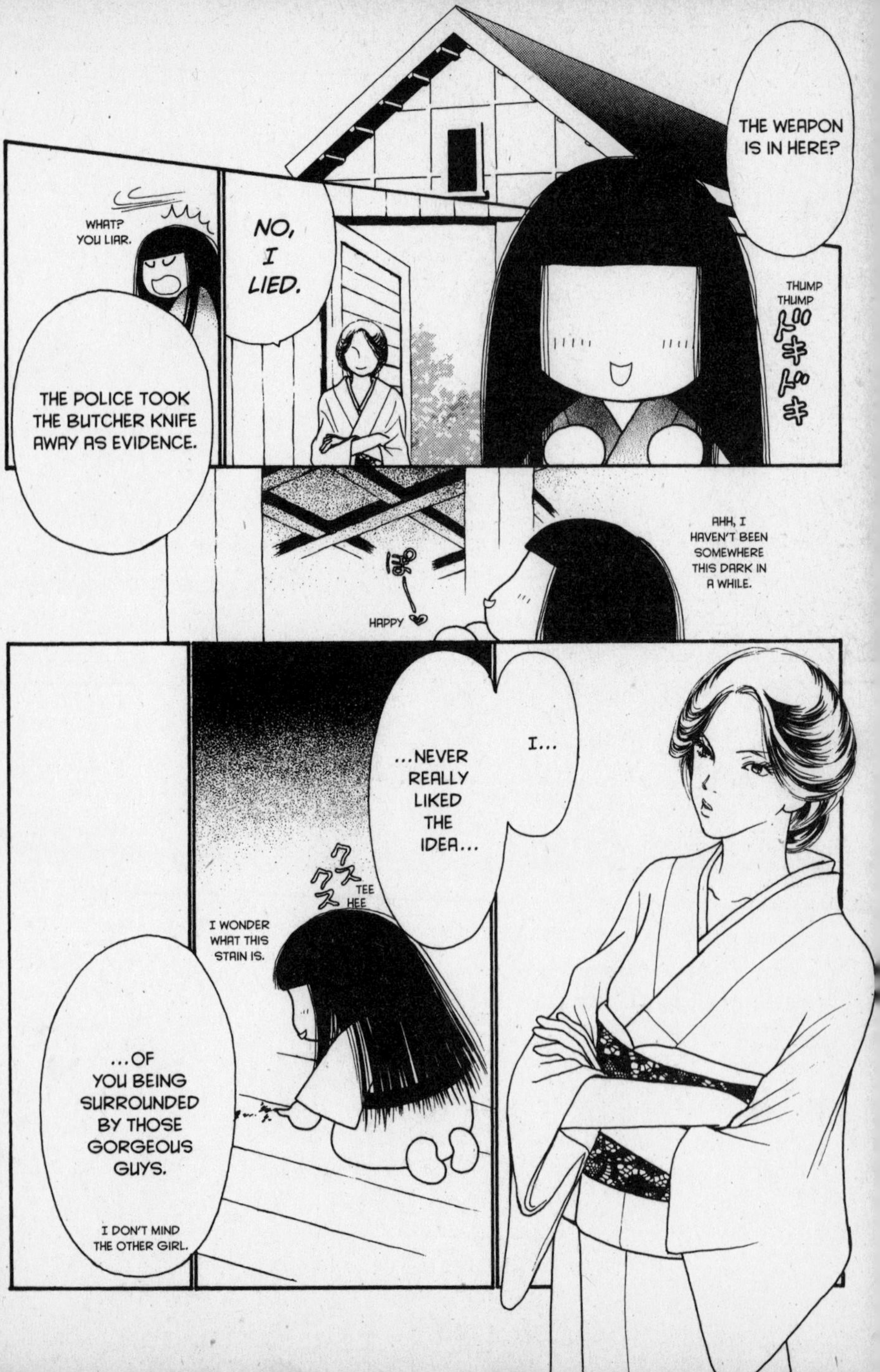
THE WEAPON IS IN HERE?
THUMP THUMP
ドキドキ
NO, I LIED.
WHAT? YOU LIAR.
THE POLICE TOOK THE BUTCHER KNIFE AWAY AS EVIDENCE.
AHH, I HAVEN'T BEEN SOMEWHERE THIS DARK IN A WHILE.
ぽ
HAPPY
I...
...NEVER REALLY LIKED THE IDEA...
クスクス
TEE HEE
I WONDER WHAT THIS STAIN IS.
...OF YOU BEING SURROUNDED BY THOSE GORGEOUS GUYS.
I DON'T MIND THE OTHER GIRL.

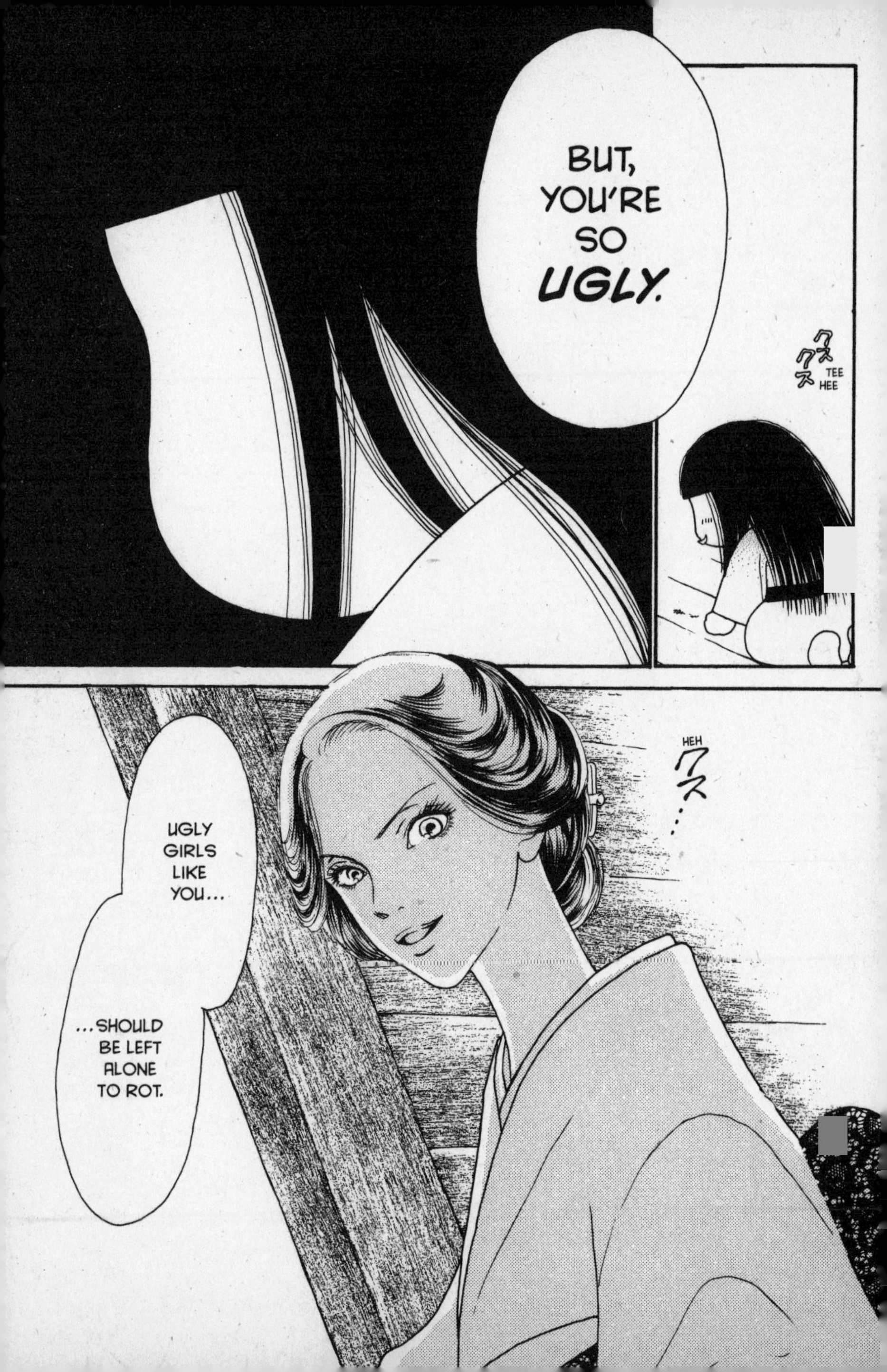
クスクス TEE HEE
BUT, YOU'RE SO UGLY.
HEH クス...
UGLY GIRLS LIKE YOU...
...SHOULD BE LEFT ALONE TO ROT.

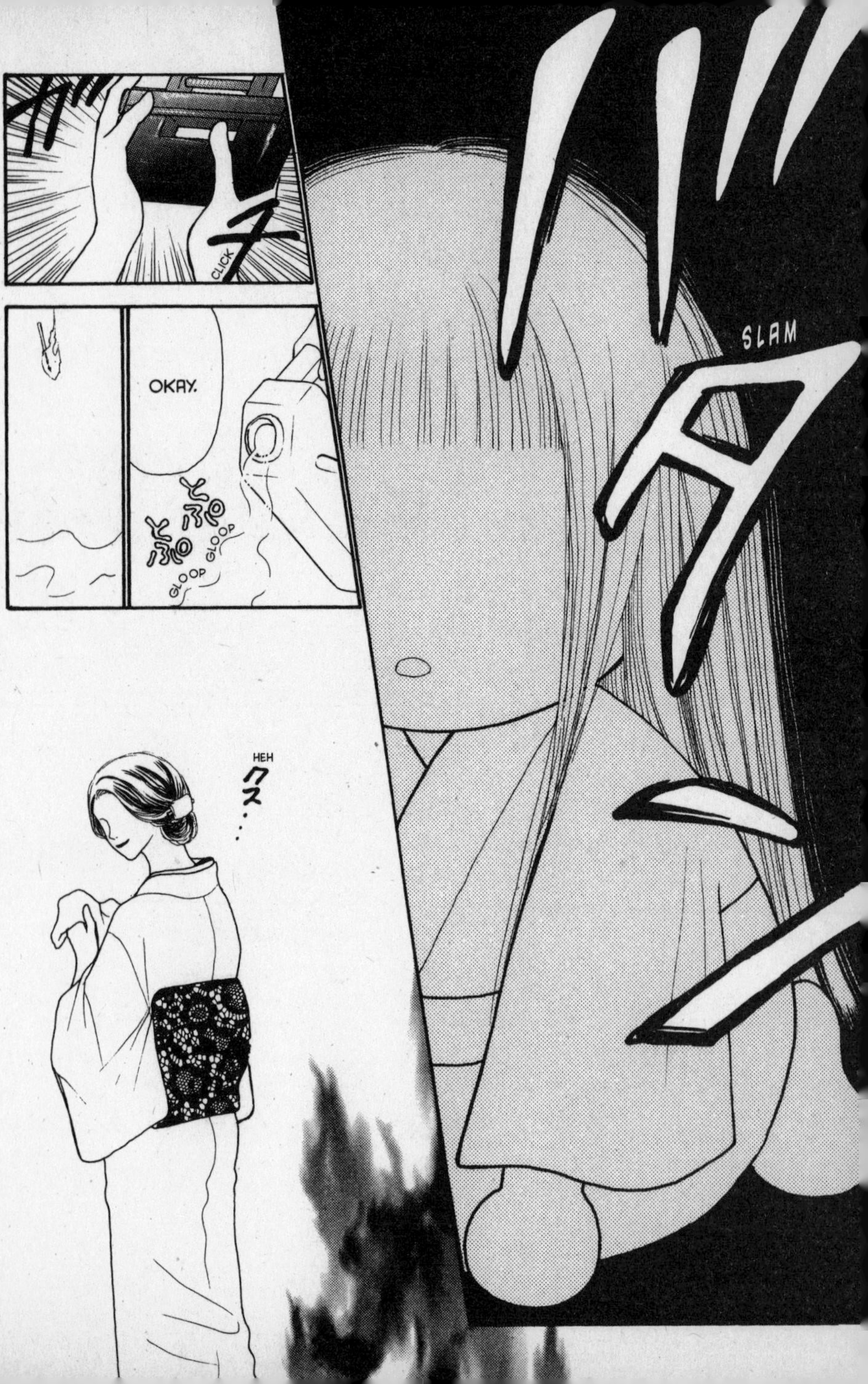
SLAM
CLICK
OKAY.
とぷ とぷ
GLOOP GLOOP
HEH
クス…

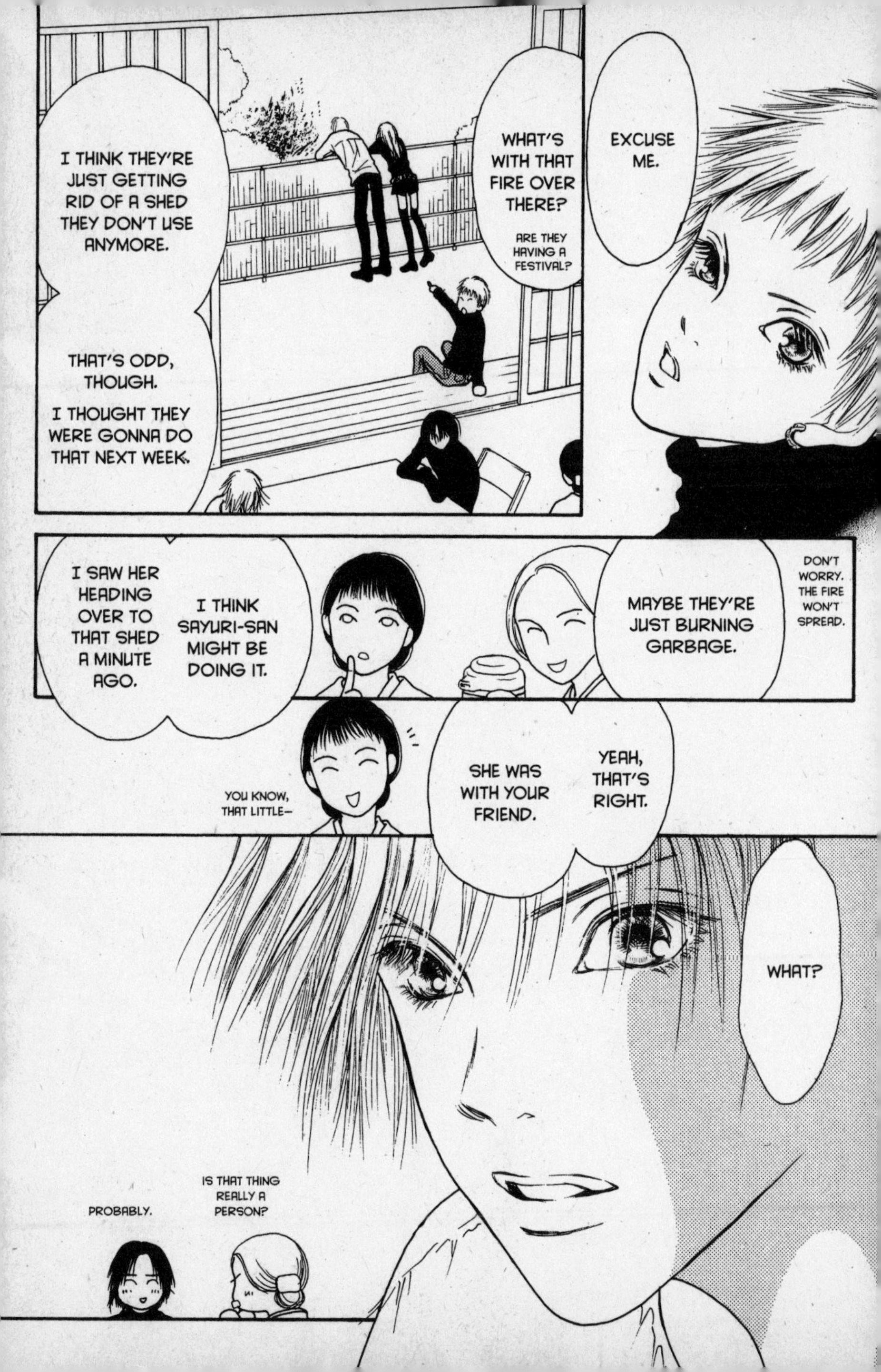
EXCUSE ME.
WHAT'S WITH THAT FIRE OVER THERE?
ARE THEY HAVING A FESTIVAL?
I THINK THEY'RE JUST GETTING RID OF A SHED THEY DON'T USE ANYMORE.
THAT'S ODD, THOUGH.
I THOUGHT THEY WERE GONNA DO THAT NEXT WEEK.
DON'T WORRY. THE FIRE WON'T SPREAD.
MAYBE THEY'RE JUST BURNING GARBAGE.
I THINK SAYURI-SAN MIGHT BE DOING IT.
I SAW HER HEADING OVER TO THAT SHED A MINUTE AGO.
YEAH, THAT'S RIGHT.
SHE WAS WITH YOUR FRIEND.
YOU KNOW, THAT LITTLE—
WHAT?
IS THAT THING REALLY A PERSON?
PROBABLY.

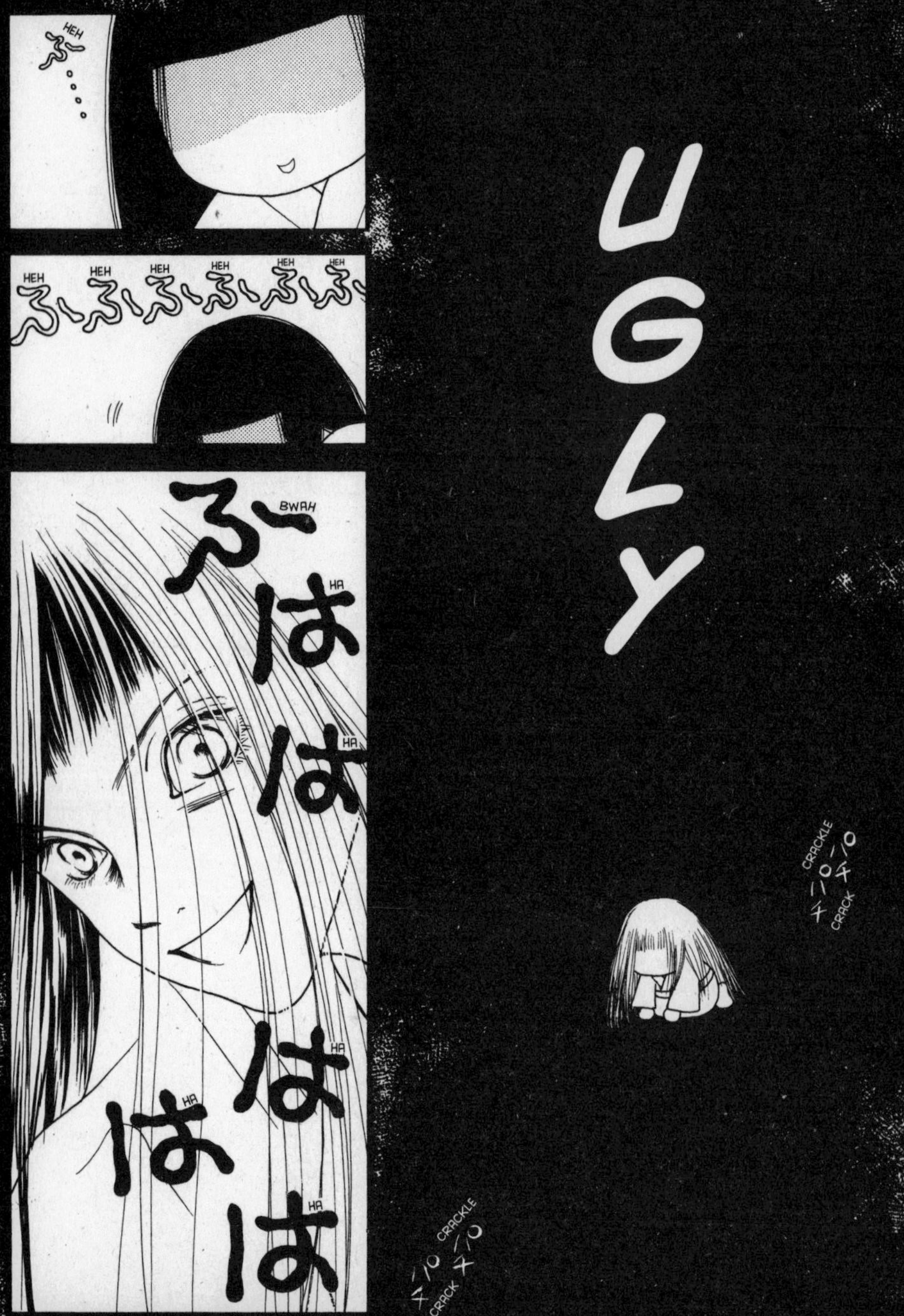
UGLY
CRACKLE CRACK
HEH
ふ……
HEH HEH HEH HEH HEH HEH
ふふふふふふ
BWAH HA HA HA HA
ふははは
CRACKLE CRACK

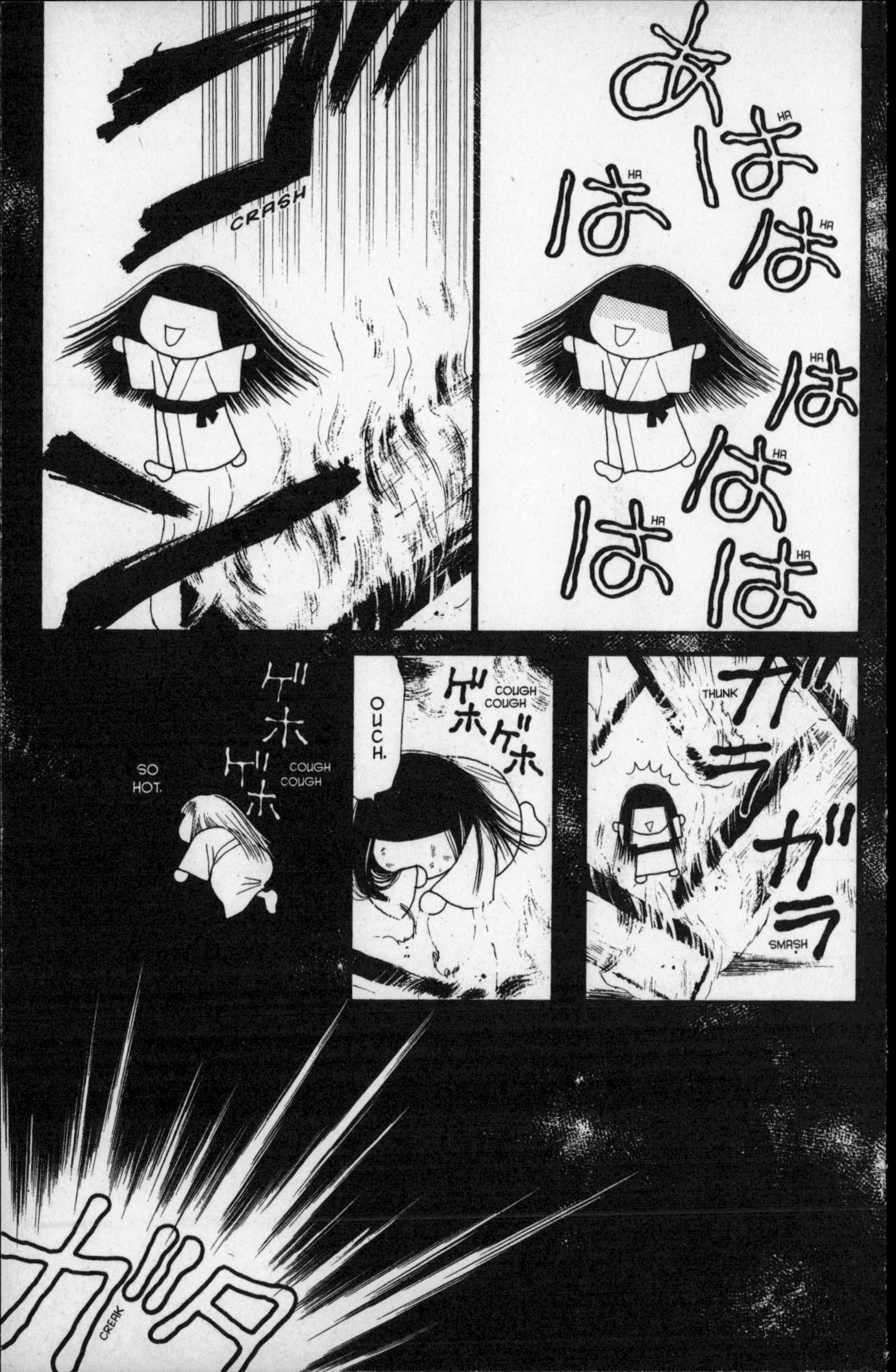

あははははははは
HA HA HA HA HA HA HA
CRASH
THUNK
ガラガラ
SMASH
ゲホゲホ
COUGH COUGH
OUCH.
ゲホゲホ
COUGH COUGH
SO HOT.
CREAK

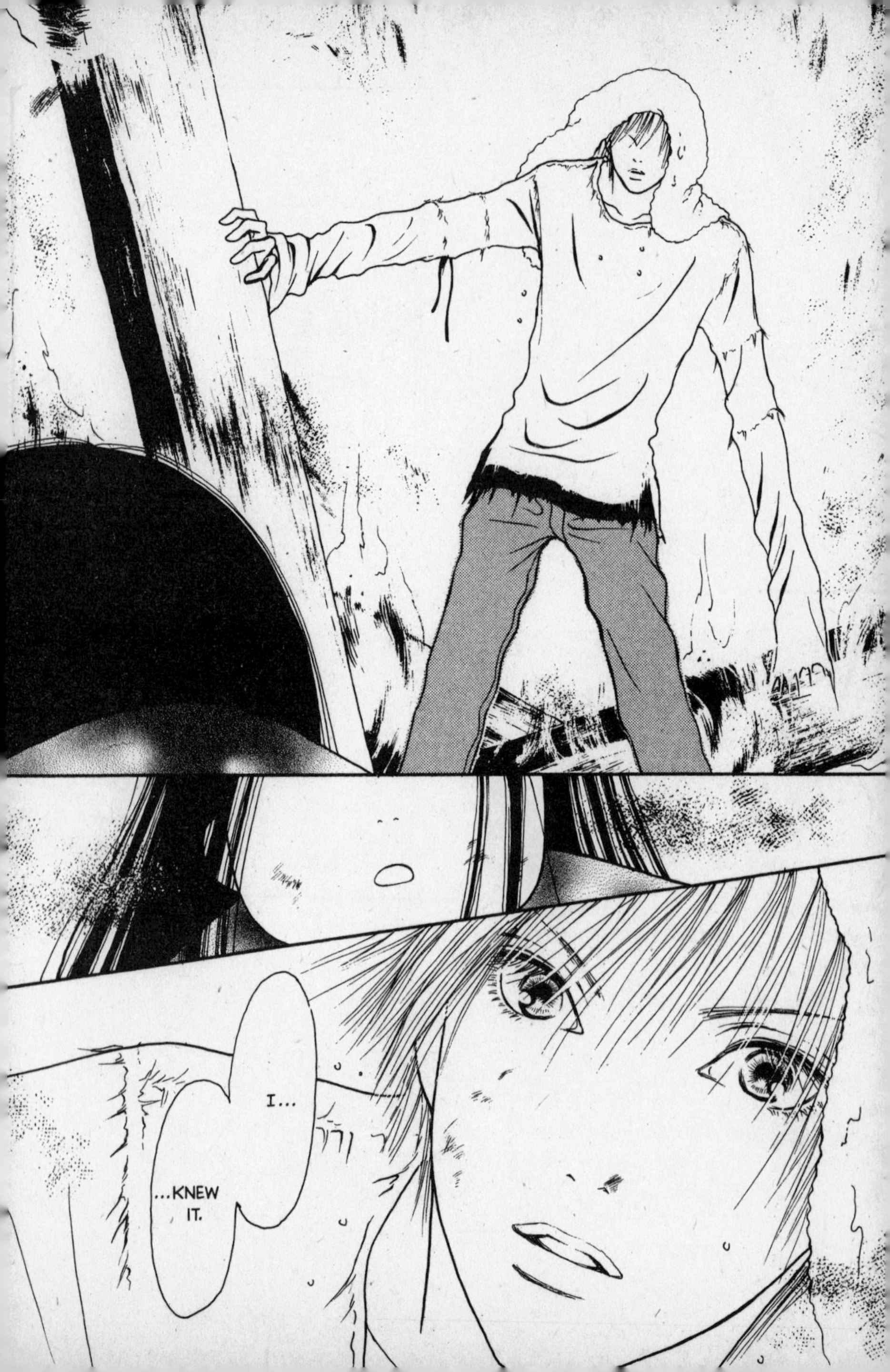
I... ...KNEW IT.

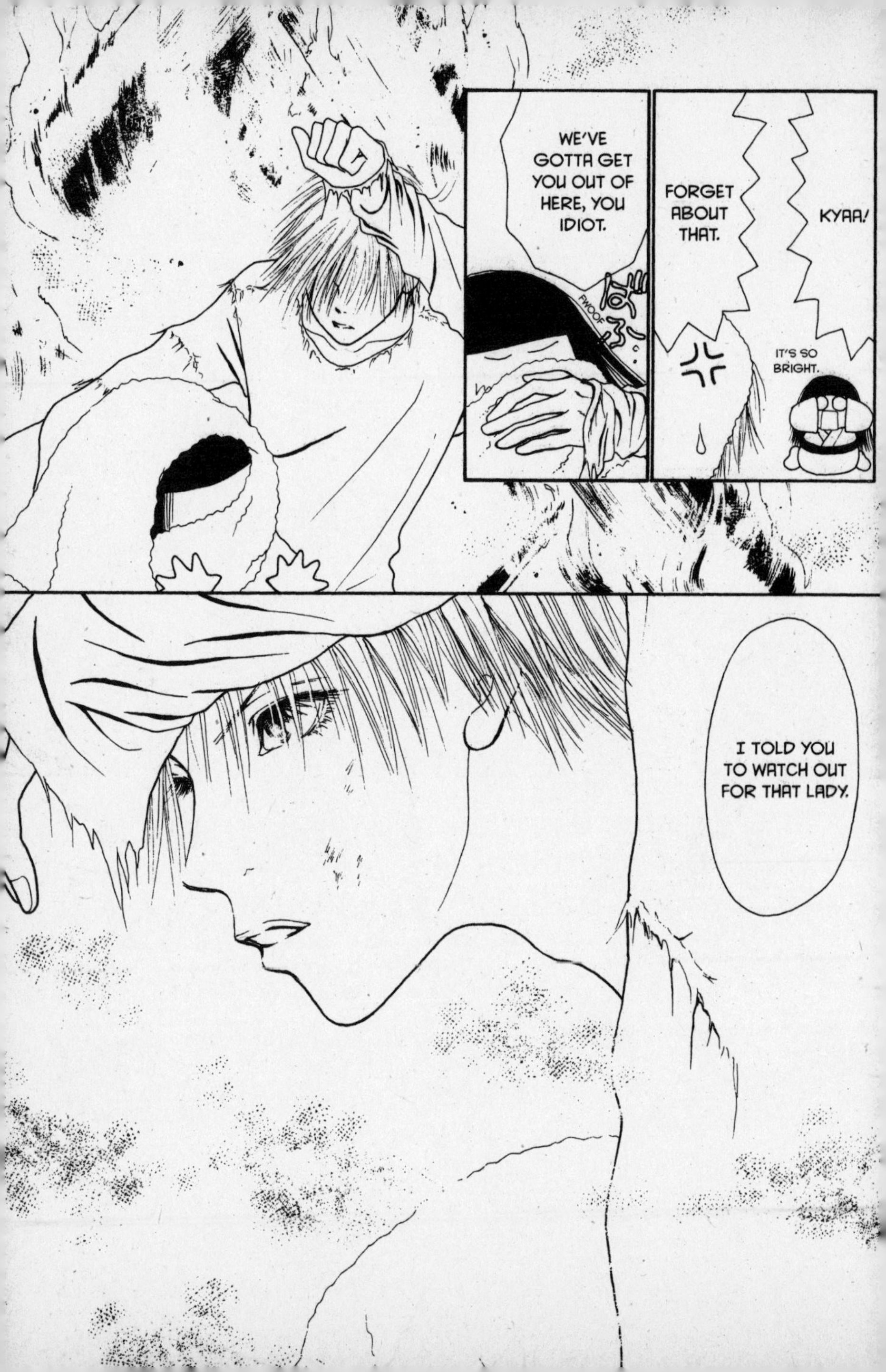
KYAA!
FORGET ABOUT THAT.
IT'S SO BRIGHT.
WE'VE GOTTA GET YOU OUT OF HERE, YOU IDIOT.
PWOOF
I TOLD YOU TO WATCH OUT FOR THAT LADY.

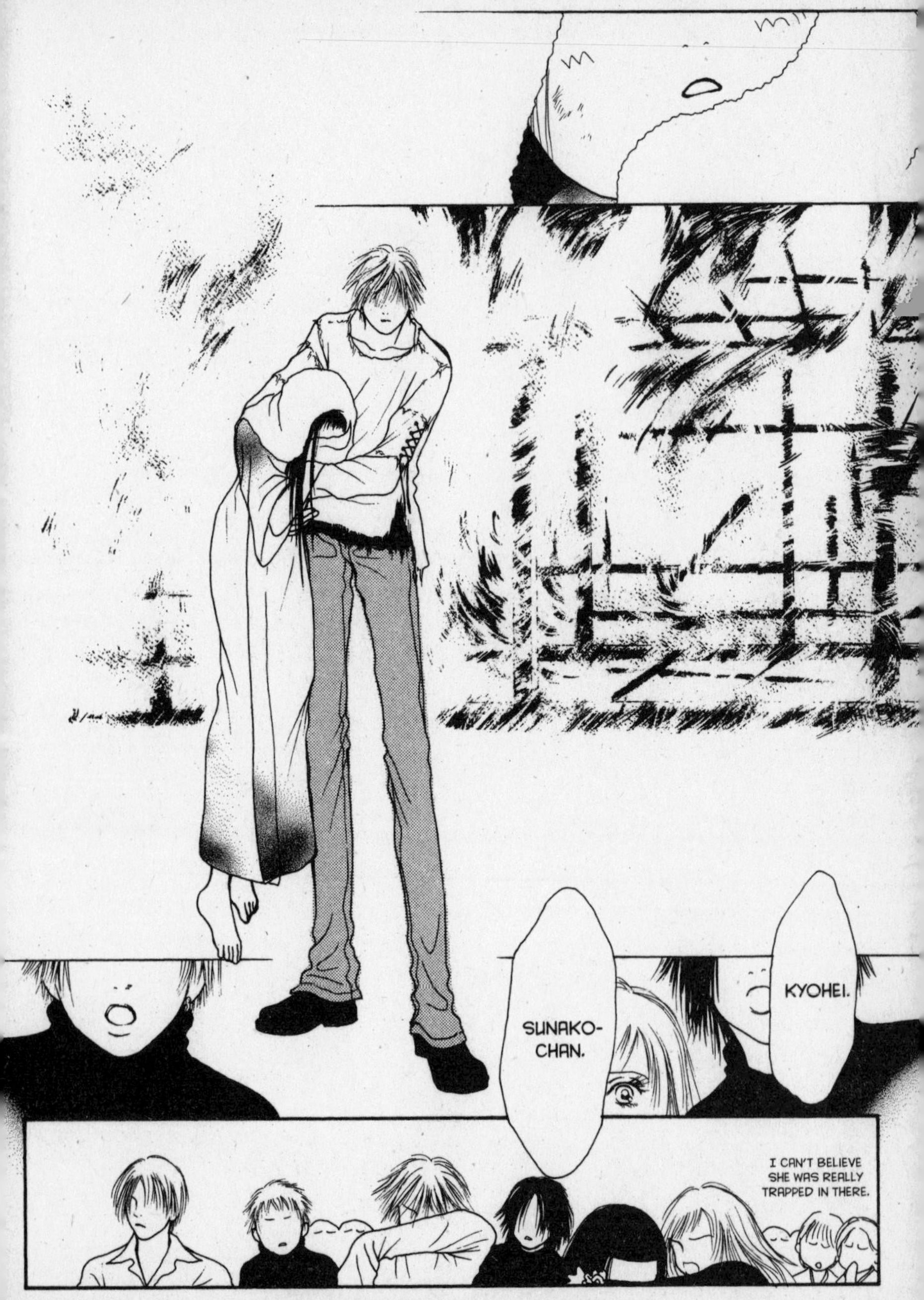
KYOHEI.
SUNAKO-CHAN.
I CAN'T BELIEVE SHE WAS REALLY TRAPPED IN THERE.

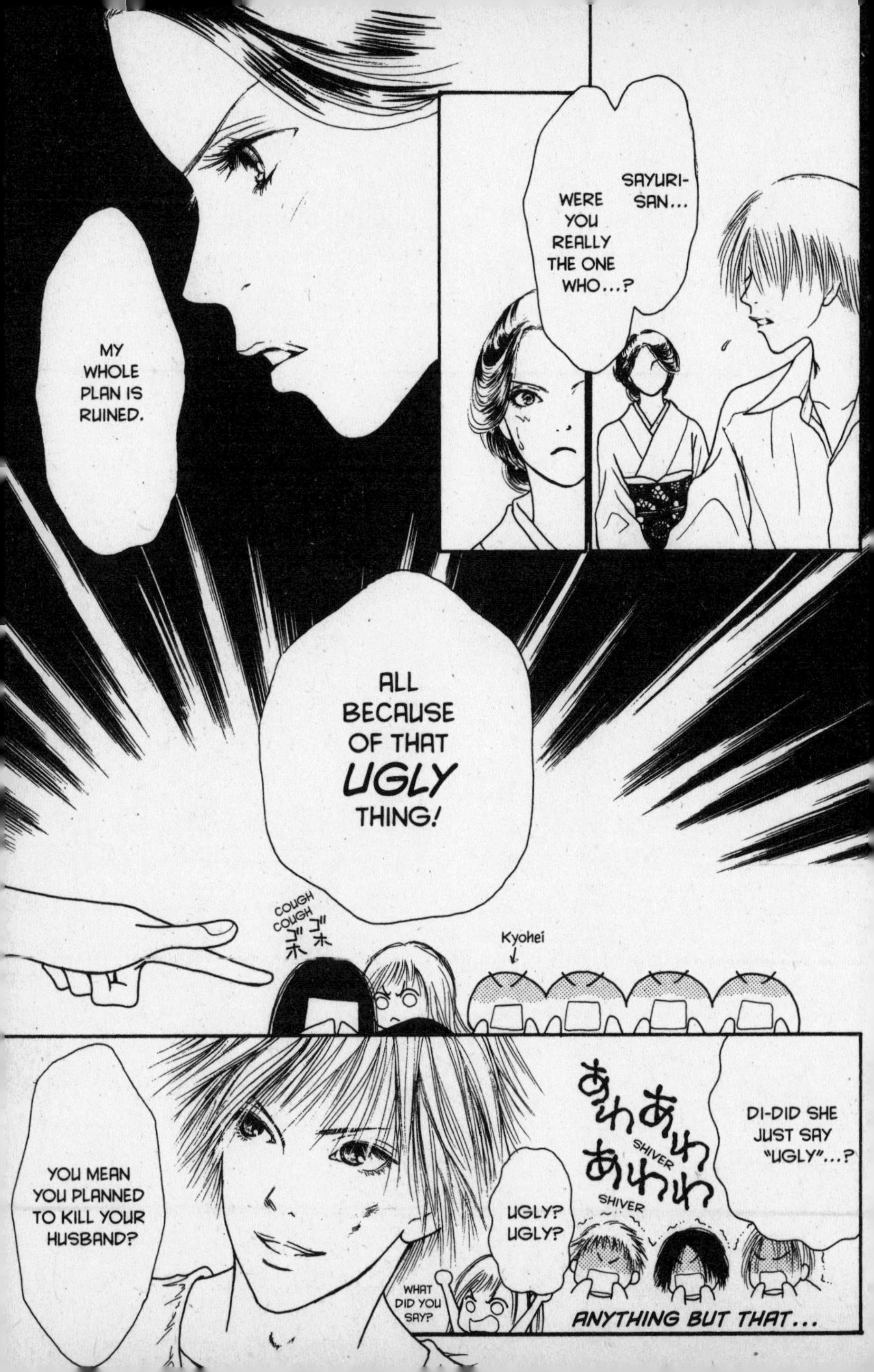
SAYURI-SAN... WERE YOU REALLY THE ONE WHO...?
MY WHOLE PLAN IS RUINED.
ALL BECAUSE OF THAT UGLY THING!
COUGH COUGH
ゴホゴホ
Kyohei
DI-DID SHE JUST SAY "UGLY"...?
あわあわあわわ
SHIVER
SHIVER
UGLY? UGLY?
WHAT DID YOU SAY?
ANYTHING BUT THAT...
YOU MEAN YOU PLANNED TO KILL YOUR HUSBAND?

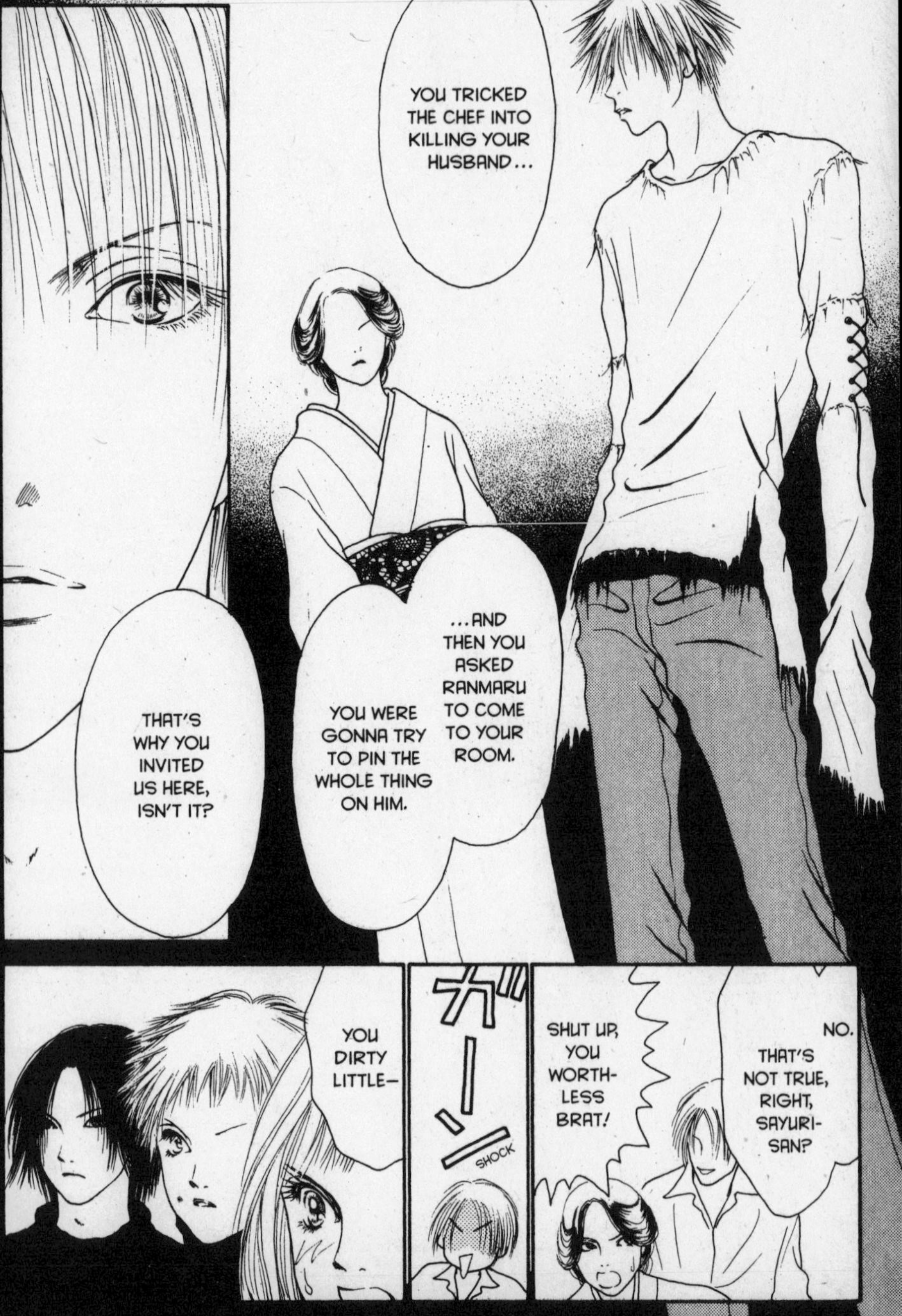
YOU TRICKED THE CHEF INTO KILLING YOUR HUSBAND...
...AND THEN YOU ASKED RANMARU TO COME TO YOUR ROOM.
YOU WERE GONNA TRY TO PIN THE WHOLE THING ON HIM.
THAT'S WHY YOU INVITED US HERE, ISN'T IT?
NO. THAT'S NOT TRUE, RIGHT, SAYURI-SAN?
SHUT UP, YOU WORTHLESS BRAT!
ガーン
SHOCK
YOU DIRTY LITTLE—

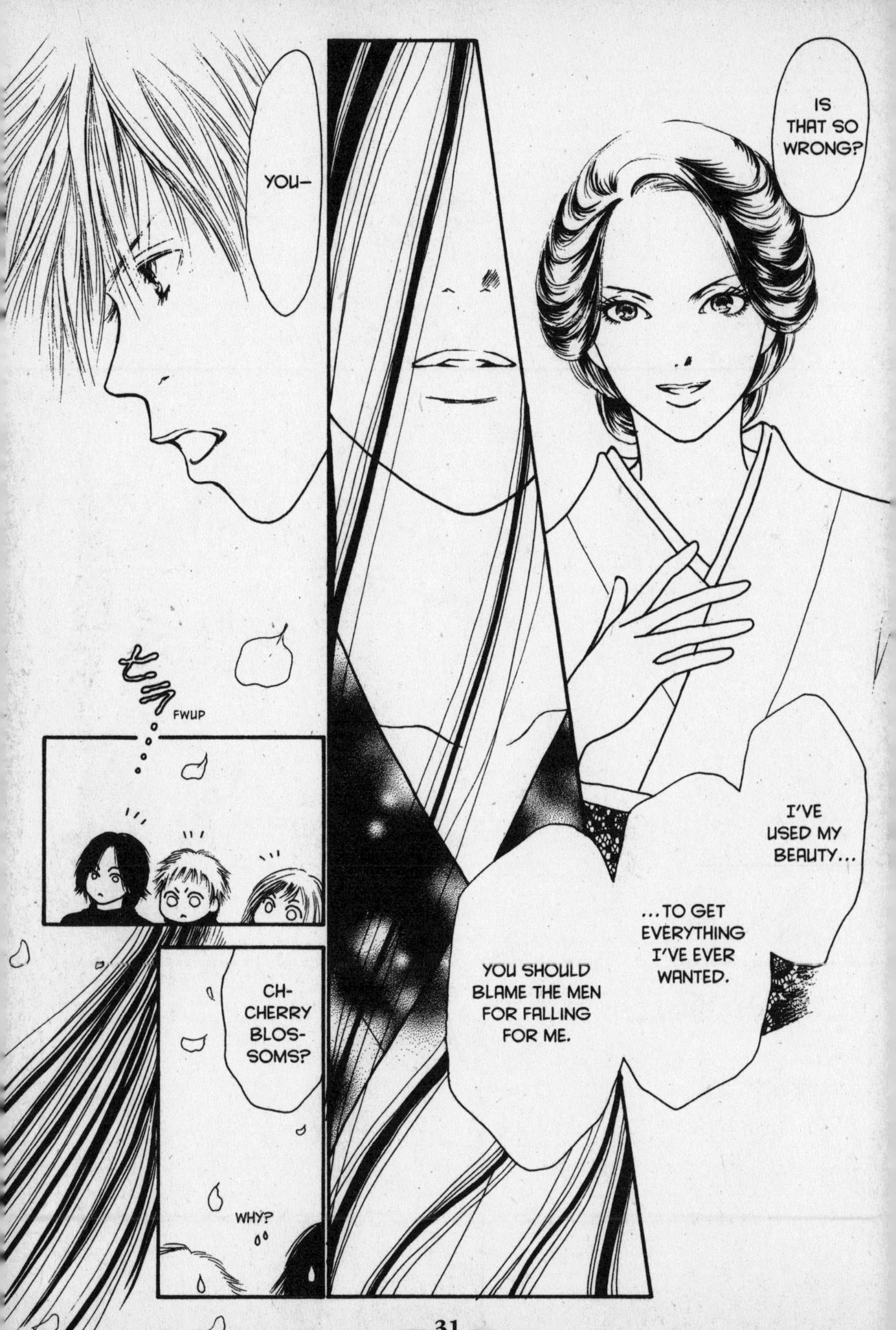
IS THAT SO WRONG?
I'VE USED MY BEAUTY...
...TO GET EVERYTHING I'VE EVER WANTED.
YOU SHOULD BLAME THE MEN FOR FALLING FOR ME.
YOU-
FWUP
CH-CHERRY BLOS-SOMS?
WHY?

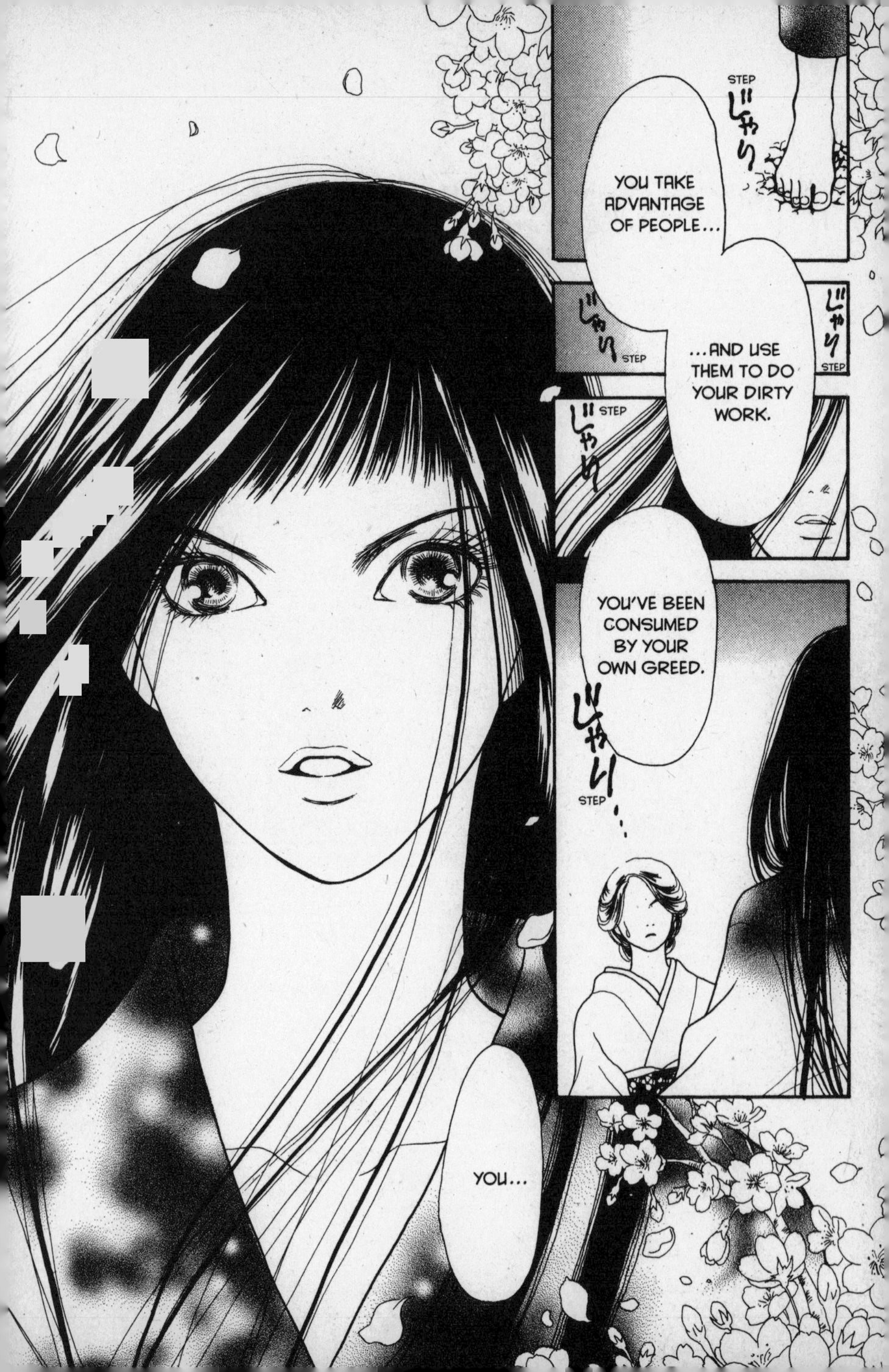
STEP
じゃり
YOU TAKE ADVANTAGE OF PEOPLE...
じゃり
STEP
じゃり
STEP
...AND USE THEM TO DO YOUR DIRTY WORK.
じゃり
STEP
YOU'VE BEEN CONSUMED BY YOUR OWN GREED.
じゃり
STEP
YOU...

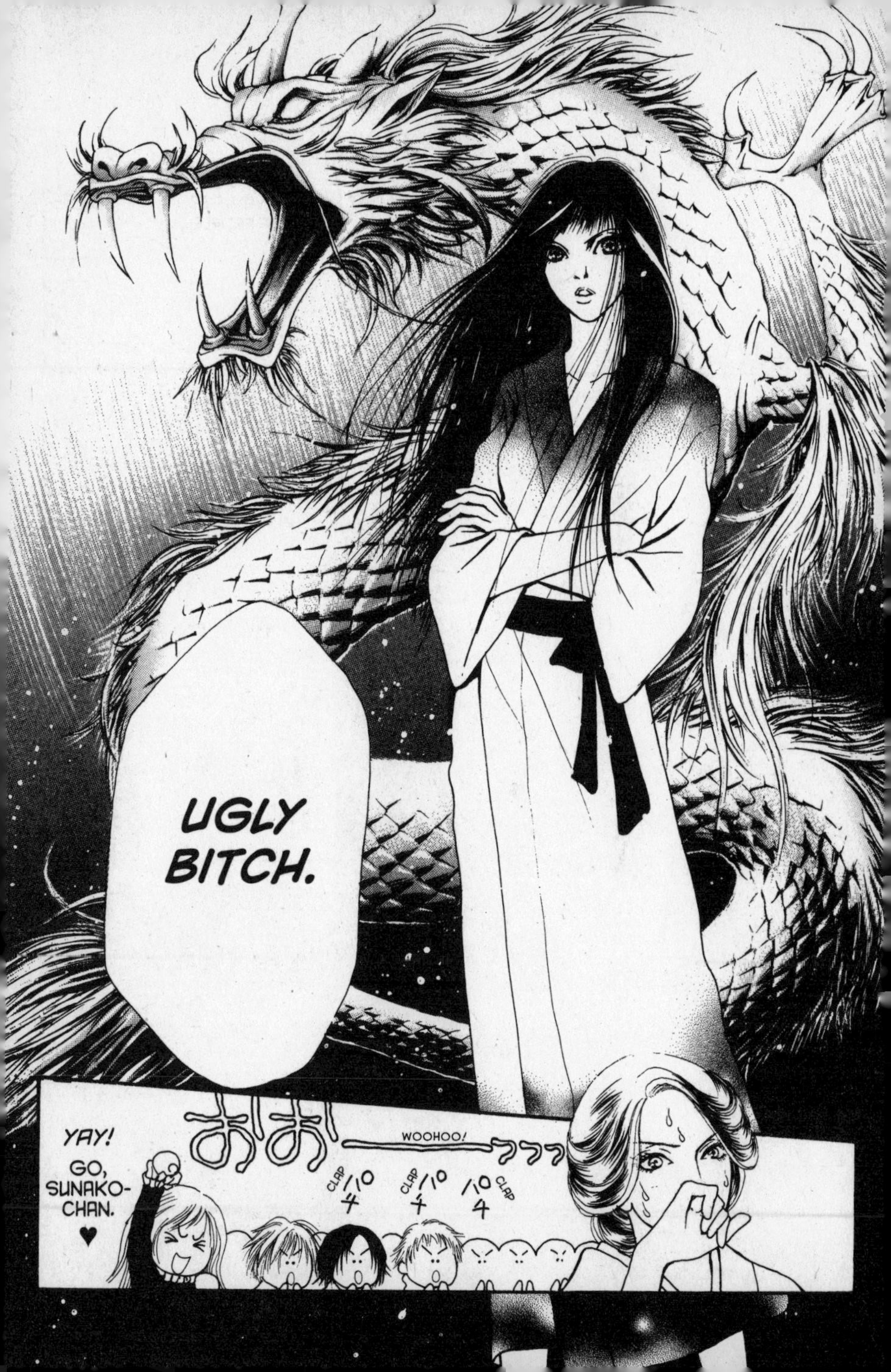
UGLY BITCH.
WOOHOO!
CLAP
CLAP
CLAP
YAY! GO, SUNAKO-CHAN. ♥

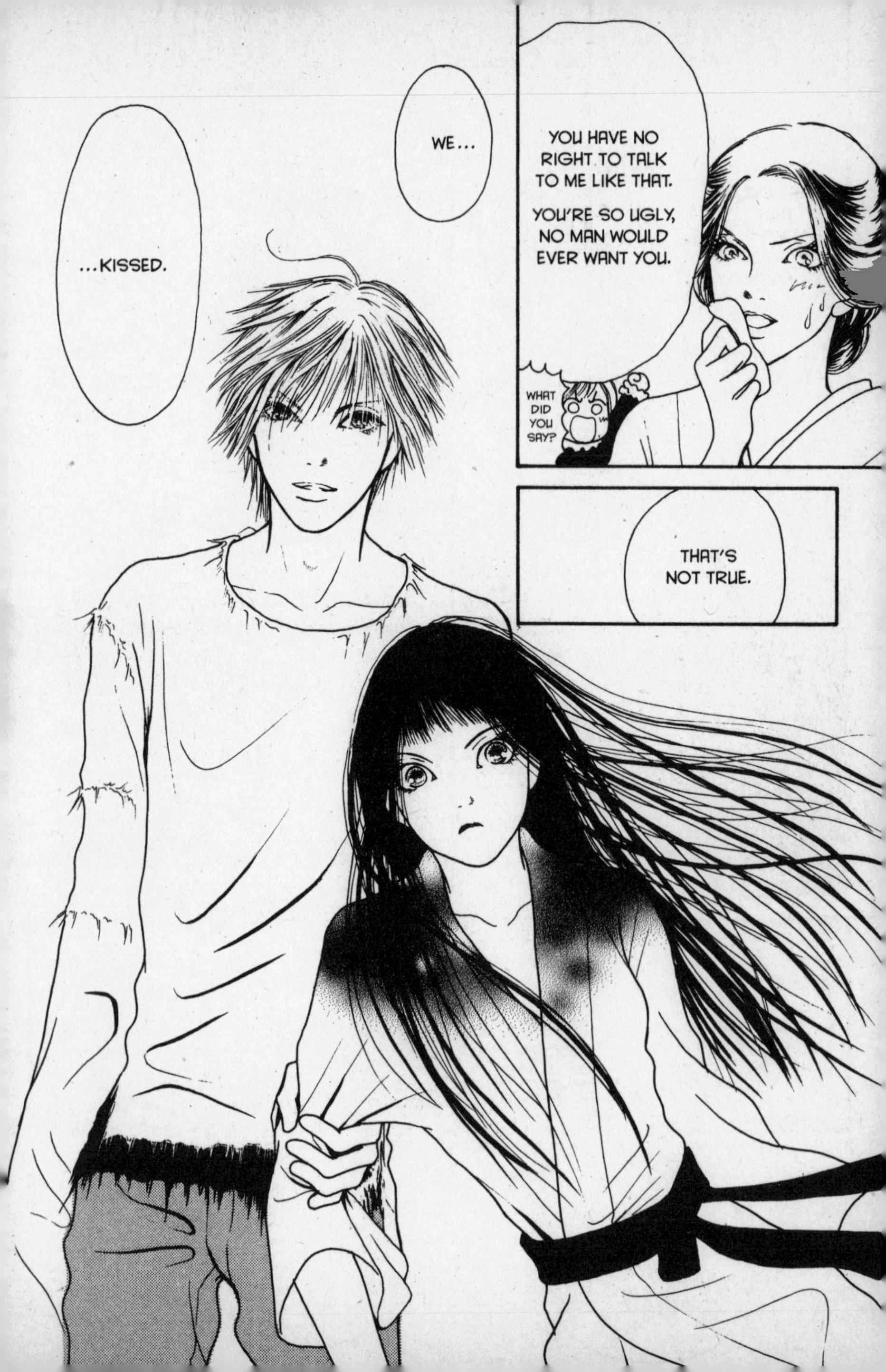
YOU HAVE NO RIGHT TO TALK TO ME LIKE THAT.
YOU'RE SO UGLY, NO MAN WOULD EVER WANT YOU.
WHAT DID YOU SAY?
THAT'S NOT TRUE.
WE...
...KISSED.

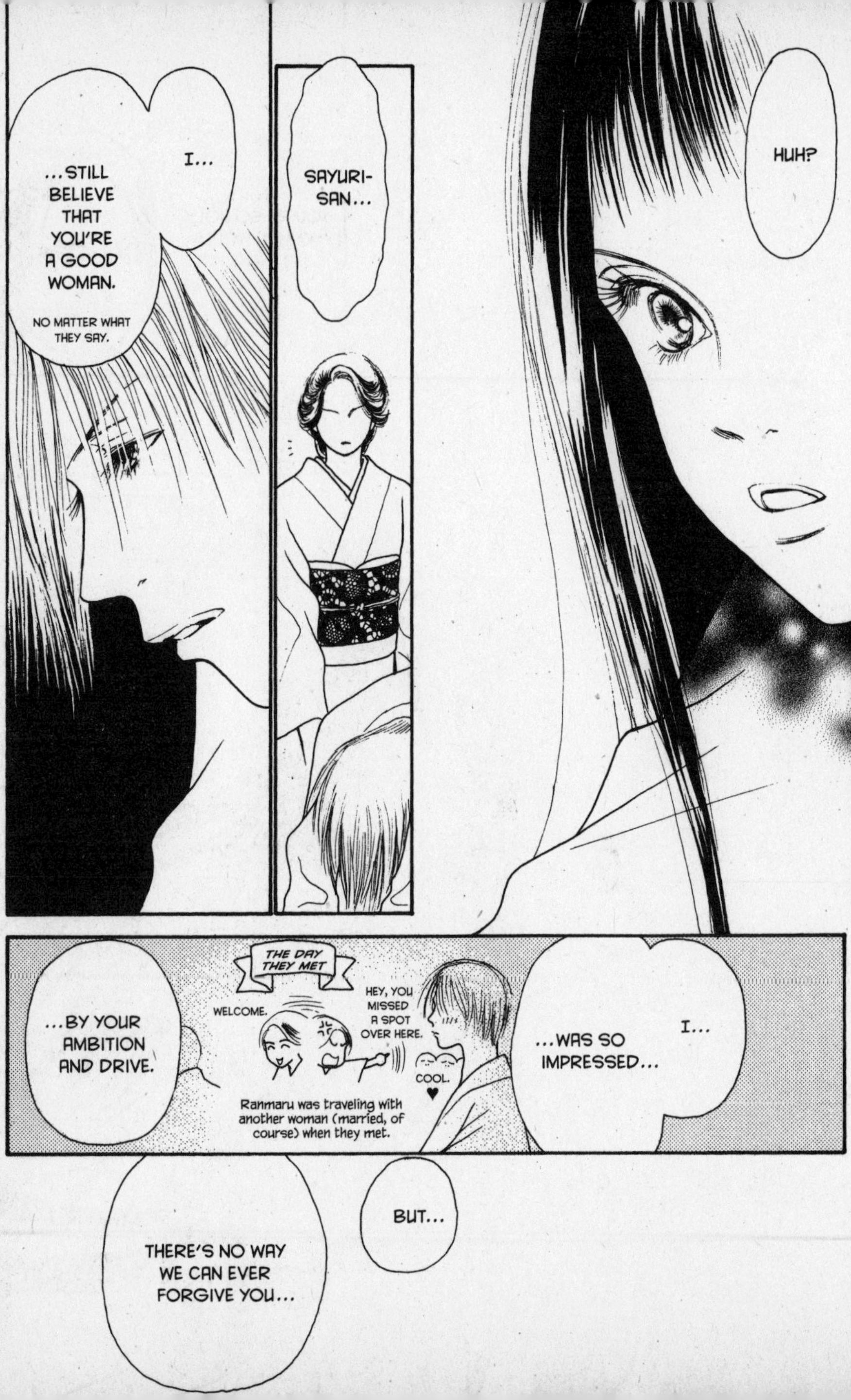
HUH?
SAYURI-SAN...
I...
...STILL BELIEVE THAT YOU'RE A GOOD WOMAN.
NO MATTER WHAT THEY SAY.
I...
...WAS SO IMPRESSED...
THE DAY THEY MET
HEY, YOU MISSED A SPOT OVER HERE.
WELCOME.
COOL.
Ranmaru was traveling with another woman (married, of course) when they met.
...BY YOUR AMBITION AND DRIVE.
BUT...
THERE'S NO WAY WE CAN EVER FORGIVE YOU...

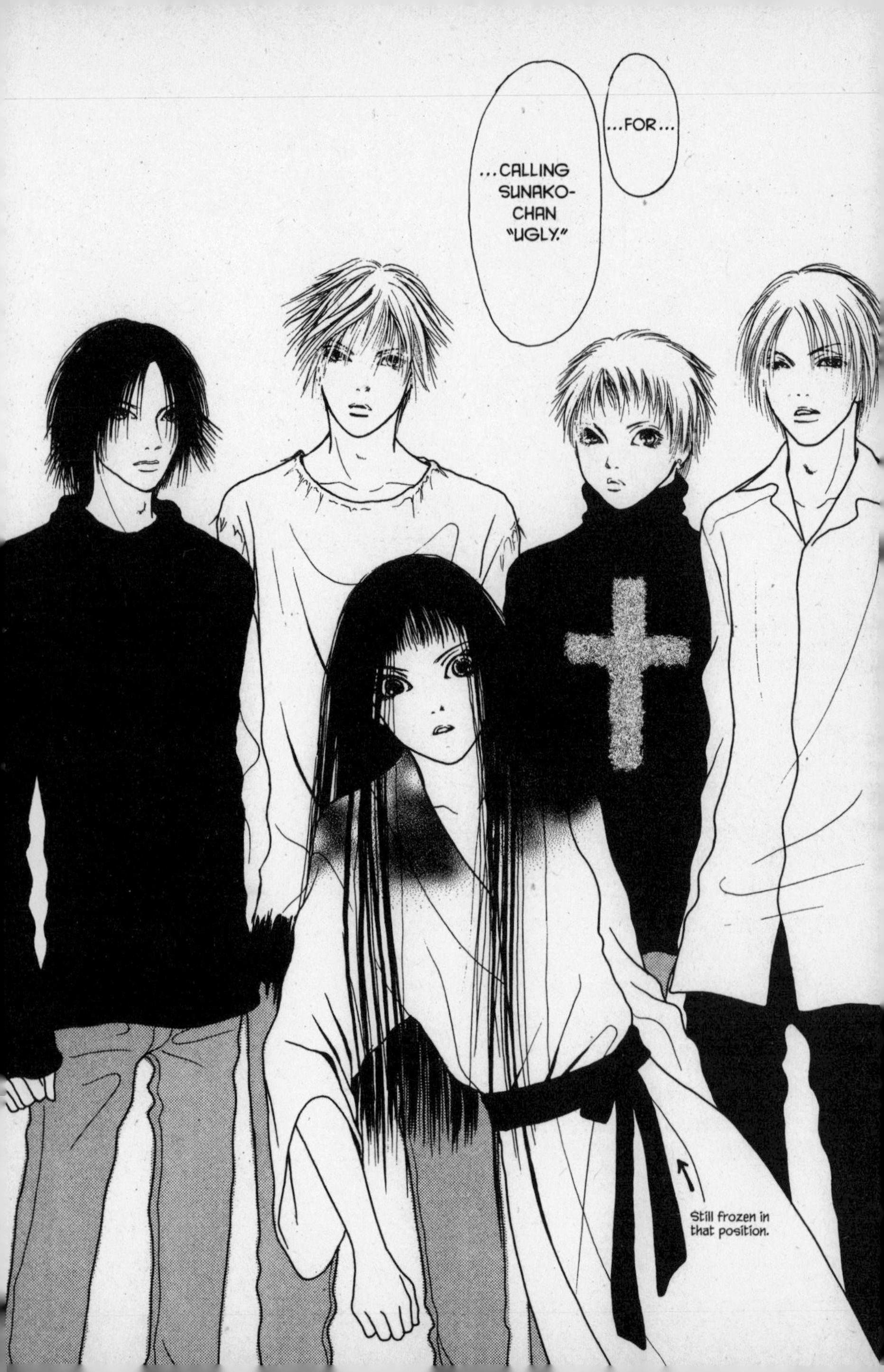
...FOR...
...CALLING SUNAKO-CHAN "UGLY."
Still frozen in that position.

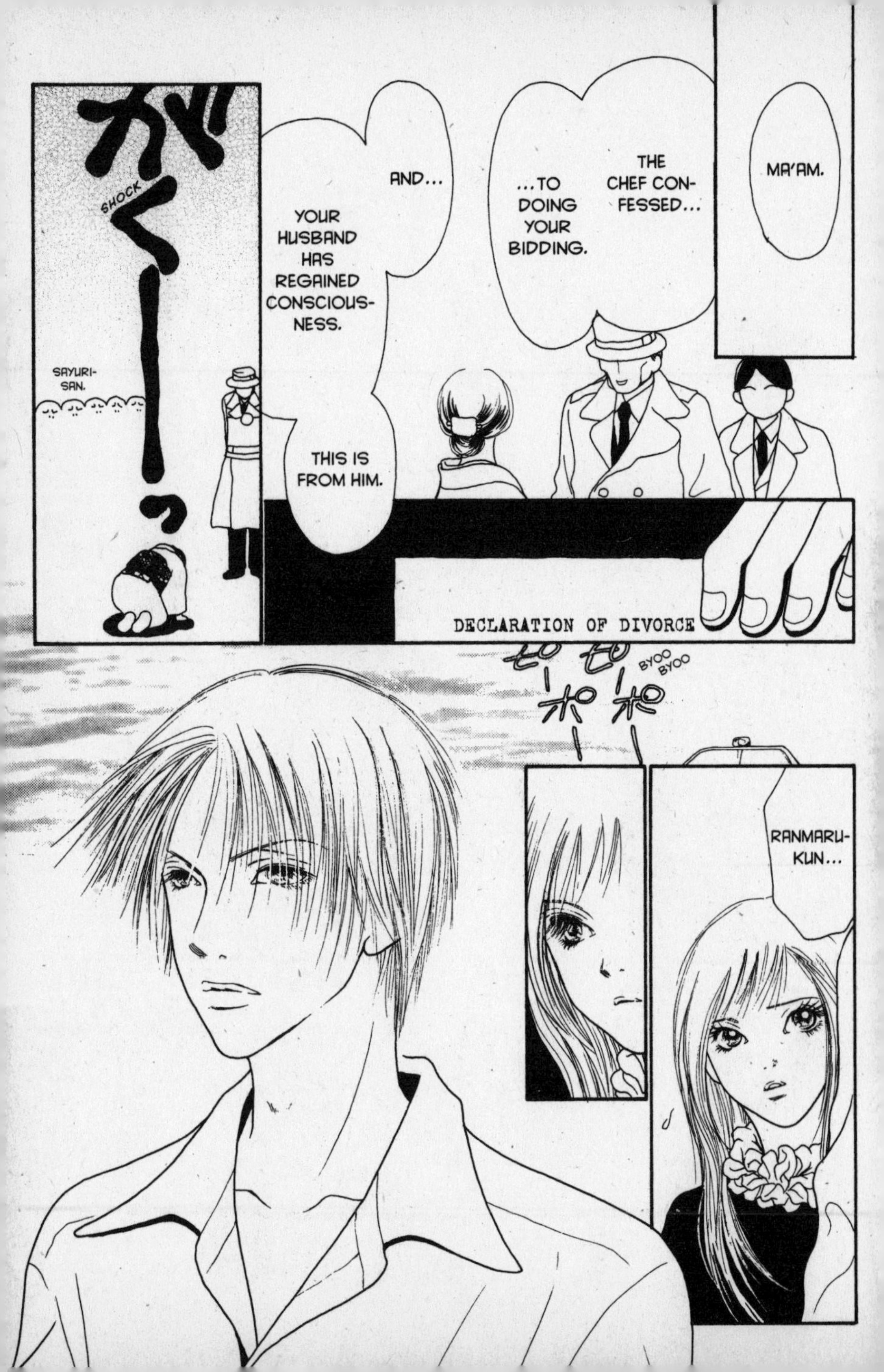
MA'AM.
THE CHEF CON-FESSED...
...TO DOING YOUR BIDDING.
AND...
YOUR HUSBAND HAS REGAINED CONSCIOUS-NESS.
THIS IS FROM HIM.
DECLARATION OF DIVORCE
SHOCK
SAYURI-SAN.
RANMARU-KUN...
BYOO BYOO

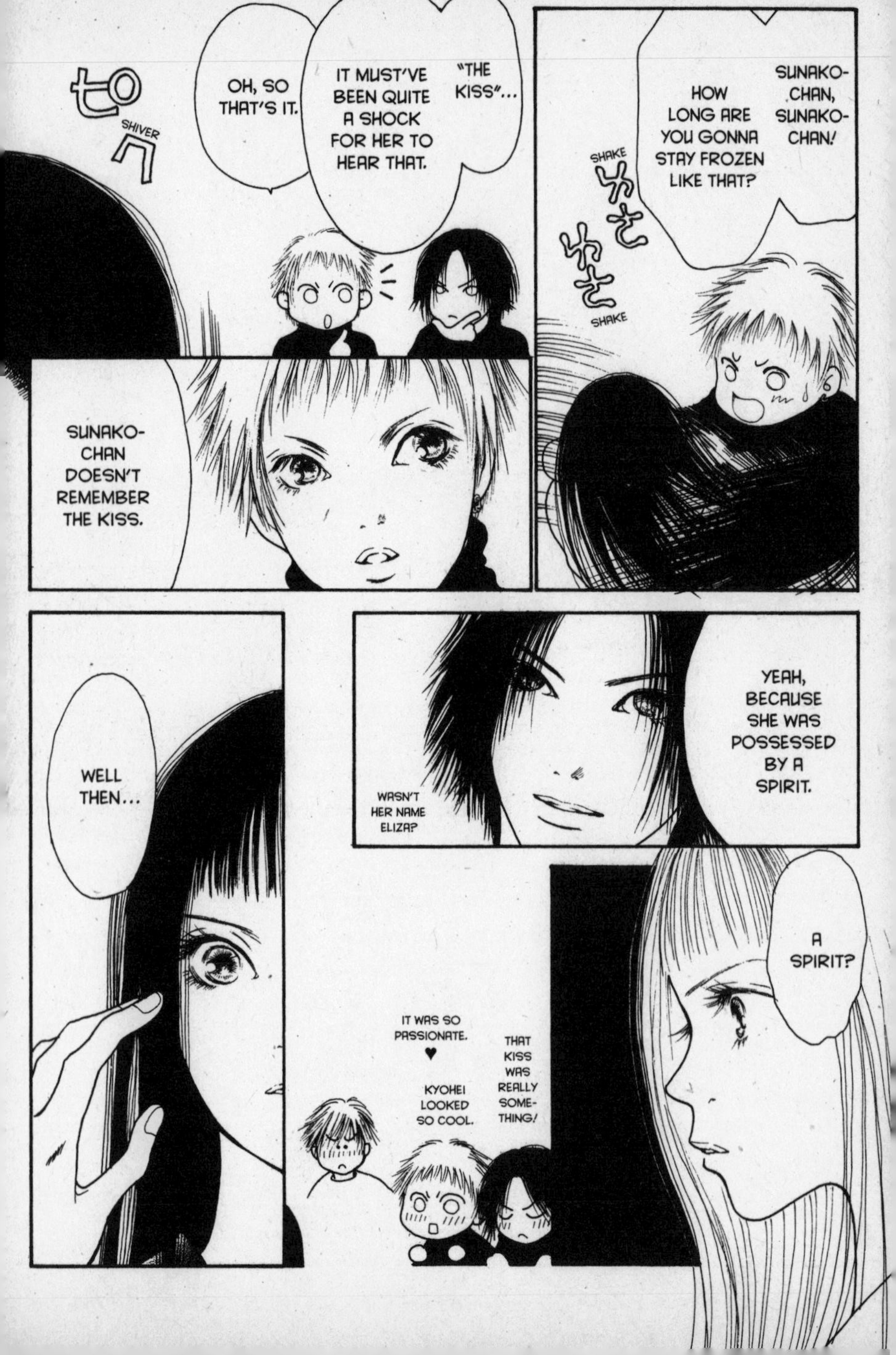
SUNAKO-CHAN, SUNAKO-CHAN!
HOW LONG ARE YOU GONNA STAY FROZEN LIKE THAT?
SHAKE
SHAKE
"THE KISS"...
IT MUST'VE BEEN QUITE A SHOCK FOR HER TO HEAR THAT.
OH, SO THAT'S IT.
SHIVER
SUNAKO-CHAN DOESN'T REMEMBER THE KISS.
YEAH, BECAUSE SHE WAS POSSESSED BY A SPIRIT.
WASN'T HER NAME ELIZA?
A SPIRIT?
THAT KISS WAS REALLY SOME-THING!
IT WAS SO PASSIONATE. ♥
KYOHEI LOOKED SO COOL.
WELL THEN...

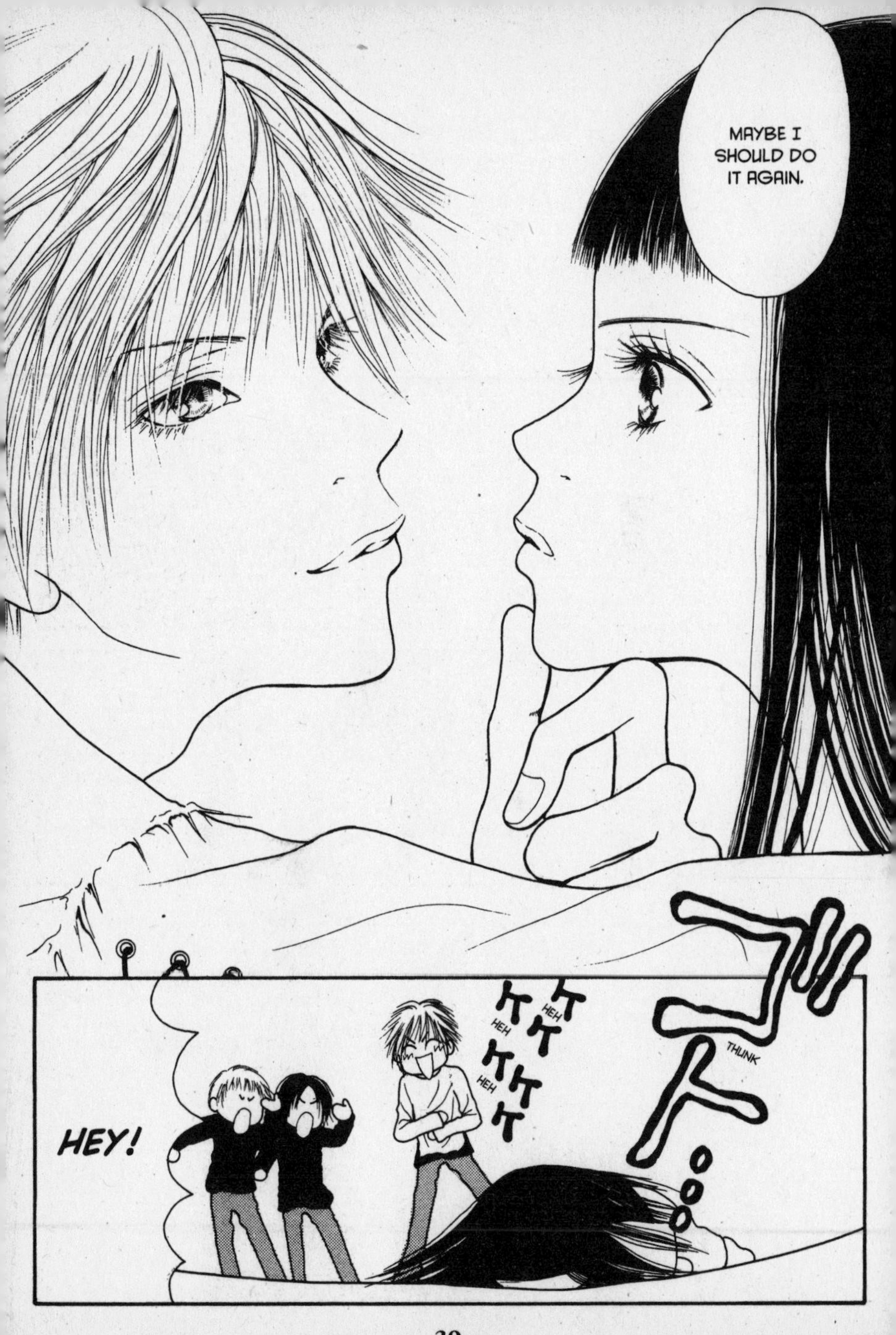
MAYBE I SHOULD DO IT AGAIN.
THUNK
HEH HEH HEH
HEY!

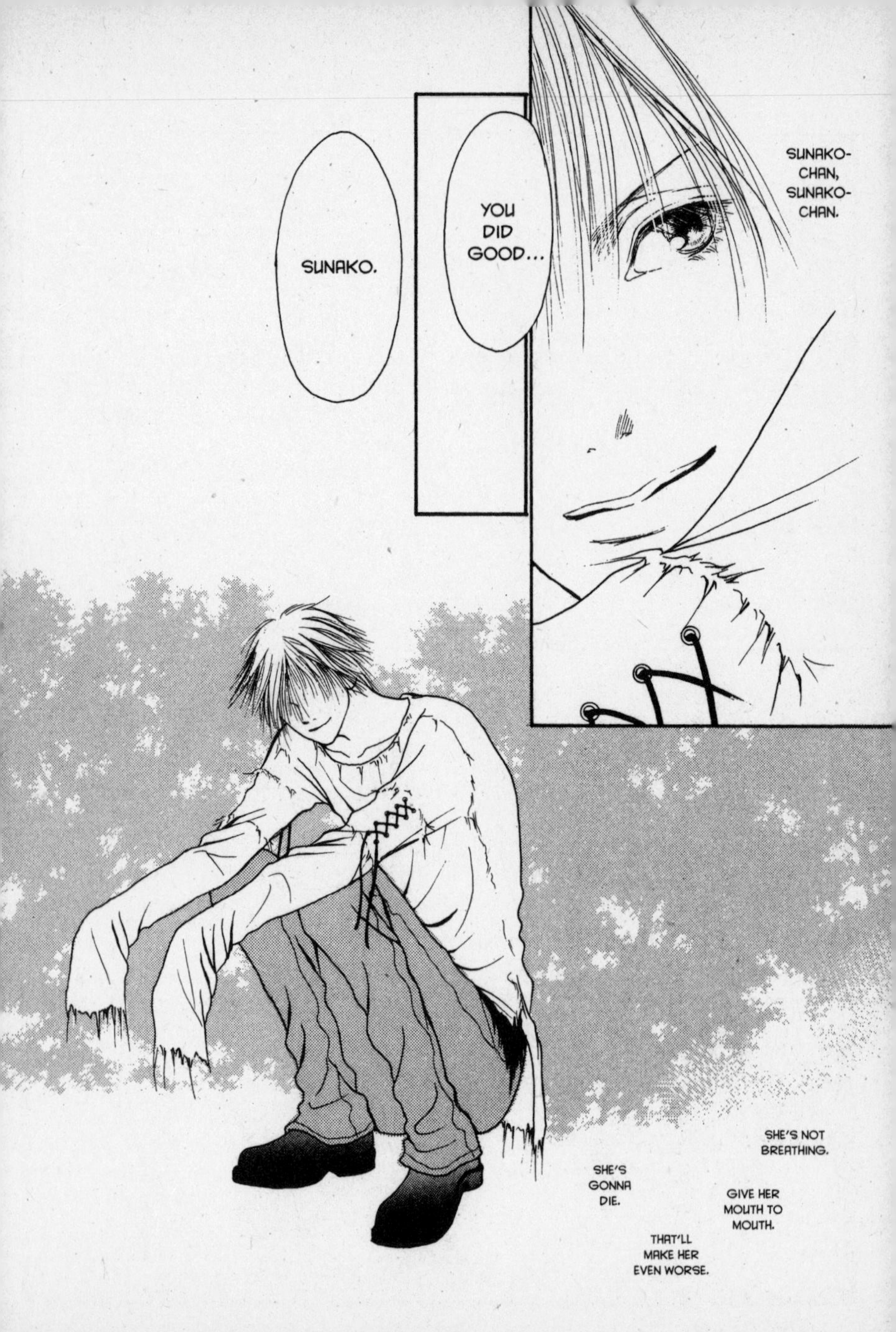
SUNAKO-CHAN, SUNAKO-CHAN.
YOU DID GOOD...
SUNAKO.
SHE'S NOT BREATHING.
GIVE HER MOUTH TO MOUTH.
SHE'S GONNA DIE.
THAT'LL MAKE HER EVEN WORSE.

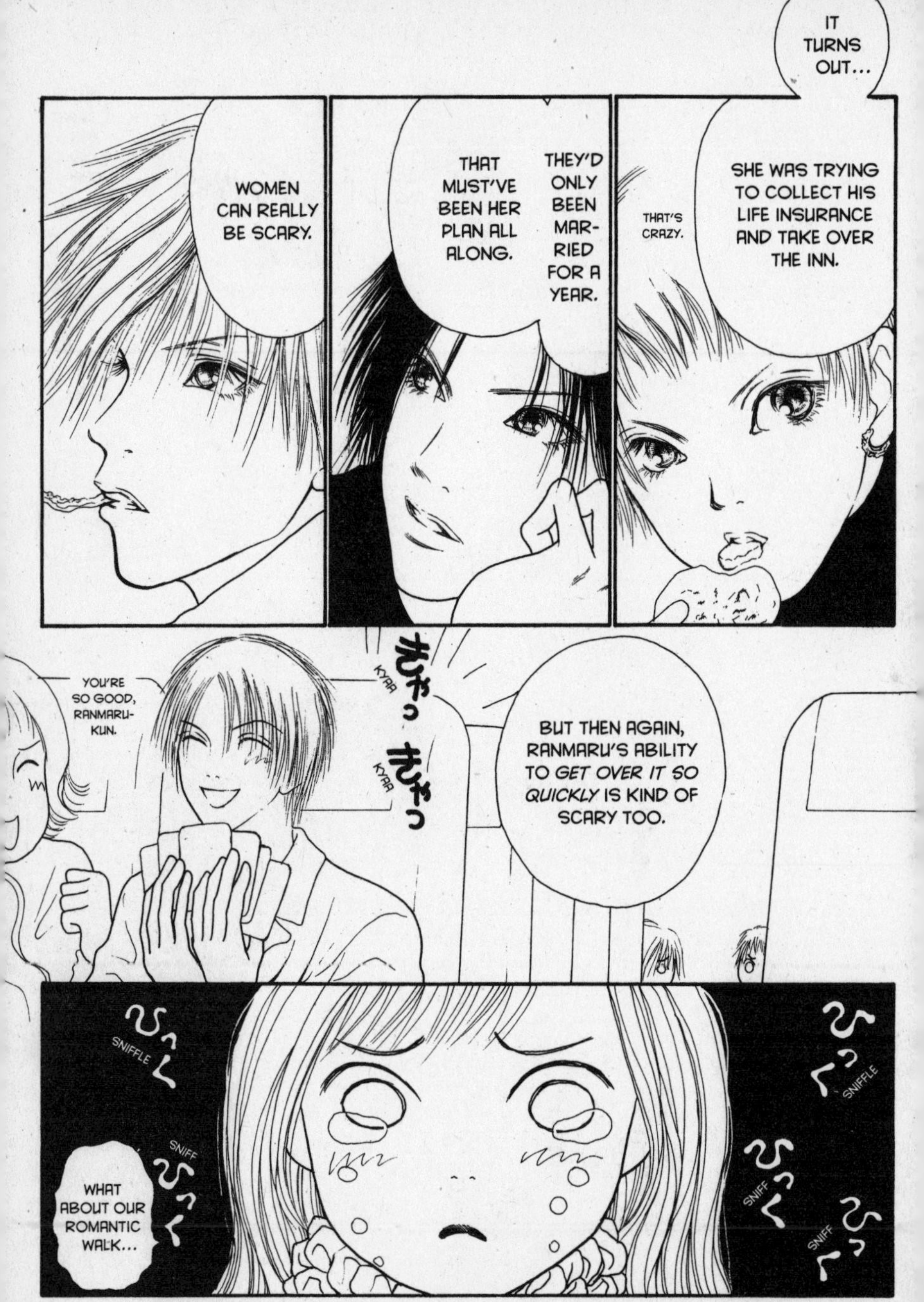

IT TURNS OUT...
SHE WAS TRYING TO COLLECT HIS LIFE INSURANCE AND TAKE OVER THE INN.
THAT'S CRAZY.
THEY'D ONLY BEEN MAR-RIED FOR A YEAR.
THAT MUST'VE BEEN HER PLAN ALL ALONG.
WOMEN CAN REALLY BE SCARY.
BUT THEN AGAIN, RANMARU'S ABILITY TO *GET OVER IT SO QUICKLY* IS KIND OF SCARY TOO.
KYAA
KYAA
YOU'RE SO GOOD, RANMARU-KUN.
SNIFFLE
SNIFF
SNIFF
SNIFF
WHAT ABOUT OUR ROMANTIC WALK...
SNIFFLE

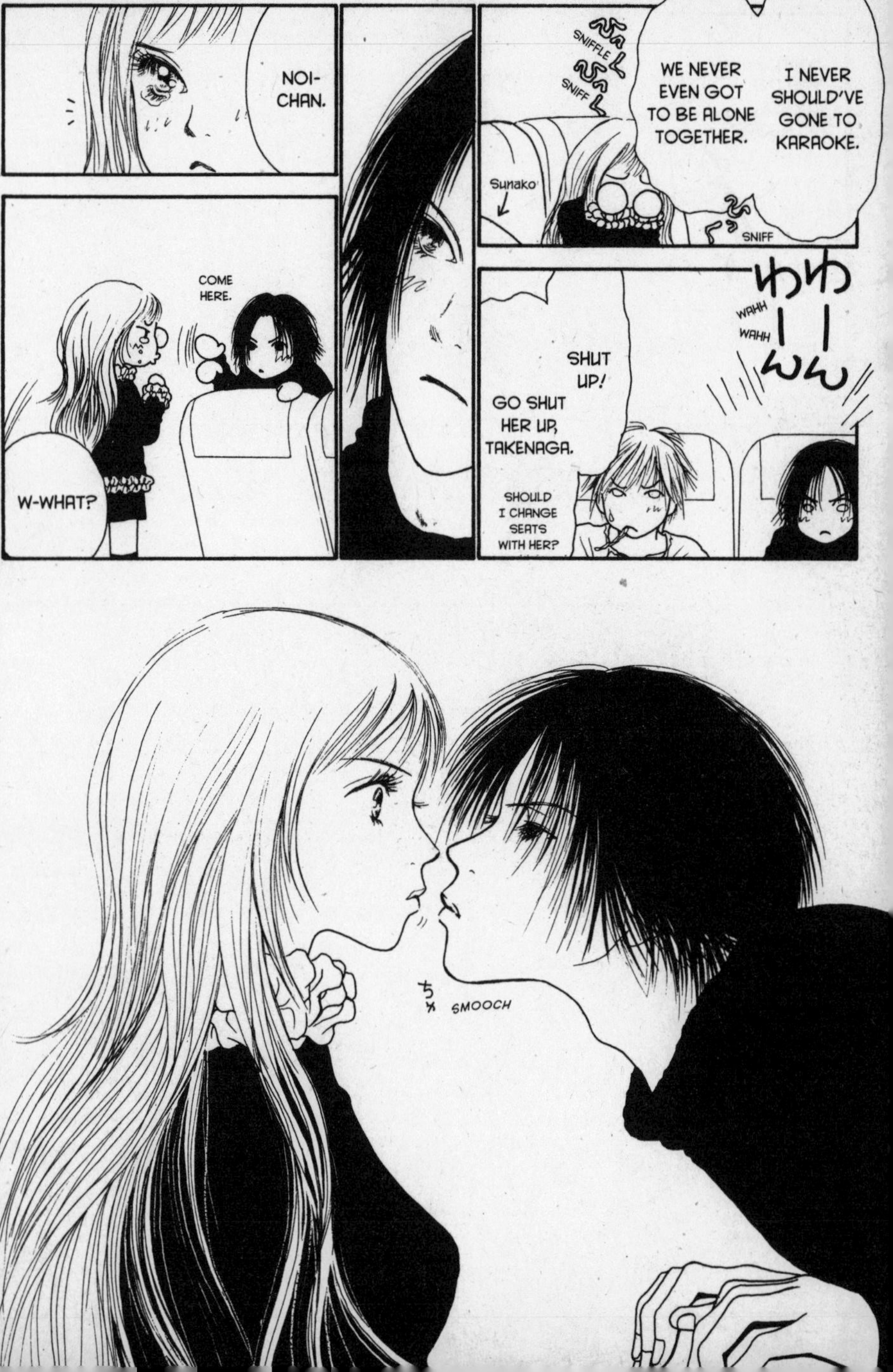
SNIFFLE
SNIFF
I NEVER SHOULD'VE GONE TO KARAOKE.
WE NEVER EVEN GOT TO BE ALONE TOGETHER.
Sunako
SNIFF
わーん わーん
WAHH
WAHH
SHUT UP!
GO SHUT HER UP, TAKENAGA.
SHOULD I CHANGE SEATS WITH HER?
NOI-CHAN.
COME HERE.
W-WHAT?
ちゅ
SMOOCH

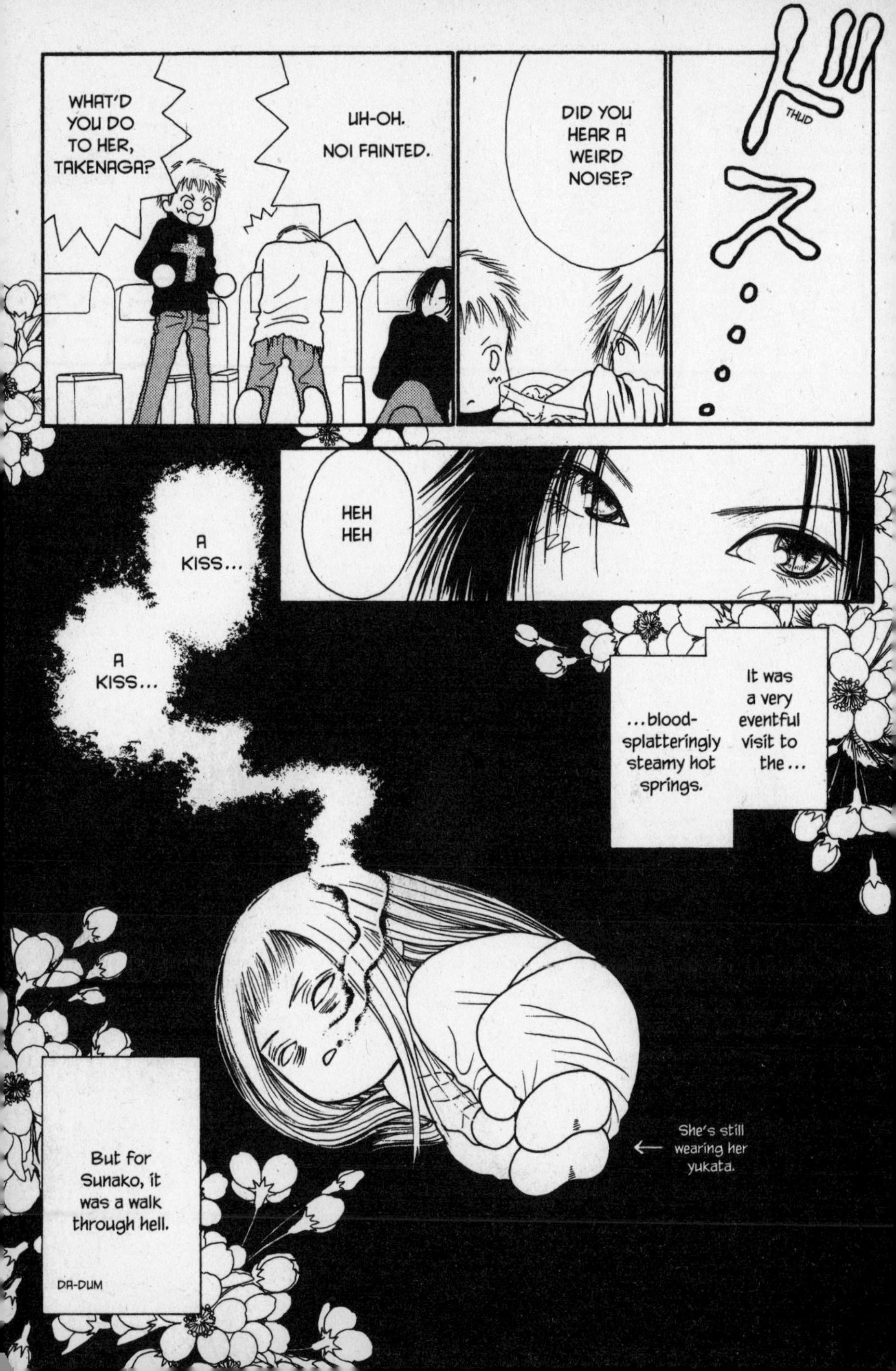
THUD
DID YOU HEAR A WEIRD NOISE?
UH-OH.
NOI FAINTED.
WHAT'D YOU DO TO HER, TAKENAGA?
HEH HEH
A KISS...
A KISS...
It was a very eventful visit to the...
...blood-splatteringly steamy hot springs.
She's still wearing her yukata.
But for Sunako, it was a walk through hell.
DA-DUM

A picture taken aboard the train.

Chapter 11

Who's the Real Enemy... Kyohei or the Test?

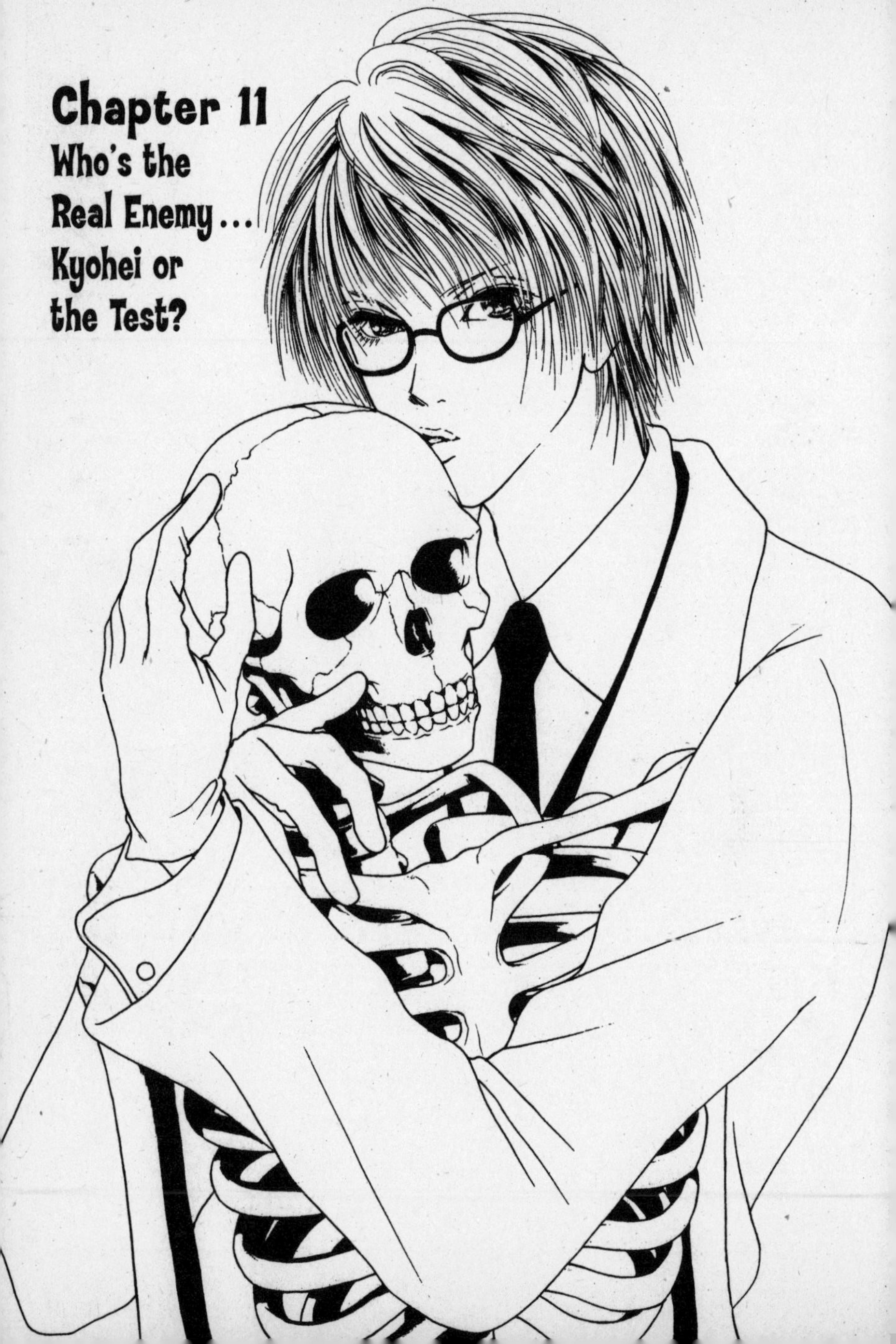

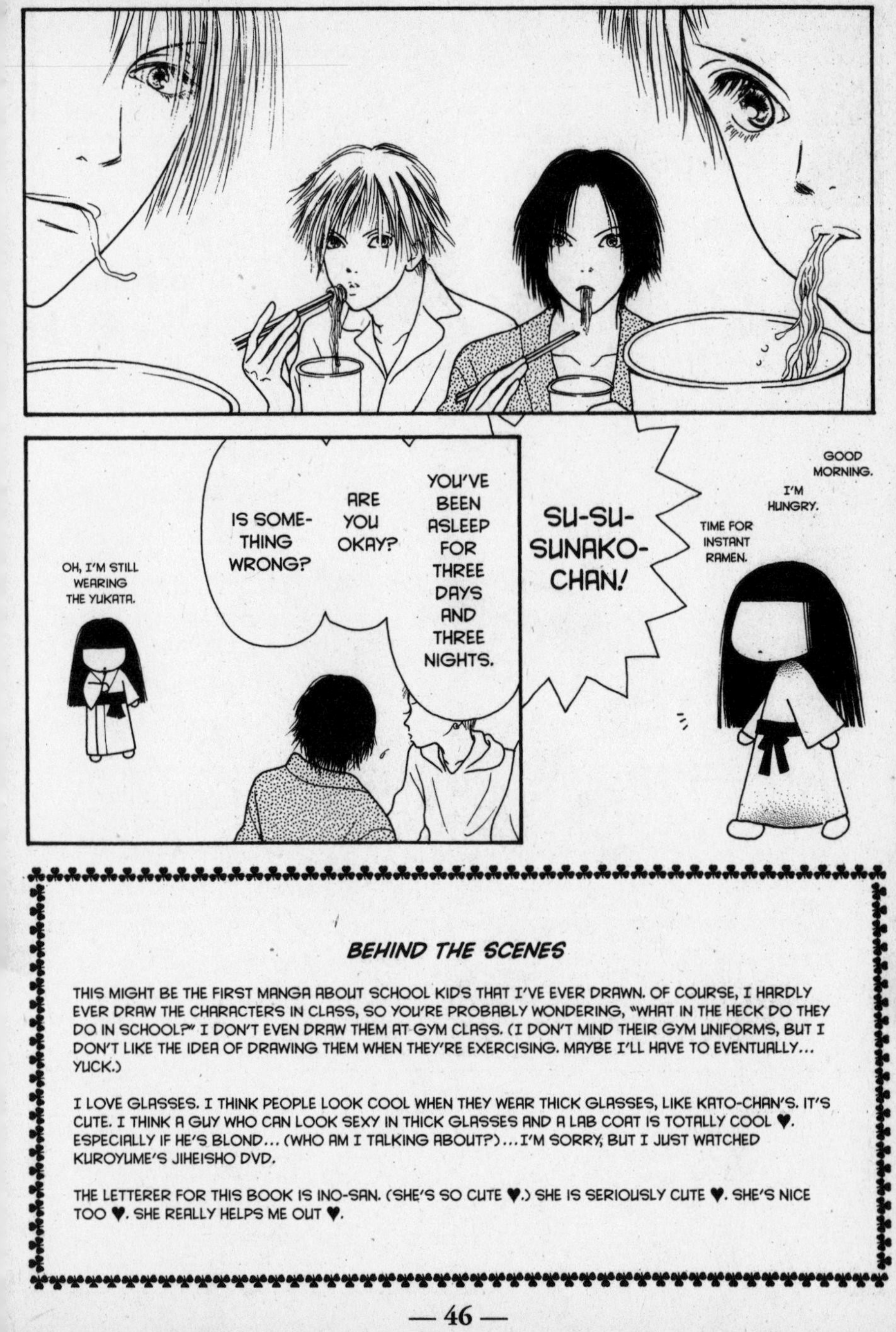
GOOD MORNING.
I'M HUNGRY.
TIME FOR INSTANT RAMEN.
SU-SU-SUNAKO-CHAN!
YOU'VE BEEN ASLEEP FOR THREE DAYS AND THREE NIGHTS.
ARE YOU OKAY?
IS SOME-THING WRONG?
OH, I'M STILL WEARING THE YUKATA.

BEHIND THE SCENES

THIS MIGHT BE THE FIRST MANGA ABOUT SCHOOL KIDS THAT I'VE EVER DRAWN. OF COURSE, I HARDLY EVER DRAW THE CHARACTERS IN CLASS, SO YOU'RE PROBABLY WONDERING, "WHAT IN THE HECK DO THEY DO IN SCHOOL?" I DON'T EVEN DRAW THEM AT GYM CLASS. (I DON'T MIND THEIR GYM UNIFORMS, BUT I DON'T LIKE THE IDEA OF DRAWING THEM WHEN THEY'RE EXERCISING. MAYBE I'LL HAVE TO EVENTUALLY... YUCK.)

I LOVE GLASSES. I THINK PEOPLE LOOK COOL WHEN THEY WEAR THICK GLASSES, LIKE KATO-CHAN'S. IT'S CUTE. I THINK A GUY WHO CAN LOOK SEXY IN THICK GLASSES AND A LAB COAT IS TOTALLY COOL ♥. ESPECIALLY IF HE'S BLOND... (WHO AM I TALKING ABOUT?)...I'M SORRY, BUT I JUST WATCHED KUROYUME'S JIHEISHO DVD.

THE LETTERER FOR THIS BOOK IS INO-SAN. (SHE'S SO CUTE ♥.) SHE IS SERIOUSLY CUTE ♥. SHE'S NICE TOO ♥. SHE REALLY HELPS ME OUT ♥.

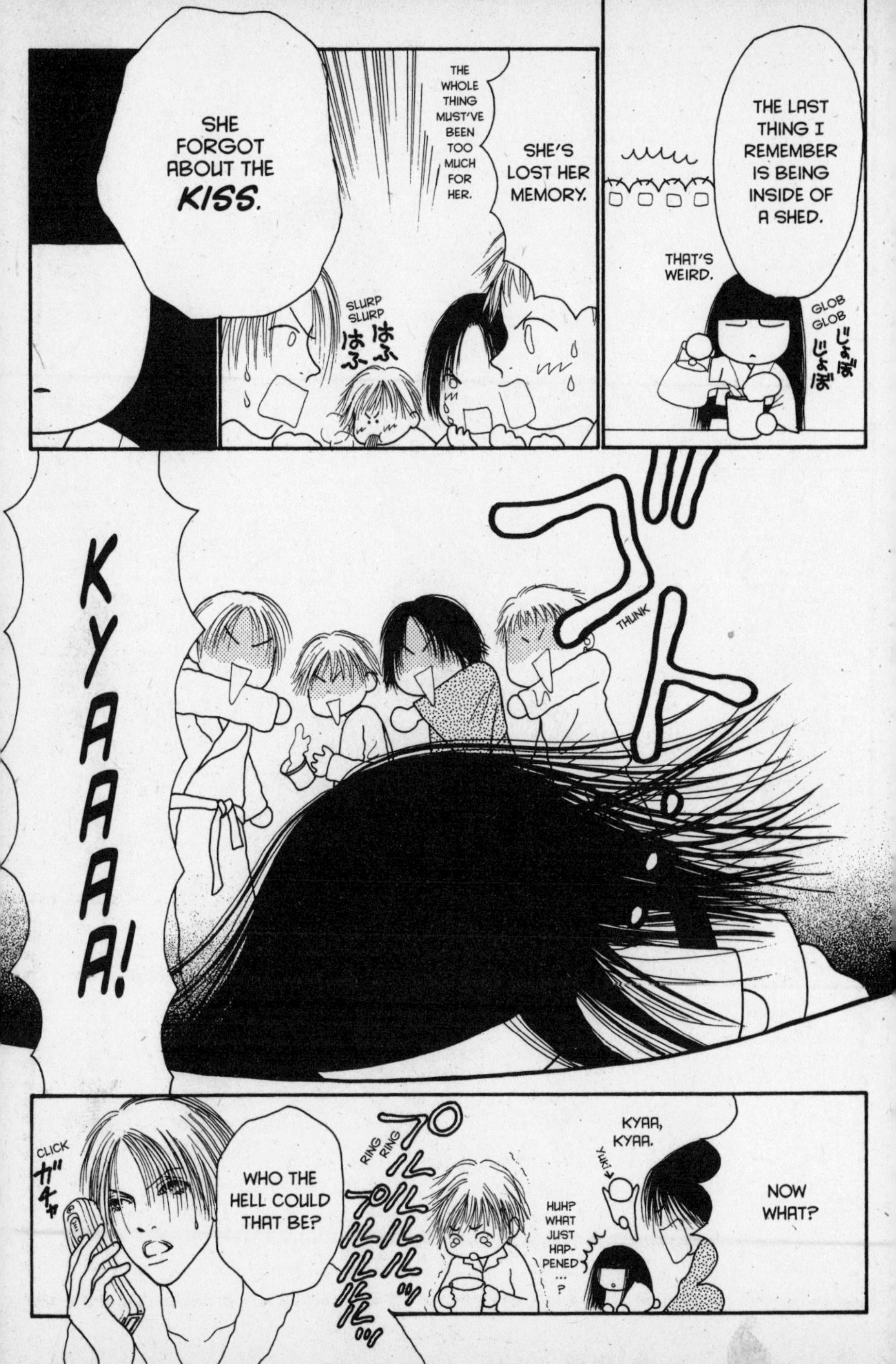
THE LAST THING I REMEMBER IS BEING INSIDE OF A SHED.
THAT'S WEIRD.
GLOB GLOB
じょぼ じょぼ
SHE'S LOST HER MEMORY.
THE WHOLE THING MUST'VE BEEN TOO MUCH FOR HER.
SLURP SLURP
はふ はふ
SHE FORGOT ABOUT THE KISS.
ゴト
THUNK
KYAAAAA!
NOW WHAT?
KYAA, KYAA.
KYA
HUH? WHAT JUST HAP-PENED...?
RING RING
プルルル プルルルル...
WHO THE HELL COULD THAT BE?
CLICK
ガチャ

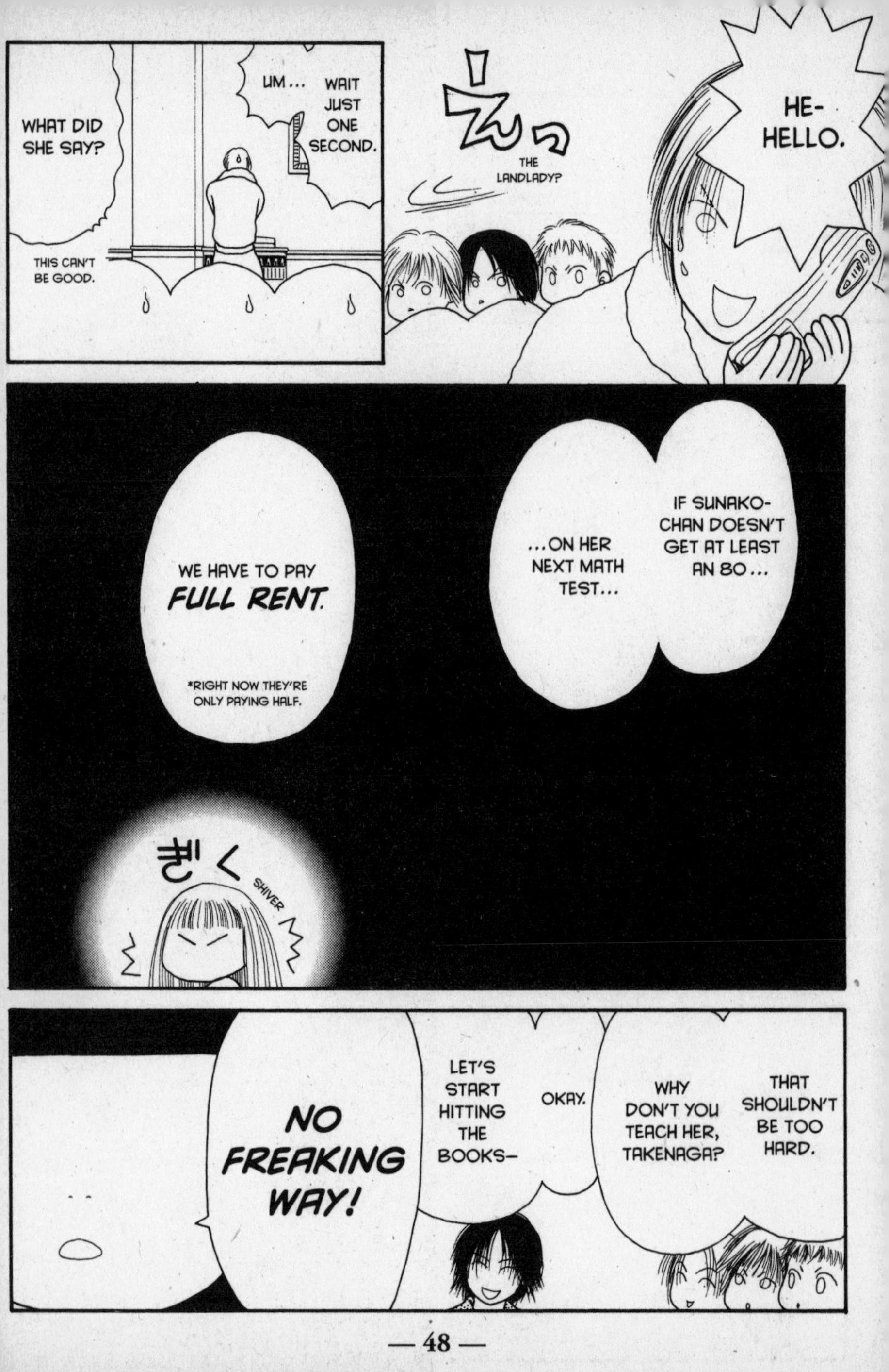
HE-HELLO.
えっ
THE LANDLADY?
UM...
WAIT JUST ONE SECOND.
WHAT DID SHE SAY?
THIS CAN'T BE GOOD.
IF SUNAKO-CHAN DOESN'T GET AT LEAST AN 80...
...ON HER NEXT MATH TEST...
WE HAVE TO PAY *FULL RENT*.
*RIGHT NOW THEY'RE ONLY PAYING HALF.
ぎく
SHIVER
THAT SHOULDN'T BE TOO HARD.
WHY DON'T YOU TEACH HER, TAKENAGA?
OKAY.
LET'S START HITTING THE BOOKS—
NO FREAKING WAY!

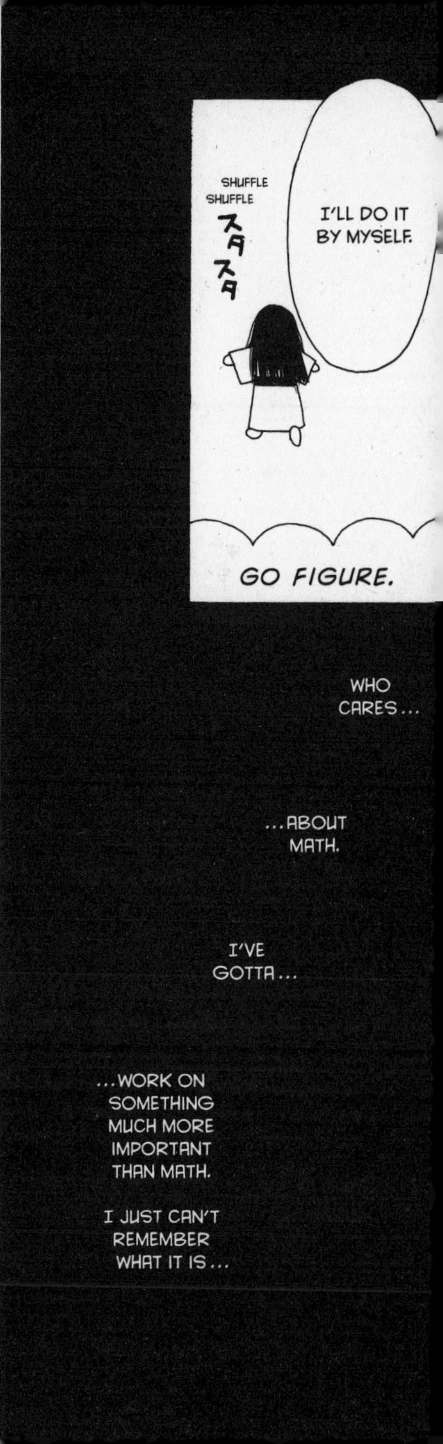
I'LL DO IT BY MYSELF.
SHUFFLE SHUFFLE
スタスタ
GO FIGURE.
WHO CARES...
...ABOUT MATH.
I'VE GOTTA...
...WORK ON SOMETHING MUCH MORE IMPORTANT THAN MATH.
I JUST CAN'T REMEMBER WHAT IT IS...
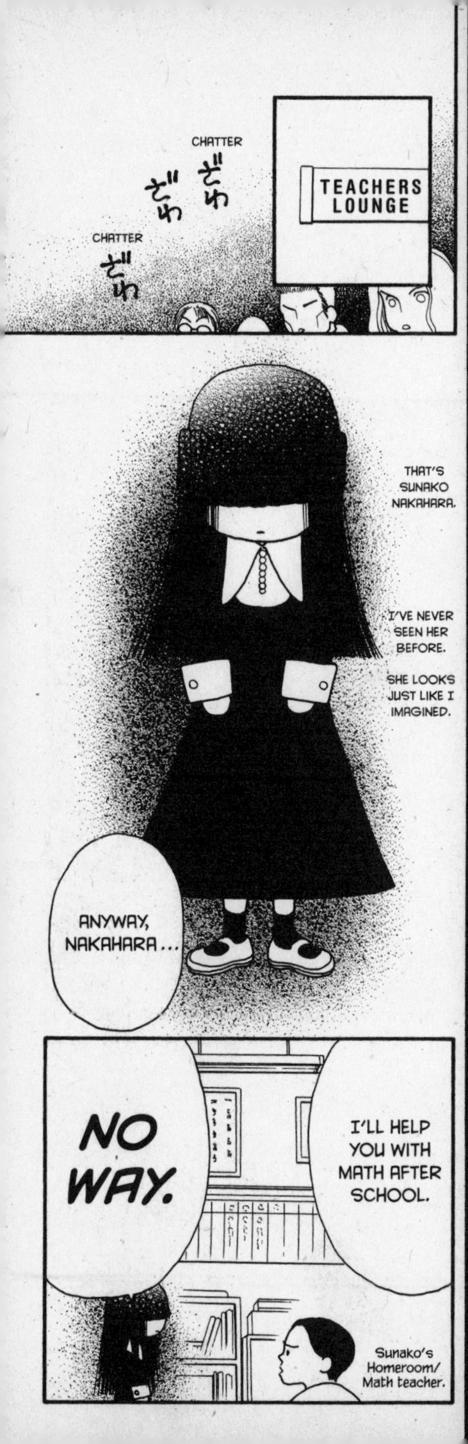
TEACHERS LOUNGE
CHATTER
ざわ
CHATTER
ざわ
THAT'S SUNAKO NAKAHARA.
I'VE NEVER SEEN HER BEFORE.
SHE LOOKS JUST LIKE I IMAGINED.
ANYWAY, NAKAHARA...
I'LL HELP YOU WITH MATH AFTER SCHOOL.
NO WAY.
Sunako's Homeroom/Math teacher.

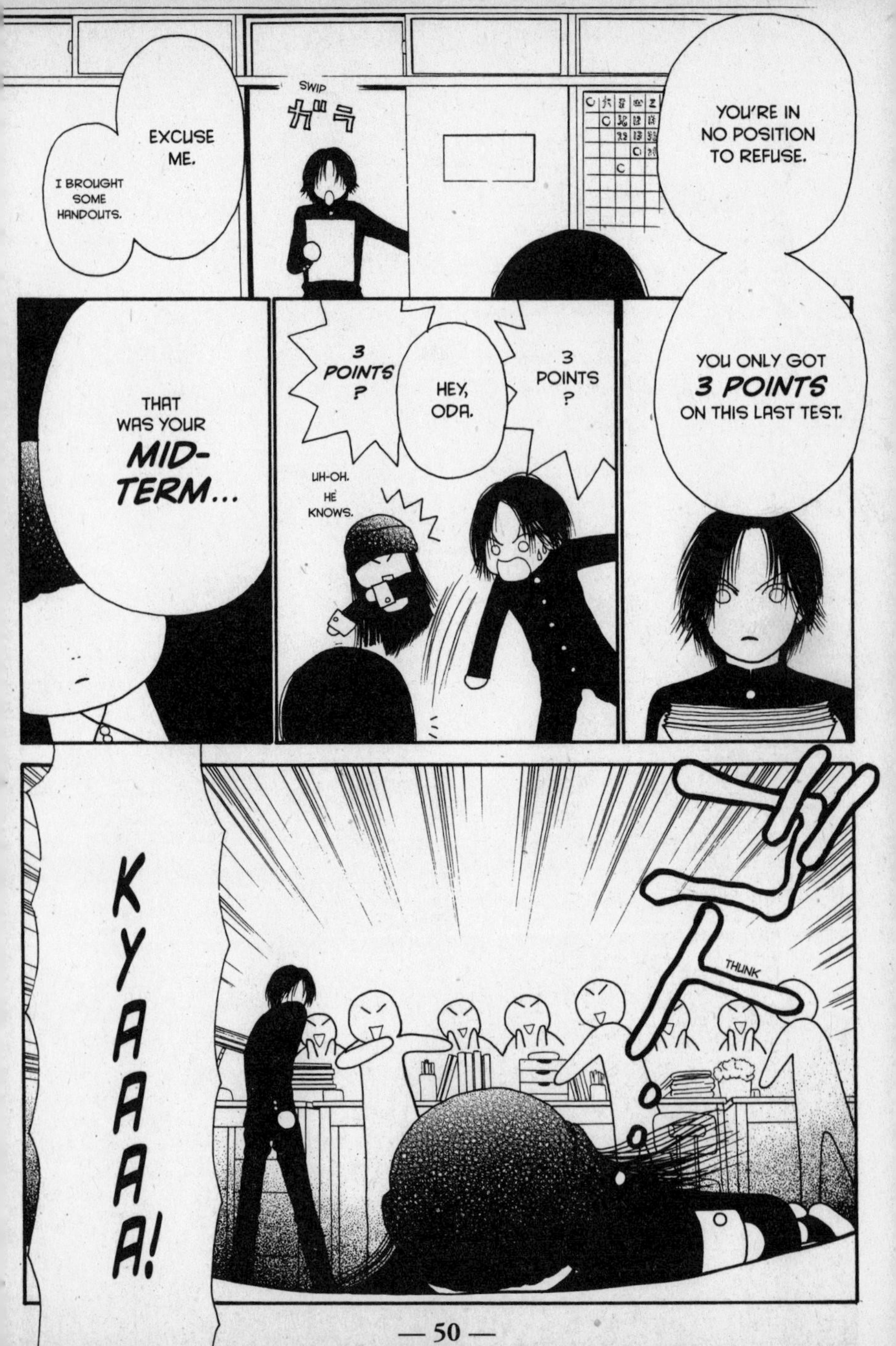
YOU'RE IN NO POSITION TO REFUSE.
SWIP
ガラ
EXCUSE ME.
I BROUGHT SOME HANDOUTS.
YOU ONLY GOT **3 POINTS** ON THIS LAST TEST.
3 POINTS ?
HEY, ODA.
3 POINTS ?
UH-OH. HE KNOWS.
THAT WAS YOUR *MID-TERM...*
THUNK
KYAAAAA!

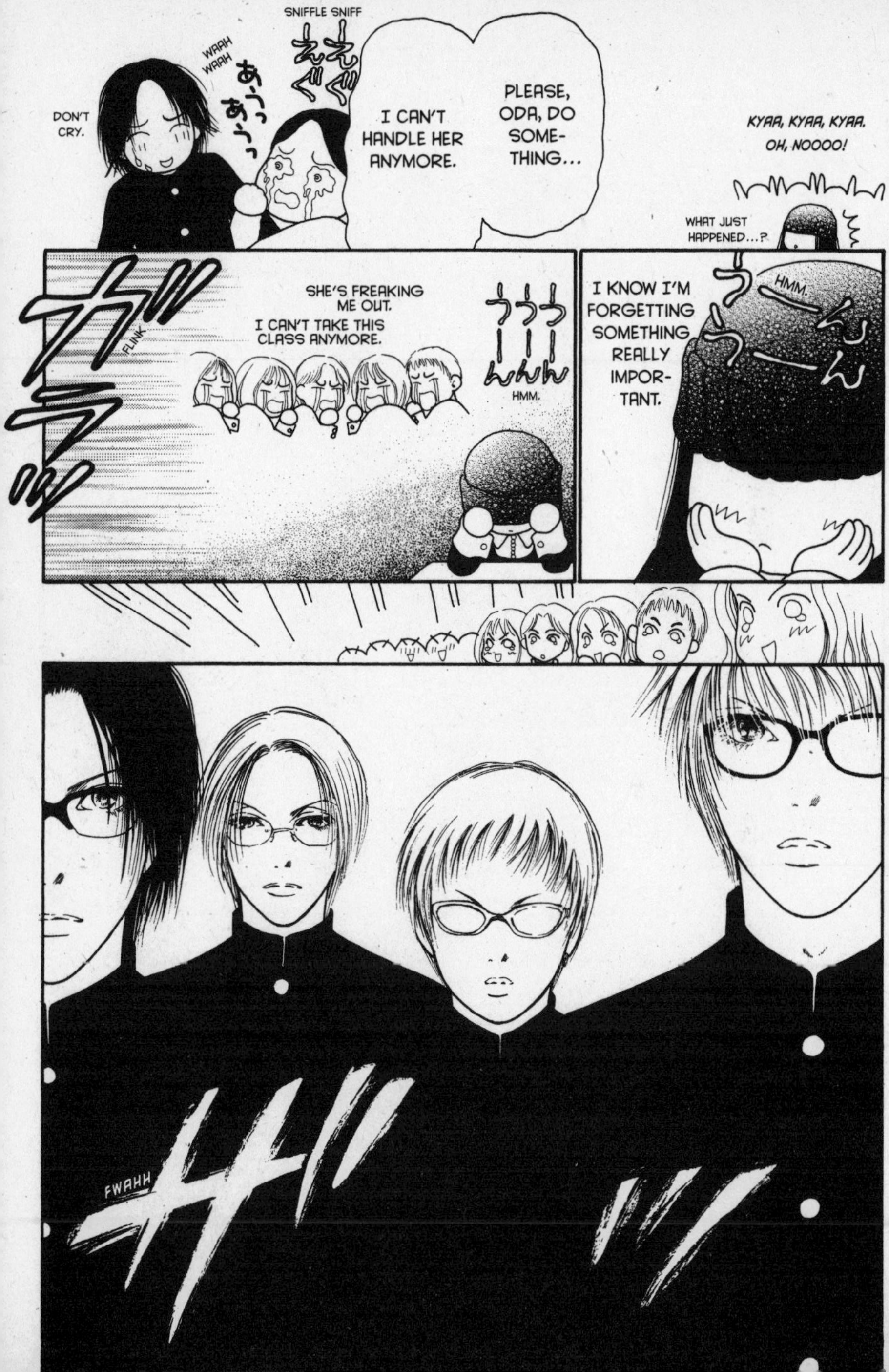
KYAA, KYAA, KYAA. OH, NOOOO!
WHAT JUST HAPPENED...?
PLEASE, ODA, DO SOMETHING...
I CAN'T HANDLE HER ANYMORE.
SNIFFLE SNIFF
WAAH WAAH
DON'T CRY.
HMM.
I KNOW I'M FORGETTING SOMETHING REALLY IMPORTANT.
HMM.
SHE'S FREAKING ME OUT.
I CAN'T TAKE THIS CLASS ANYMORE.
FLINK
FWAHH

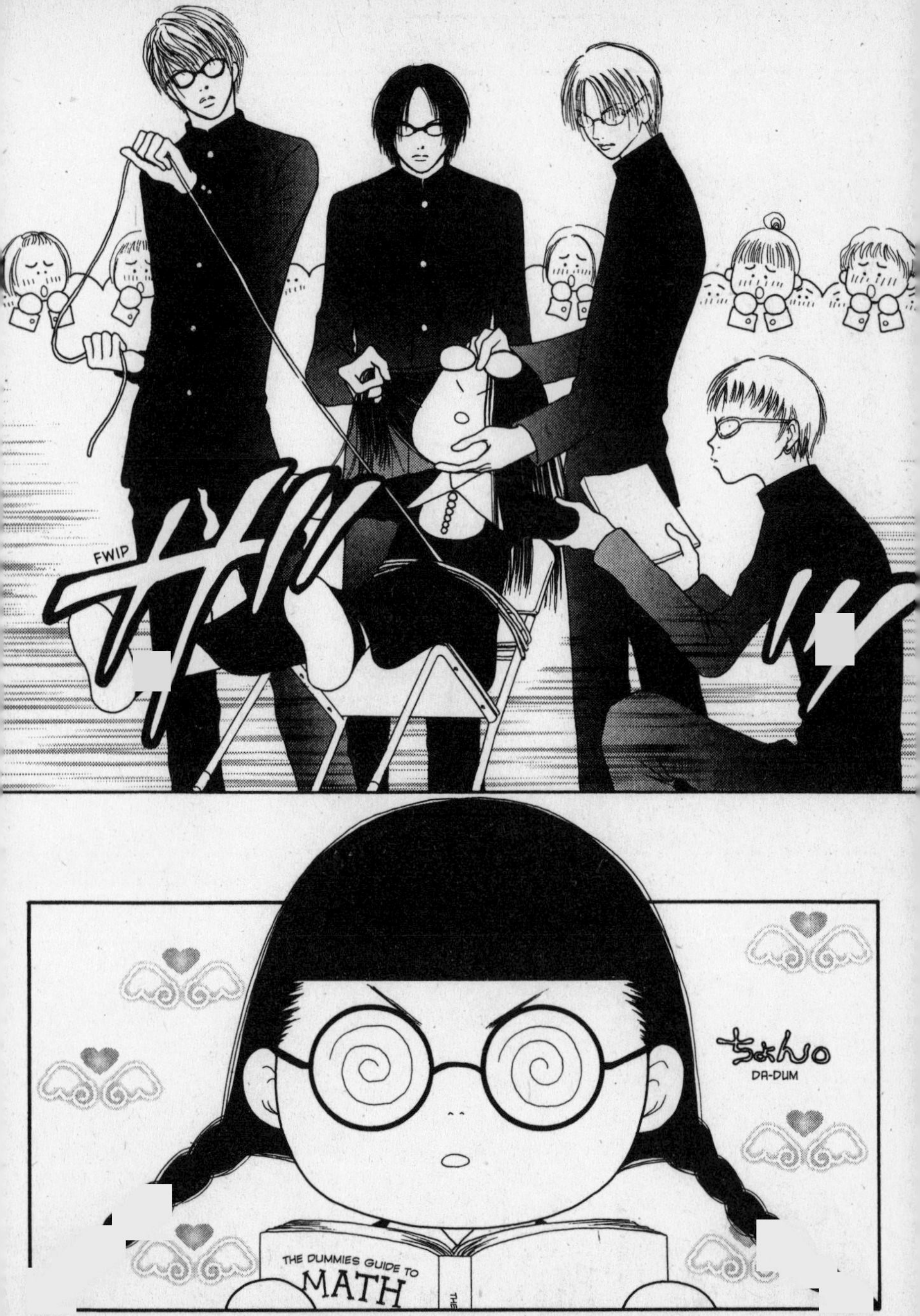
FWIP
DA-DUM
THE DUMMIES GUIDE TO MATH

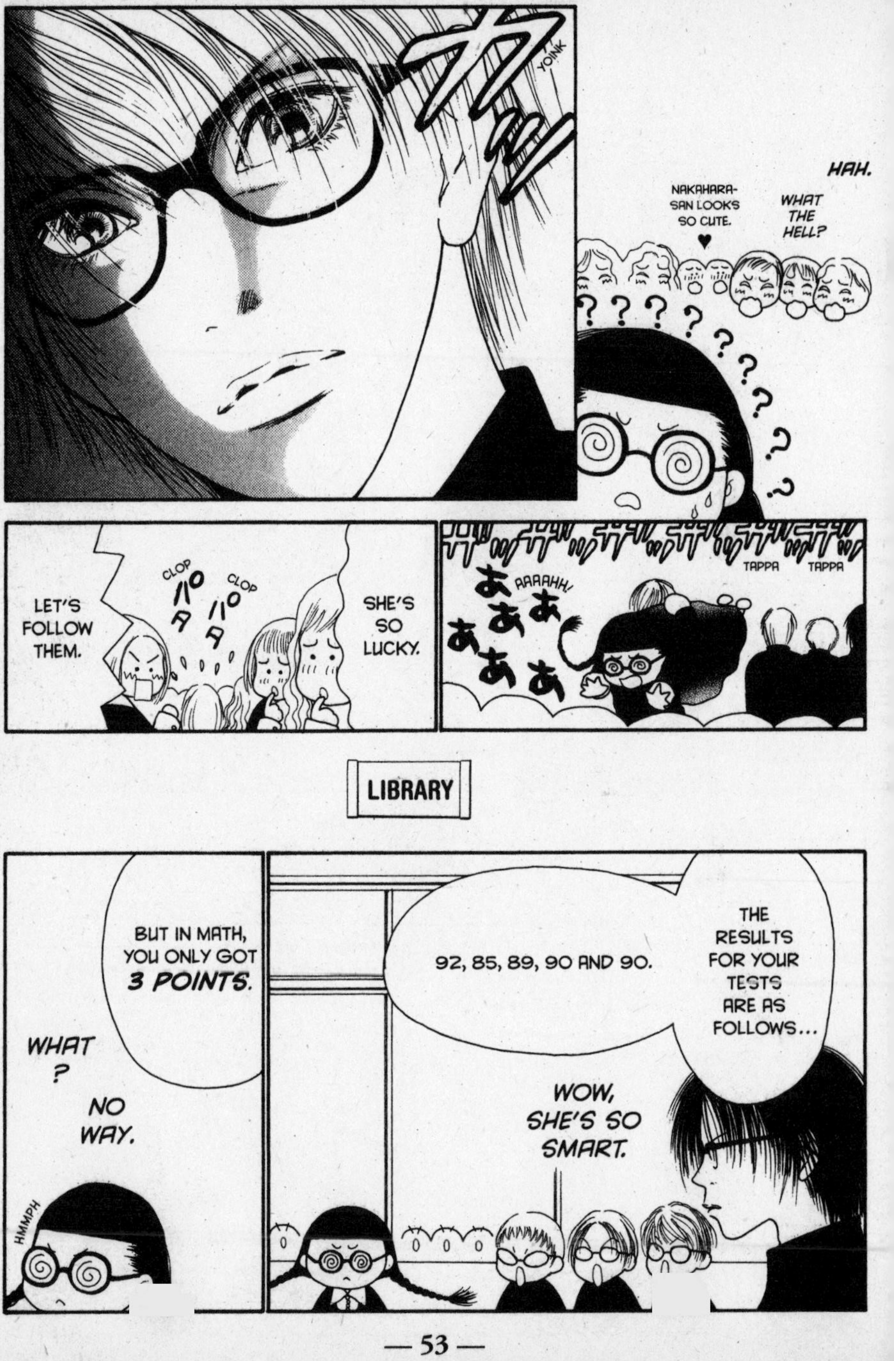
HAH.
WHAT THE HELL?
NAKAHARA-SAN LOOKS SO CUTE. ♥
YOINK
TAPPA
TAPPA
AAAAAHH!
SHE'S SO LUCKY.
CLOP
CLOP
LET'S FOLLOW THEM.
LIBRARY
THE RESULTS FOR YOUR TESTS ARE AS FOLLOWS...
92, 85, 89, 90 AND 90.
WOW, SHE'S SO SMART.
BUT IN MATH, YOU ONLY GOT 3 POINTS.
WHAT?
NO WAY.
HMMPH

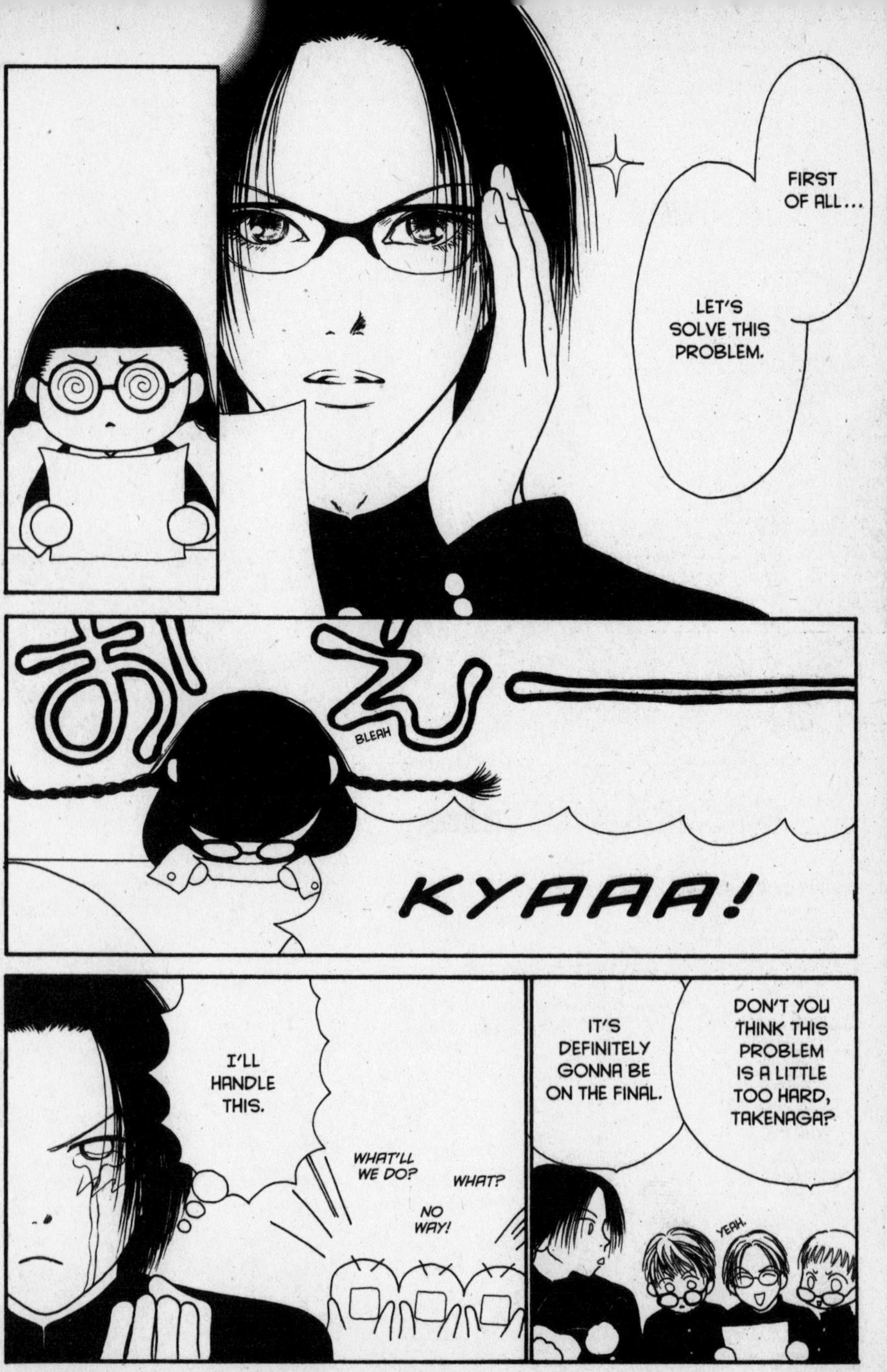
FIRST OF ALL...
LET'S SOLVE THIS PROBLEM.
おえー
BLEAH
KYAAA!
DON'T YOU THINK THIS PROBLEM IS A LITTLE TOO HARD, TAKENAGA?
IT'S DEFINITELY GONNA BE ON THE FINAL.
YEAH.
I'LL HANDLE THIS.
WHAT?
WHAT'LL WE DO?
NO WAY!

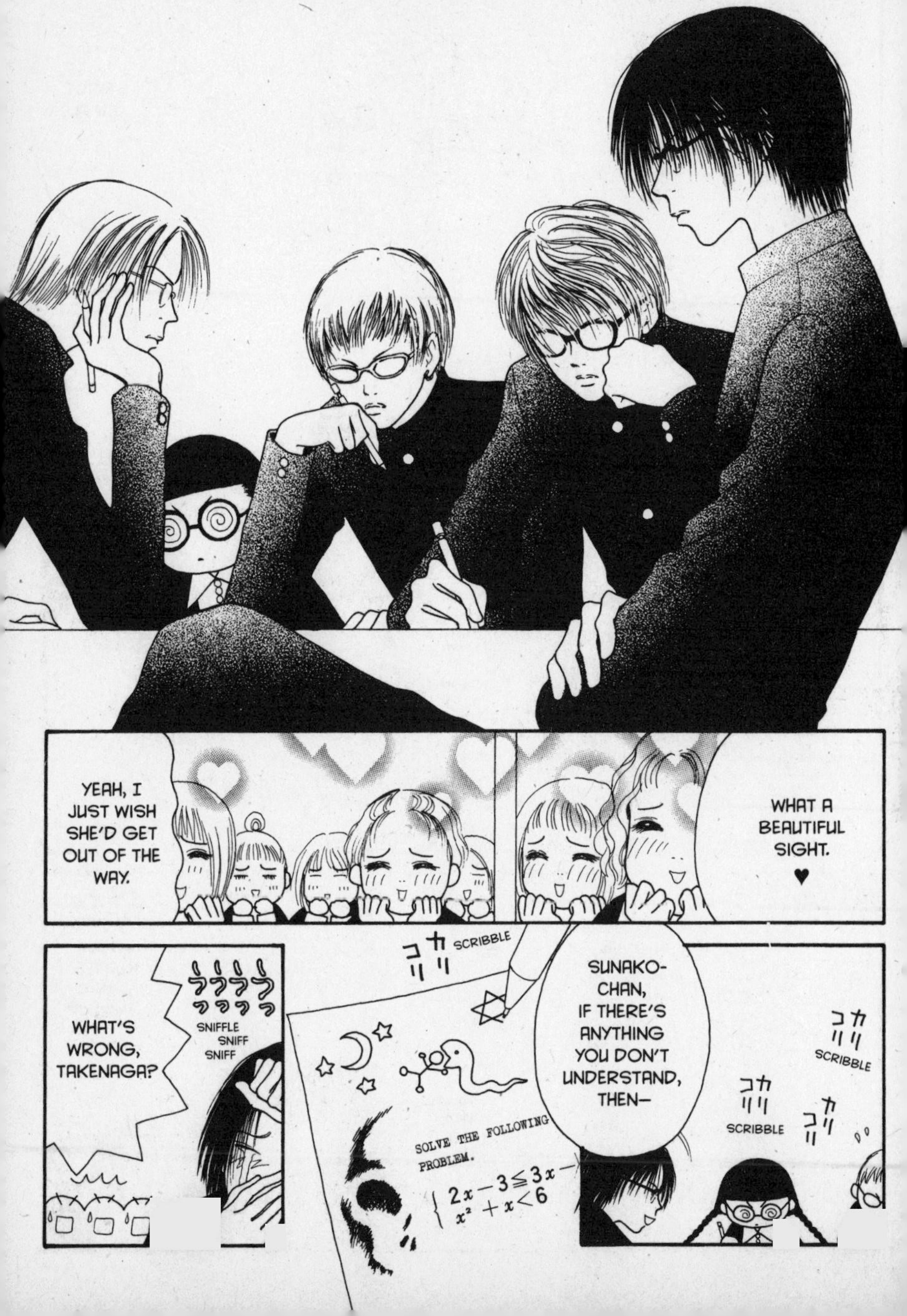
WHAT A BEAUTIFUL SIGHT. ♥
YEAH, I JUST WISH SHE'D GET OUT OF THE WAY.
SCRIBBLE
SCRIBBLE
SUNAKO-CHAN, IF THERE'S ANYTHING YOU DON'T UNDERSTAND, THEN—
SCRIBBLE
SOLVE THE FOLLOWING PROBLEM.
$2x - 3 \leqq 3x -$
$x^2 + x < 6$
SNIFFLE SNIFF SNIFF
WHAT'S WRONG, TAKENAGA?

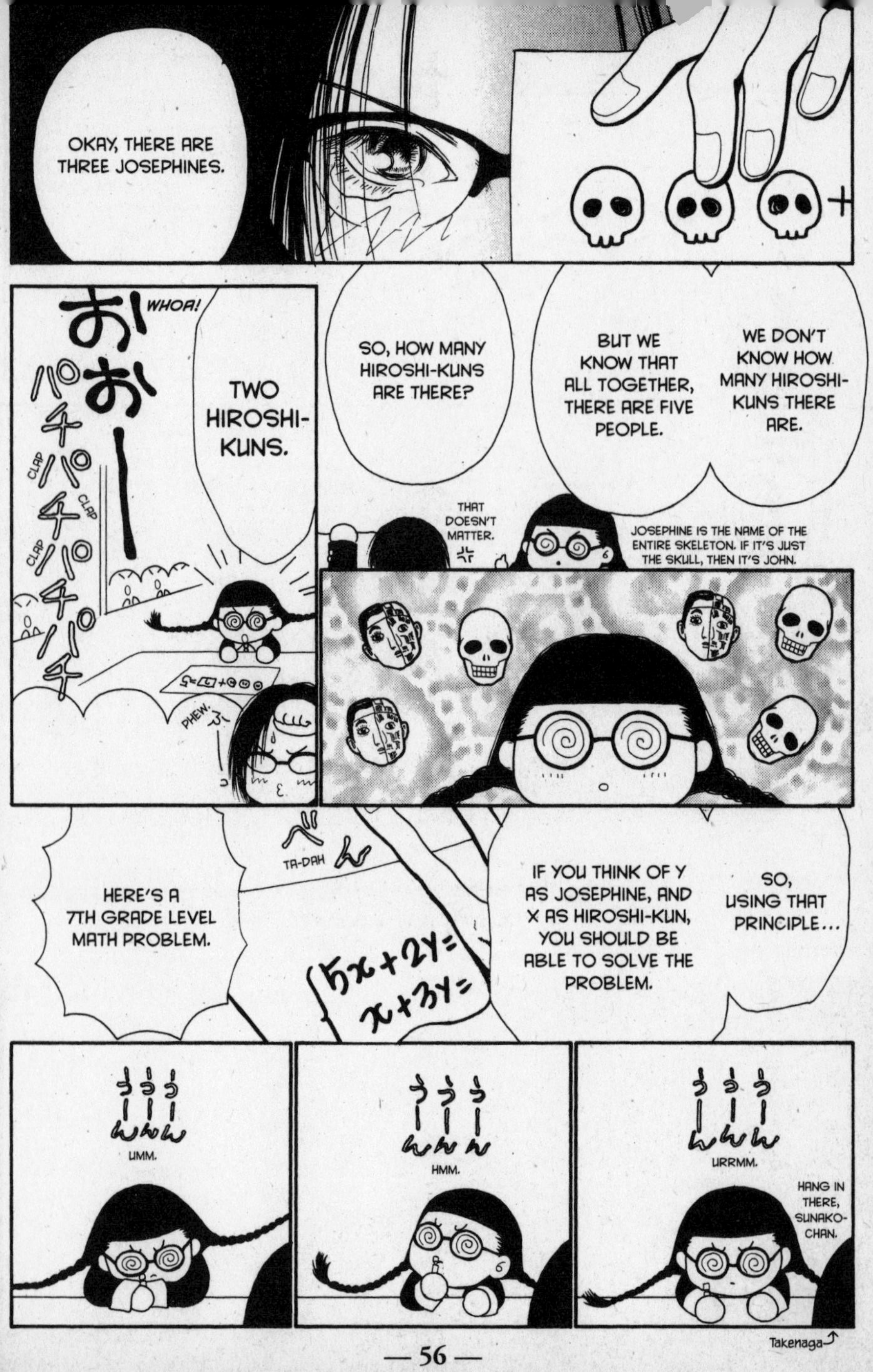

OKAY, THERE ARE THREE JOSEPHINES.
WE DON'T KNOW HOW MANY HIROSHI-KUNS THERE ARE.
BUT WE KNOW THAT ALL TOGETHER, THERE ARE FIVE PEOPLE.
SO, HOW MANY HIROSHI-KUNS ARE THERE?
JOSEPHINE IS THE NAME OF THE ENTIRE SKELETON. IF IT'S JUST THE SKULL, THEN IT'S JOHN.
THAT DOESN'T MATTER.
TWO HIROSHI-KUNS.
おおー WHOA!
パチパチパチパチ CLAP CLAP CLAP
ふー PHEW.
SO, USING THAT PRINCIPLE...
IF YOU THINK OF Y AS JOSEPHINE, AND X AS HIROSHI-KUN, YOU SHOULD BE ABLE TO SOLVE THE PROBLEM.
べん TA-DAH
HERE'S A 7TH GRADE LEVEL MATH PROBLEM.
5x+2y=
x+3y=
うーん URRMM.
HANG IN THERE, SUNAKO-CHAN.
Takenaga
うーん HMM.
うーん UMM.

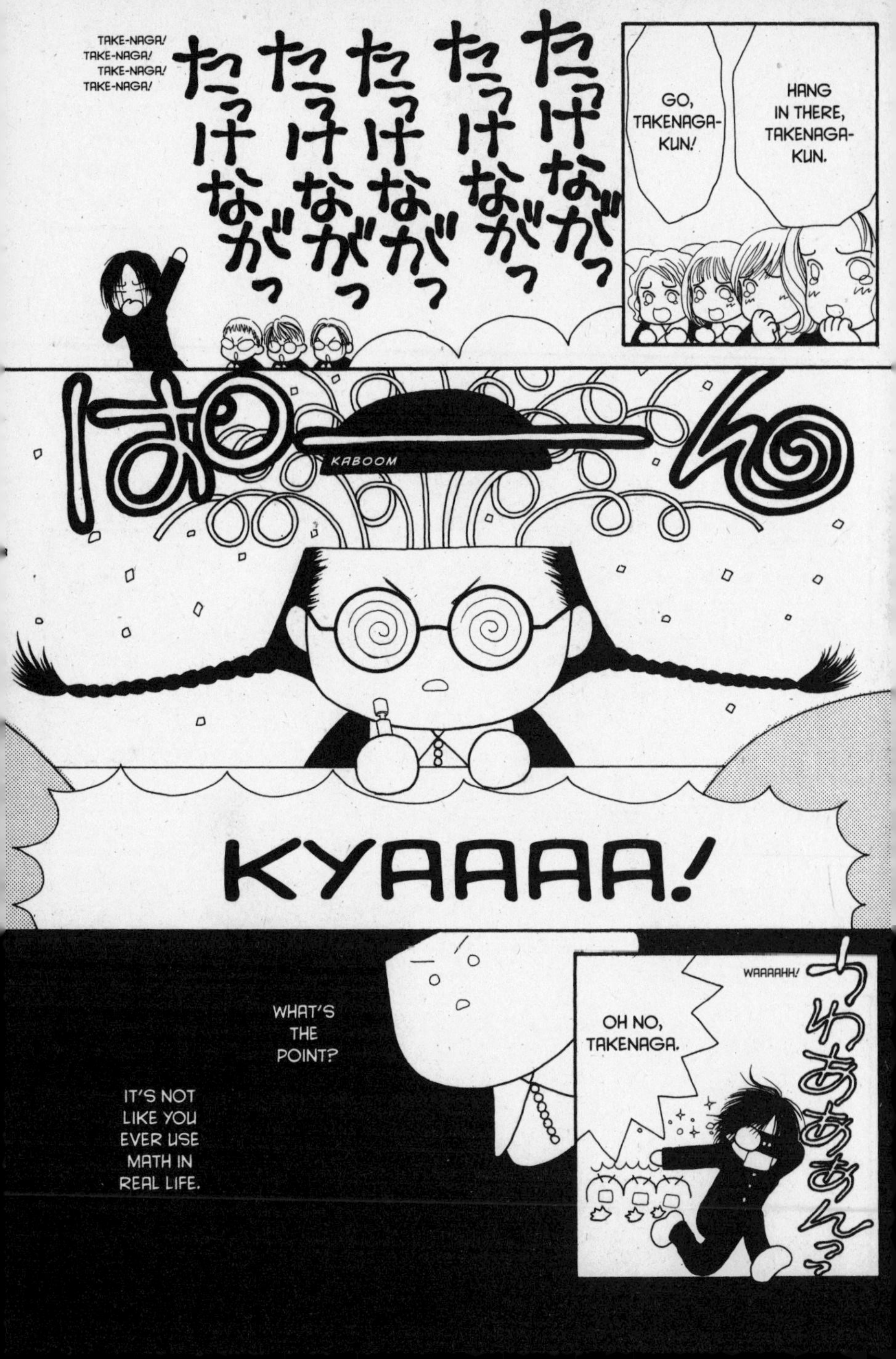
HANG IN THERE, TAKENAGA-KUN.
GO, TAKENAGA-KUN!
たっけながっ
たっけながっ
たっけながっ
たっけながっ
TAKE-NAGA!
TAKE-NAGA!
TAKE-NAGA!
TAKE-NAGA!
ぱーん
KABOOM
KYAAAAA!
うわあああんっ
WAAAAHH!
OH NO, TAKENAGA.
WHAT'S THE POINT?
IT'S NOT LIKE YOU EVER USE MATH IN REAL LIFE.

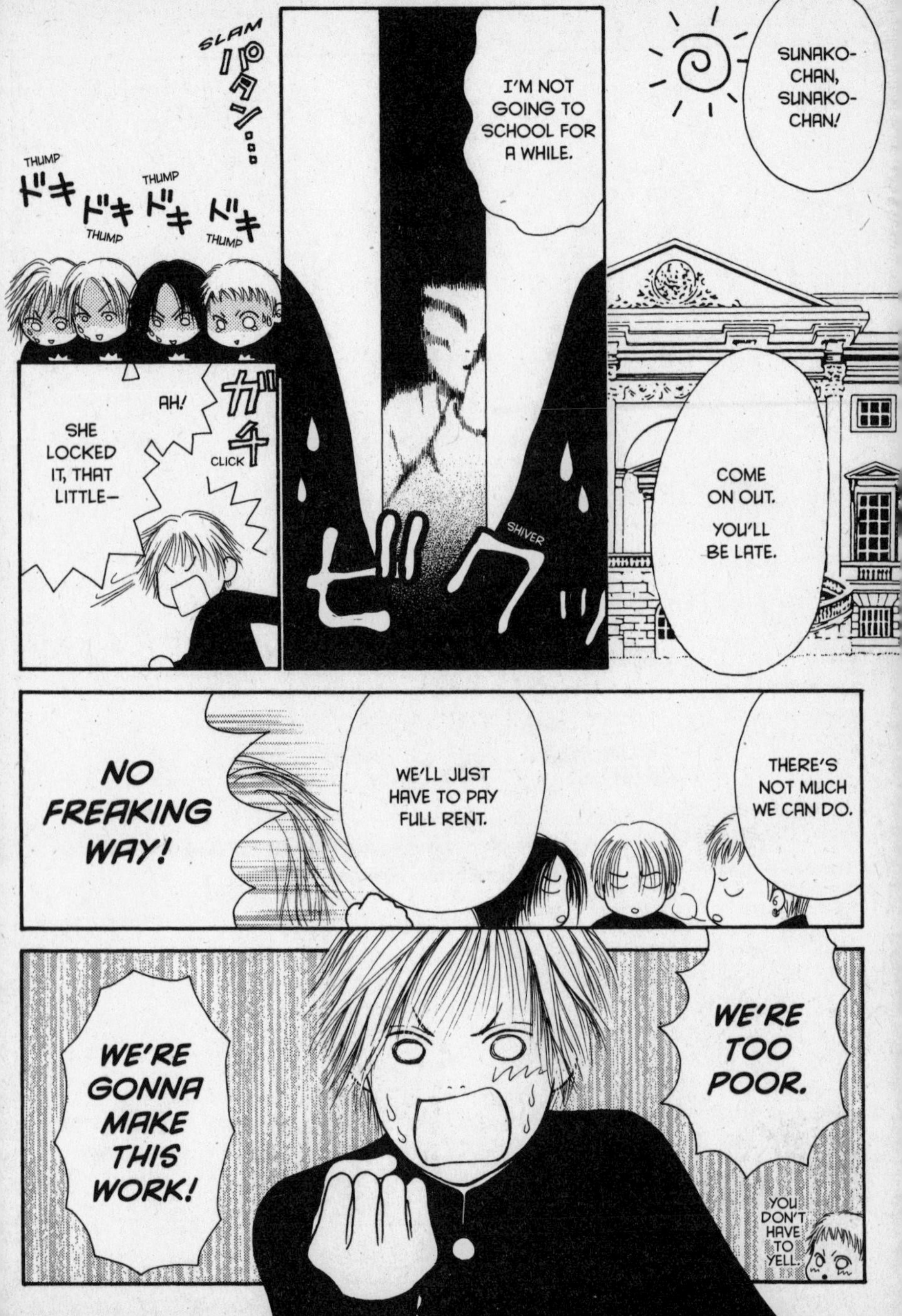

SUNAKO-CHAN, SUNAKO-CHAN!
COME ON OUT. YOU'LL BE LATE.
I'M NOT GOING TO SCHOOL FOR A WHILE.
SHIVER
ビクッ
SLAM
パタン…
THUMP
ドキ ドキ ドキ ドキ
THUMP THUMP THUMP
ガチ
CLICK
AH!
SHE LOCKED IT, THAT LITTLE—
THERE'S NOT MUCH WE CAN DO.
WE'LL JUST HAVE TO PAY FULL RENT.
NO FREAKING WAY!
WE'RE TOO POOR.
YOU DON'T HAVE TO YELL.
WE'RE GONNA MAKE THIS WORK!

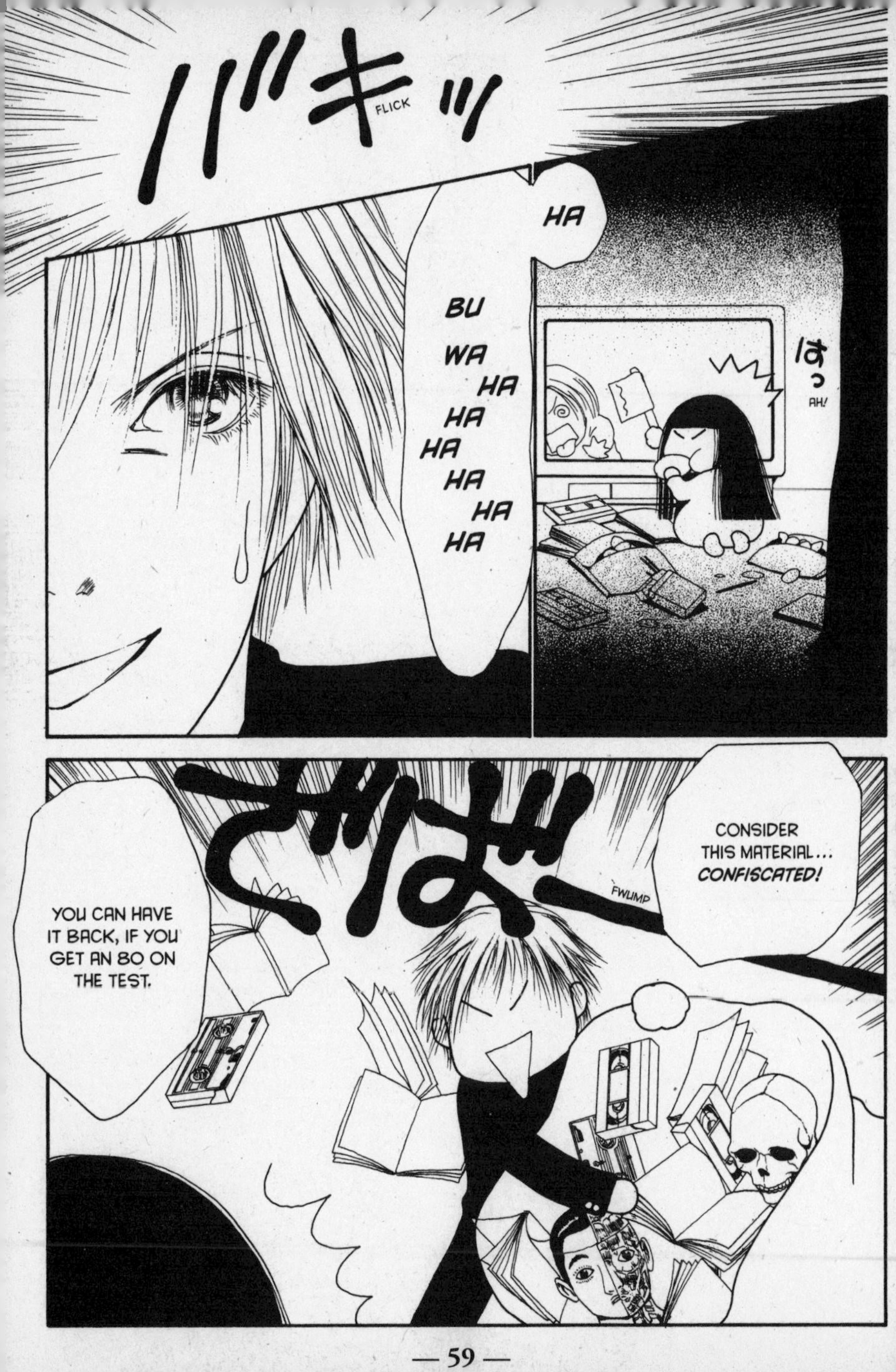
バキッ
FLICK
HA
BU WA HA HA HA HA HA HA
はっ
AH!
FWUMP
CONSIDER THIS MATERIAL... *CONFISCATED!*
YOU CAN HAVE IT BACK, IF YOU GET AN 80 ON THE TEST.

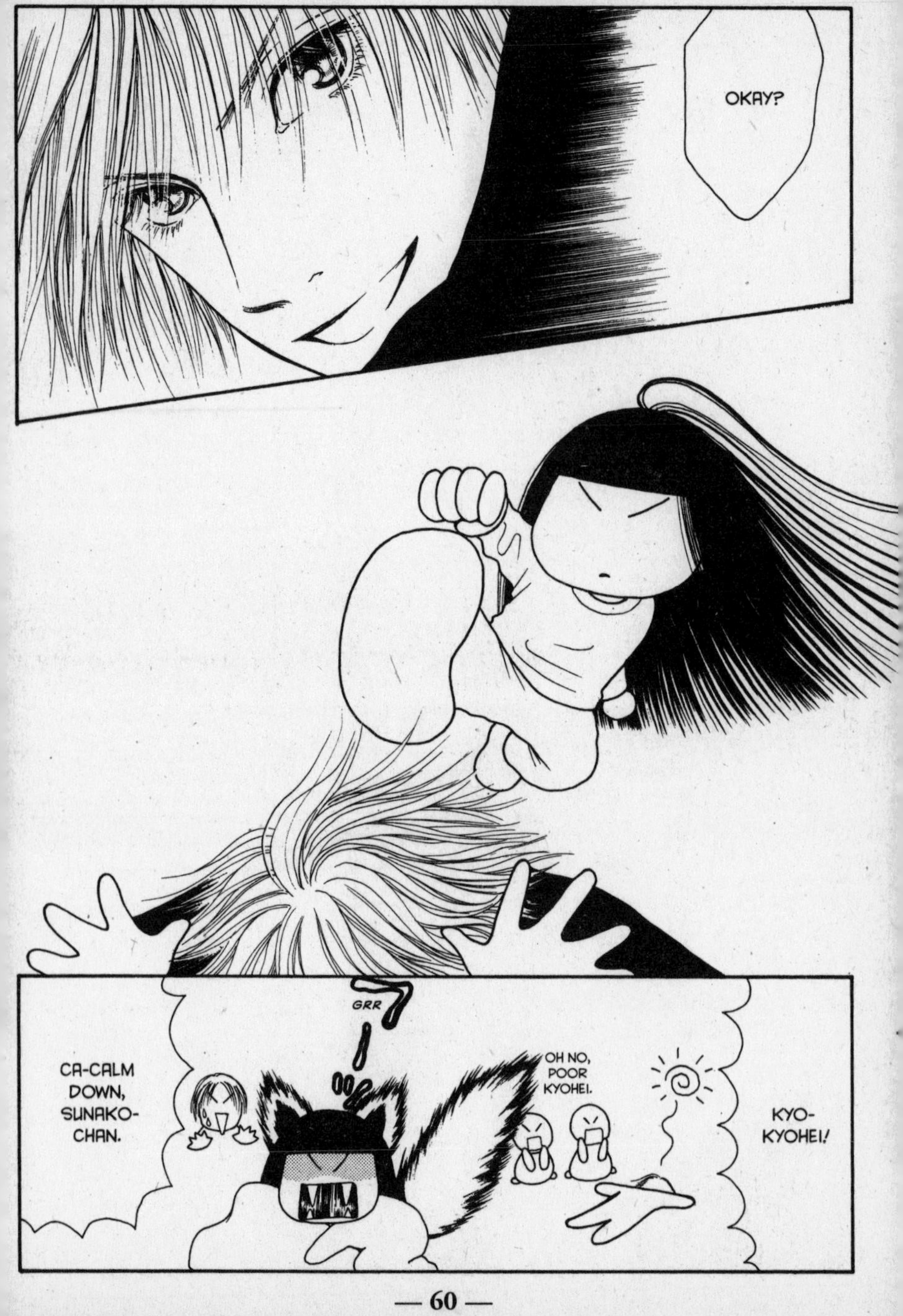
OKAY?
KYO-KYOHEI!
OH NO, POOR KYOHEI.
GRR
CA-CALM DOWN, SUNAKO-CHAN.

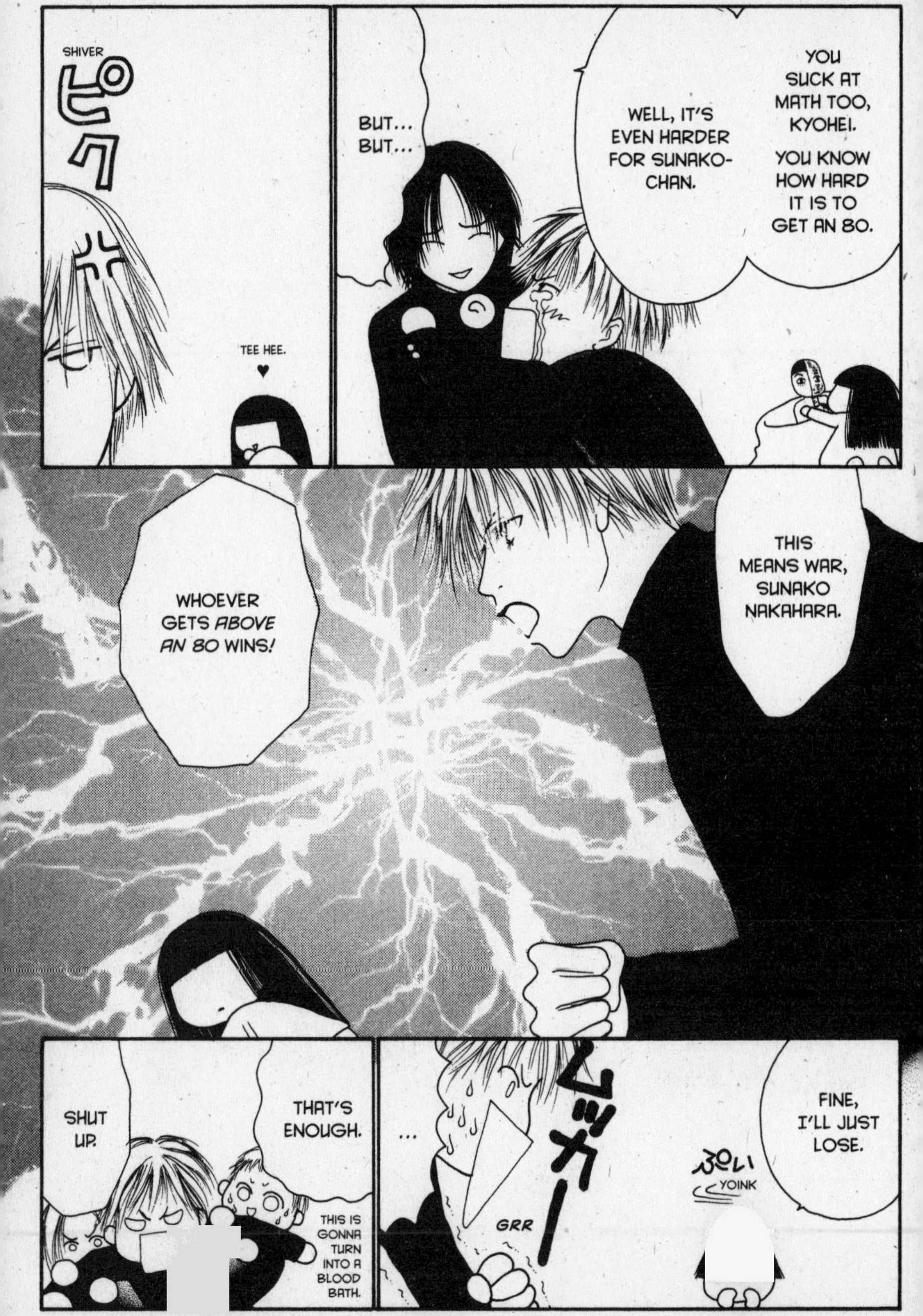
YOU SUCK AT MATH TOO, KYOHEI.
YOU KNOW HOW HARD IT IS TO GET AN 80.
WELL, IT'S EVEN HARDER FOR SUNAKO-CHAN.
BUT... BUT...
SHIVER
ピク
TEE HEE. ♥
THIS MEANS WAR, SUNAKO NAKAHARA.
WHOEVER GETS *ABOVE* AN 80 WINS!
FINE, I'LL JUST LOSE.
ぷい
YOINK
ムッカー
GRR
...
THAT'S ENOUGH.
SHUT UP.
THIS IS GONNA TURN INTO A BLOOD BATH.

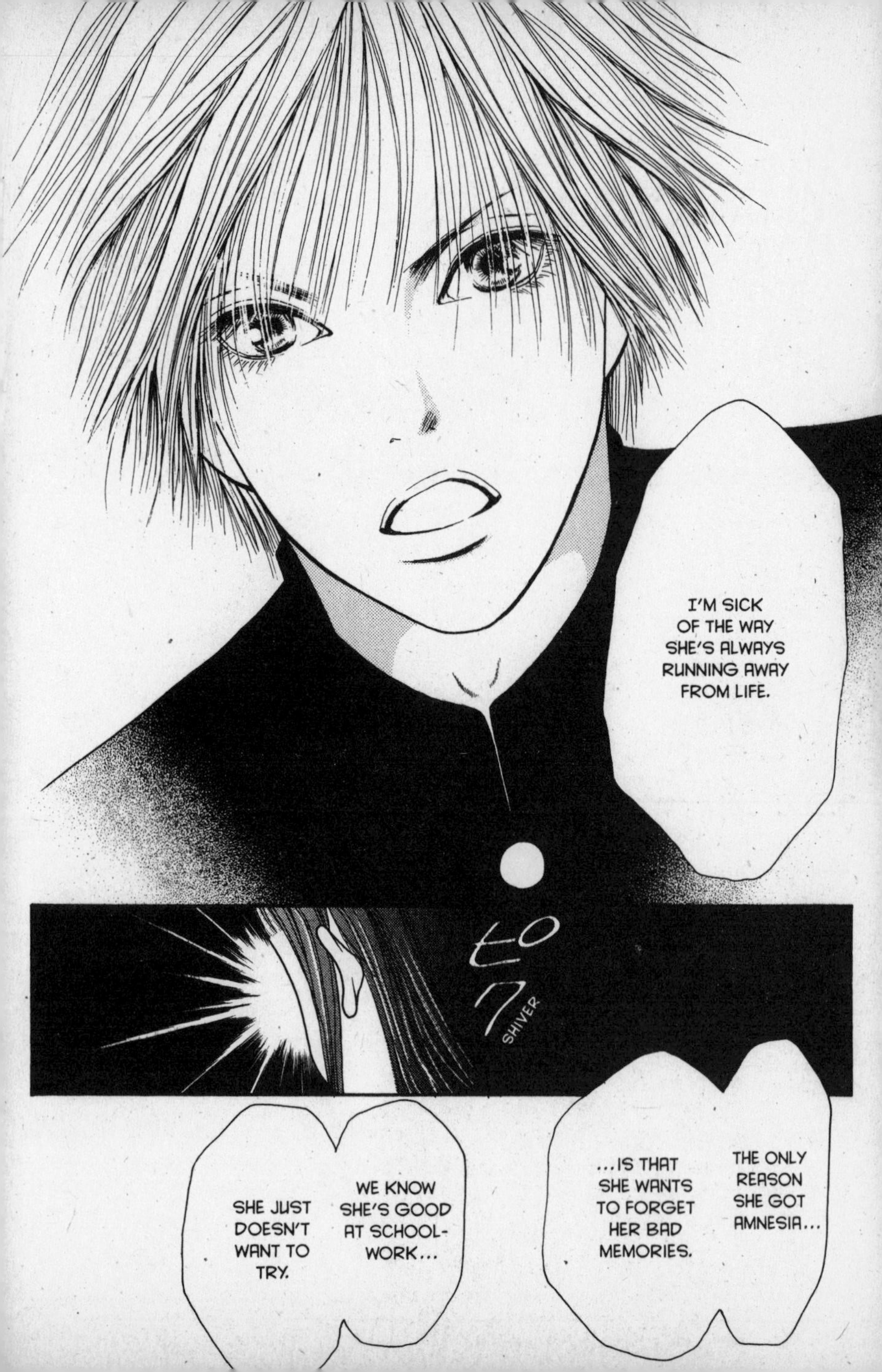
I'M SICK OF THE WAY SHE'S ALWAYS RUNNING AWAY FROM LIFE.
SHIVER
THE ONLY REASON SHE GOT AMNESIA...
...IS THAT SHE WANTS TO FORGET HER BAD MEMORIES.
WE KNOW SHE'S GOOD AT SCHOOL-WORK...
SHE JUST DOESN'T WANT TO TRY.

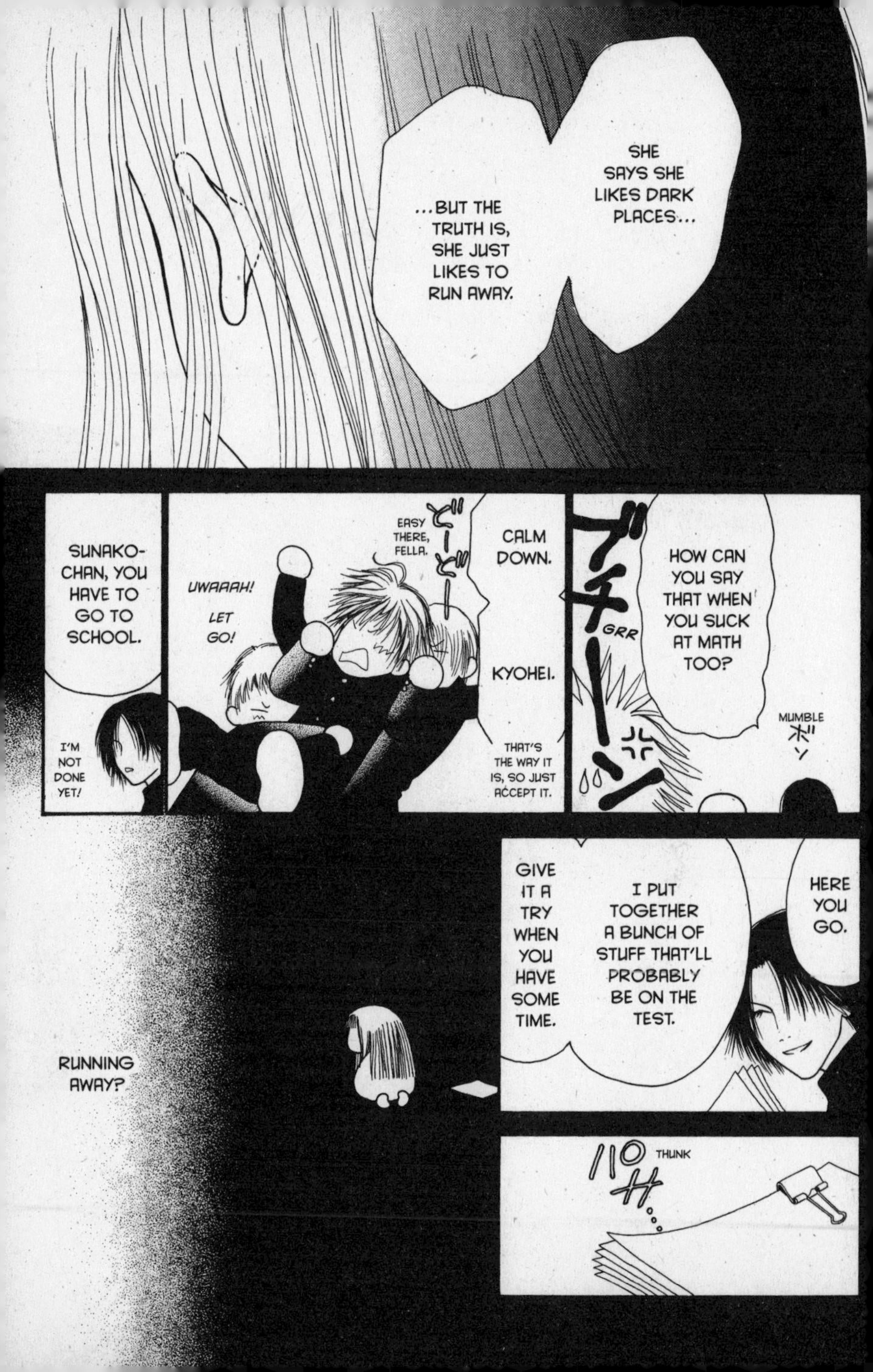
SHE SAYS SHE LIKES DARK PLACES...
...BUT THE TRUTH IS, SHE JUST LIKES TO RUN AWAY.
HOW CAN YOU SAY THAT WHEN YOU SUCK AT MATH TOO?
GRR
MUMBLE
CALM DOWN.
KYOHEI.
THAT'S THE WAY IT IS, SO JUST ACCEPT IT.
EASY THERE, FELLA.
UWAAAH!
LET GO!
SUNAKO-CHAN, YOU HAVE TO GO TO SCHOOL.
I'M NOT DONE YET!
HERE YOU GO.
I PUT TOGETHER A BUNCH OF STUFF THAT'LL PROBABLY BE ON THE TEST.
GIVE IT A TRY WHEN YOU HAVE SOME TIME.
THUNK
RUNNING AWAY?

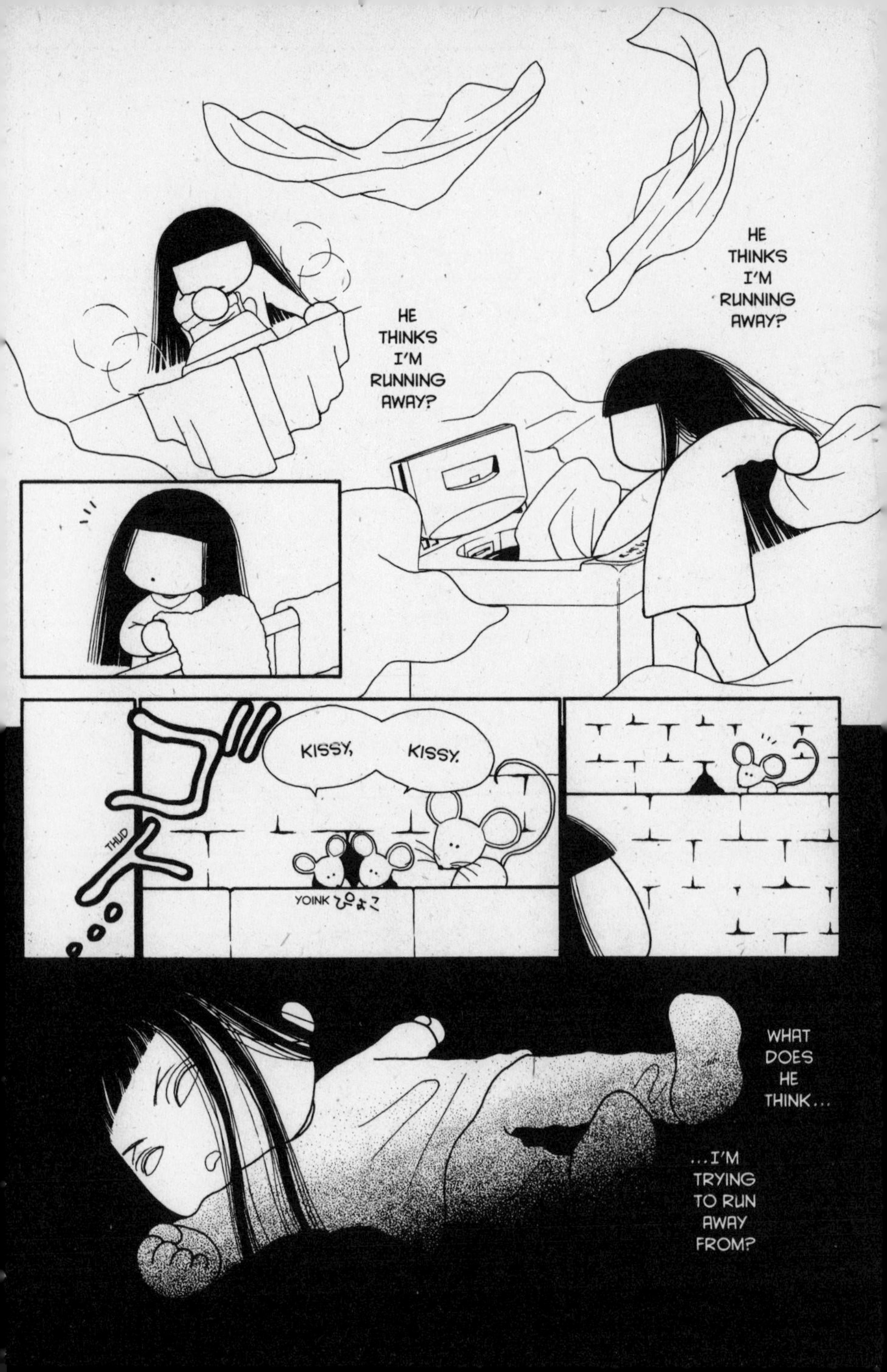
HE THINKS I'M RUNNING AWAY?
HE THINKS I'M RUNNING AWAY?
KISSY, KISSY.
THUD
YOINK ぴょこ
WHAT DOES HE THINK...
...I'M TRYING TO RUN AWAY FROM?

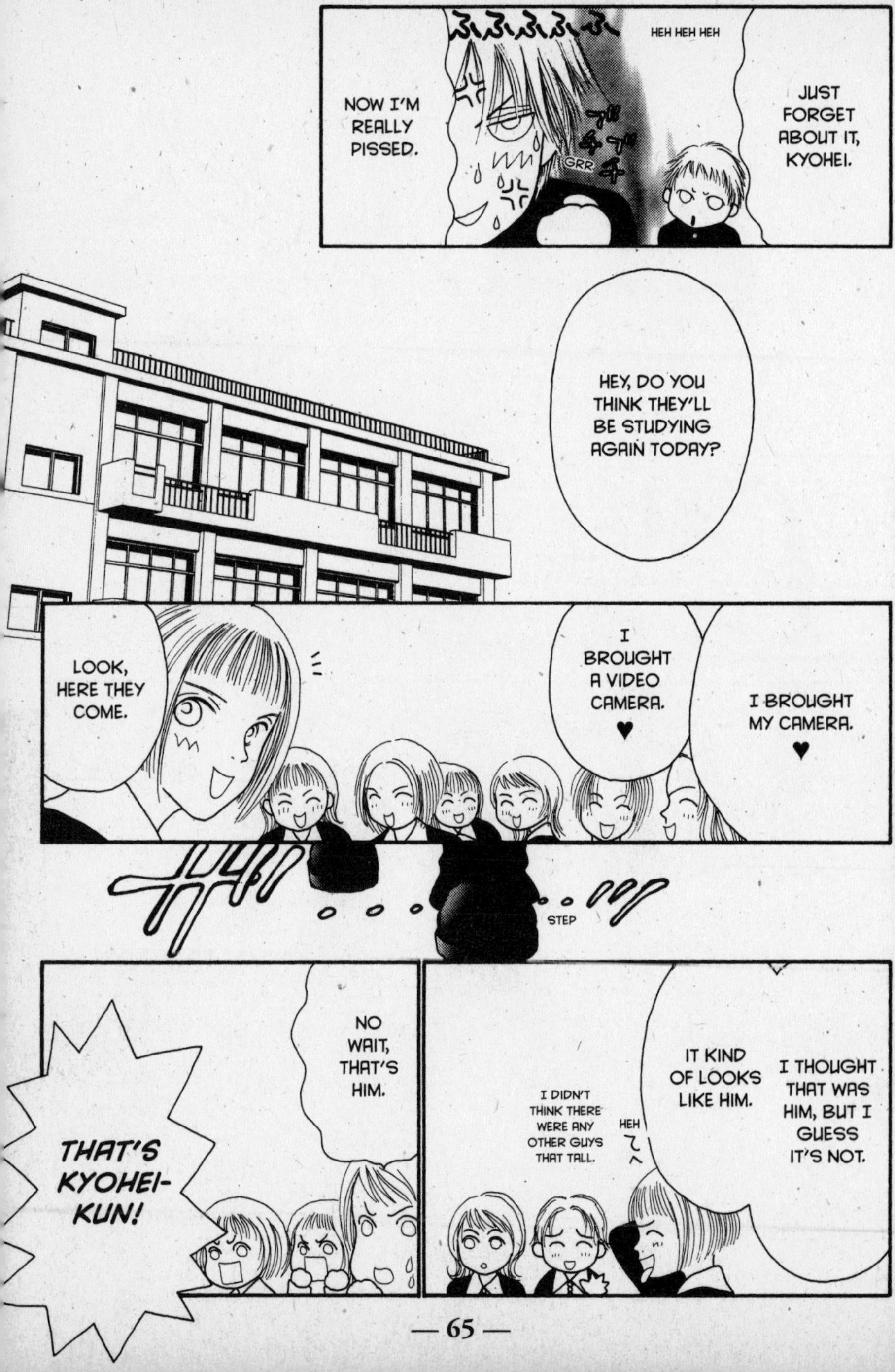
JUST FORGET ABOUT IT, KYOHEI.
ふふふふふ
HEH HEH HEH
GRR
NOW I'M REALLY PISSED.
HEY, DO YOU THINK THEY'LL BE STUDYING AGAIN TODAY?
I BROUGHT MY CAMERA. ♥
I BROUGHT A VIDEO CAMERA. ♥
LOOK, HERE THEY COME.
STEP
I THOUGHT THAT WAS HIM, BUT I GUESS IT'S NOT.
IT KIND OF LOOKS LIKE HIM.
HEH
I DIDN'T THINK THERE WERE ANY OTHER GUYS THAT TALL.
NO WAIT, THAT'S HIM.
THAT'S KYOHEI-KUN!

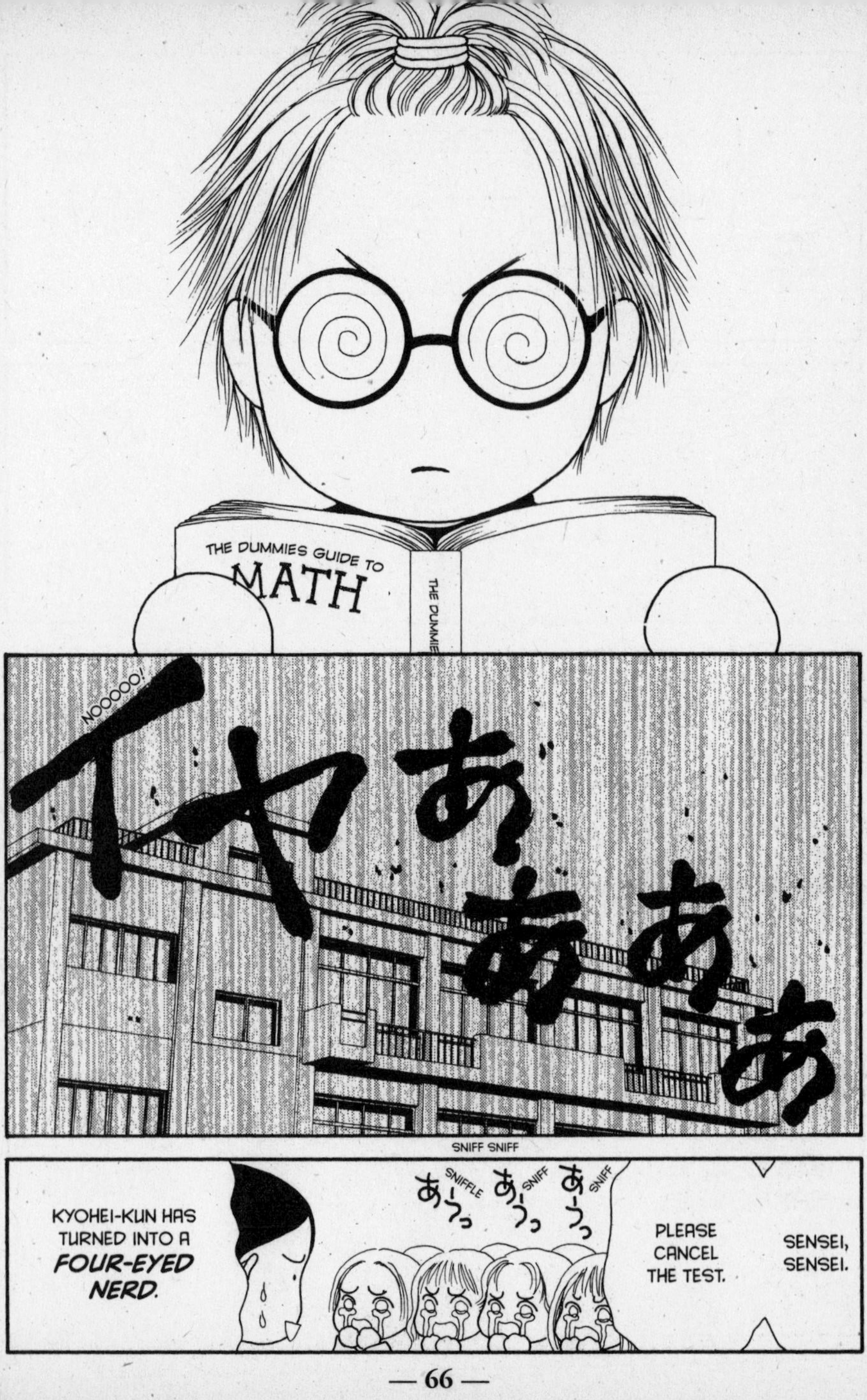
THE DUMMIES GUIDE TO MATH
THE DUMMIE
NOOOOO!
イヤああああ
SNIFF SNIFF
SENSEI, SENSEI.
PLEASE CANCEL THE TEST.
あうっ SNIFF
あうっ SNIFF
あうっ SNIFFLE
KYOHEI-KUN HAS TURNED INTO A *FOUR-EYED NERD*.

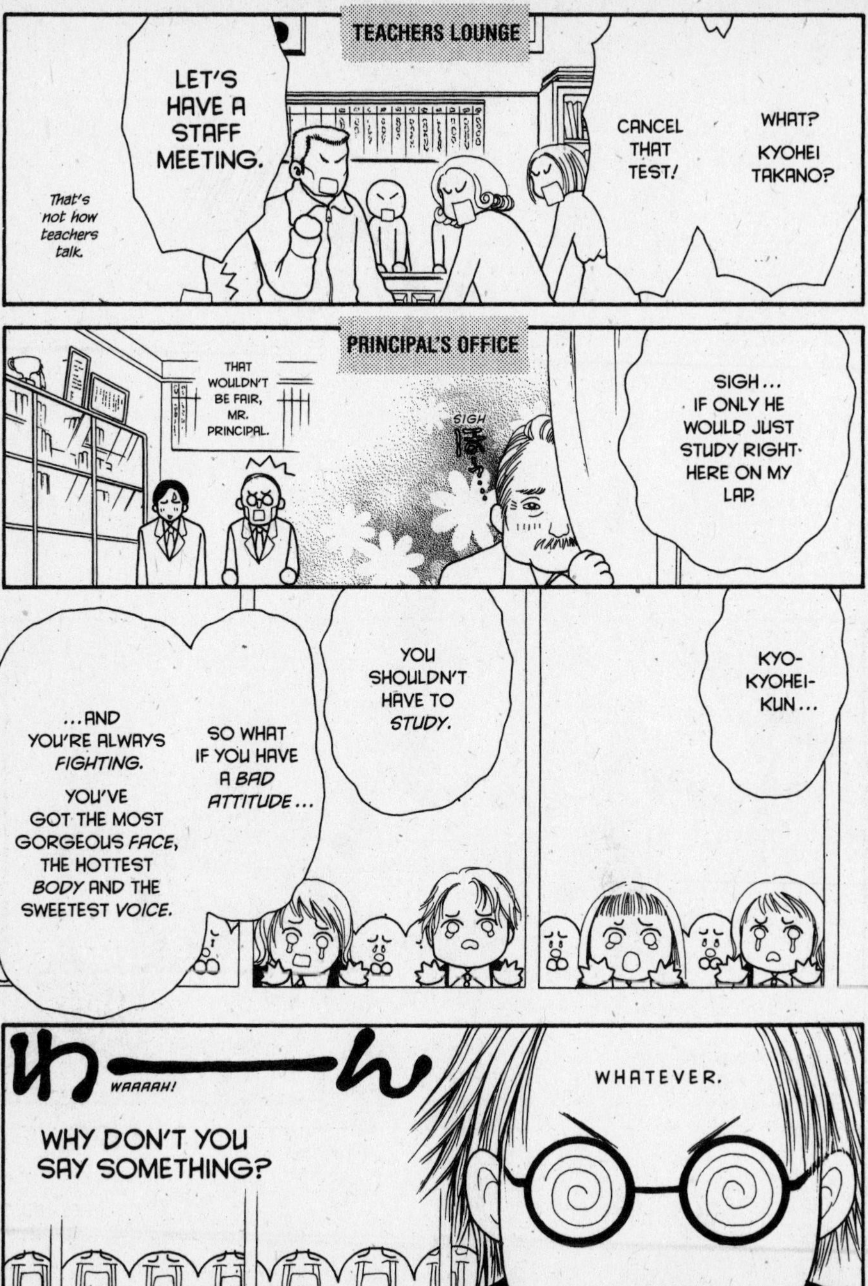
TEACHERS LOUNGE
WHAT? KYOHEI TAKANO?
CANCEL THAT TEST!
LET'S HAVE A STAFF MEETING.
That's not how teachers talk.
PRINCIPAL'S OFFICE
SIGH... IF ONLY HE WOULD JUST STUDY RIGHT HERE ON MY LAP.
SIGH
THAT WOULDN'T BE FAIR, MR. PRINCIPAL.
KYO-KYOHEI-KUN...
YOU SHOULDN'T HAVE TO STUDY.
SO WHAT IF YOU HAVE A BAD ATTITUDE...
...AND YOU'RE ALWAYS FIGHTING.
YOU'VE GOT THE MOST GORGEOUS FACE, THE HOTTEST BODY AND THE SWEETEST VOICE.
WHATEVER.
わーん
WAAAAH!
WHY DON'T YOU SAY SOMETHING?

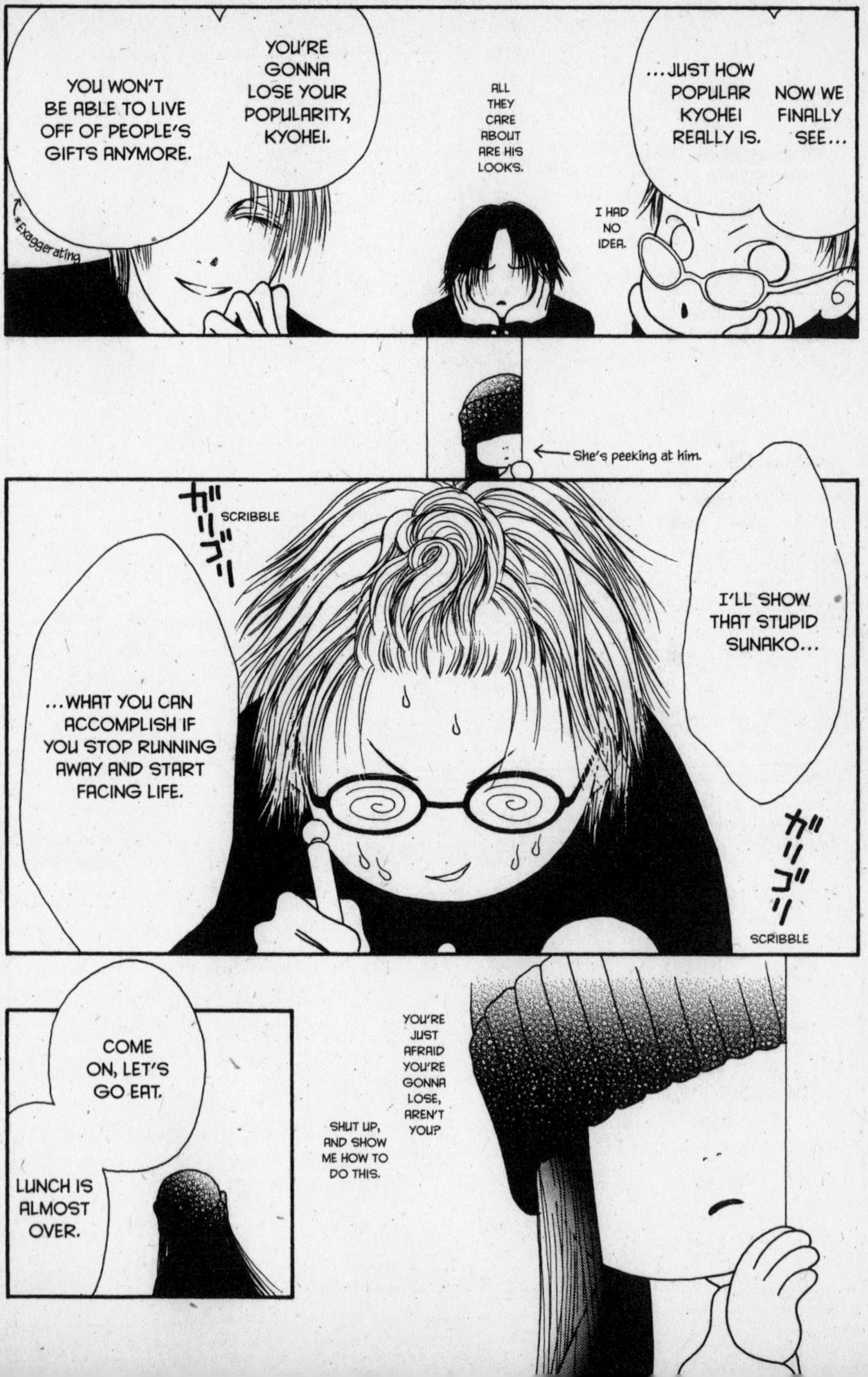
NOW WE FINALLY SEE...
...JUST HOW POPULAR KYOHEI REALLY IS.
I HAD NO IDEA.
ALL THEY CARE ABOUT ARE HIS LOOKS.
YOU'RE GONNA LOSE YOUR POPULARITY, KYOHEI.
YOU WON'T BE ABLE TO LIVE OFF OF PEOPLE'S GIFTS ANYMORE.
*Exaggerating
She's peeking at him.
SCRIBBLE
I'LL SHOW THAT STUPID SUNAKO...
...WHAT YOU CAN ACCOMPLISH IF YOU STOP RUNNING AWAY AND START FACING LIFE.
SCRIBBLE
YOU'RE JUST AFRAID YOU'RE GONNA LOSE, AREN'T YOU?
SHUT UP, AND SHOW ME HOW TO DO THIS.
COME ON, LET'S GO EAT.
LUNCH IS ALMOST OVER.

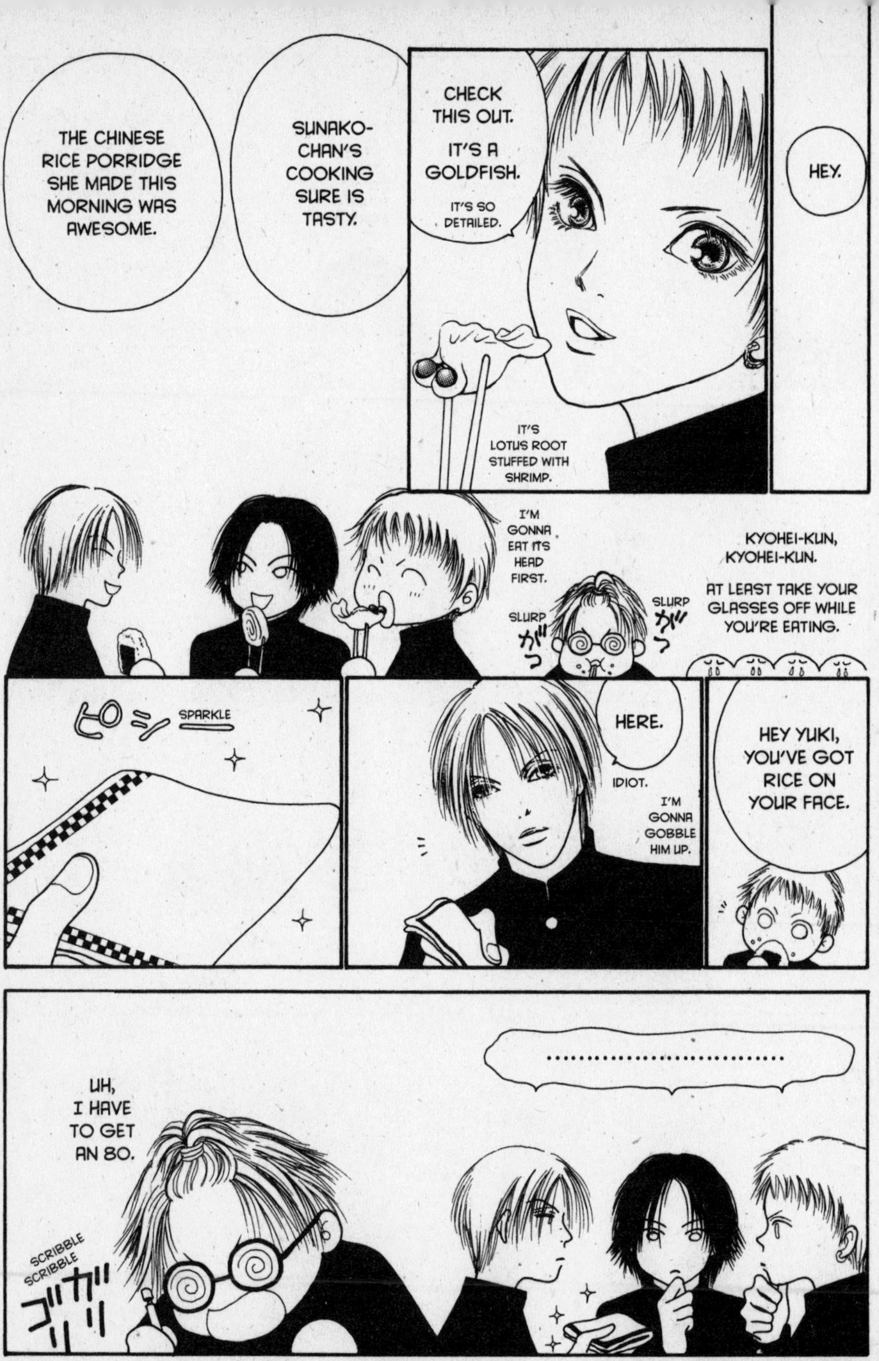
HEY.
CHECK THIS OUT. IT'S A GOLDFISH.
IT'S SO DETAILED.
IT'S LOTUS ROOT STUFFED WITH SHRIMP.
SUNAKO-CHAN'S COOKING SURE IS TASTY.
THE CHINESE RICE PORRIDGE SHE MADE THIS MORNING WAS AWESOME.
KYOHEI-KUN, KYOHEI-KUN.
AT LEAST TAKE YOUR GLASSES OFF WHILE YOU'RE EATING.
SLURP
SLURP
I'M GONNA EAT ITS HEAD FIRST.
HEY YUKI, YOU'VE GOT RICE ON YOUR FACE.
HERE.
IDIOT.
I'M GONNA GOBBLE HIM UP.
SPARKLE
....
UH, I HAVE TO GET AN 80.
SCRIBBLE SCRIBBLE

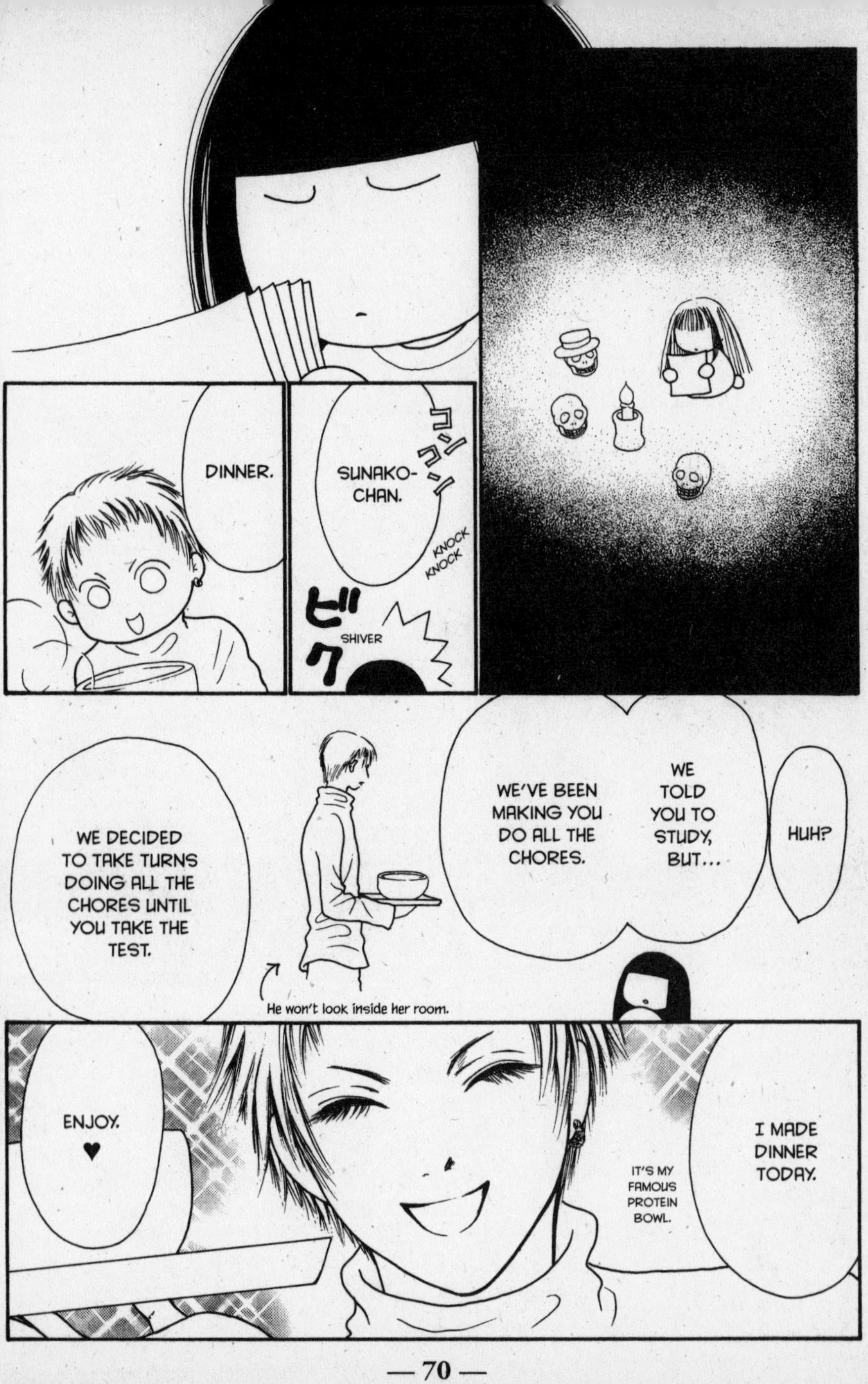
コンコン
KNOCK KNOCK
SUNAKO-CHAN.
ビク
SHIVER
DINNER.
HUH?
WE TOLD YOU TO STUDY, BUT...
WE'VE BEEN MAKING YOU DO ALL THE CHORES.
WE DECIDED TO TAKE TURNS DOING ALL THE CHORES UNTIL YOU TAKE THE TEST.
He won't look inside her room.
I MADE DINNER TODAY.
IT'S MY FAMOUS PROTEIN BOWL.
ENJOY. ♥

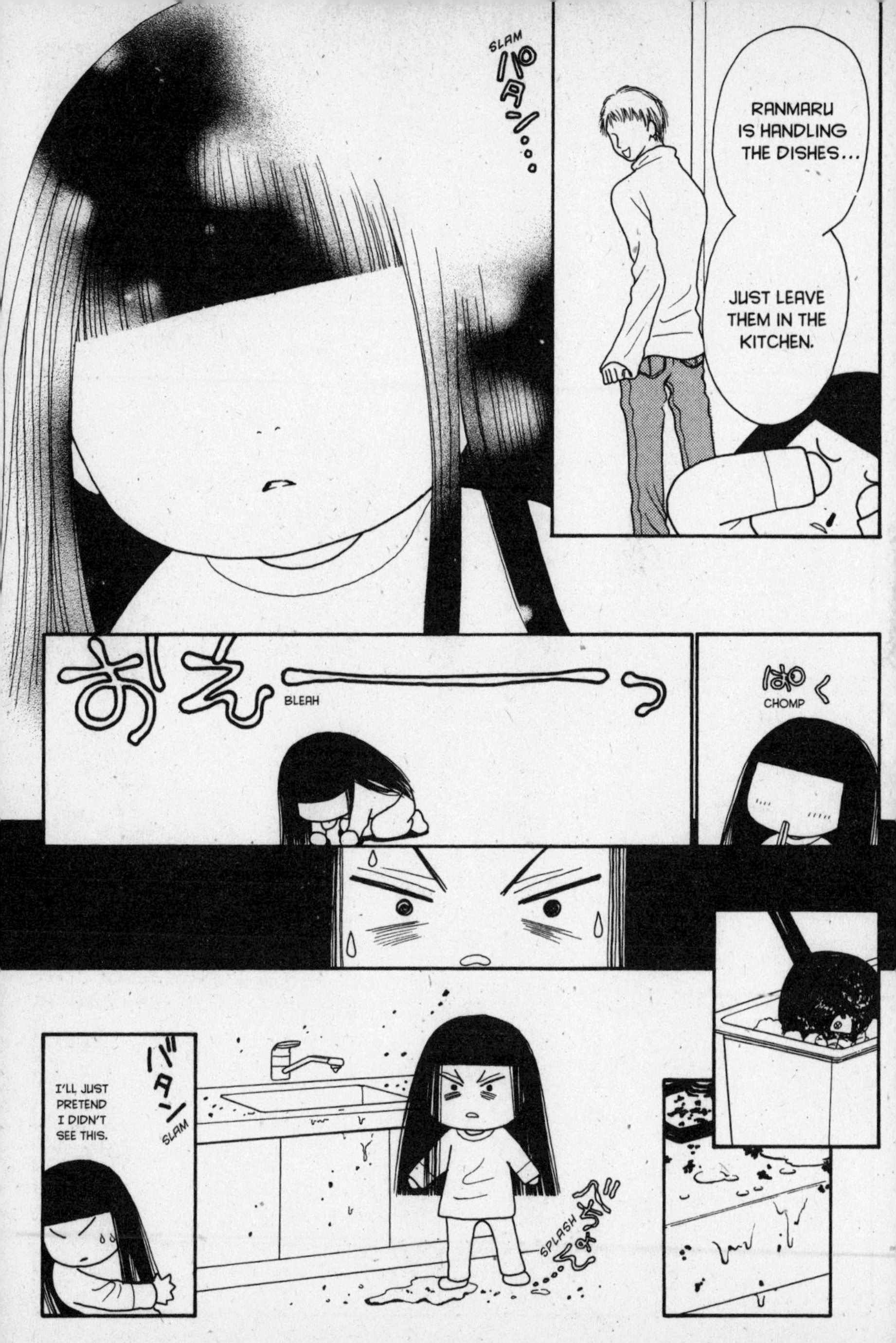
RANMARU IS HANDLING THE DISHES...
JUST LEAVE THEM IN THE KITCHEN.
パタン...
SLAM
ぱく
CHOMP
おえーっ
BLEAH
SPLASH
バタン
SLAM
I'LL JUST PRETEND I DIDN'T SEE THIS.

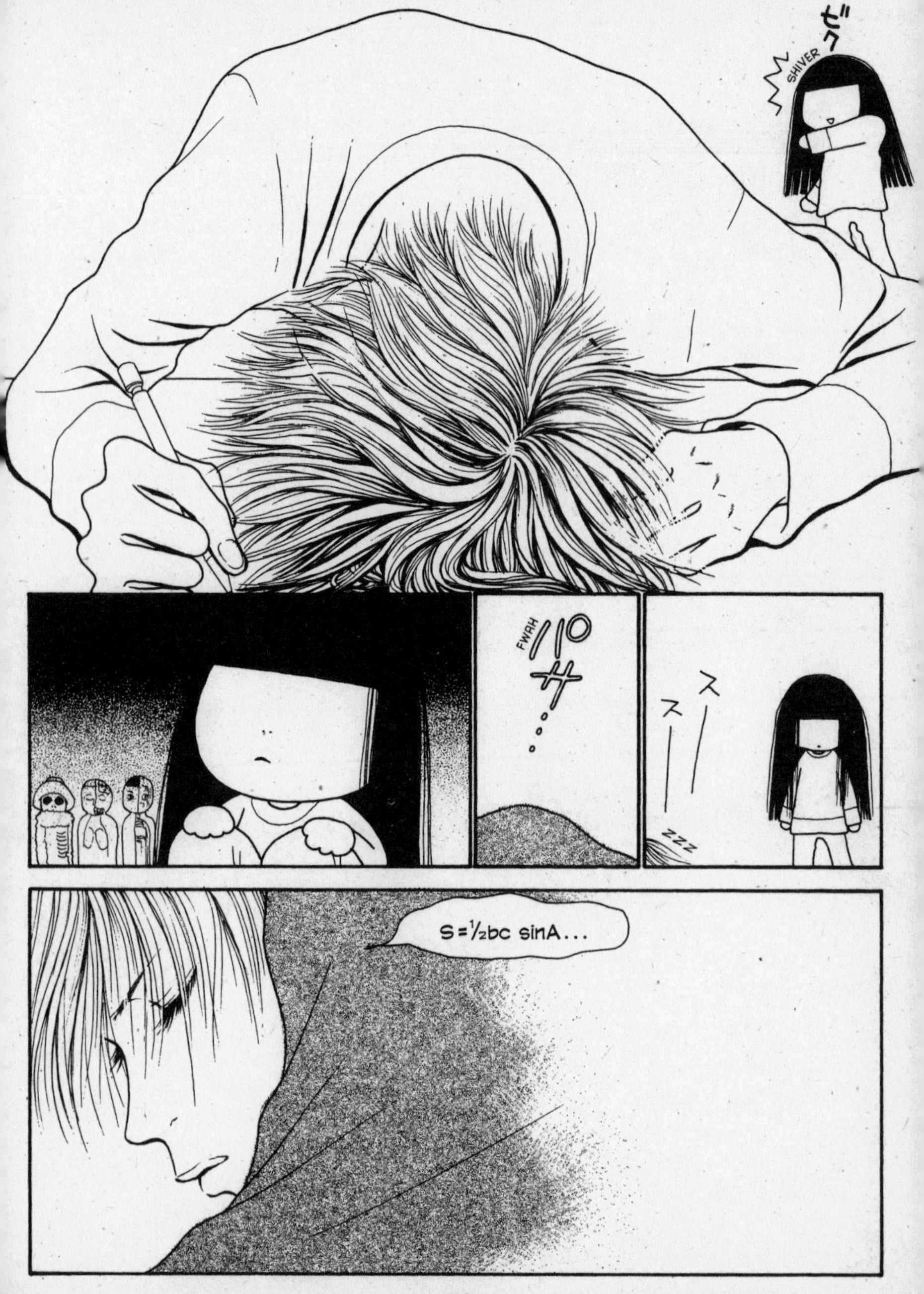
ビク
SHIVER
スー スー
ZZZ
パサ…
FWAH
S=½bc sinA...

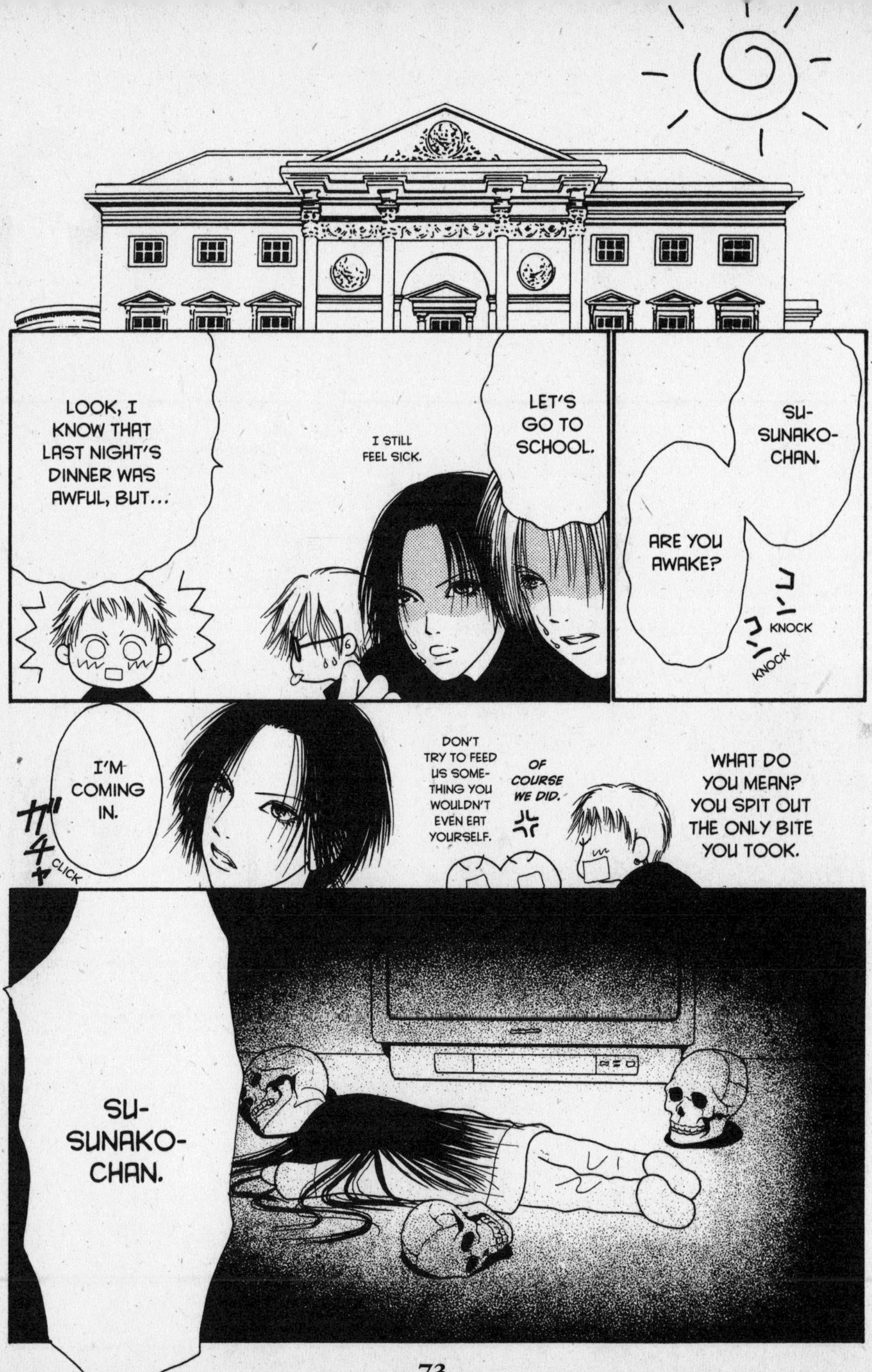
SU-SUNAKO-CHAN.
ARE YOU AWAKE?
コン KNOCK
コン KNOCK
LET'S GO TO SCHOOL.
I STILL FEEL SICK.
LOOK, I KNOW THAT LAST NIGHT'S DINNER WAS AWFUL, BUT...
WHAT DO YOU MEAN? YOU SPIT OUT THE ONLY BITE YOU TOOK.
OF COURSE WE DID.
DON'T TRY TO FEED US SOME-THING YOU WOULDN'T EVEN EAT YOURSELF.
I'M COMING IN.
ガチャ CLICK
SU-SUNAKO-CHAN.

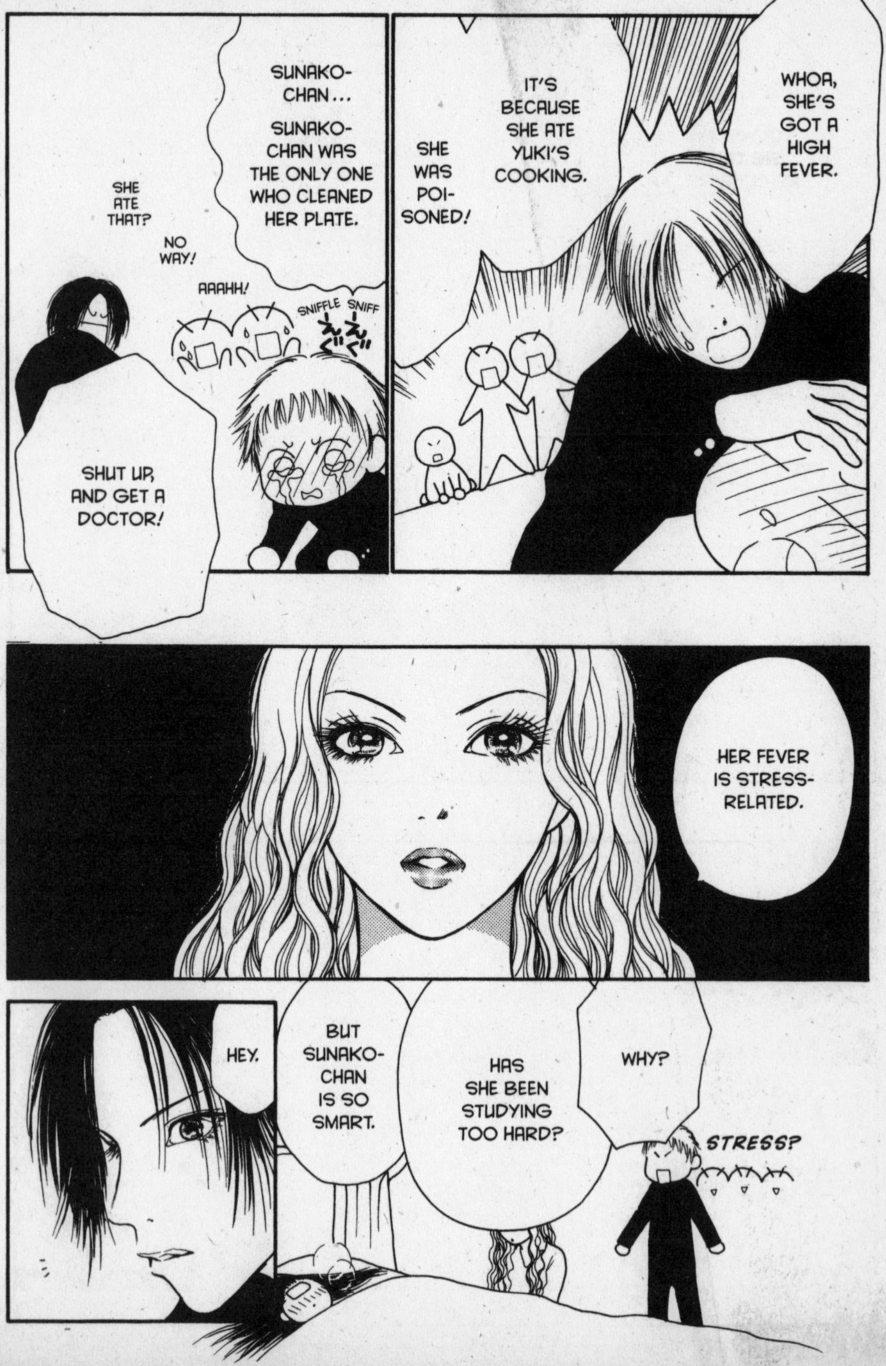
WHOA, SHE'S GOT A HIGH FEVER.
IT'S BECAUSE SHE ATE YUKI'S COOKING.
SHE WAS POI-SONED!
SUNAKO-CHAN... SUNAKO-CHAN WAS THE ONLY ONE WHO CLEANED HER PLATE.
SHE ATE THAT?
NO WAY!
AAAHH!
SNIFFLE SNIFF
SHUT UP, AND GET A DOCTOR!
HER FEVER IS STRESS-RELATED.
WHY?
STRESS?
HAS SHE BEEN STUDYING TOO HARD?
BUT SUNAKO-CHAN IS SO SMART.
HEY.

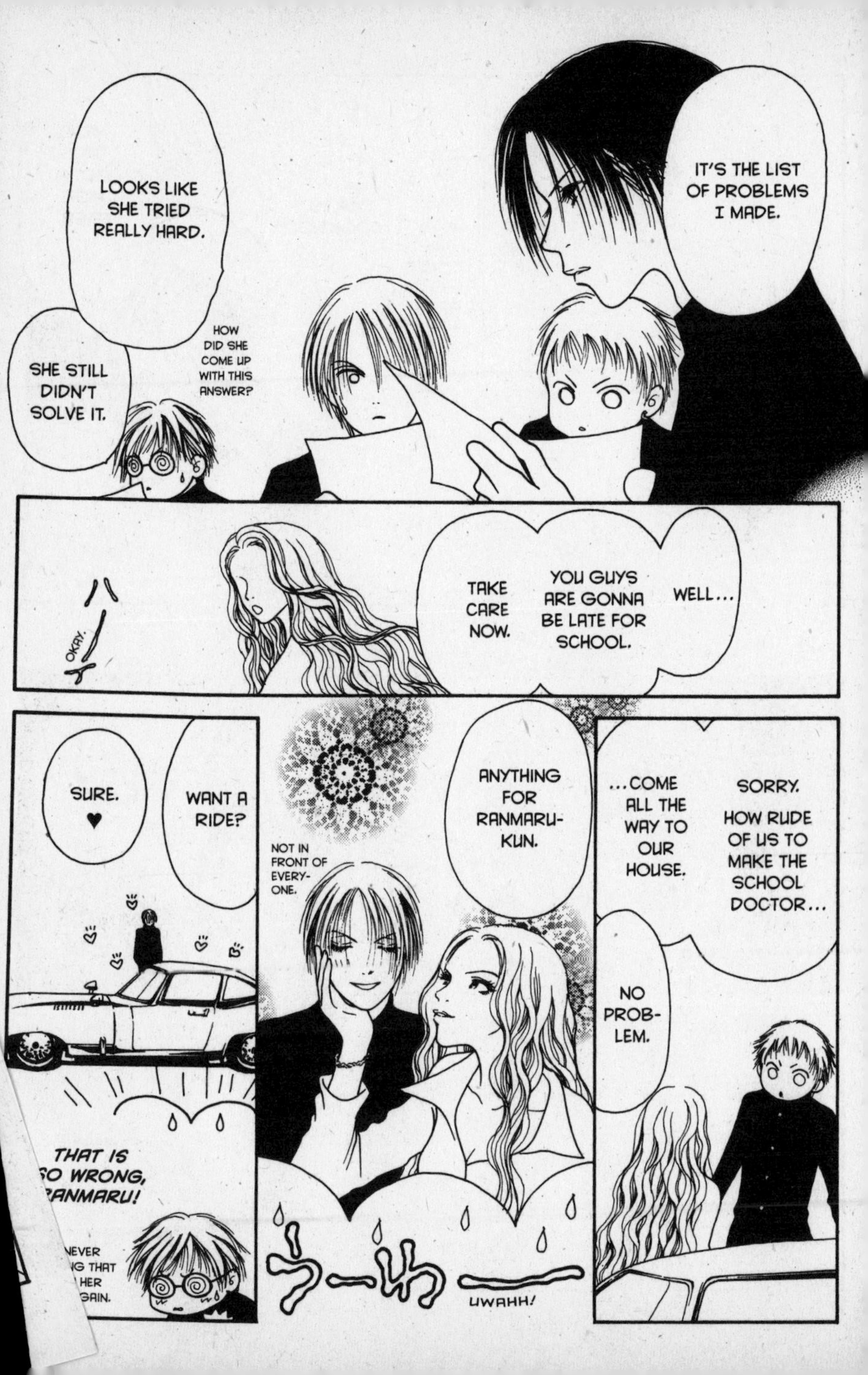

IT'S THE LIST OF PROBLEMS I MADE.
LOOKS LIKE SHE TRIED REALLY HARD.
HOW DID SHE COME UP WITH THIS ANSWER?
SHE STILL DIDN'T SOLVE IT.
WELL...
YOU GUYS ARE GONNA BE LATE FOR SCHOOL.
TAKE CARE NOW.
OKAY.
SORRY. HOW RUDE OF US TO MAKE THE SCHOOL DOCTOR...
...COME ALL THE WAY TO OUR HOUSE.
NO PROBLEM.
ANYTHING FOR RANMARU-KUN.
NOT IN FRONT OF EVERYONE.
うーわー
UWAHH!
WANT A RIDE?
SURE. ♥
THAT IS SO WRONG, RANMARU!

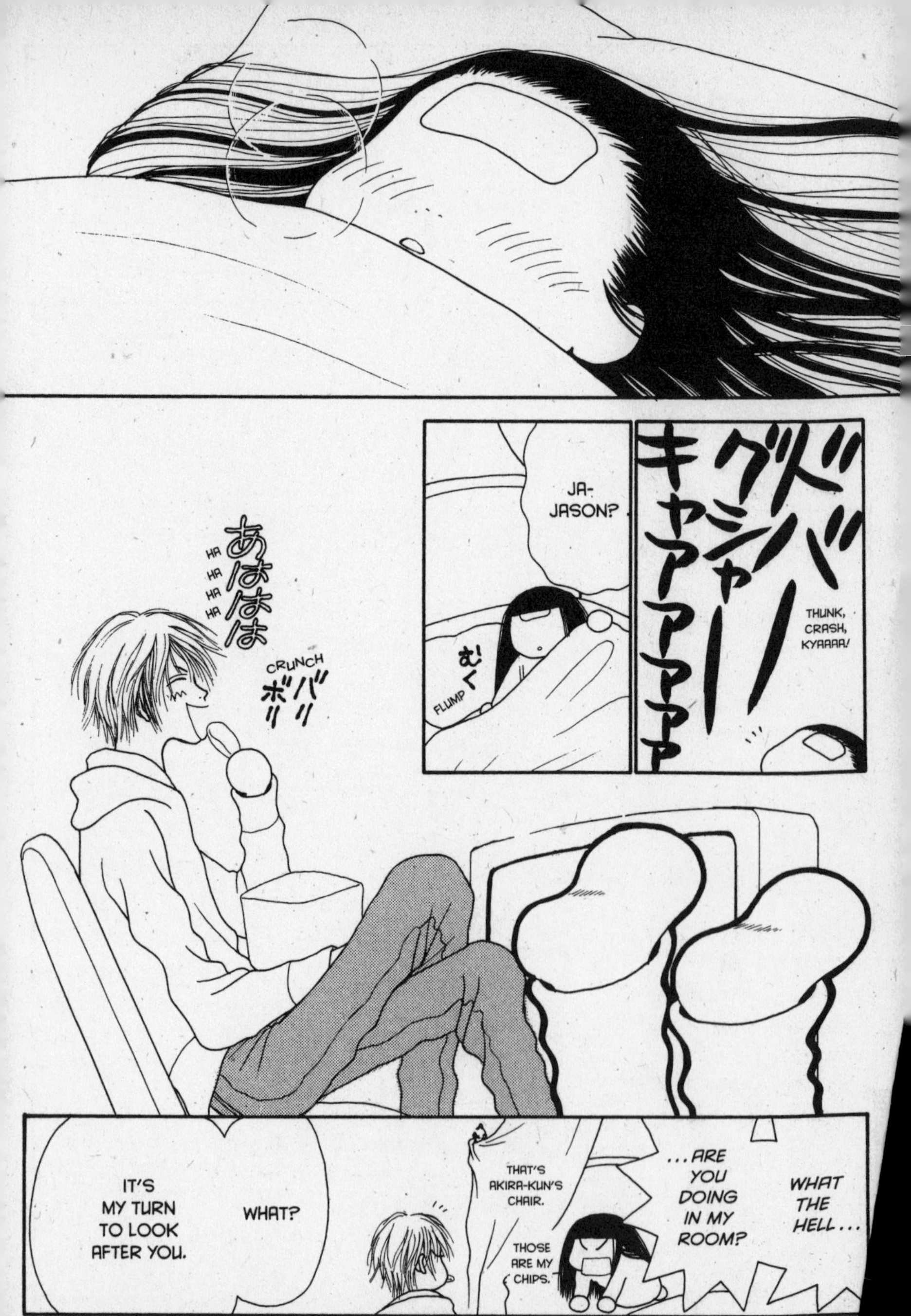
ドバン
グシャー
キャアアアア
THUNK, CRASH, KYAAAA!
JA-JASON?
むく
FLUMP
あははは
HA HA HA HA
ボリボリ
CRUNCH
WHAT THE HELL...
...ARE YOU DOING IN MY ROOM?
THAT'S AKIRA-KUN'S CHAIR.
THOSE ARE MY CHIPS.
WHAT?
IT'S MY TURN TO LOOK AFTER YOU.

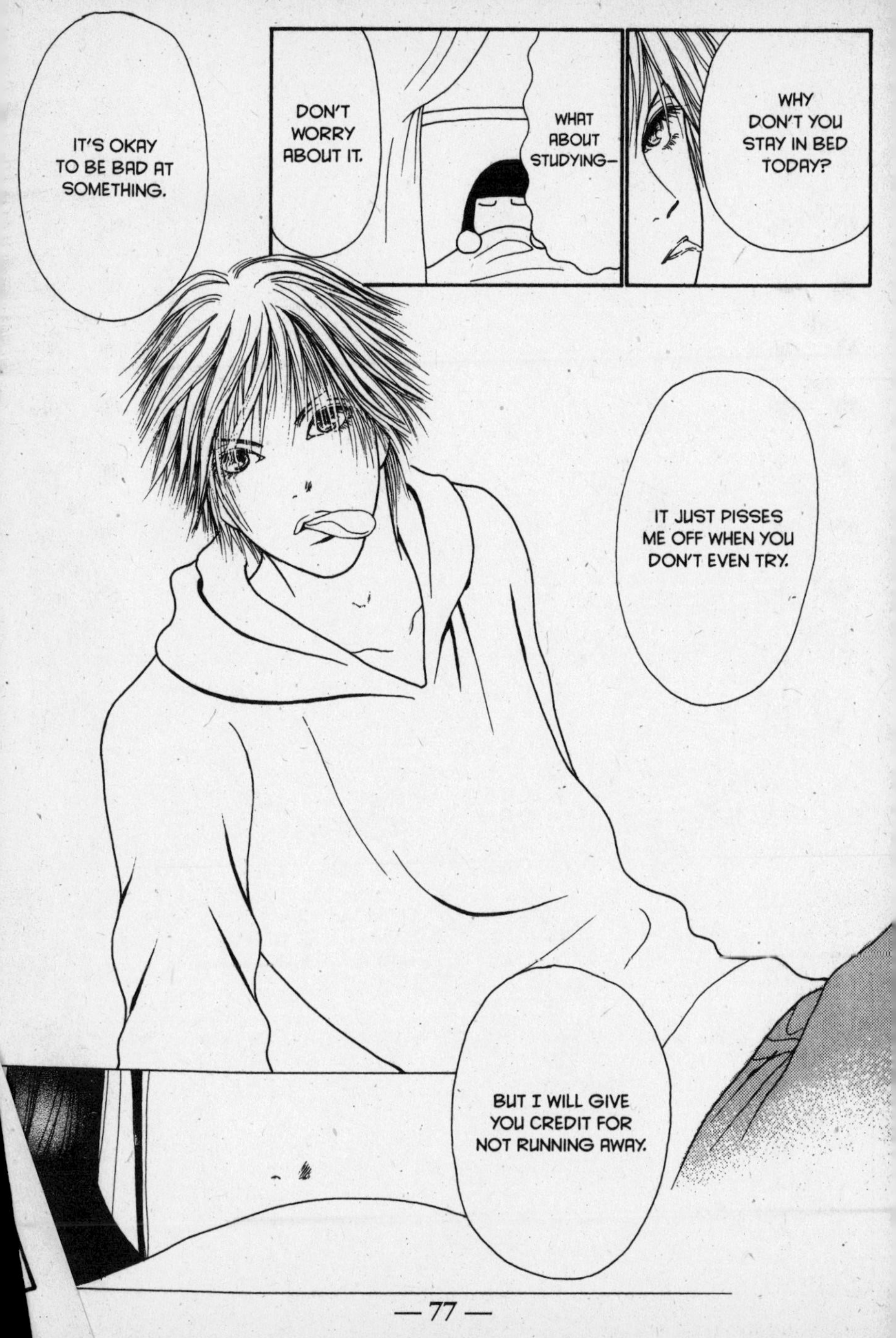
WHY DON'T YOU STAY IN BED TODAY?
WHAT ABOUT STUDYING—
DON'T WORRY ABOUT IT.
IT'S OKAY TO BE BAD AT SOMETHING.
IT JUST PISSES ME OFF WHEN YOU DON'T EVEN TRY.
BUT I WILL GIVE YOU CREDIT FOR NOT RUNNING AWAY.

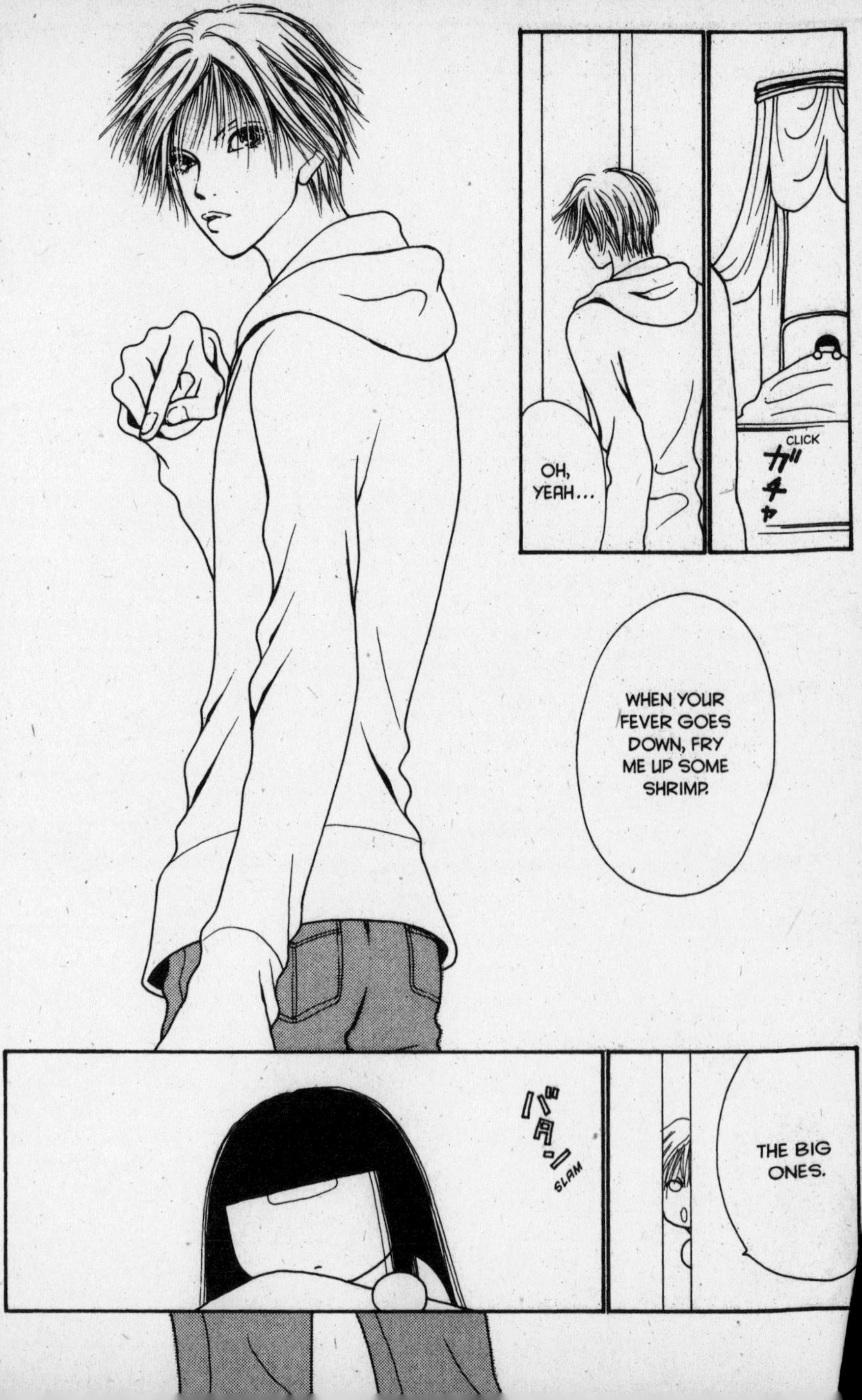
CLICK
ガチャ
OH, YEAH...
WHEN YOUR FEVER GOES DOWN, FRY ME UP SOME SHRIMP.
THE BIG ONES.
バタン
SLAM

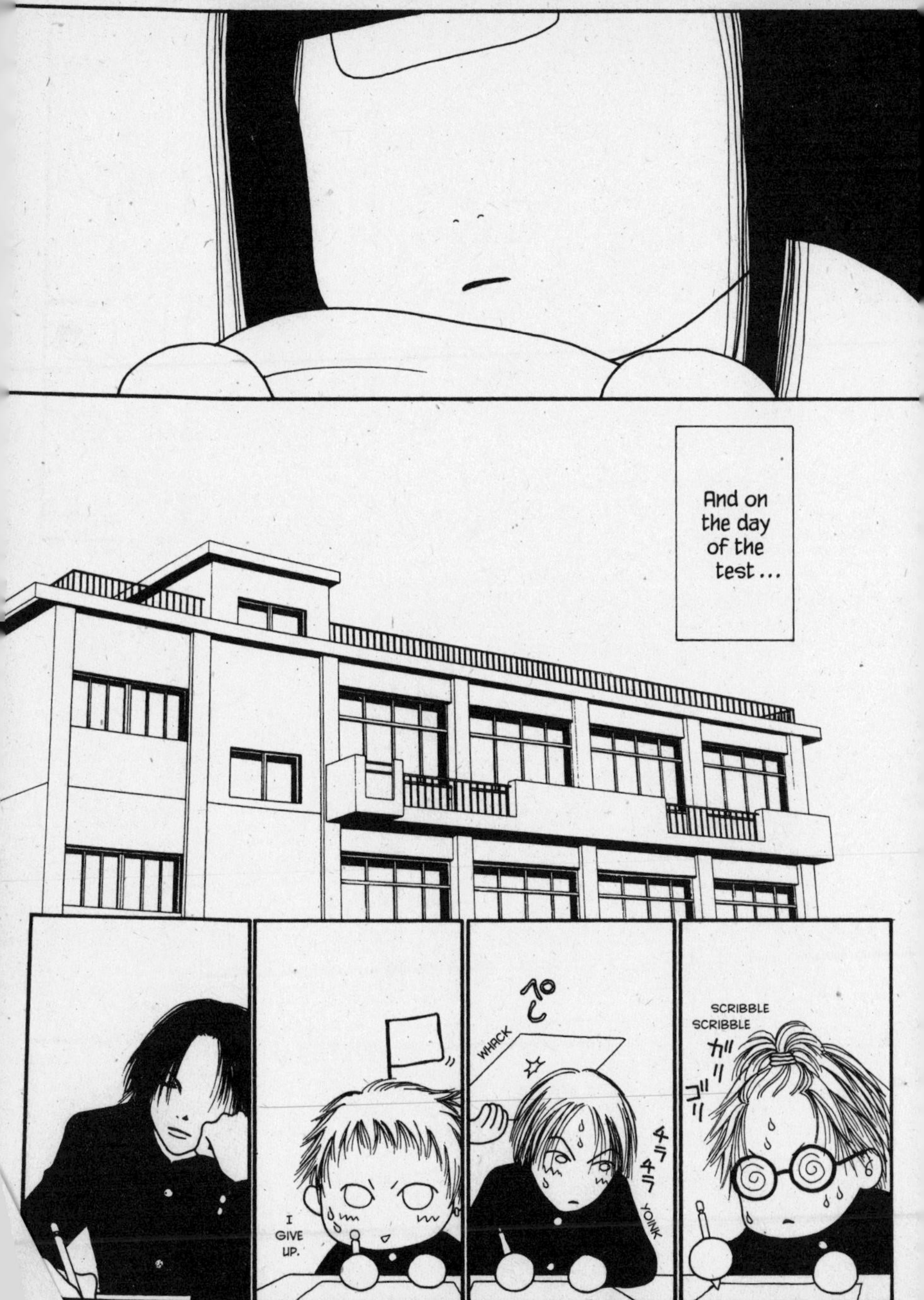

And on the day of the test...
SCRIBBLE SCRIBBLE
WHACK
YOINK
I GIVE UP.

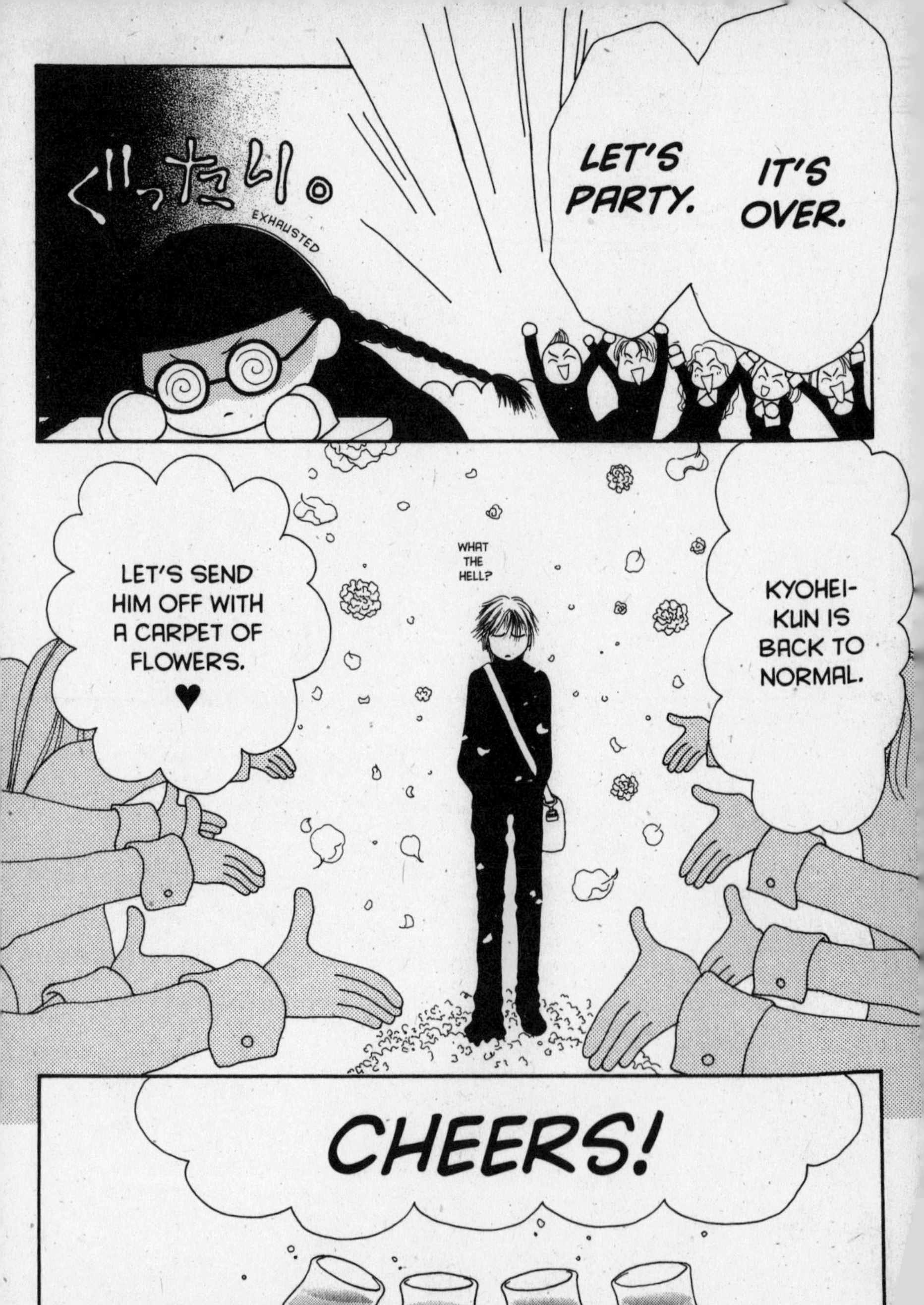
IT'S OVER.
LET'S PARTY.
ぐったり。
EXHAUSTED
KYOHEI-KUN IS BACK TO NORMAL.
WHAT THE HELL?
LET'S SEND HIM OFF WITH A CARPET OF FLOWERS. ♥
CHEERS!

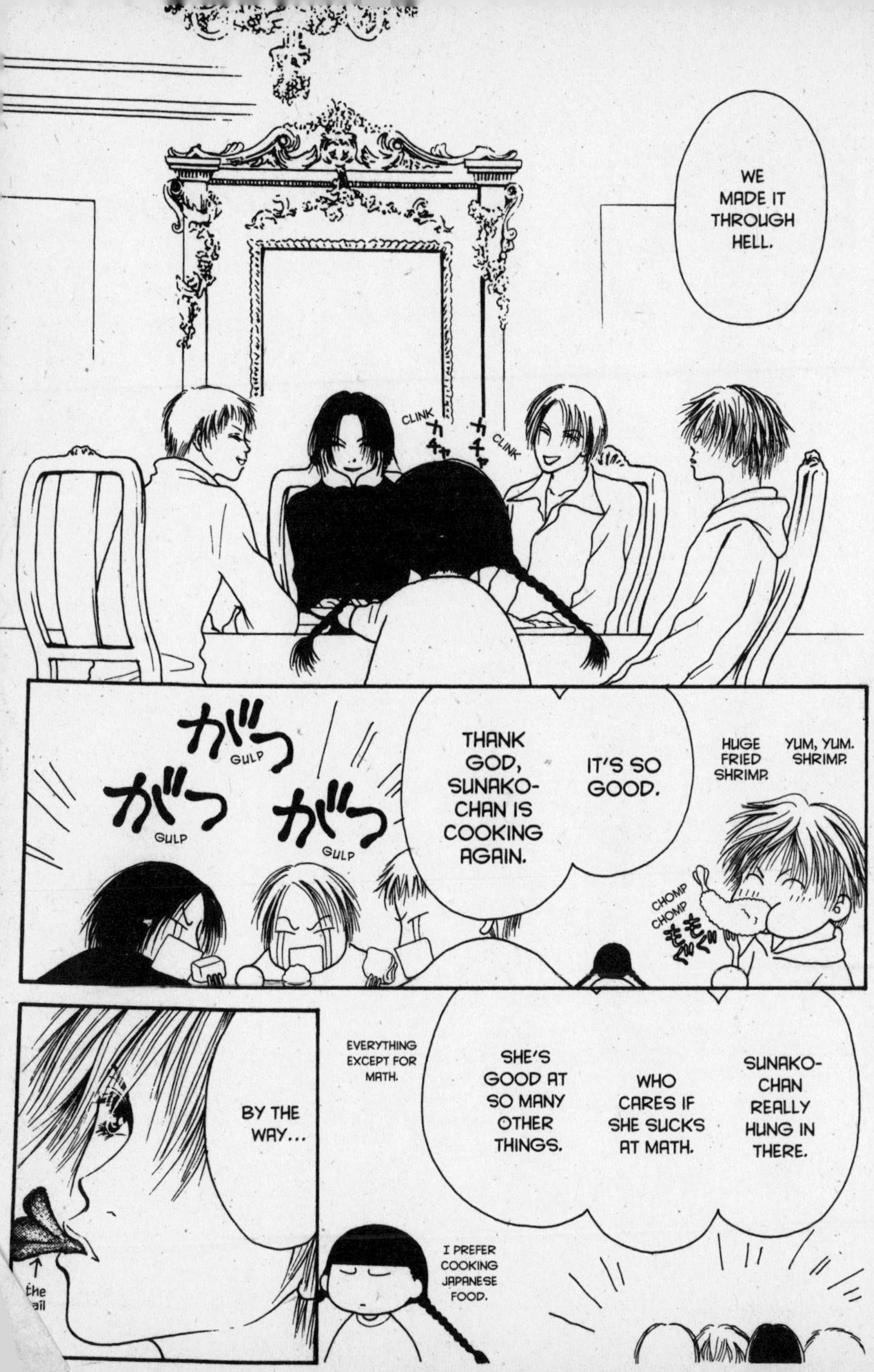
WE MADE IT THROUGH HELL.
CLINK カチャ
CLINK カチャ
THANK GOD, SUNAKO-CHAN IS COOKING AGAIN.
IT'S SO GOOD.
HUGE FRIED SHRIMP.
YUM, YUM. SHRIMP.
がつ GULP
がつ GULP
がつ GULP
CHOMP CHOMP もぐもぐ
SUNAKO-CHAN REALLY HUNG IN THERE.
WHO CARES IF SHE SUCKS AT MATH.
SHE'S GOOD AT SO MANY OTHER THINGS.
EVERYTHING EXCEPT FOR MATH.
I PREFER COOKING JAPANESE FOOD.
BY THE WAY...

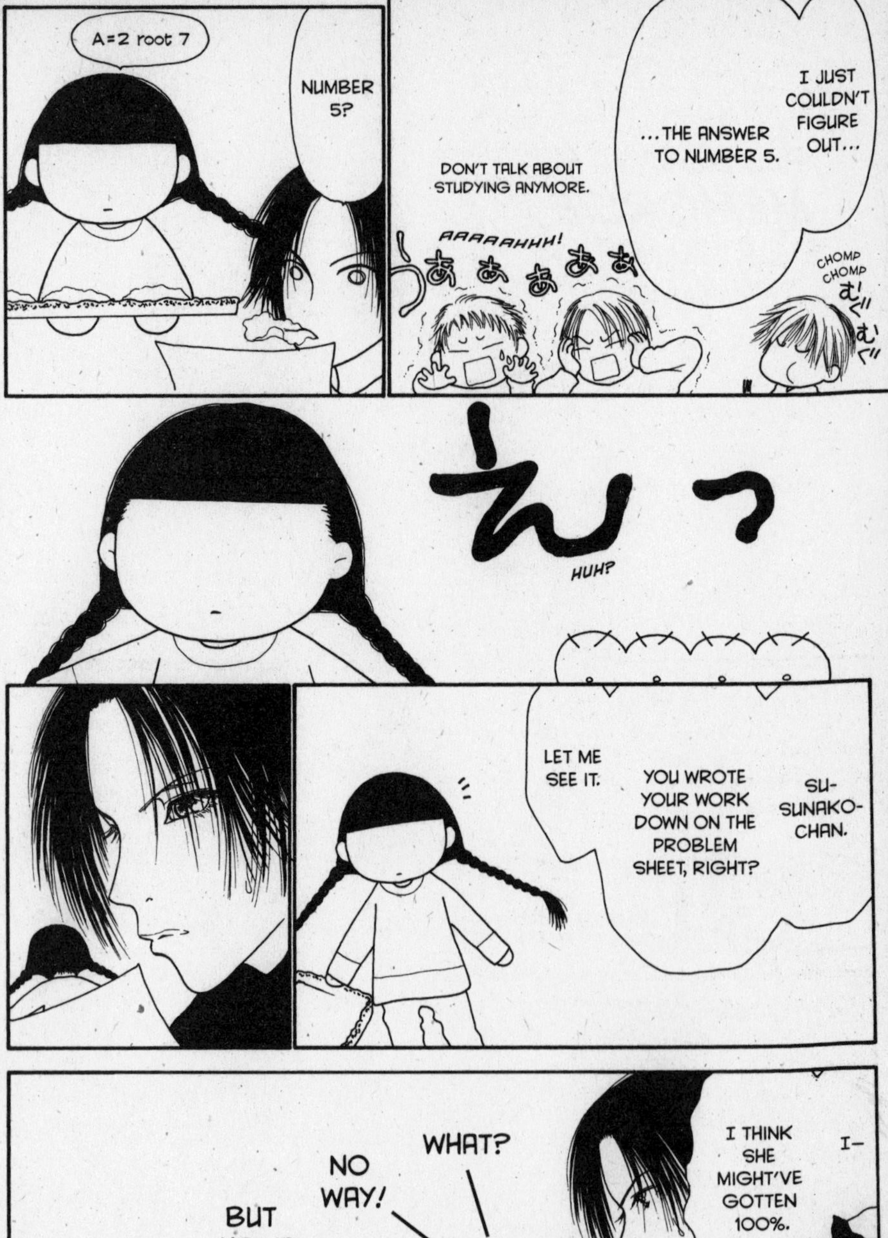
I JUST COULDN'T FIGURE OUT... ...THE ANSWER TO NUMBER 5.
DON'T TALK ABOUT STUDYING ANYMORE.
うあああああ
AAAAAHHH!
むぐむぐ
CHOMP CHOMP
NUMBER 5?
A=2 root 7
えっ
HUH?
SU-SUNAKO-CHAN.
YOU WROTE YOUR WORK DOWN ON THE PROBLEM SHEET, RIGHT?
LET ME SEE IT.
I—
I THINK SHE MIGHT'VE GOTTEN 100%.
WHAT?
NO WAY!
BUT HOW?

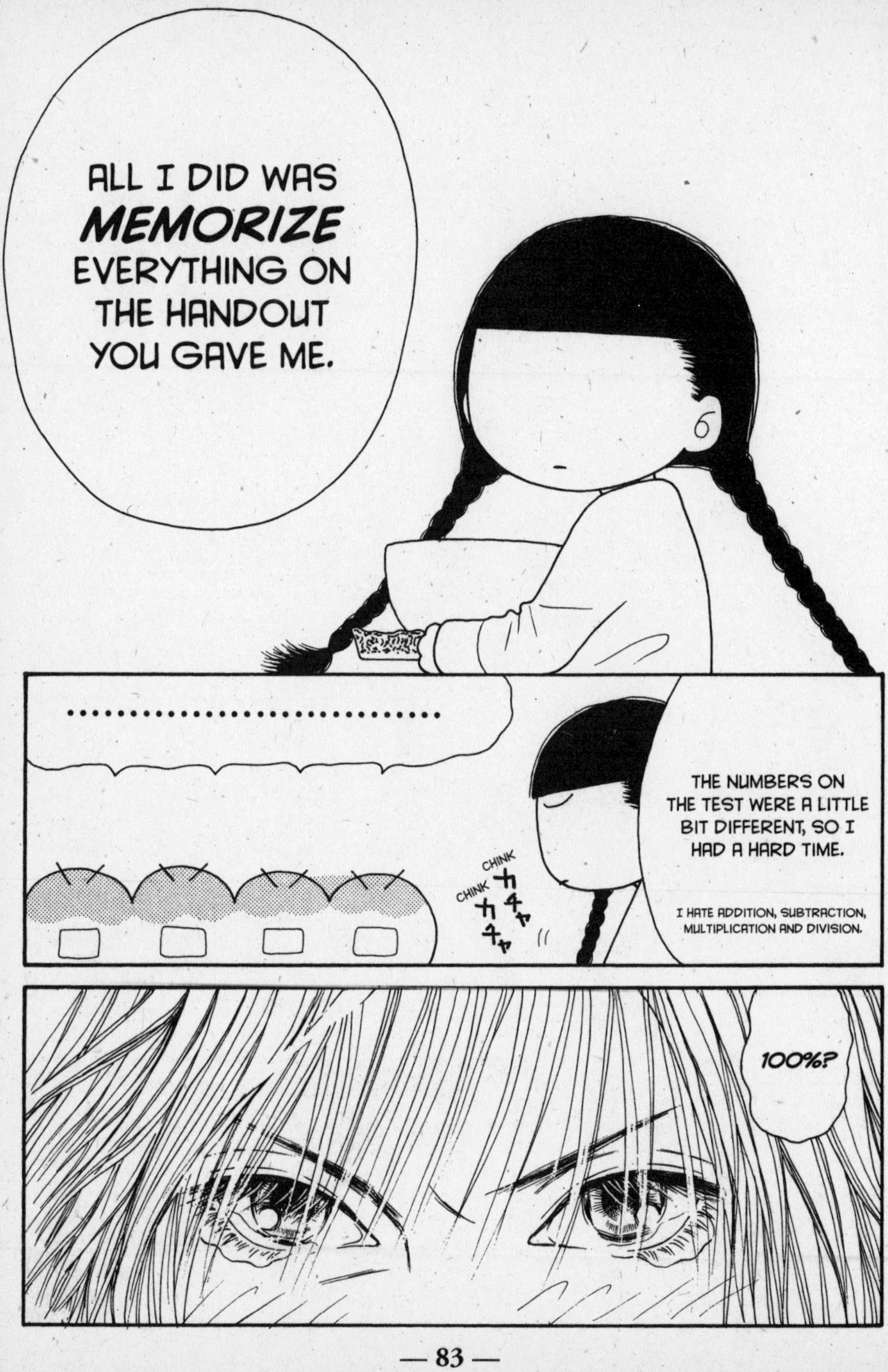
ALL I DID WAS *MEMORIZE* EVERYTHING ON THE HANDOUT YOU GAVE ME.
THE NUMBERS ON THE TEST WERE A LITTLE BIT DIFFERENT, SO I HAD A HARD TIME.
I HATE ADDITION, SUBTRACTION, MULTIPLICATION AND DIVISION.
CHINK カチャ
CHINK カチャ
....
100%?

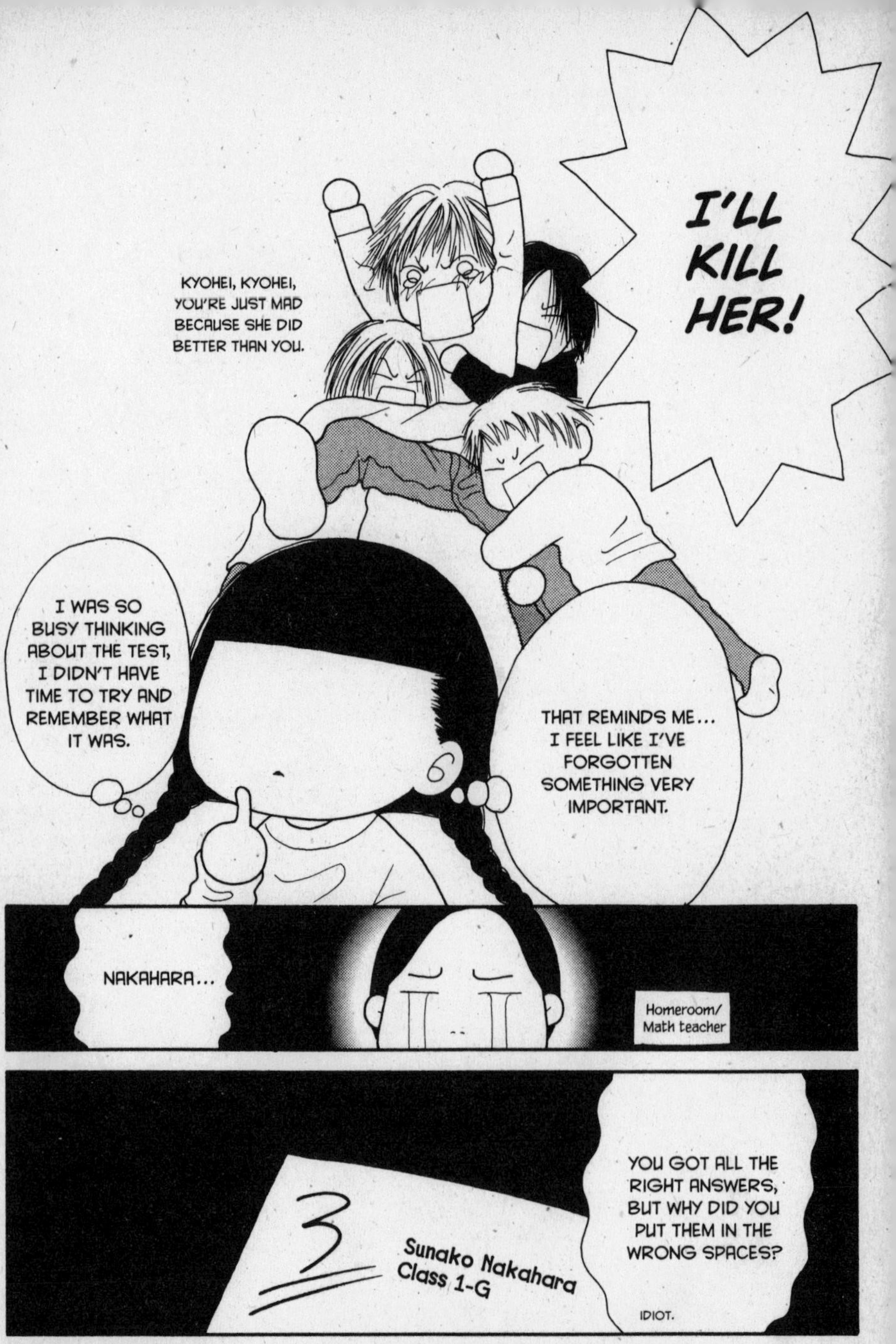
I'LL KILL HER!
KYOHEI, KYOHEI, YOU'RE JUST MAD BECAUSE SHE DID BETTER THAN YOU.
THAT REMINDS ME... I FEEL LIKE I'VE FORGOTTEN SOMETHING VERY IMPORTANT.
I WAS SO BUSY THINKING ABOUT THE TEST, I DIDN'T HAVE TIME TO TRY AND REMEMBER WHAT IT WAS.
Homeroom/ Math teacher
NAKAHARA...
YOU GOT ALL THE RIGHT ANSWERS, BUT WHY DID YOU PUT THEM IN THE WRONG SPACES?
IDIOT.
3
Sunako Nakahara Class 1-G

Chapter 12
The Girl in the Storm

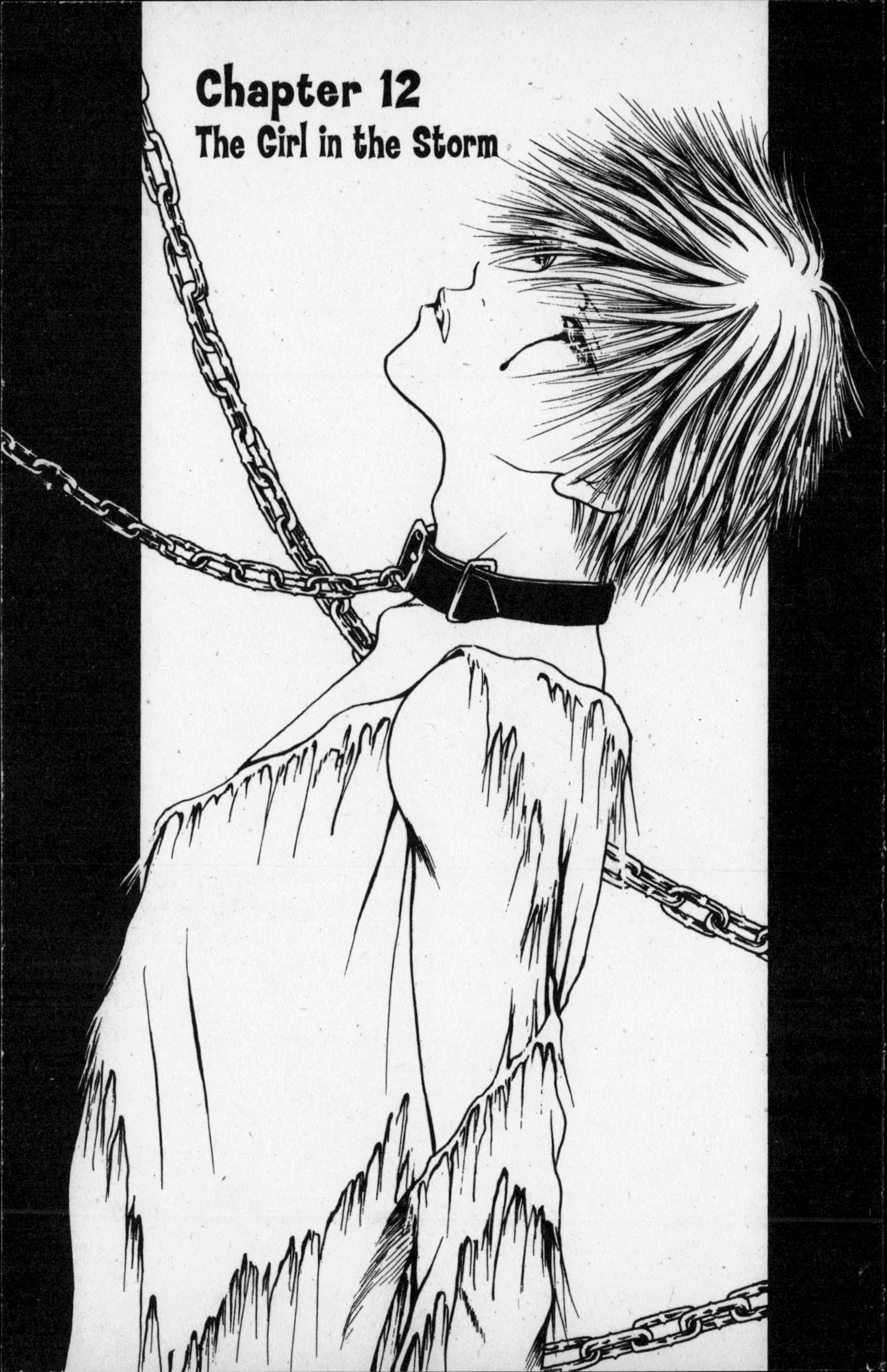

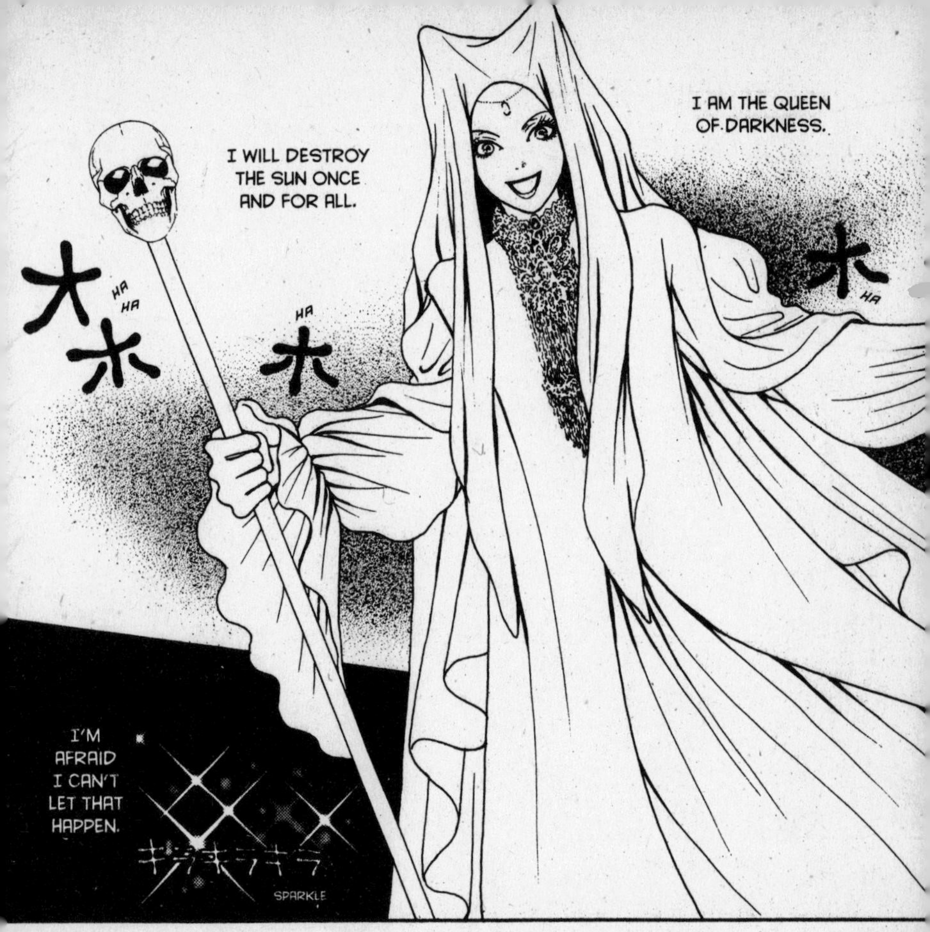
I AM THE QUEEN OF DARKNESS.
HA
I WILL DESTROY THE SUN ONCE AND FOR ALL.
HA
HA HA
I'M AFRAID I CAN'T LET THAT HAPPEN.
SPARKLE

BEHIND THE SCENES

IT LOOKS LIKE THE ISSUE OF "THE KISS" HAS FINALLY BEEN RESOLVED. I'D BEEN WONDERING ABOUT THAT KISS EVER SINCE I DREW IT IN BOOK 2. THIS WAS YET ANOTHER CASE THAT MADE ME TRULY UNDERSTAND HOW AMAZING MY EDITOR IS.

AS FAR AS KYOHEI'S PAST GOES...APPARENTLY, HE HAD A VERY ROUGH TIME IN JUNIOR HIGH. (APPARENTLY...?) I'LL WRITE ABOUT IT SOMEDAY, IF I GET A CHANCE. I HAVEN'T EVEN WRITTEN A STORY THAT EXPLAINS WHY THE FOUR GUYS WERE SEPARATED FROM THEIR PARENTS AND SENT TO A BOARDING HOUSE. MAYBE I'LL WRITE THAT STORY TOO, SOMEDAY. I GUESS IT'S PROBABLY NOT THAT INTERESTING OF A STORY.

SOME READERS HAVE BEEN ASKING FOR AN EXTENSIVE BIO ON SUNAKO AND THE GANG. PLEASE GIVE ME SOME TIME. IS IT BECAUSE I HAVEN'T FIGURED IT OUT YET?...NO...HOW COULD YOU THINK THAT?

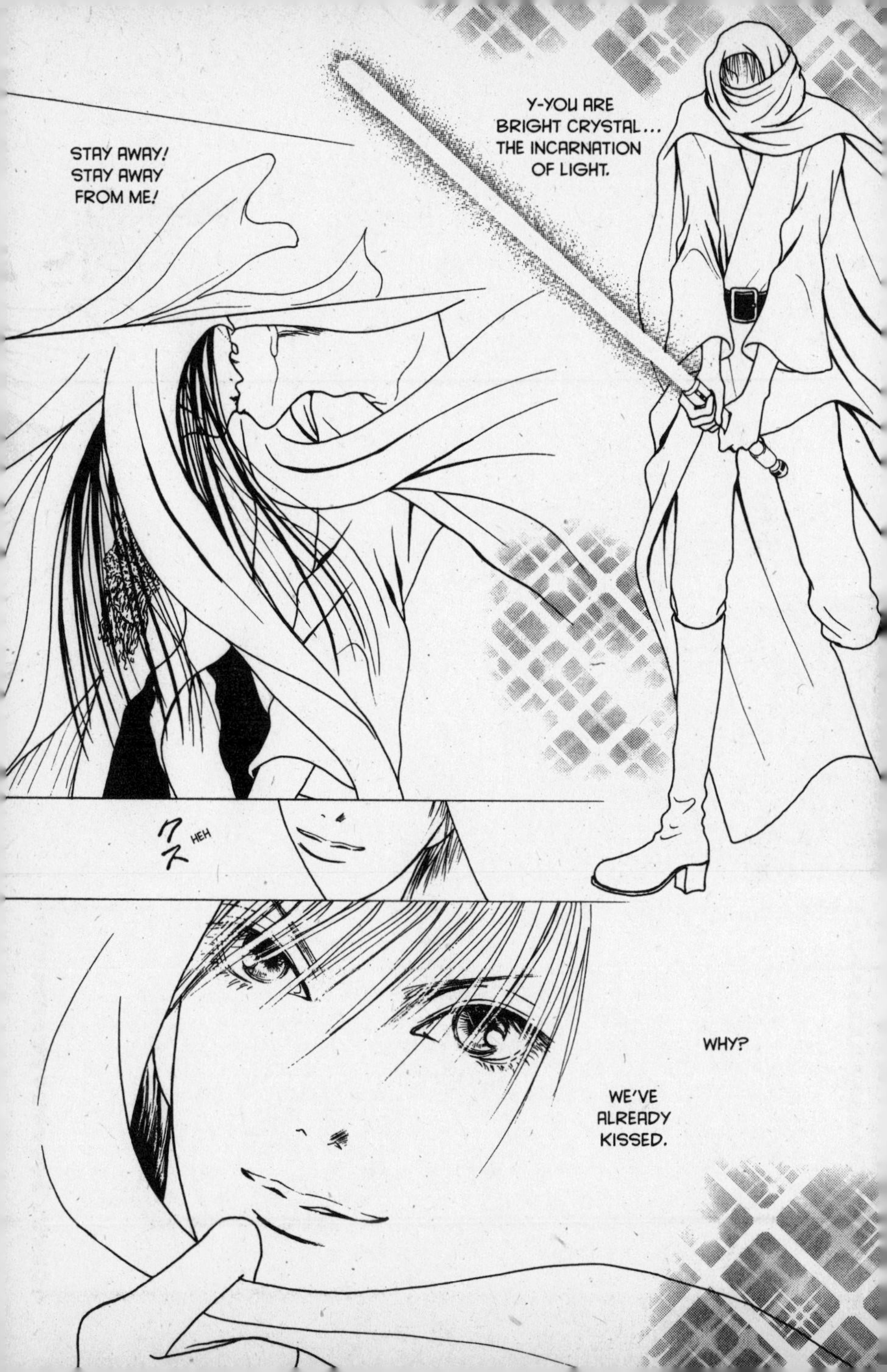
Y-YOU ARE BRIGHT CRYSTAL... THE INCARNATION OF LIGHT.
STAY AWAY! STAY AWAY FROM ME!
クス
HEH
WHY?
WE'VE ALREADY KISSED.

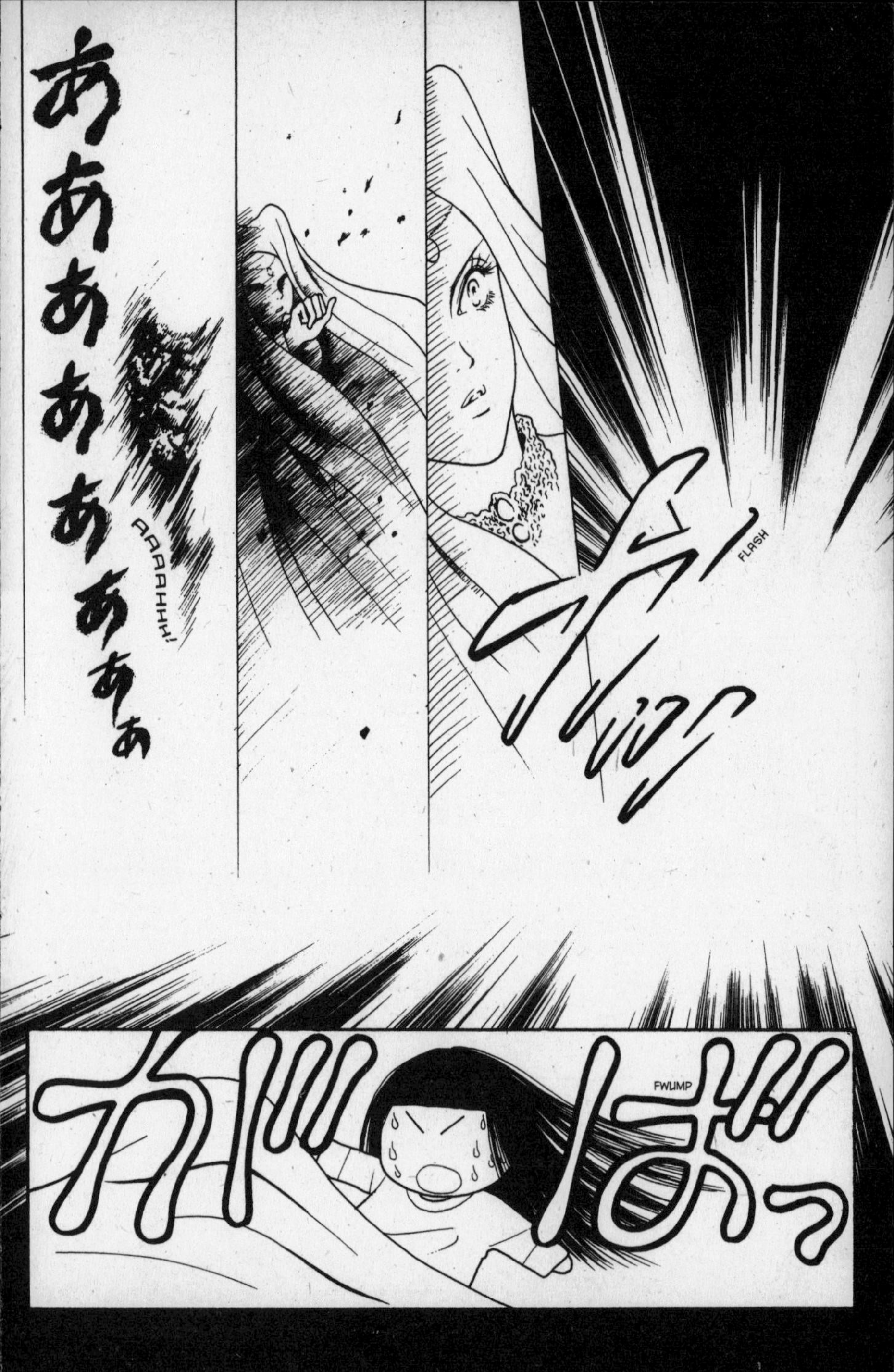
FLASH
あああああああ
AAAAHHH!
がばっ
FWUMP

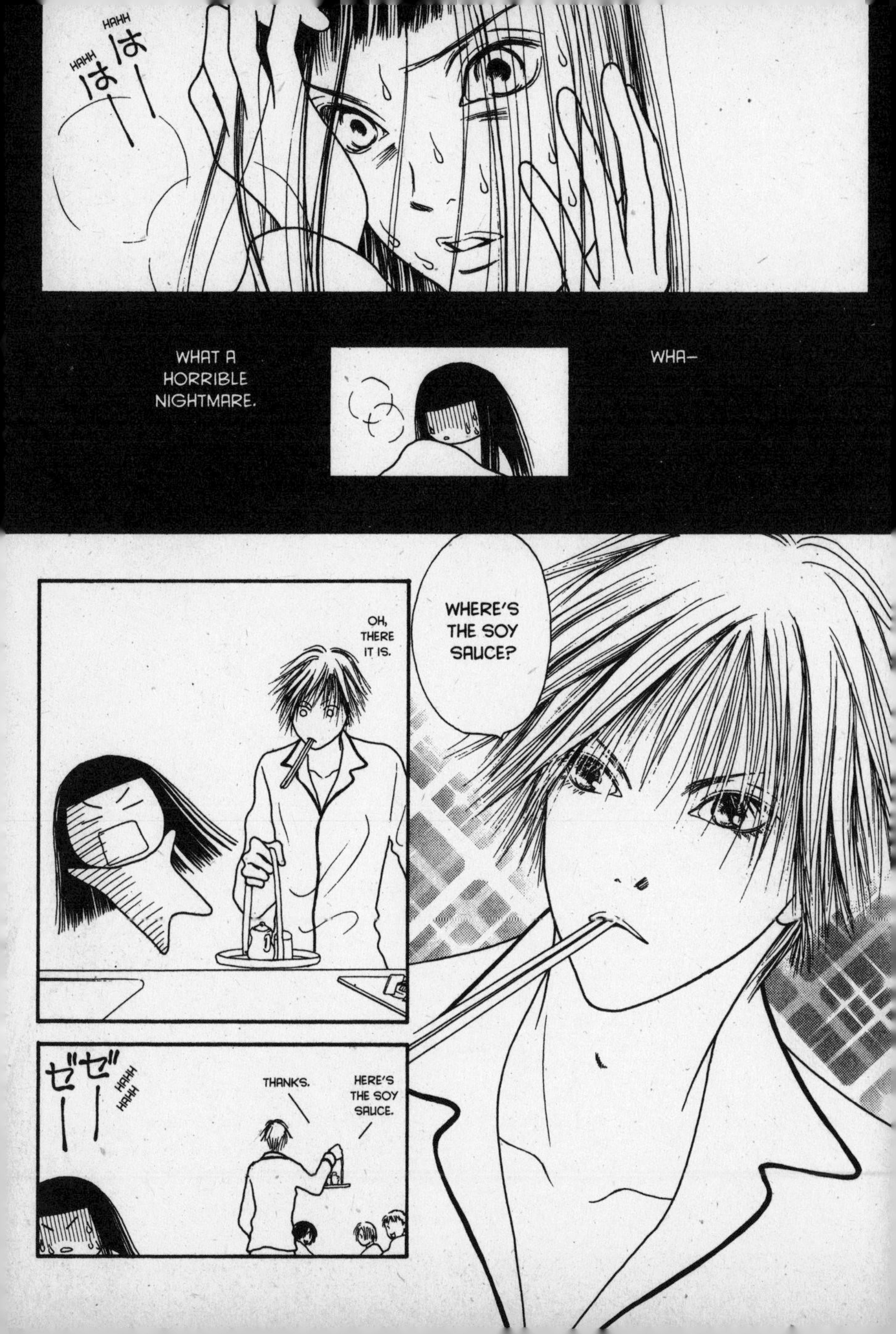
はーはー
HAHH HAHH
WHA–
WHAT A HORRIBLE NIGHTMARE.
WHERE'S THE SOY SAUCE?
OH, THERE IT IS.
HERE'S THE SOY SAUCE.
THANKS.
ゼーゼー
HAHH HAHH

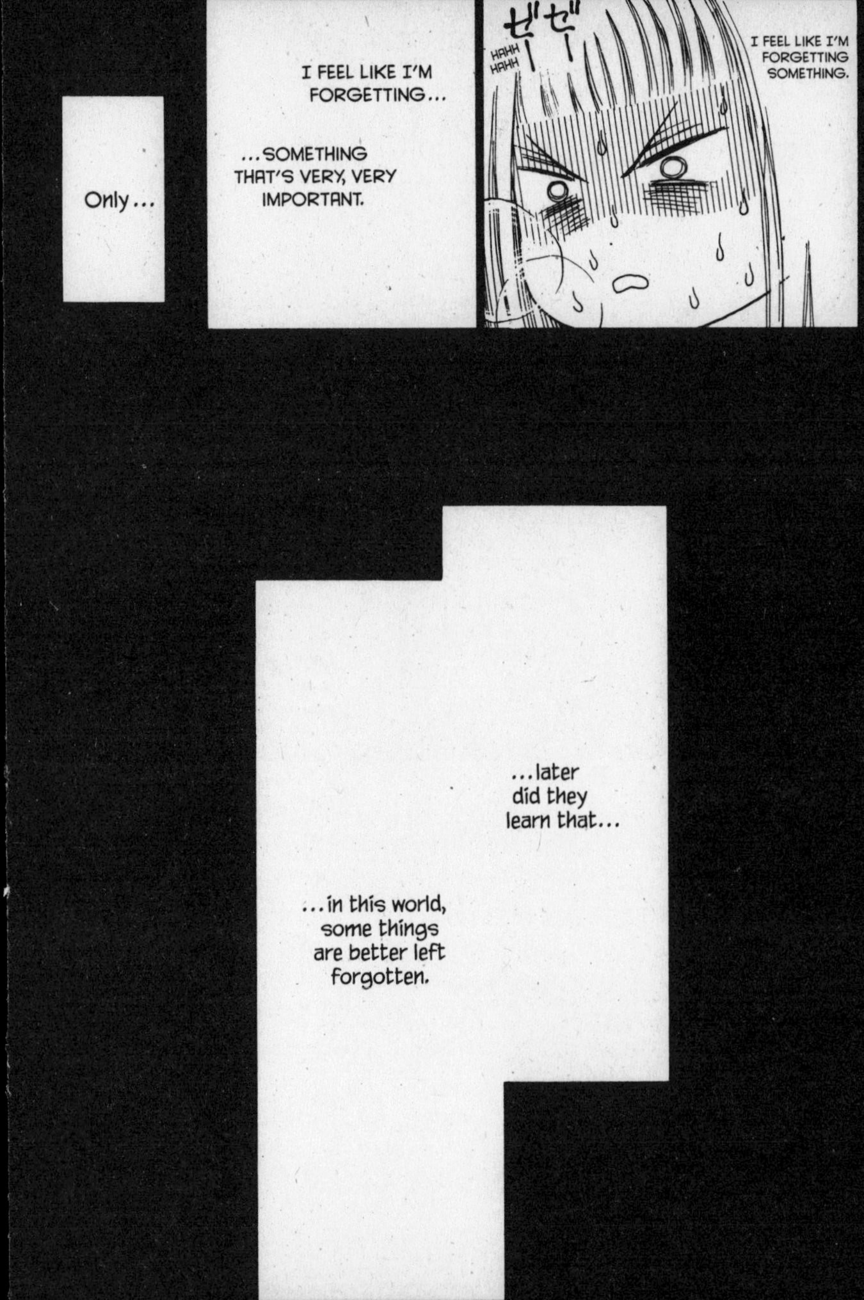
ゼゼ
HAHH HAHH
I FEEL LIKE I'M FORGETTING SOMETHING.
I FEEL LIKE I'M FORGETTING...
...SOMETHING THAT'S VERY, VERY IMPORTANT.
Only...
...later did they learn that...
...in this world, some things are better left forgotten.

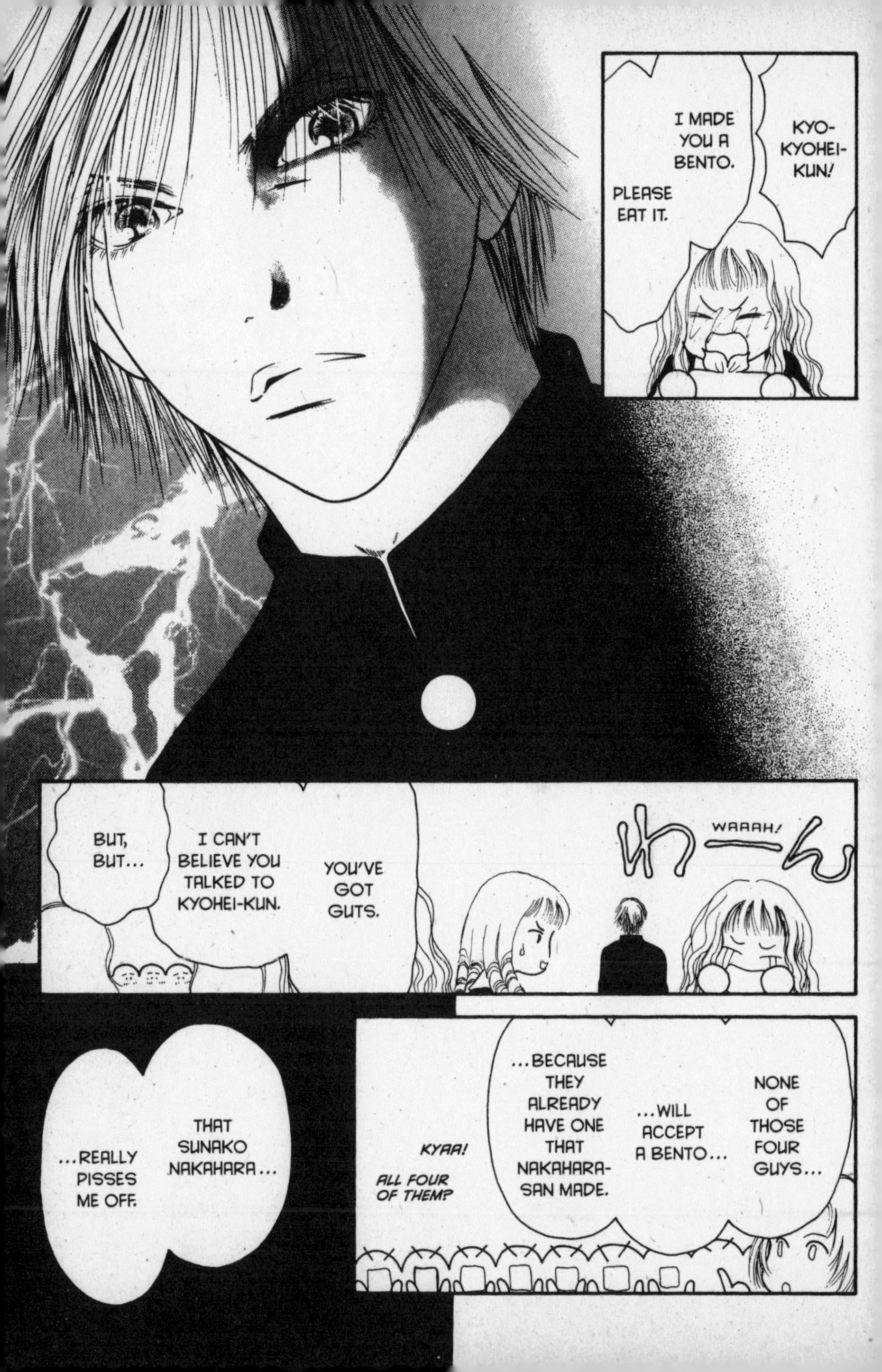
KYO-KYOHEI-KUN!
I MADE YOU A BENTO.
PLEASE EAT IT.
わーん
WAAAH!
YOU'VE GOT GUTS.
I CAN'T BELIEVE YOU TALKED TO KYOHEI-KUN.
BUT, BUT...
NONE OF THOSE FOUR GUYS...
...WILL ACCEPT A BENTO...
...BECAUSE THEY ALREADY HAVE ONE THAT NAKAHARA-SAN MADE.
KYAA!
ALL FOUR OF THEM?
THAT SUNAKO NAKAHARA...
...REALLY PISSES ME OFF.

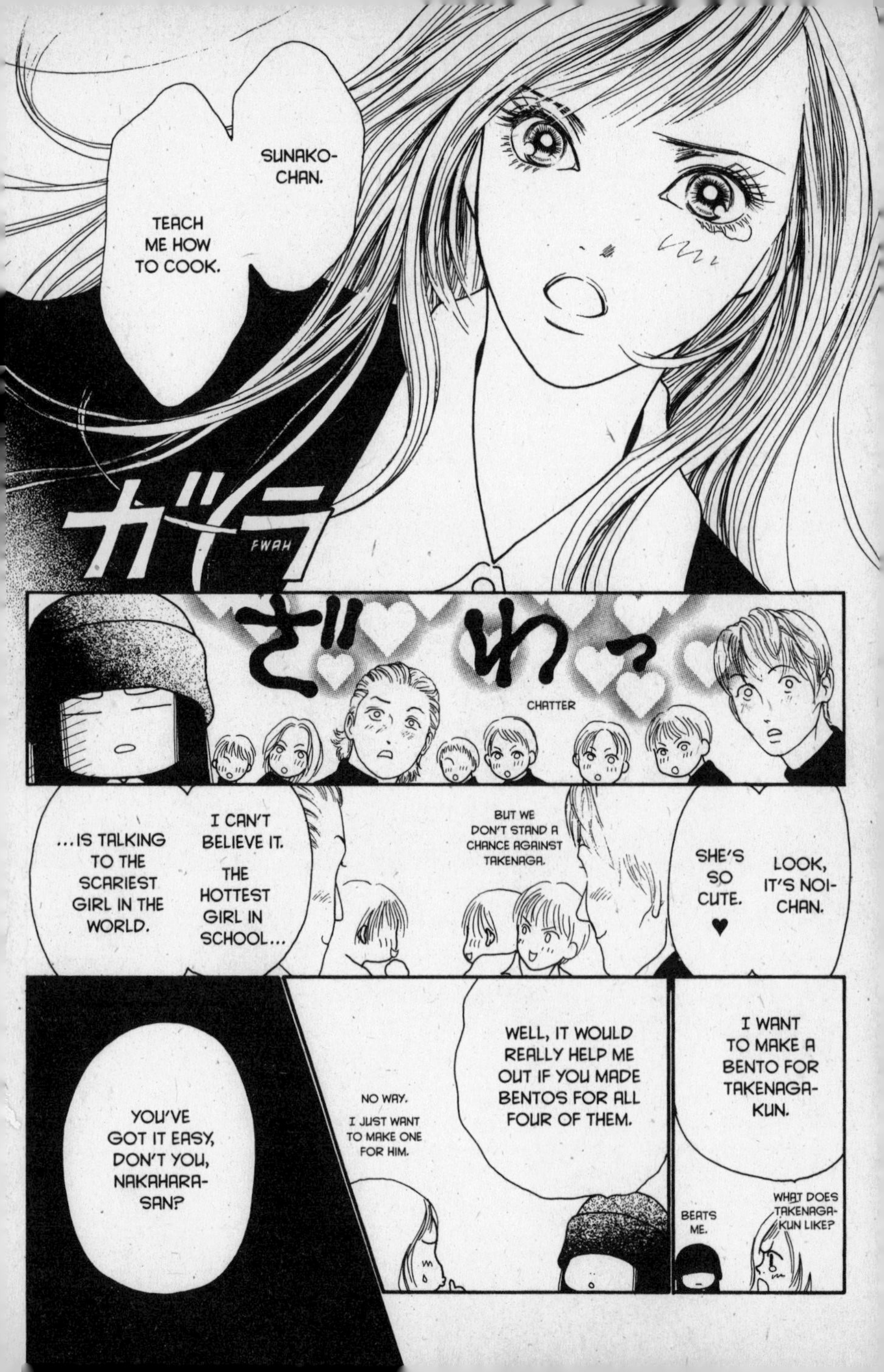
SUNAKO-CHAN.
TEACH ME HOW TO COOK.
ガラ
FWAH
ざわっ
CHATTER
LOOK, IT'S NOI-CHAN.
SHE'S SO CUTE. ♥
BUT WE DON'T STAND A CHANCE AGAINST TAKENAGA.
I CAN'T BELIEVE IT.
THE HOTTEST GIRL IN SCHOOL...
...IS TALKING TO THE SCARIEST GIRL IN THE WORLD.
I WANT TO MAKE A BENTO FOR TAKENAGA-KUN.
WHAT DOES TAKENAGA-KUN LIKE?
BEATS ME.
WELL, IT WOULD REALLY HELP ME OUT IF YOU MADE BENTOS FOR ALL FOUR OF THEM.
NO WAY.
I JUST WANT TO MAKE ONE FOR HIM.
YOU'VE GOT IT EASY, DON'T YOU, NAKAHARA-SAN?

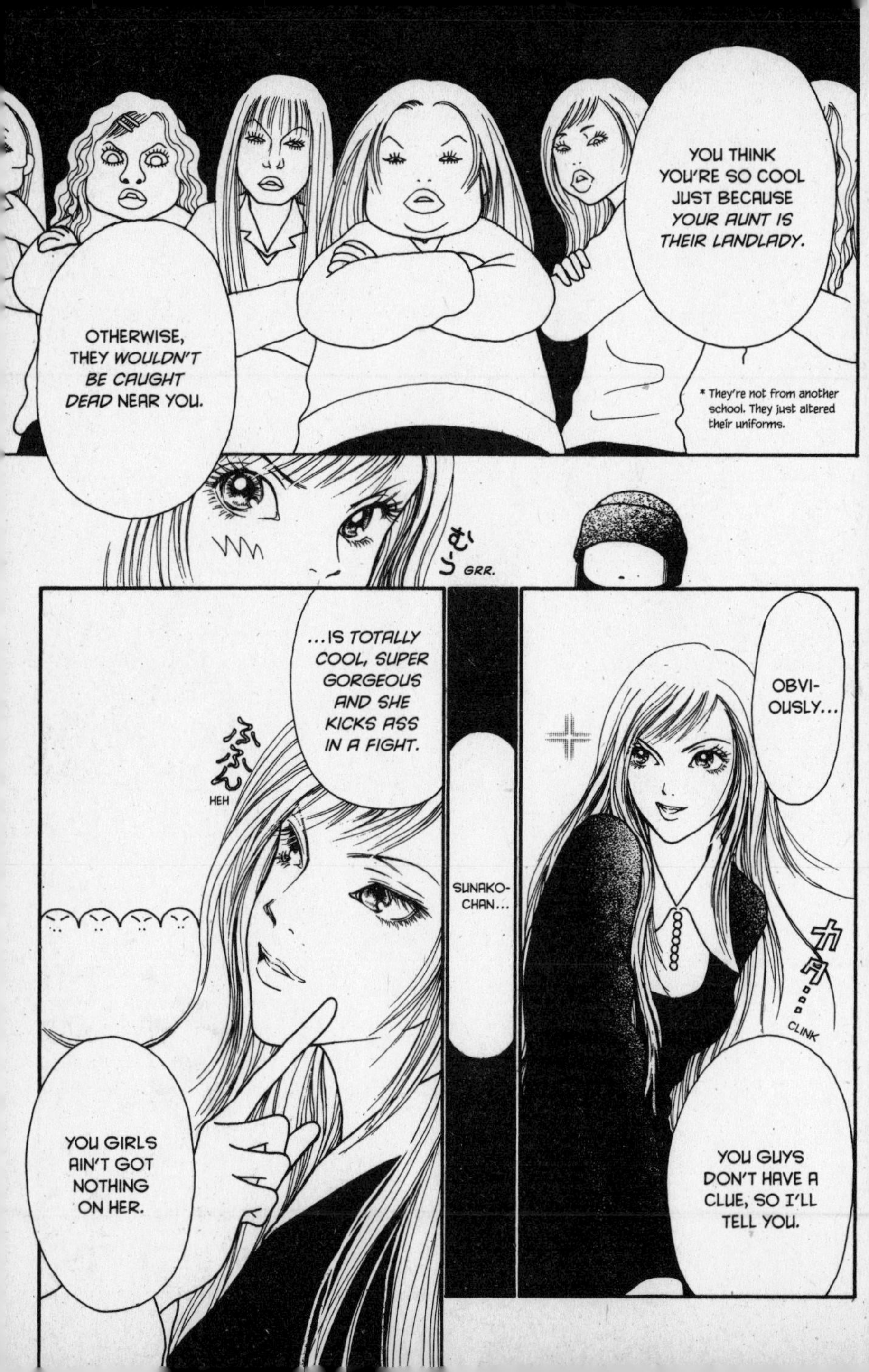
YOU THINK YOU'RE SO COOL JUST BECAUSE YOUR AUNT IS THEIR LANDLADY.
* They're not from another school. They just altered their uniforms.
OTHERWISE, THEY WOULDN'T BE CAUGHT DEAD NEAR YOU.
むー GRR.
OBVI-OUSLY...
カタ... CLINK
YOU GUYS DON'T HAVE A CLUE, SO I'LL TELL YOU.
SUNAKO-CHAN...
...IS TOTALLY COOL, SUPER GORGEOUS AND SHE KICKS ASS IN A FIGHT.
ふふん HEH
YOU GIRLS AIN'T GOT NOTHING ON HER.

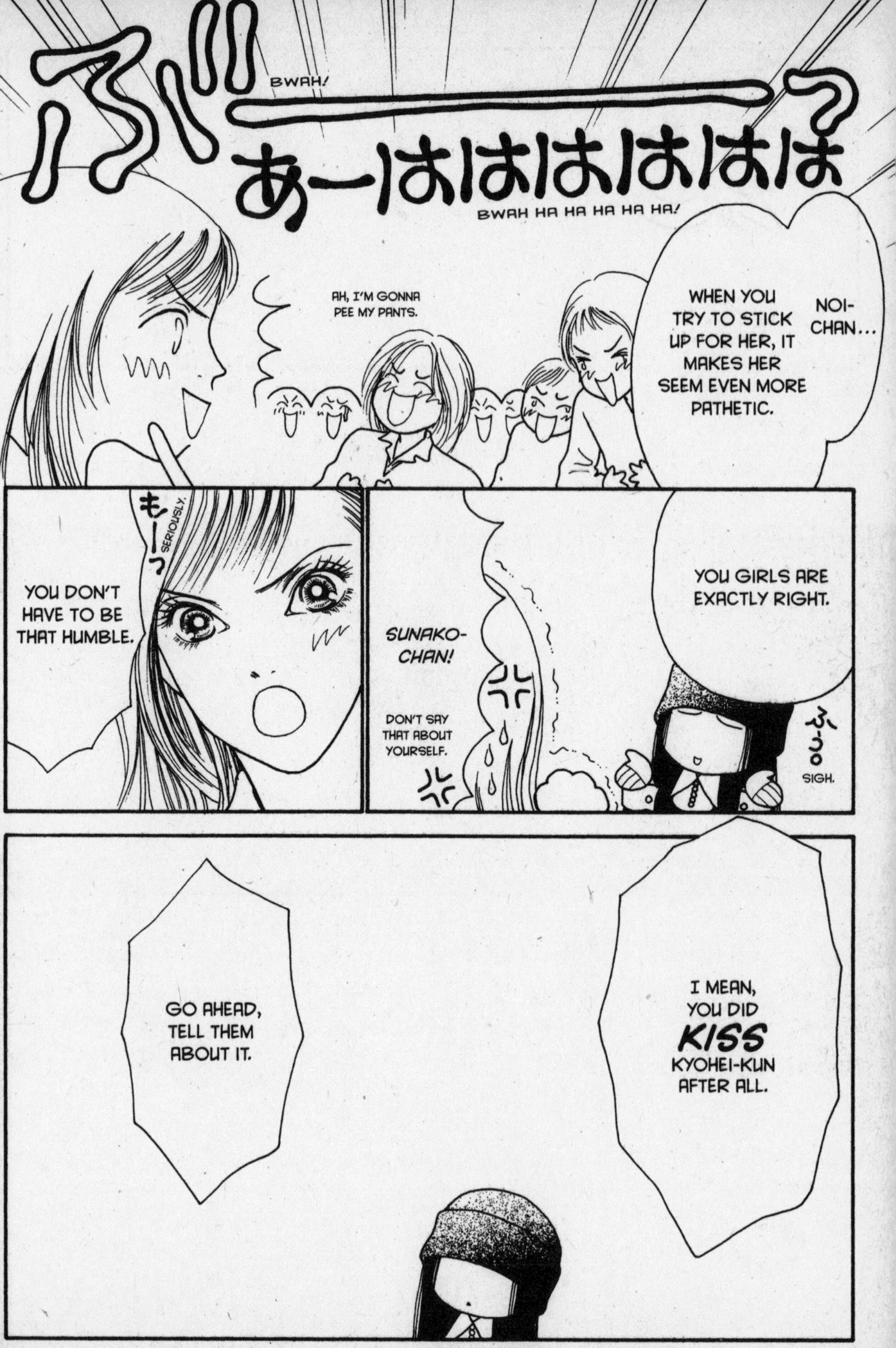
ぶーっ
BWAH!
あーはははははは
BWAH HA HA HA HA HA!
NOI-CHAN...
WHEN YOU TRY TO STICK UP FOR HER, IT MAKES HER SEEM EVEN MORE PATHETIC.
AH, I'M GONNA PEE MY PANTS.
YOU GIRLS ARE EXACTLY RIGHT.
ふーっ
SIGH.
SUNAKO-CHAN!
DON'T SAY THAT ABOUT YOURSELF.
もーっ
SERIOUSLY.
YOU DON'T HAVE TO BE THAT HUMBLE.
I MEAN, YOU DID **KISS** KYOHEI-KUN AFTER ALL.
GO AHEAD, TELL THEM ABOUT IT.

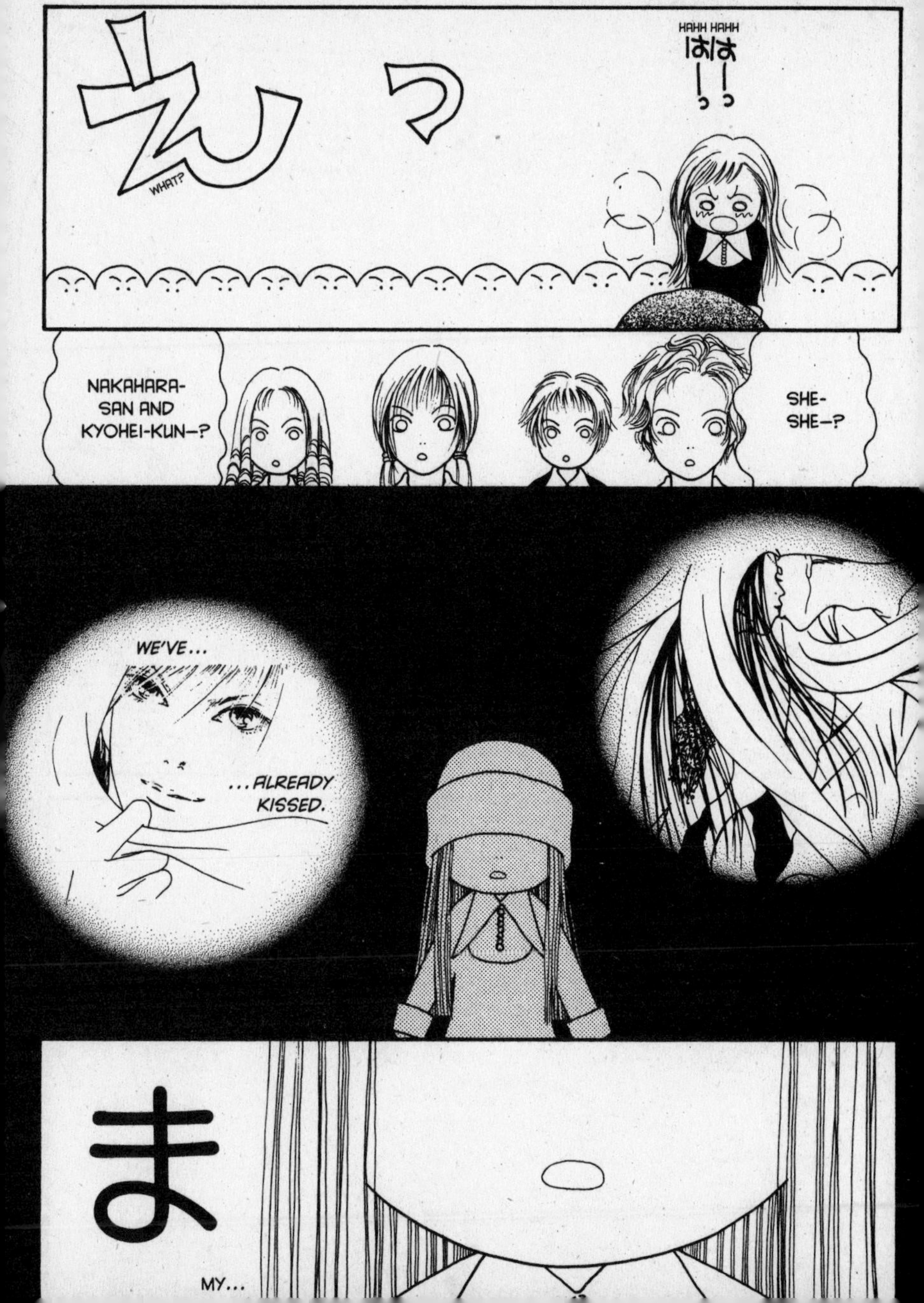
HAHH HAHH
はは!!
えっ
WHAT?
SHE-
SHE-?
NAKAHARA-
SAN AND
KYOHEI-KUN-?
WE'VE...
...ALREADY
KISSED.
ま
MY...

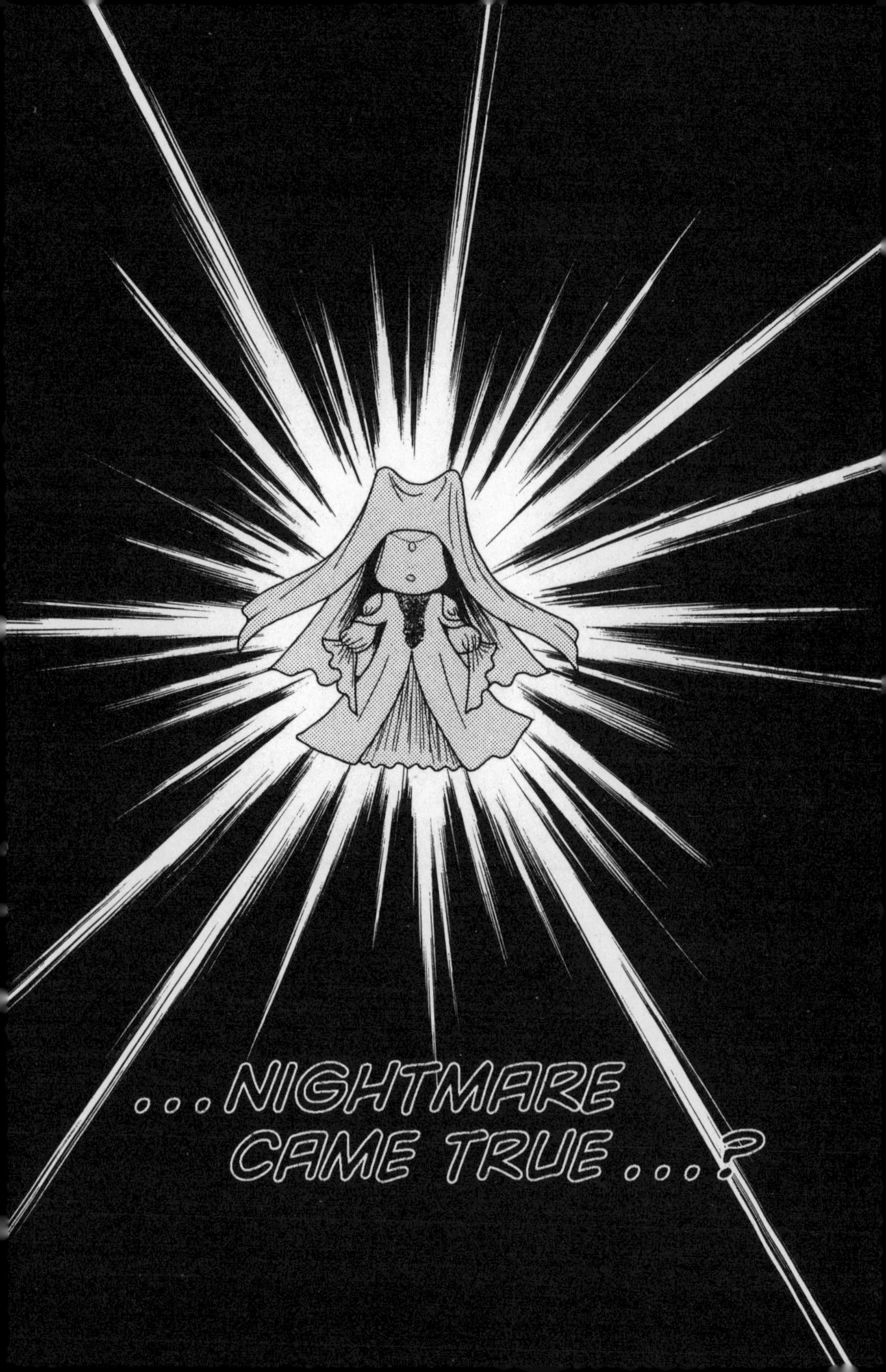
...NIGHTMARE CAME TRUE...?

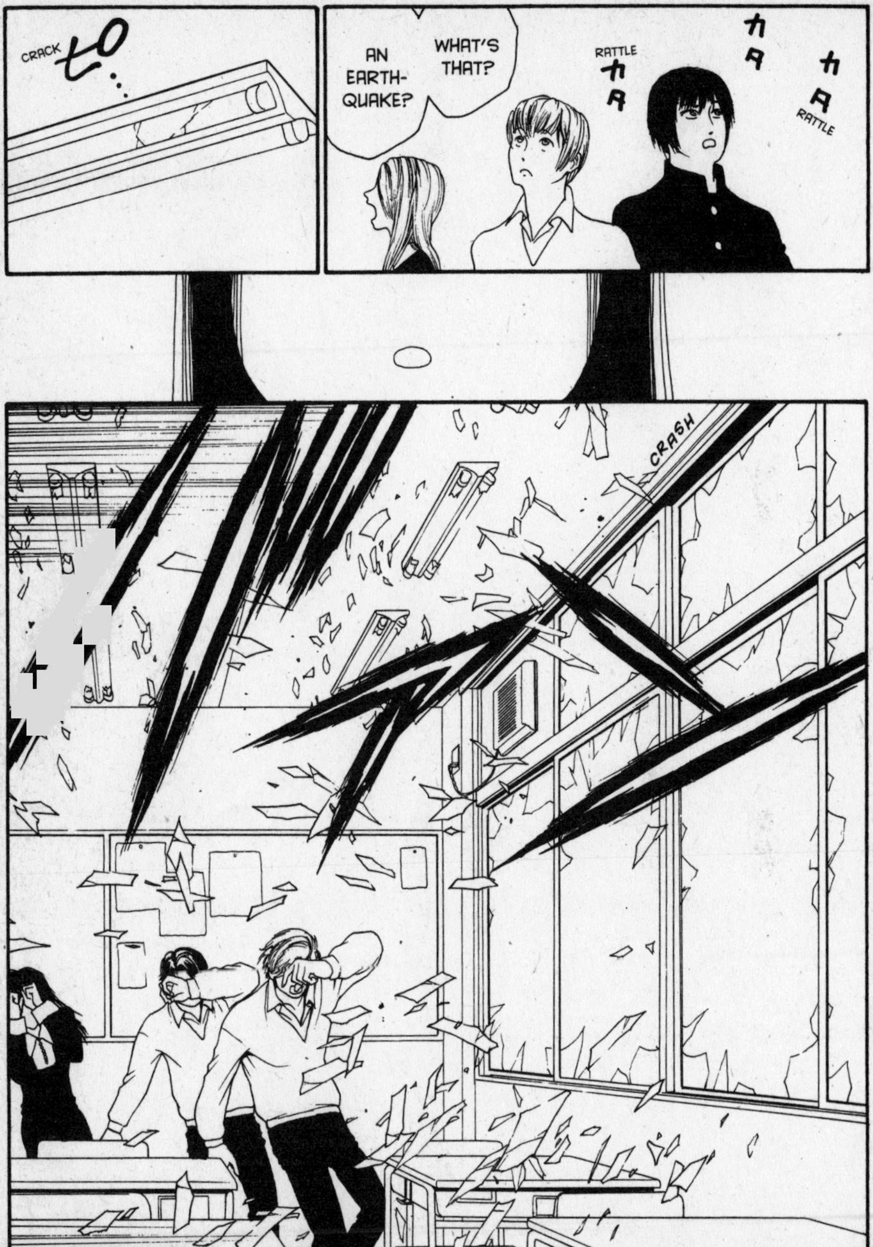

RATTLE
RATTLE
WHAT'S THAT?
AN EARTHQUAKE?
CRACK
CRASH

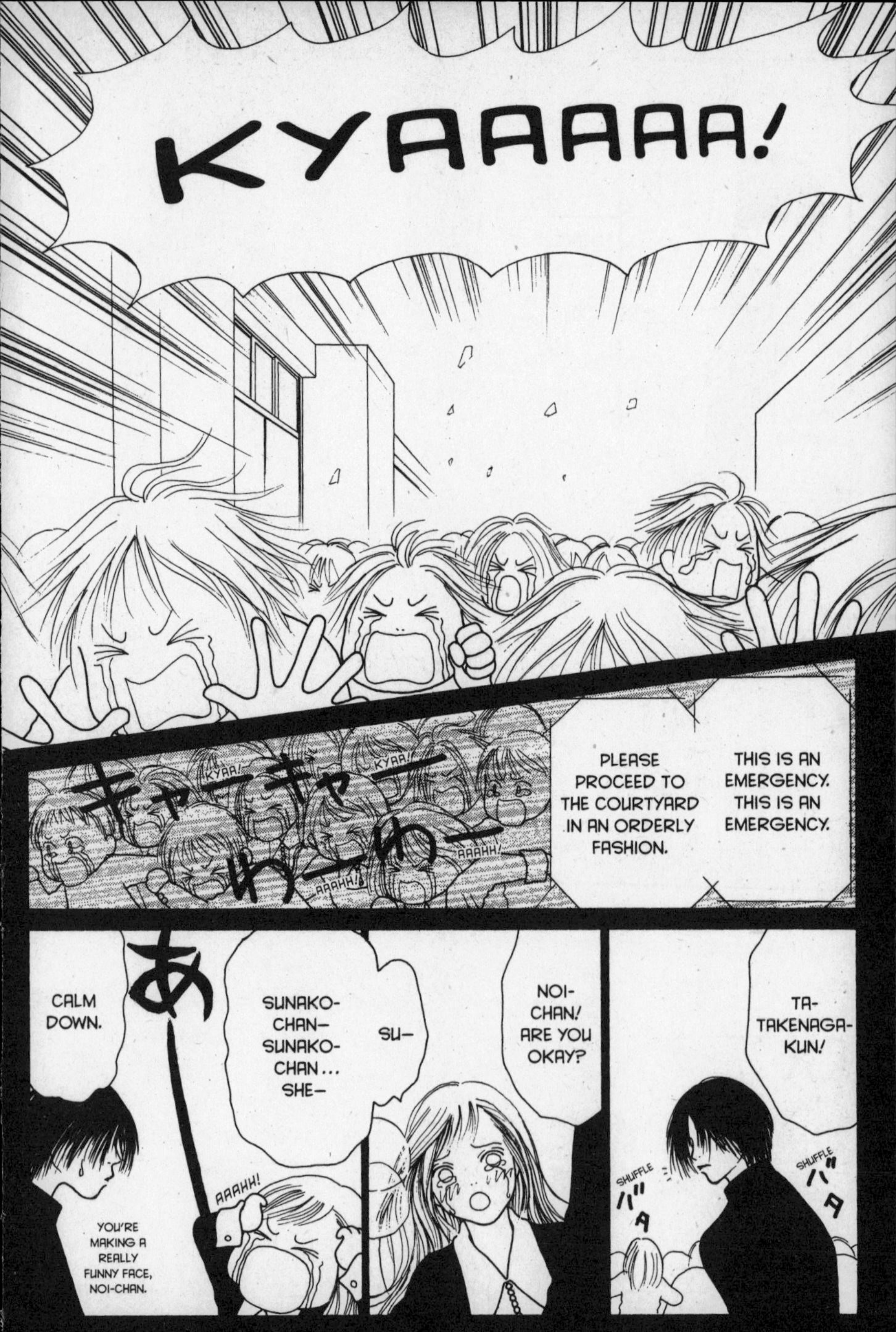
KYAAAAAA!
THIS IS AN EMERGENCY. THIS IS AN EMERGENCY.
PLEASE PROCEED TO THE COURTYARD IN AN ORDERLY FASHION.
キャーキャー
KYAA!
KYAA!
わーわー
AAAHH!
AAAHH!
TA-TAKENAGA-KUN!
SHUFFLE
バタ
SHUFFLE
バタ
NOI-CHAN! ARE YOU OKAY?
SU-
SUNAKO-CHAN-SUNAKO-CHAN... SHE-
あ
CALM DOWN.
AAAHH!
YOU'RE MAKING A REALLY FUNNY FACE, NOI-CHAN.

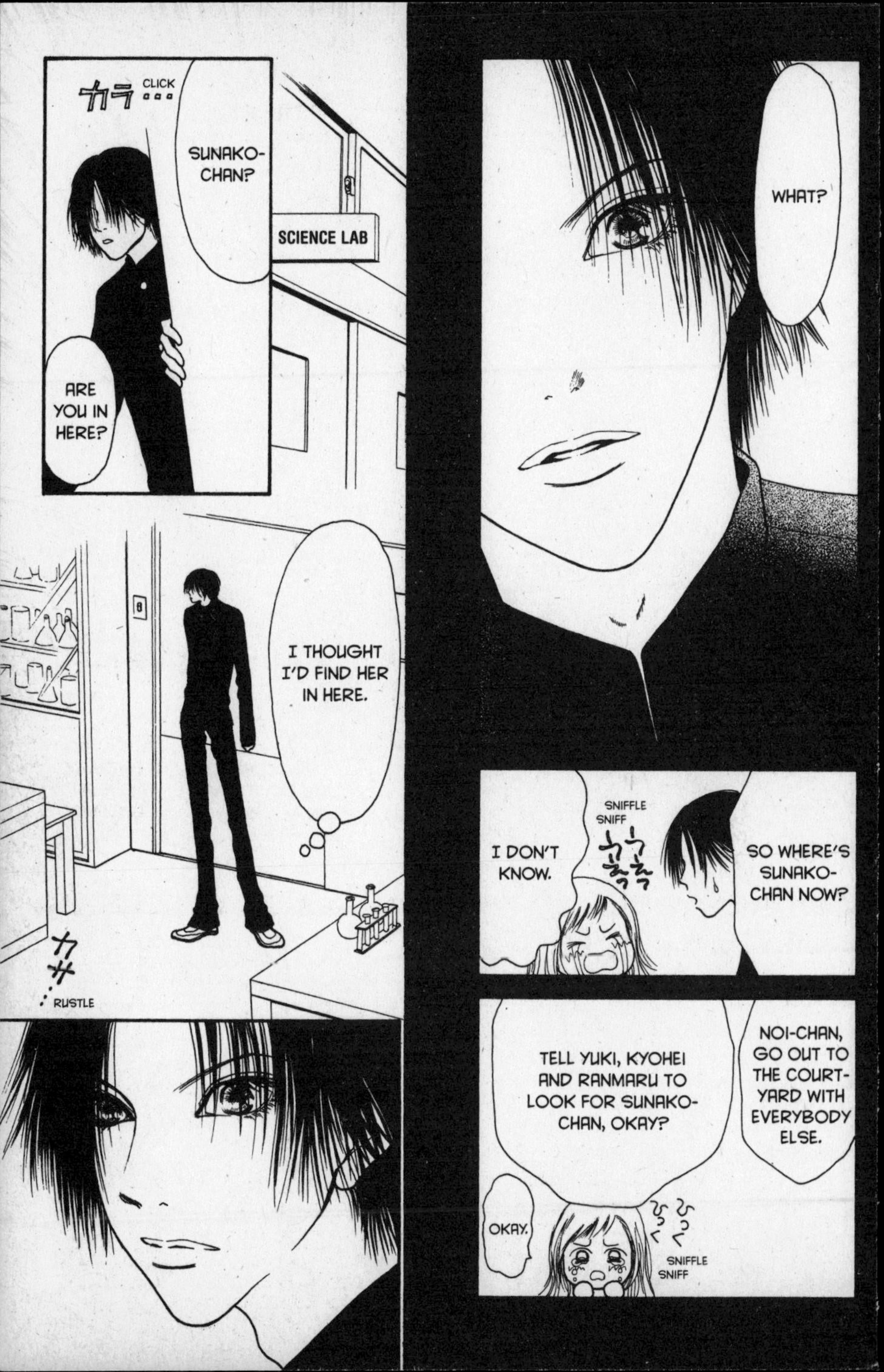
WHAT?
SO WHERE'S SUNAKO-CHAN NOW?
SNIFFLE SNIFF
I DON'T KNOW.
NOI-CHAN, GO OUT TO THE COURT-YARD WITH EVERYBODY ELSE.
TELL YUKI, KYOHEI AND RANMARU TO LOOK FOR SUNAKO-CHAN, OKAY?
OKAY.
SNIFFLE SNIFF
カラ
CLICK . . .
SUNAKO-CHAN?
SCIENCE LAB
ARE YOU IN HERE?
I THOUGHT I'D FIND HER IN HERE.
カサ
RUSTLE

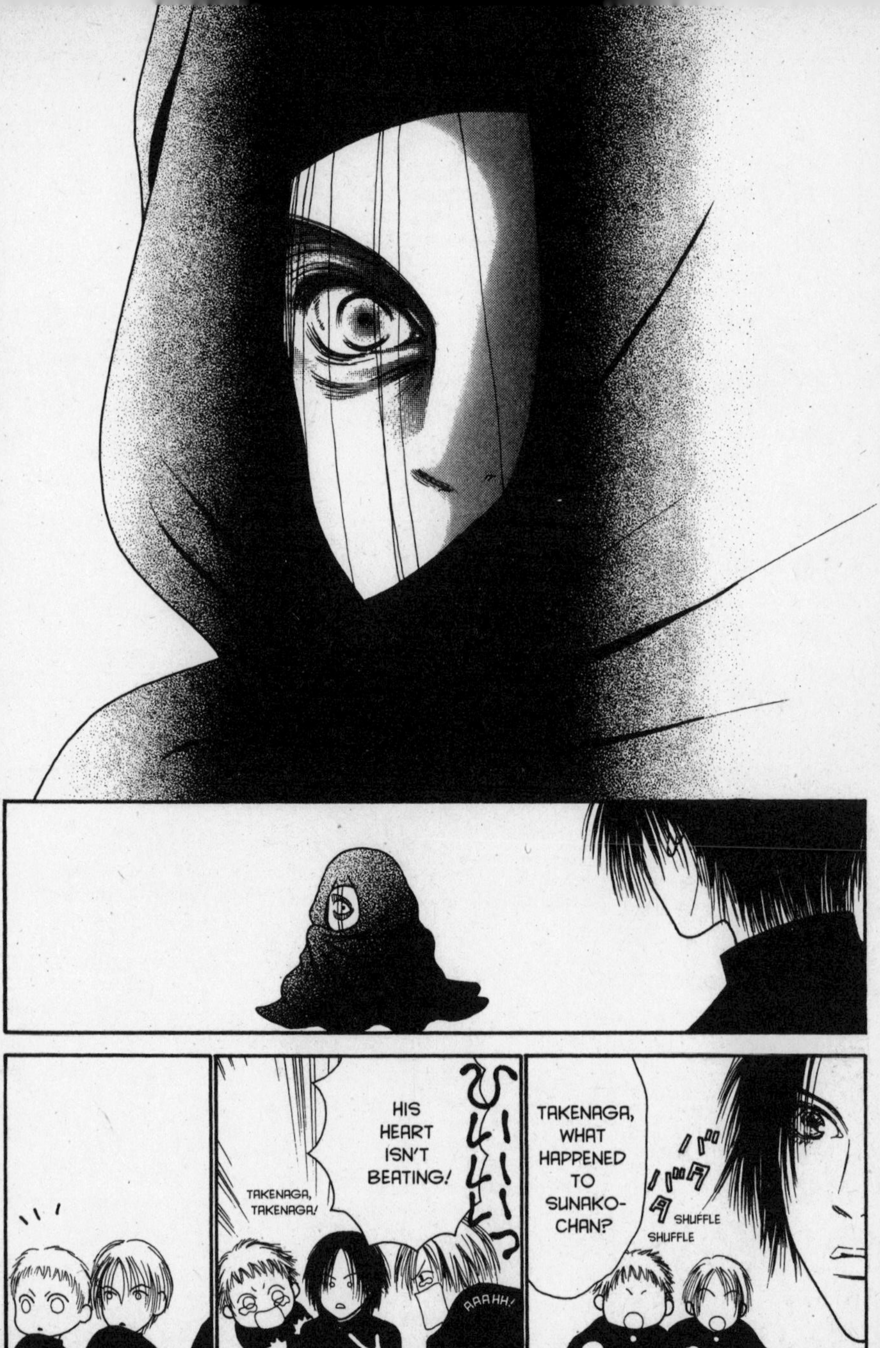
TAKENAGA, WHAT HAPPENED TO SUNAKO-CHAN?
バタ バタ
SHUFFLE
SHUFFLE
ひぃぃぃーっ
HIS HEART ISN'T BEATING!
TAKENAGA, TAKENAGA!
AAAHH!

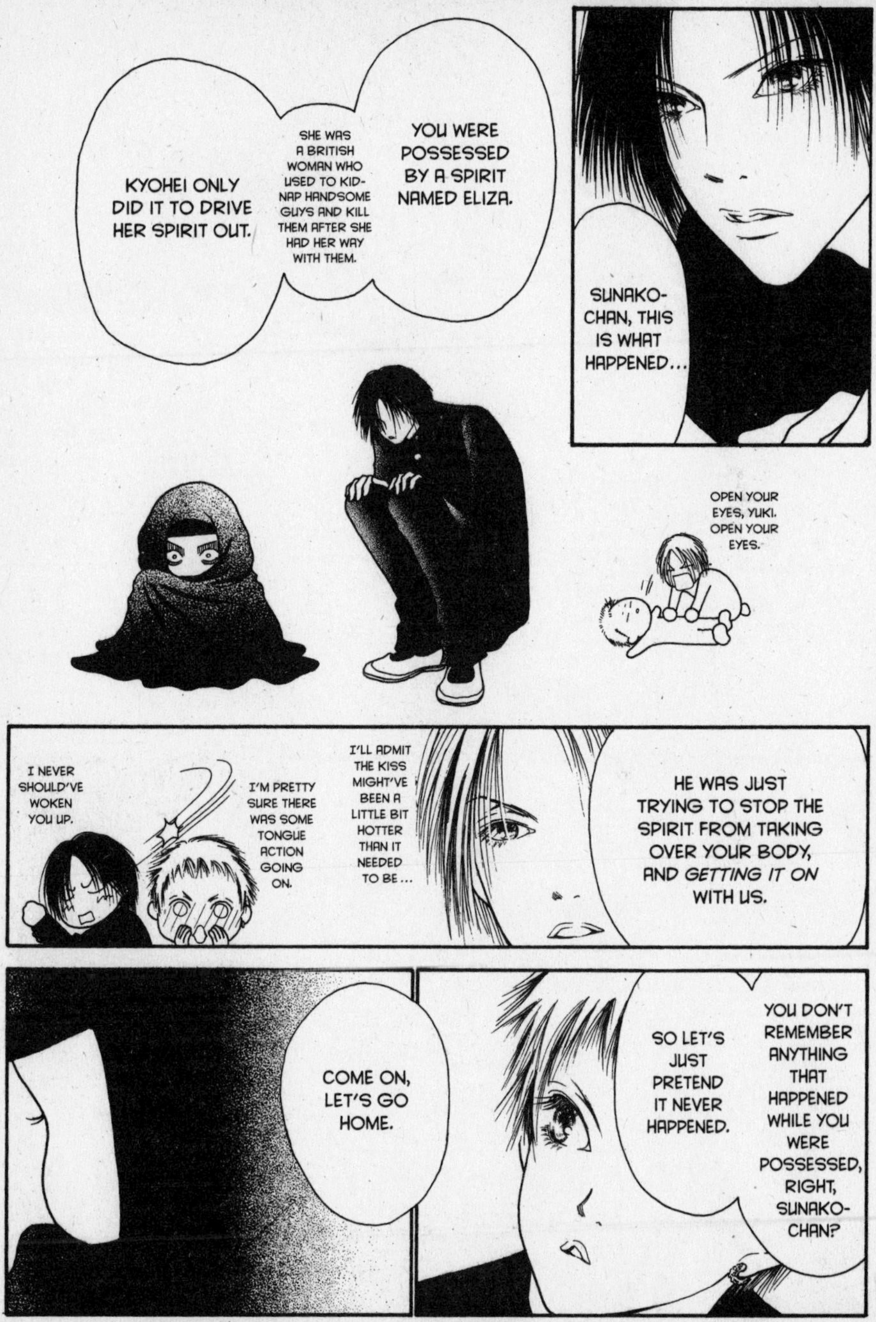
SUNAKO-CHAN, THIS IS WHAT HAPPENED...
YOU WERE POSSESSED BY A SPIRIT NAMED ELIZA.
SHE WAS A BRITISH WOMAN WHO USED TO KID-NAP HANDSOME GUYS AND KILL THEM AFTER SHE HAD HER WAY WITH THEM.
KYOHEI ONLY DID IT TO DRIVE HER SPIRIT OUT.
OPEN YOUR EYES, YUKI. OPEN YOUR EYES.
HE WAS JUST TRYING TO STOP THE SPIRIT FROM TAKING OVER YOUR BODY, AND *GETTING IT ON* WITH US.
I'LL ADMIT THE KISS MIGHT'VE BEEN A LITTLE BIT HOTTER THAN IT NEEDED TO BE...
I'M PRETTY SURE THERE WAS SOME TONGUE ACTION GOING ON.
I NEVER SHOULD'VE WOKEN YOU UP.
YOU DON'T REMEMBER ANYTHING THAT HAPPENED WHILE YOU WERE POSSESSED, RIGHT, SUNAKO-CHAN?
SO LET'S JUST PRETEND IT NEVER HAPPENED.
COME ON, LET'S GO HOME.

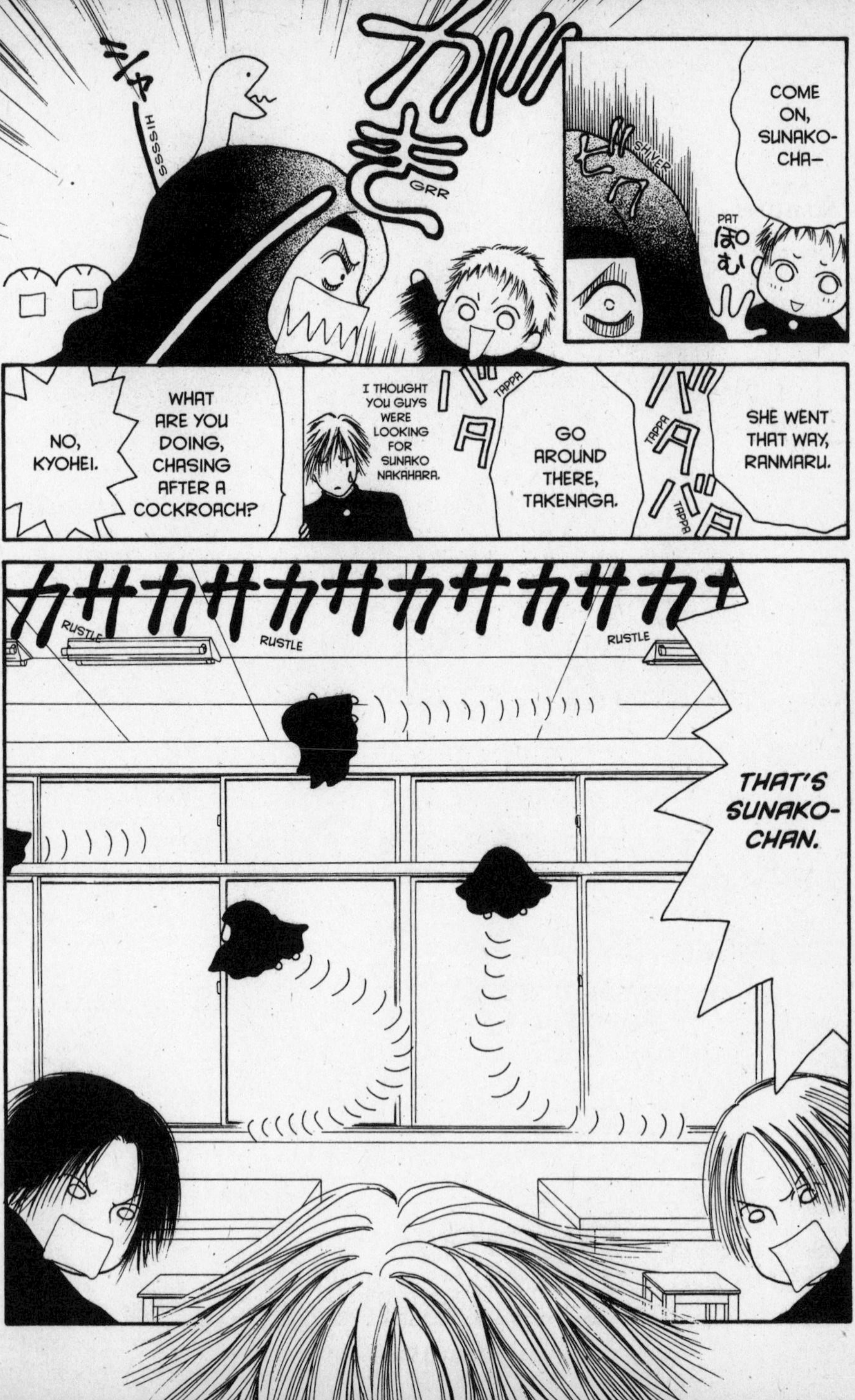
COME ON, SUNAKO-CHA—
SHIVER
PAT
ぽむ
GRR
シャ
HISSSS
SHE WENT THAT WAY, RANMARU.
TAPPA
TAPPA
GO AROUND THERE, TAKENAGA.
TAPPA
I THOUGHT YOU GUYS WERE LOOKING FOR SUNAKO NAKAHARA.
WHAT ARE YOU DOING, CHASING AFTER A COCKROACH?
NO, KYOHEI.
カサカサカサカサカサカ
RUSTLE
RUSTLE
RUSTLE
THAT'S SUNAKO-CHAN.

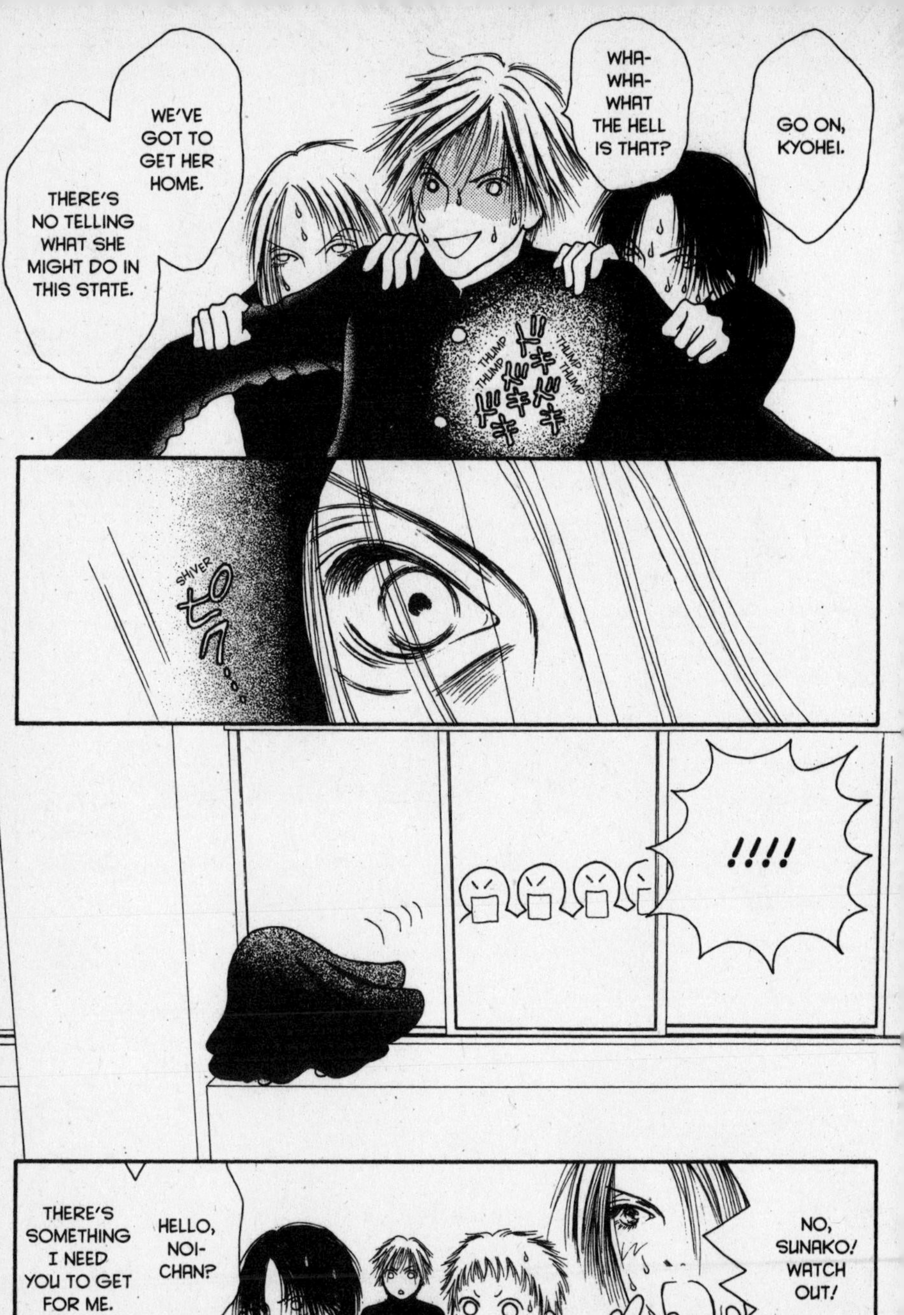
GO ON, KYOHEI.
WHA-WHA-WHAT THE HELL IS THAT?
WE'VE GOT TO GET HER HOME.
THERE'S NO TELLING WHAT SHE MIGHT DO IN THIS STATE.
THUMP THUMP THUMP THUMP
SHIVER
!!!!
NO, SUNAKO! WATCH OUT!
HELLO, NOI-CHAN?
THERE'S SOMETHING I NEED YOU TO GET FOR ME.

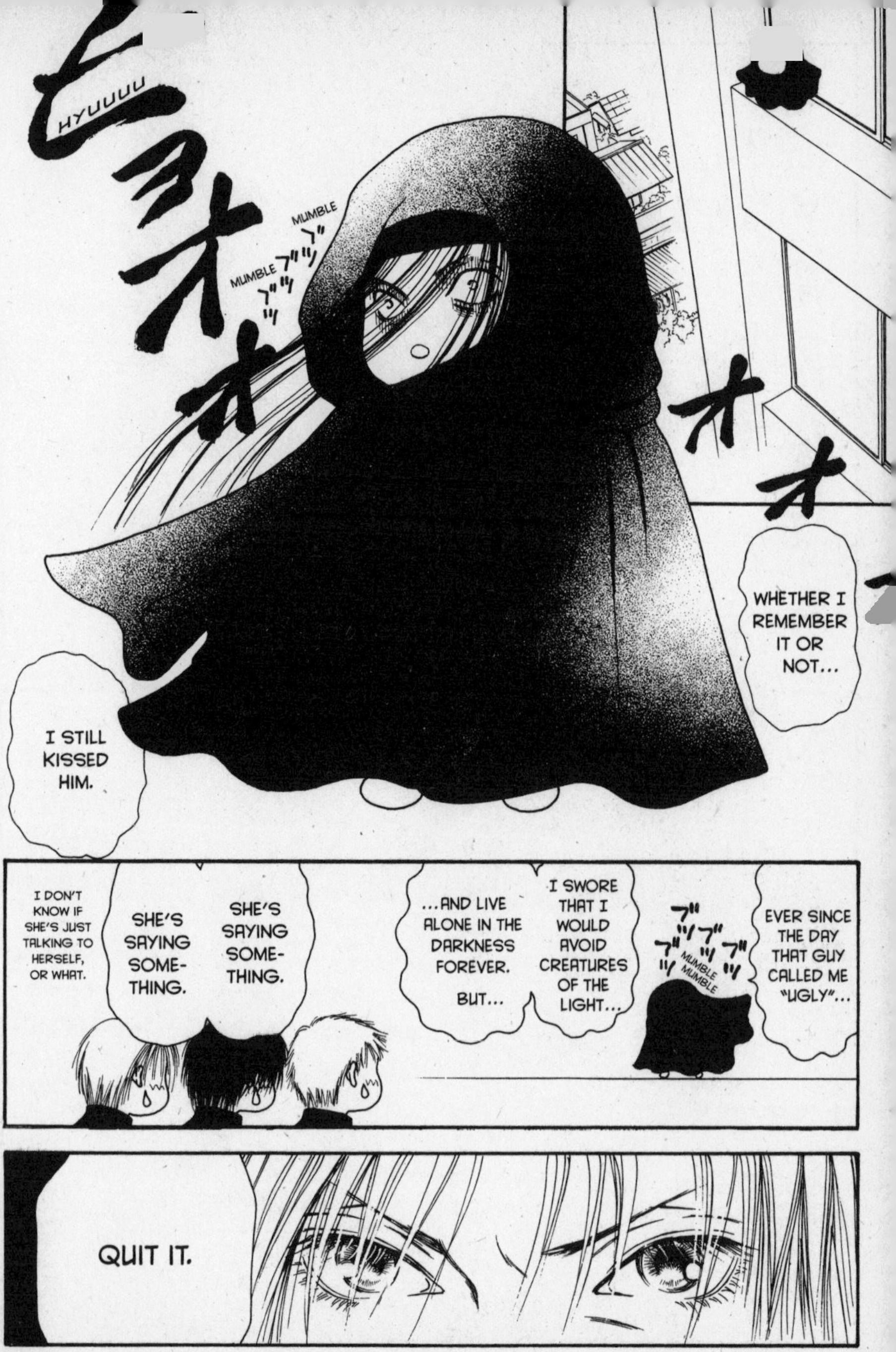
ヒョオオオ
HYUUUU
ブツブツ
MUMBLE
MUMBLE
WHETHER I REMEMBER IT OR NOT...
I STILL KISSED HIM.
EVER SINCE THE DAY THAT GUY CALLED ME "UGLY"...
MUMBLE MUMBLE
I SWORE THAT I WOULD AVOID CREATURES OF THE LIGHT...
...AND LIVE ALONE IN THE DARKNESS FOREVER. BUT...
SHE'S SAYING SOMETHING.
SHE'S SAYING SOMETHING.
I DON'T KNOW IF SHE'S JUST TALKING TO HERSELF, OR WHAT.
QUIT IT.

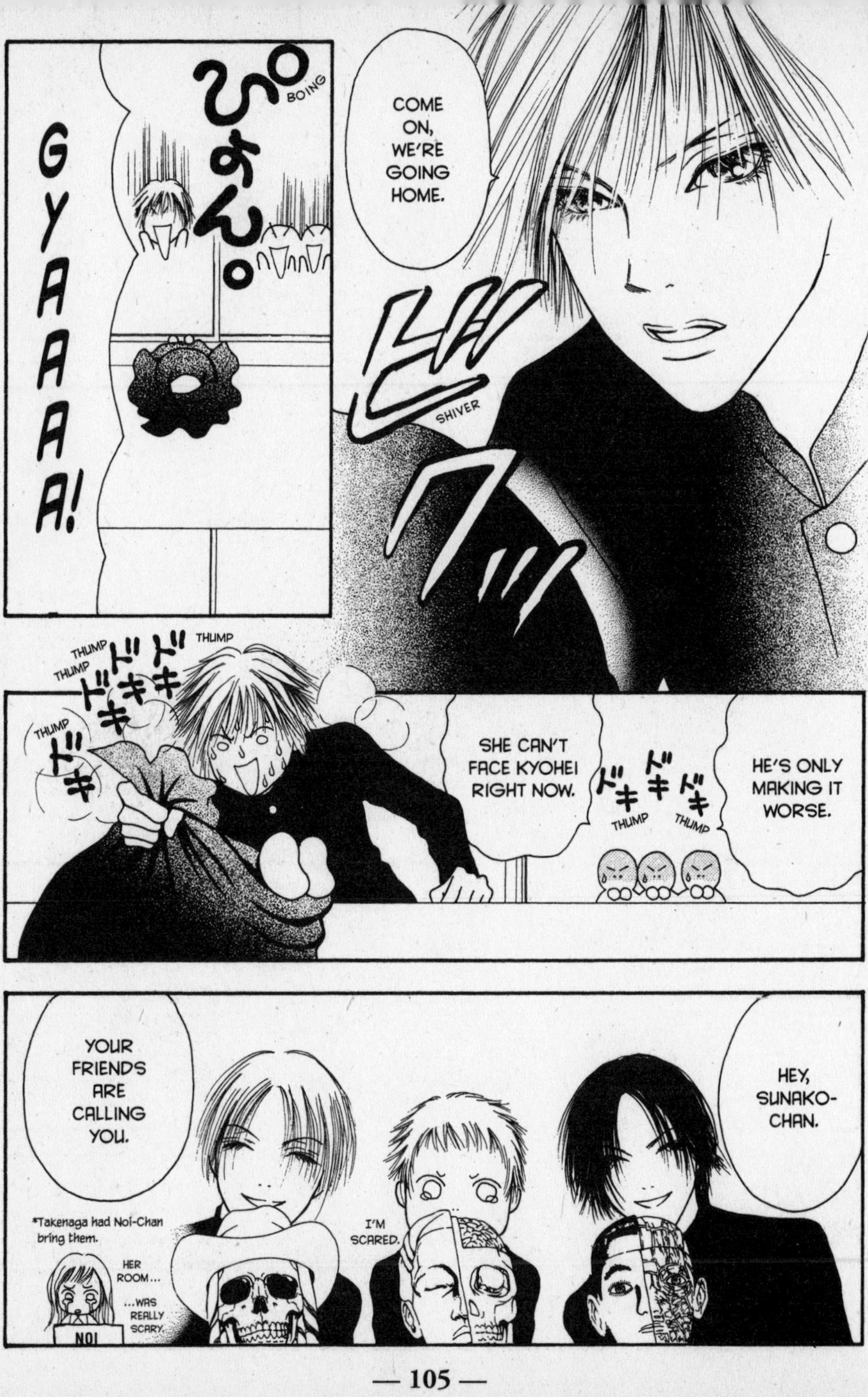
COME ON, WE'RE GOING HOME.
SHIVER
ぴょん。
BOING
GYAAAAA!
HE'S ONLY MAKING IT WORSE.
ドキドキドキ
THUMP THUMP
SHE CAN'T FACE KYOHEI RIGHT NOW.
ドキドキドキドキ
THUMP THUMP THUMP THUMP
HEY, SUNAKO-CHAN.
I'M SCARED.
YOUR FRIENDS ARE CALLING YOU.
*Takenaga had Noi-Chan bring them.
HER ROOM...
...WAS REALLY SCARY.
NOI

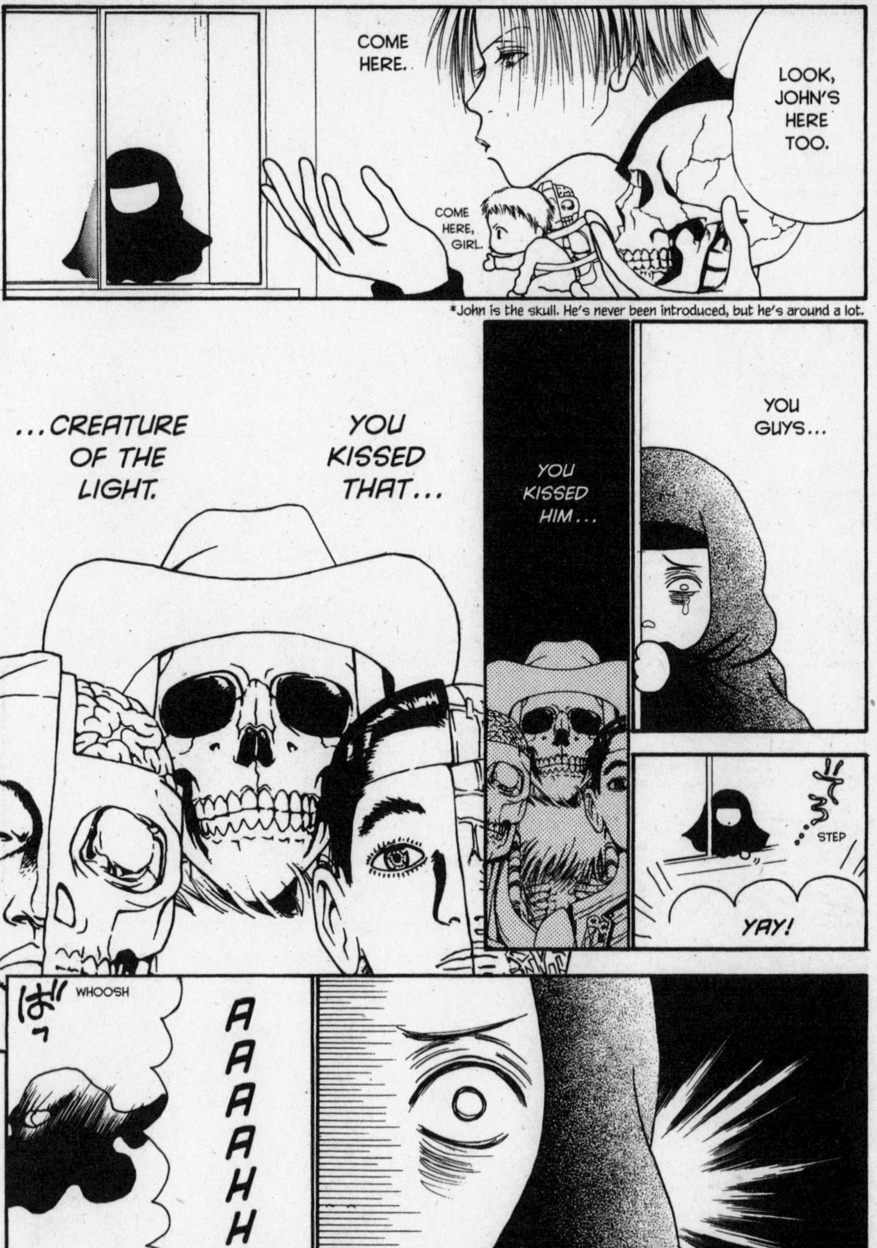
LOOK, JOHN'S HERE TOO.
COME HERE.
COME HERE, GIRL.
YOU GUYS...
STEP
YAY!
YOU KISSED HIM...
YOU KISSED THAT...
...CREATURE OF THE LIGHT.
ばっ
WHOOSH
AAAAAAHHH!

*John is the skull. He's never been introduced, but he's around a lot.

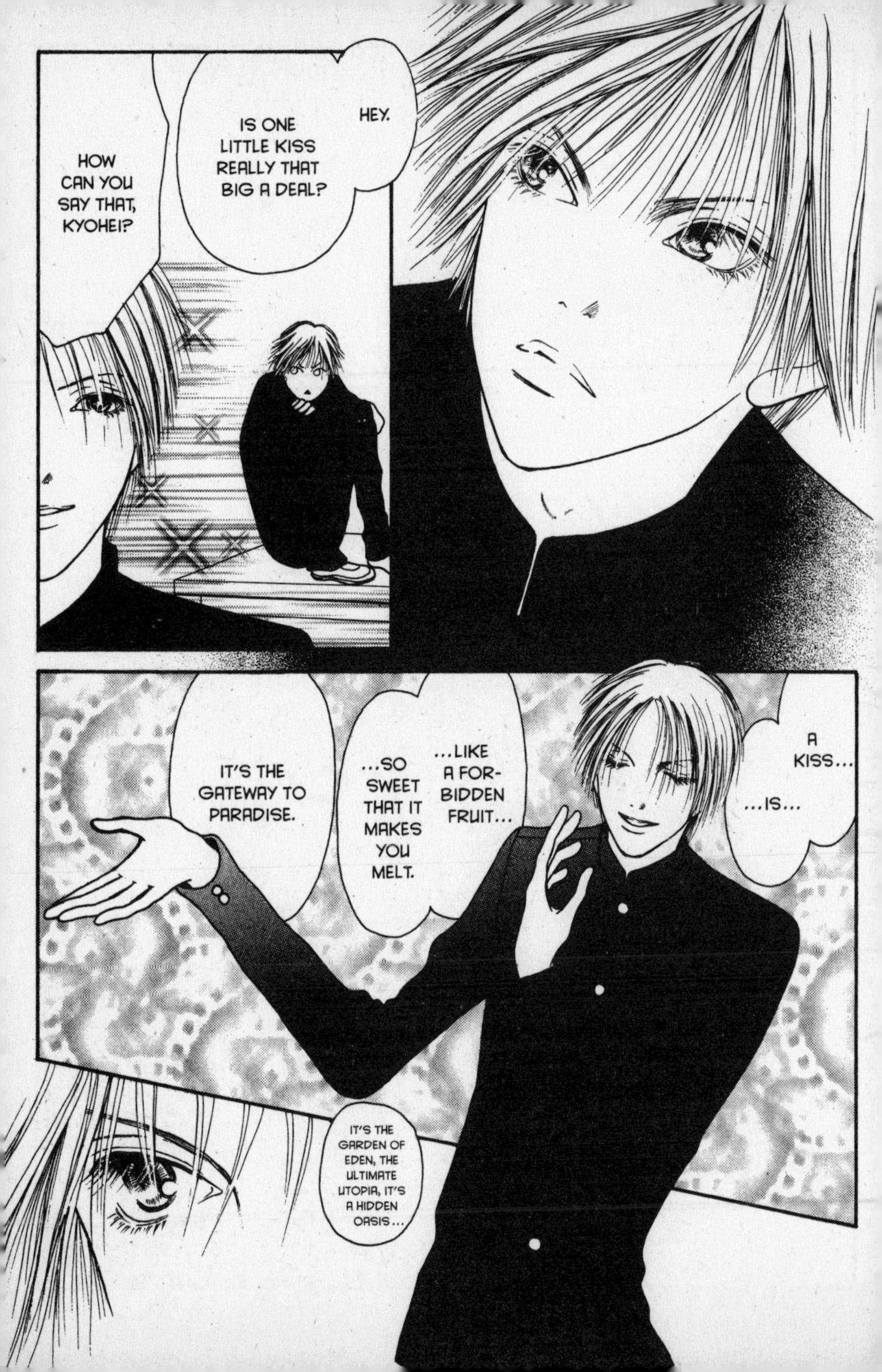
HEY.
IS ONE LITTLE KISS REALLY THAT BIG A DEAL?
HOW CAN YOU SAY THAT, KYOHEI?
A KISS...
...IS...
...LIKE A FOR-BIDDEN FRUIT...
...SO SWEET THAT IT MAKES YOU MELT.
IT'S THE GATEWAY TO PARADISE.
IT'S THE GARDEN OF EDEN, THE ULTIMATE UTOPIA, IT'S A HIDDEN OASIS...

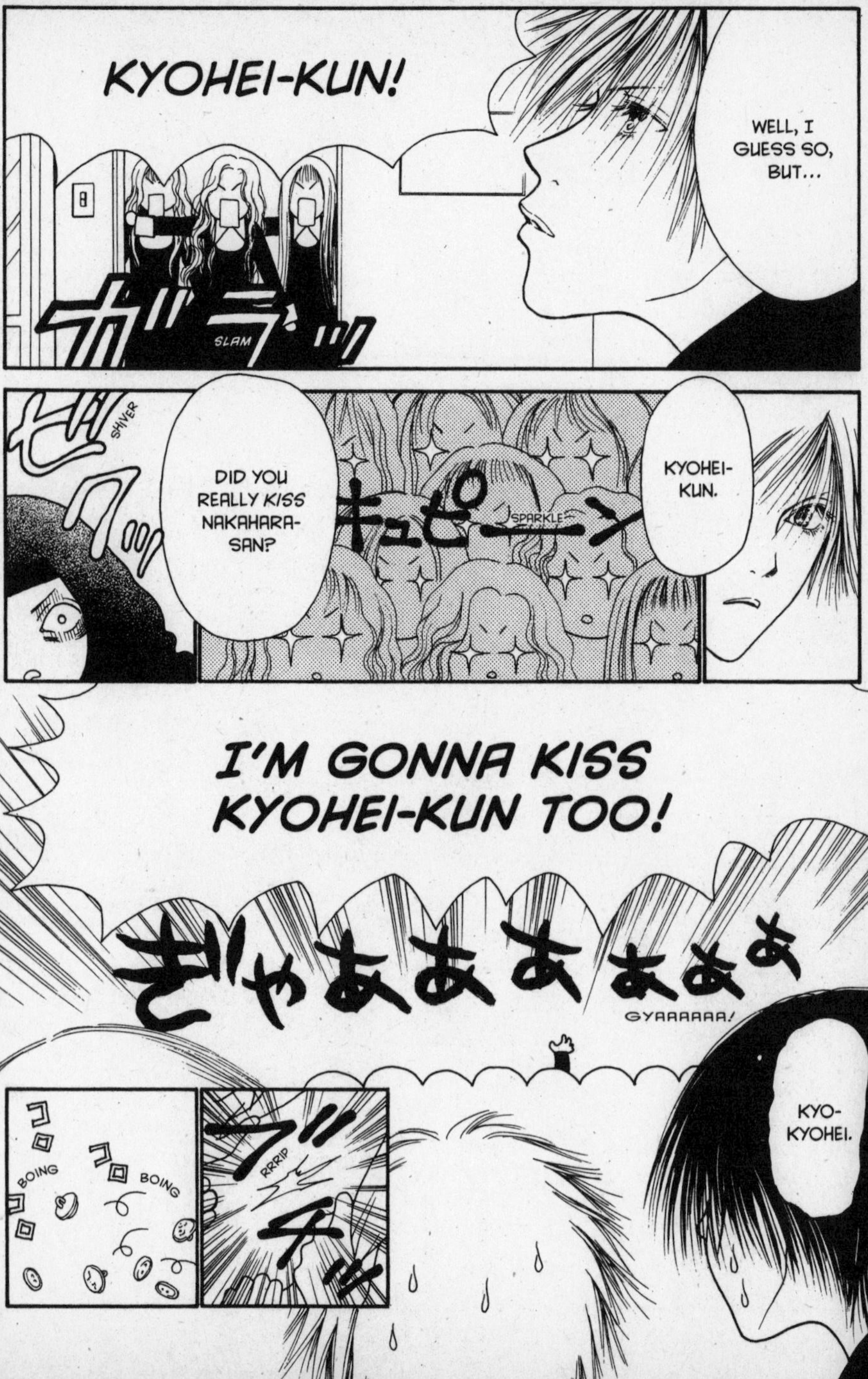
WELL, I GUESS SO, BUT...
KYOHEI-KUN!
ガラッ
SLAM
KYOHEI-KUN.
DID YOU REALLY *KISS* NAKAHARA-SAN?
キュピーン
SPARKLE
SHIVER
I'M GONNA KISS KYOHEI-KUN TOO!
ぎゃああああああ
GYAAAAAAA!
KYO-KYOHEI.
RRRIP
コロ
BOING
コロ
BOING

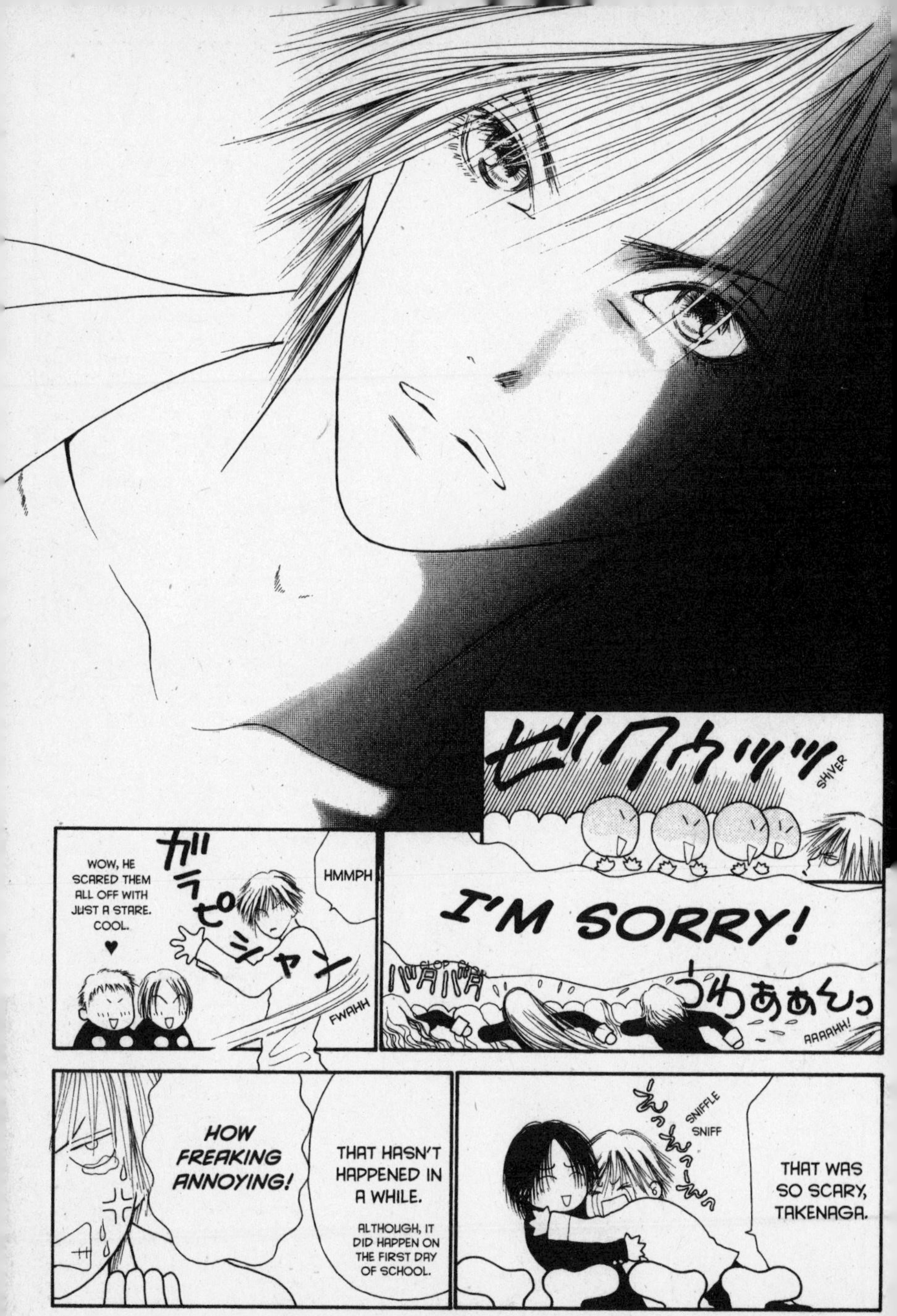
SHIVER
I'M SORRY!
CLOP CLOP
AAAHH!
HMMPH
WOW, HE SCARED THEM ALL OFF WITH JUST A STARE. COOL. ♥
FWAHH
THAT WAS SO SCARY, TAKENAGA.
SNIFFLE
SNIFF
THAT HASN'T HAPPENED IN A WHILE.
ALTHOUGH, IT DID HAPPEN ON THE FIRST DAY OF SCHOOL.
HOW FREAKING ANNOYING!

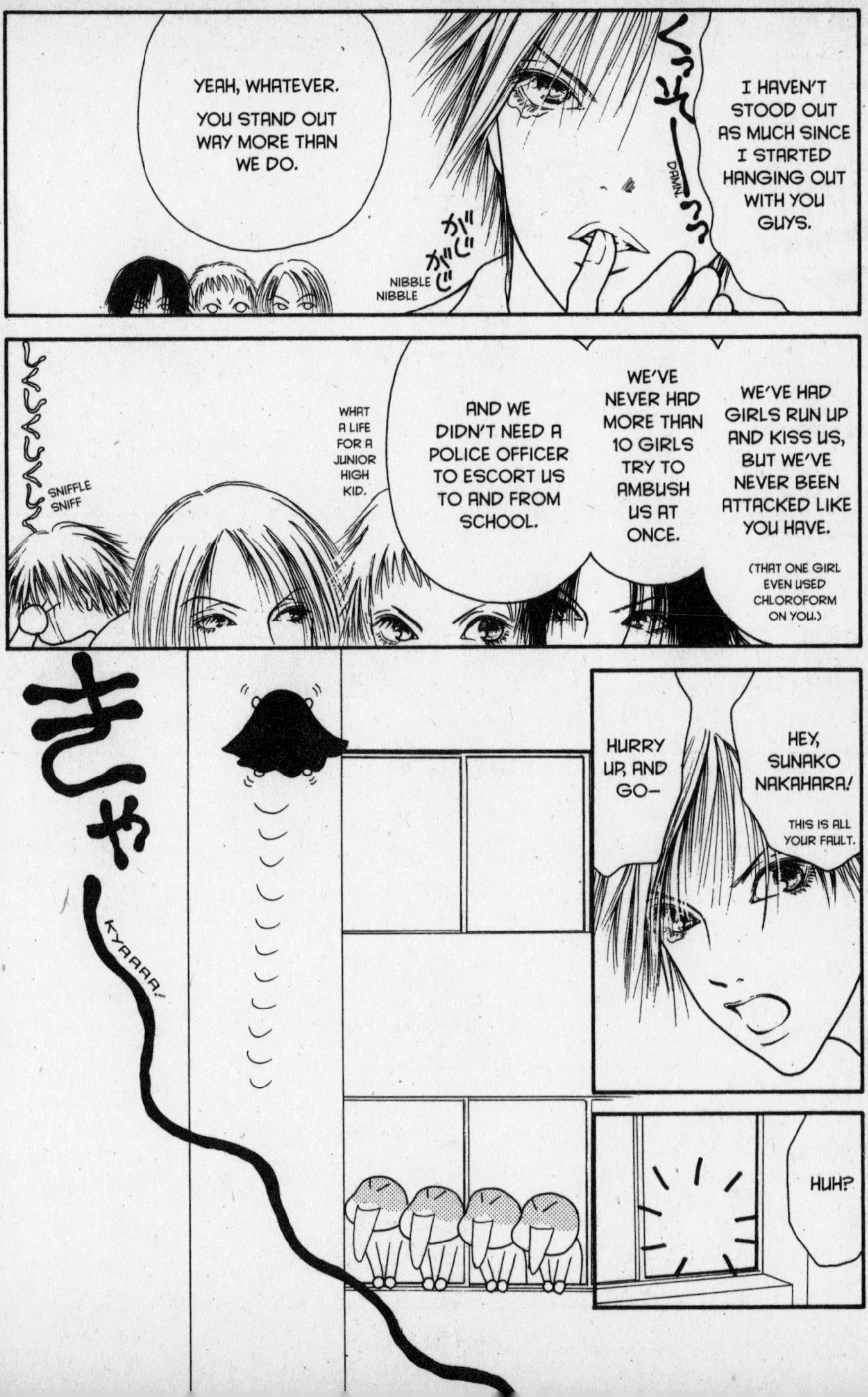

I HAVEN'T STOOD OUT AS MUCH SINCE I STARTED HANGING OUT WITH YOU GUYS.
くっそーっっ
DAMN.
がじがじ
NIBBLE NIBBLE
YEAH, WHATEVER.
YOU STAND OUT WAY MORE THAN WE DO.
WE'VE HAD GIRLS RUN UP AND KISS US, BUT WE'VE NEVER BEEN ATTACKED LIKE YOU HAVE.
(THAT ONE GIRL EVEN USED CHLOROFORM ON YOU.)
WE'VE NEVER HAD MORE THAN 10 GIRLS TRY TO AMBUSH US AT ONCE.
AND WE DIDN'T NEED A POLICE OFFICER TO ESCORT US TO AND FROM SCHOOL.
WHAT A LIFE FOR A JUNIOR HIGH KID.
しくしくしく
SNIFFLE SNIFF
HEY, SUNAKO NAKAHARA!
THIS IS ALL YOUR FAULT.
HURRY UP, AND GO-
HUH?
きゃー
KYAAAA!

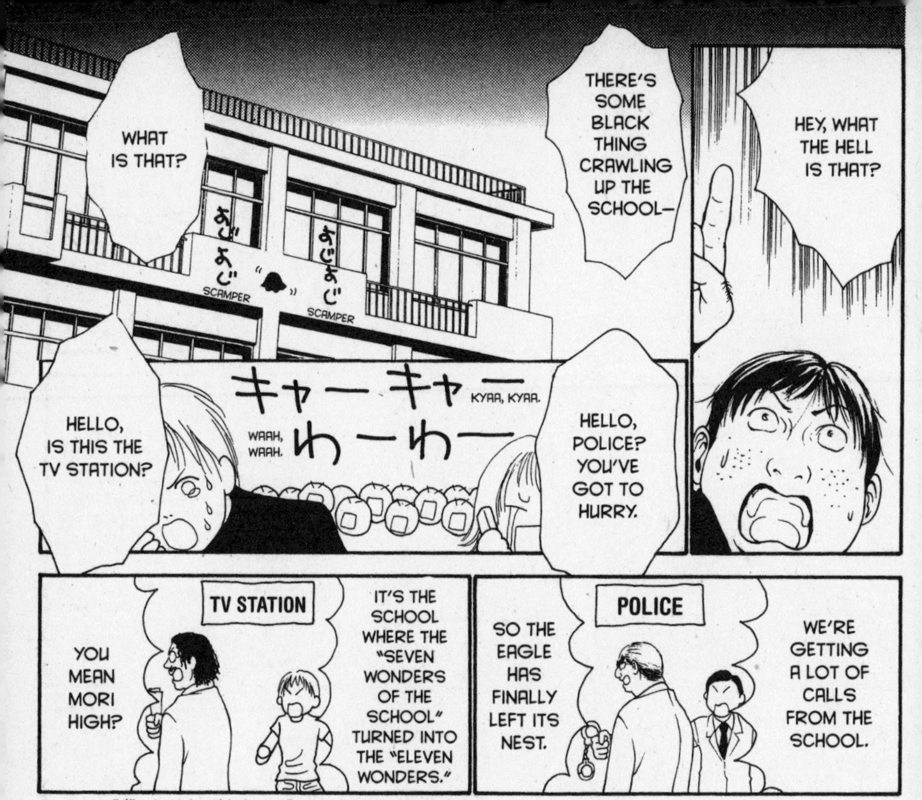
HEY, WHAT THE HELL IS THAT?
THERE'S SOME BLACK THING CRAWLING UP THE SCHOOL—
WHAT IS THAT?
SCAMPER
SCAMPER
HELLO, POLICE? YOU'VE GOT TO HURRY.
キャーキャー
KYAA, KYAA.
わーわー
WAAH, WAAH.
HELLO, IS THIS THE TV STATION?
POLICE
WE'RE GETTING A LOT OF CALLS FROM THE SCHOOL.
SO THE EAGLE HAS FINALLY LEFT ITS NEST.
TV STATION
IT'S THE SCHOOL WHERE THE "SEVEN WONDERS OF THE SCHOOL" TURNED INTO THE "ELEVEN WONDERS."
YOU MEAN MORI HIGH?

Editor's Note: This is a reference to a joke in Book 1.

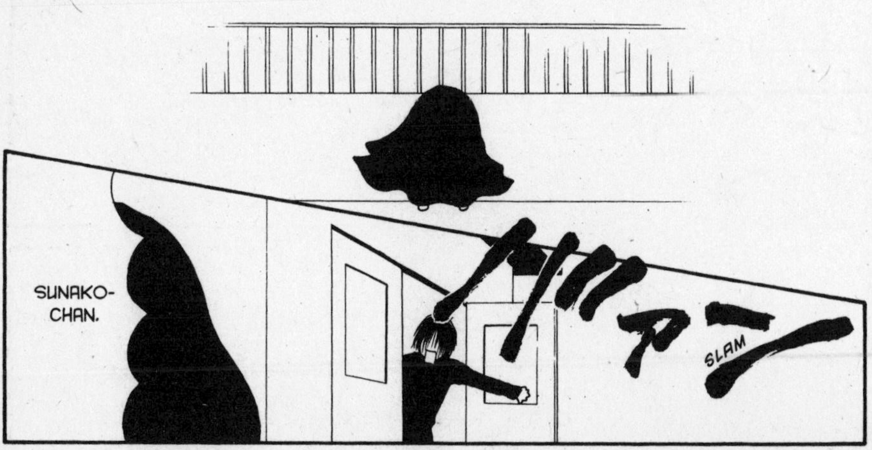
SLAM
SUNAKO-CHAN.

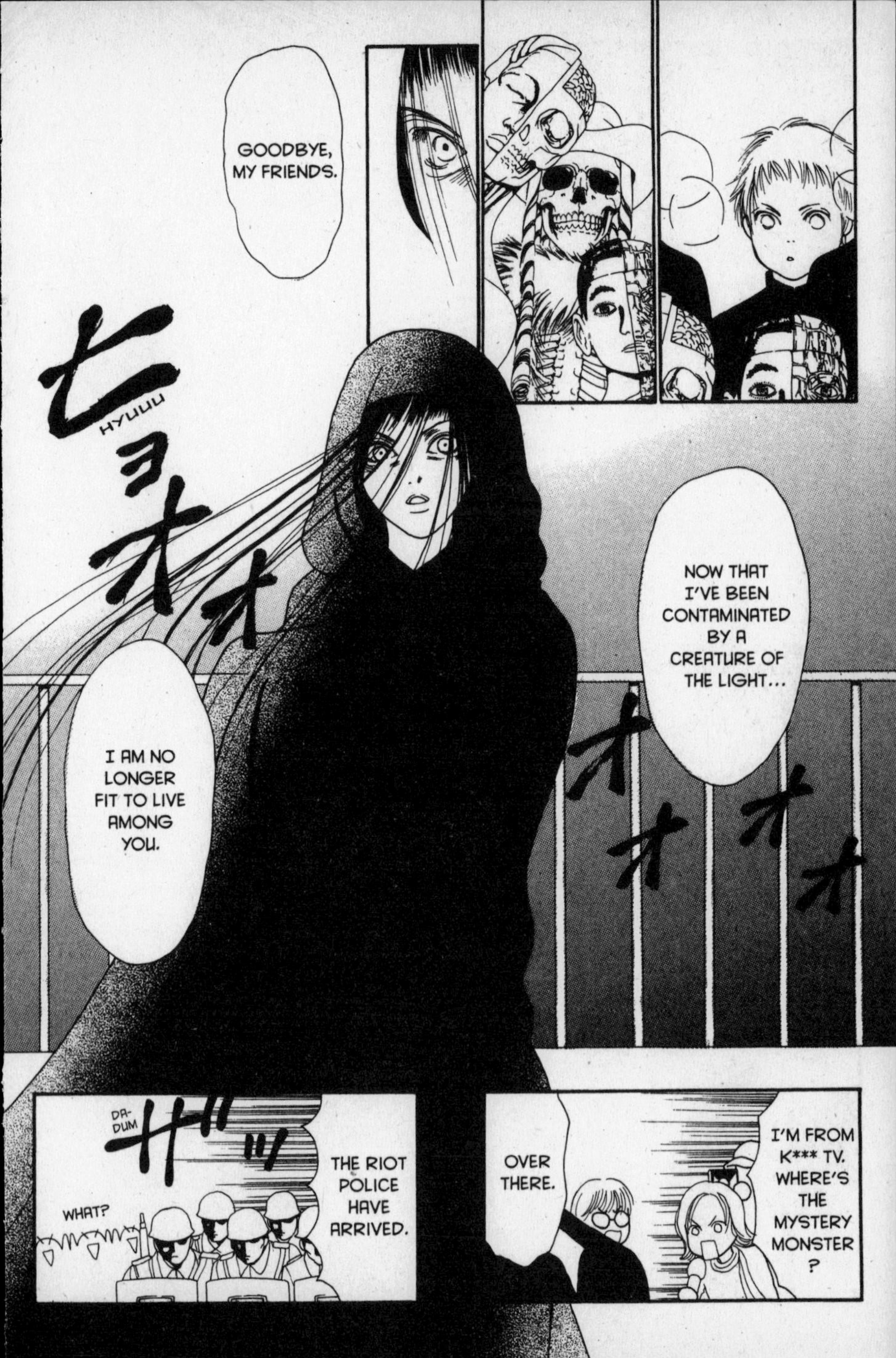
GOODBYE, MY FRIENDS.
ヒョオオオオオオ
HYUUU
NOW THAT I'VE BEEN CONTAMINATED BY A CREATURE OF THE LIGHT...
I AM NO LONGER FIT TO LIVE AMONG YOU.
I'M FROM K*** TV. WHERE'S THE MYSTERY MONSTER?
OVER THERE.
ザッ
DA-DUM
THE RIOT POLICE HAVE ARRIVED.
WHAT?

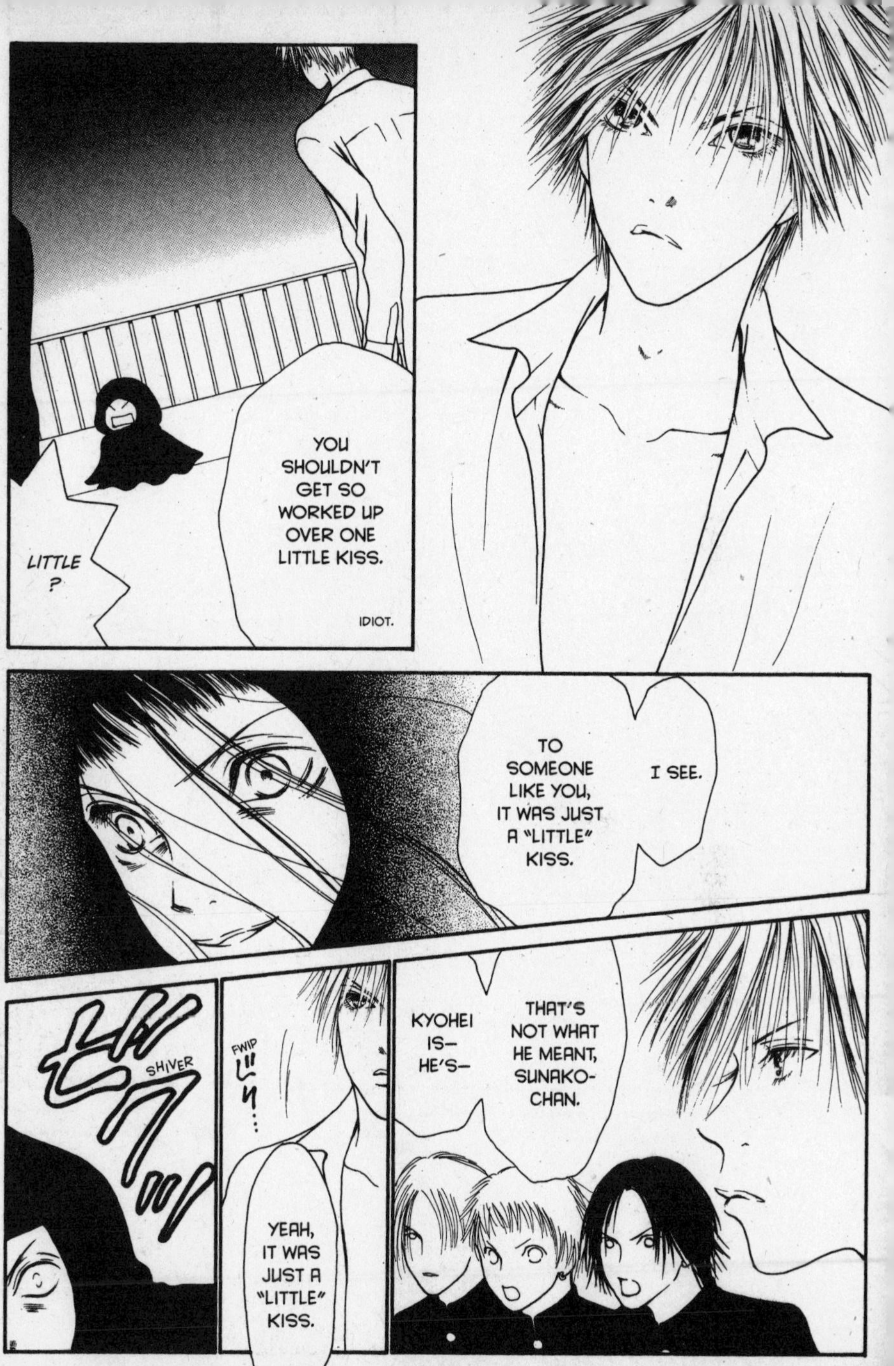
YOU SHOULDN'T GET SO WORKED UP OVER ONE LITTLE KISS.
IDIOT.
LITTLE ?
I SEE.
TO SOMEONE LIKE YOU, IT WAS JUST A "LITTLE" KISS.
THAT'S NOT WHAT HE MEANT, SUNAKO-CHAN.
KYOHEI IS— HE'S—
FWIP
YEAH, IT WAS JUST A "LITTLE" KISS.
SHIVER

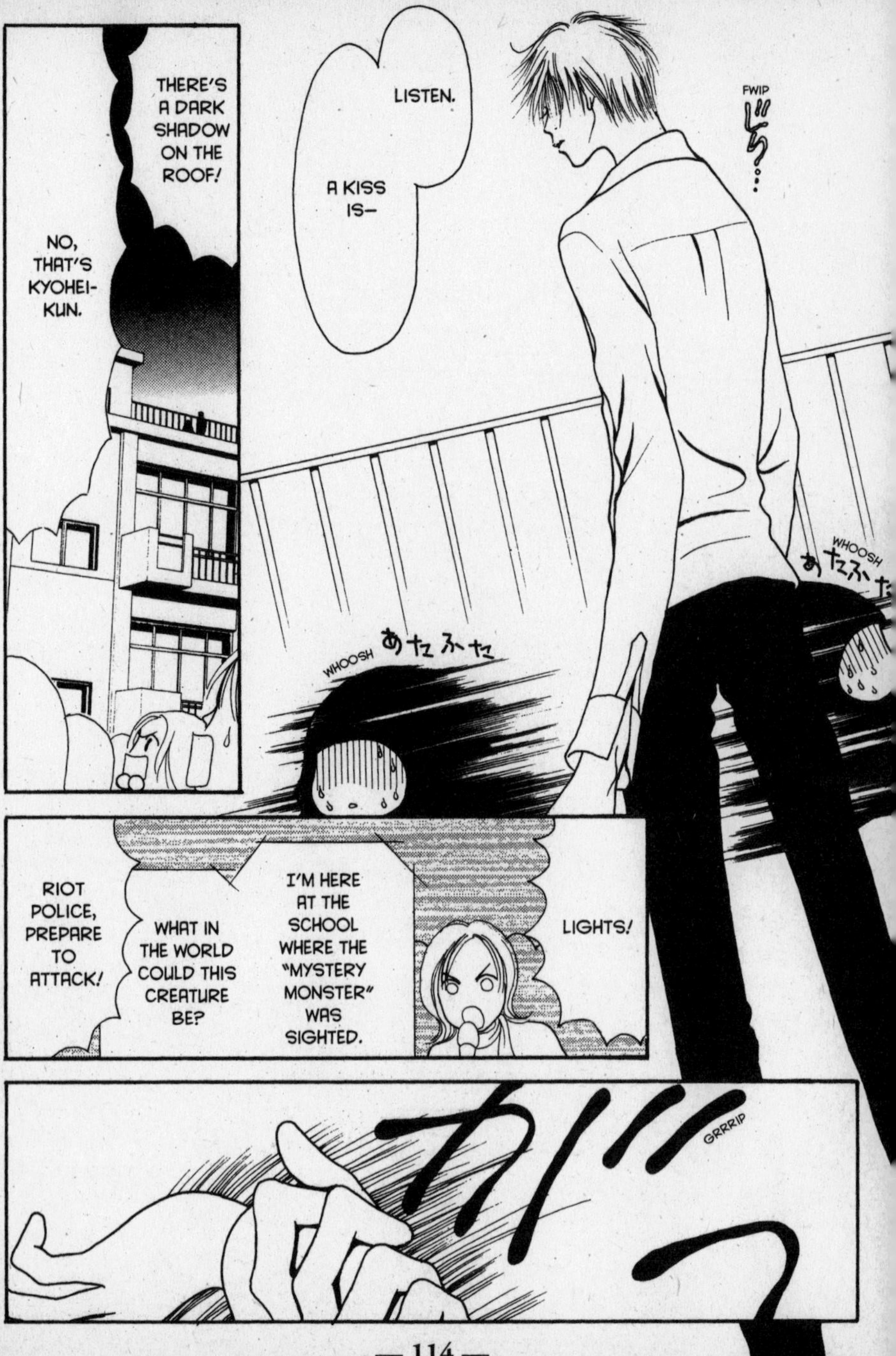
FWIP
じろ…
LISTEN.
A KISS IS—
WHOOSH
あたふた
WHOOSH
THERE'S A DARK SHADOW ON THE ROOF!
NO, THAT'S KYOHEI-KUN.
LIGHTS!
I'M HERE AT THE SCHOOL WHERE THE "MYSTERY MONSTER" WAS SIGHTED.
WHAT IN THE WORLD COULD THIS CREATURE BE?
RIOT POLICE, PREPARE TO ATTACK!
GRRRIP

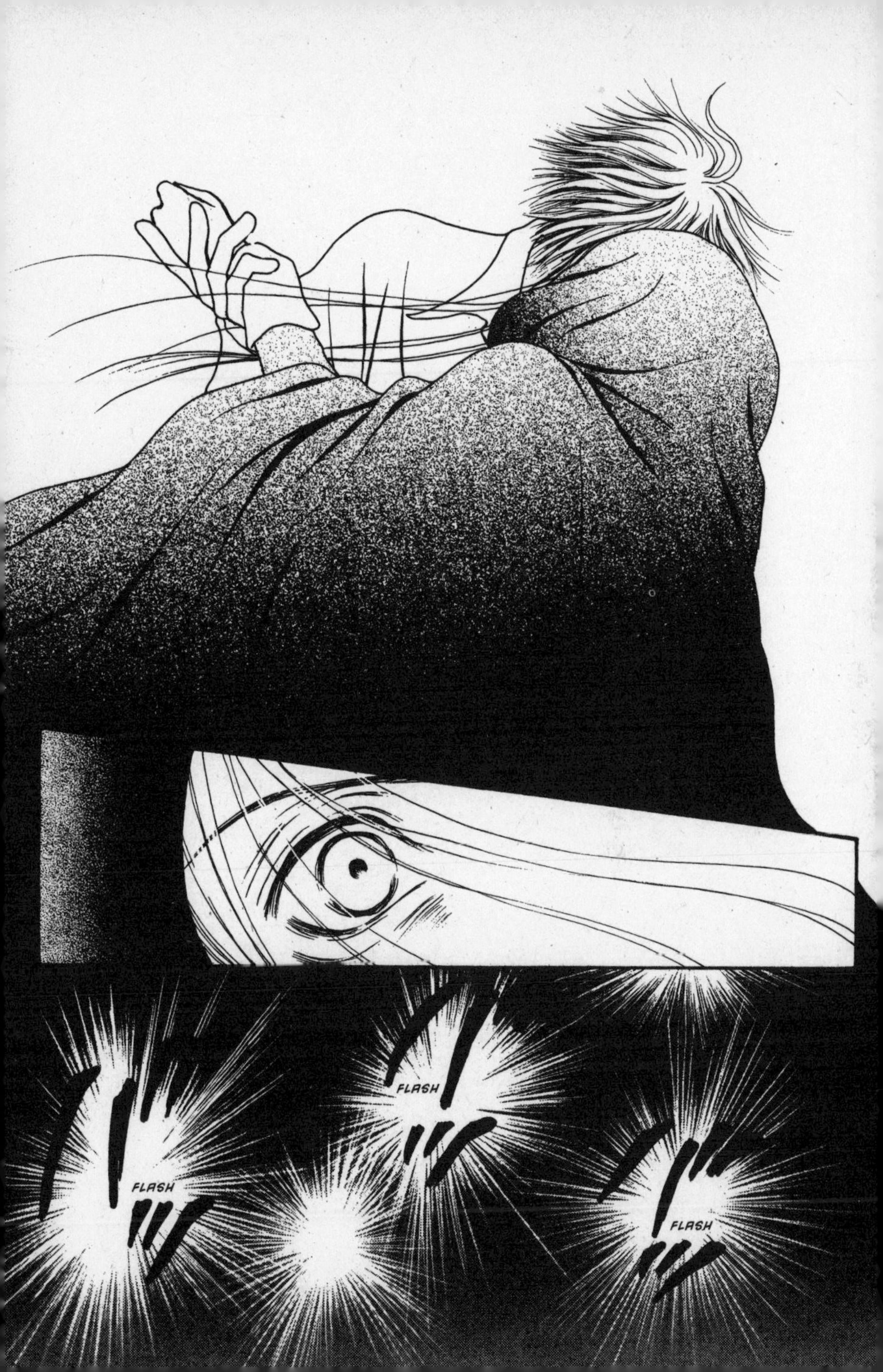
FLASH
FLASH
FLASH

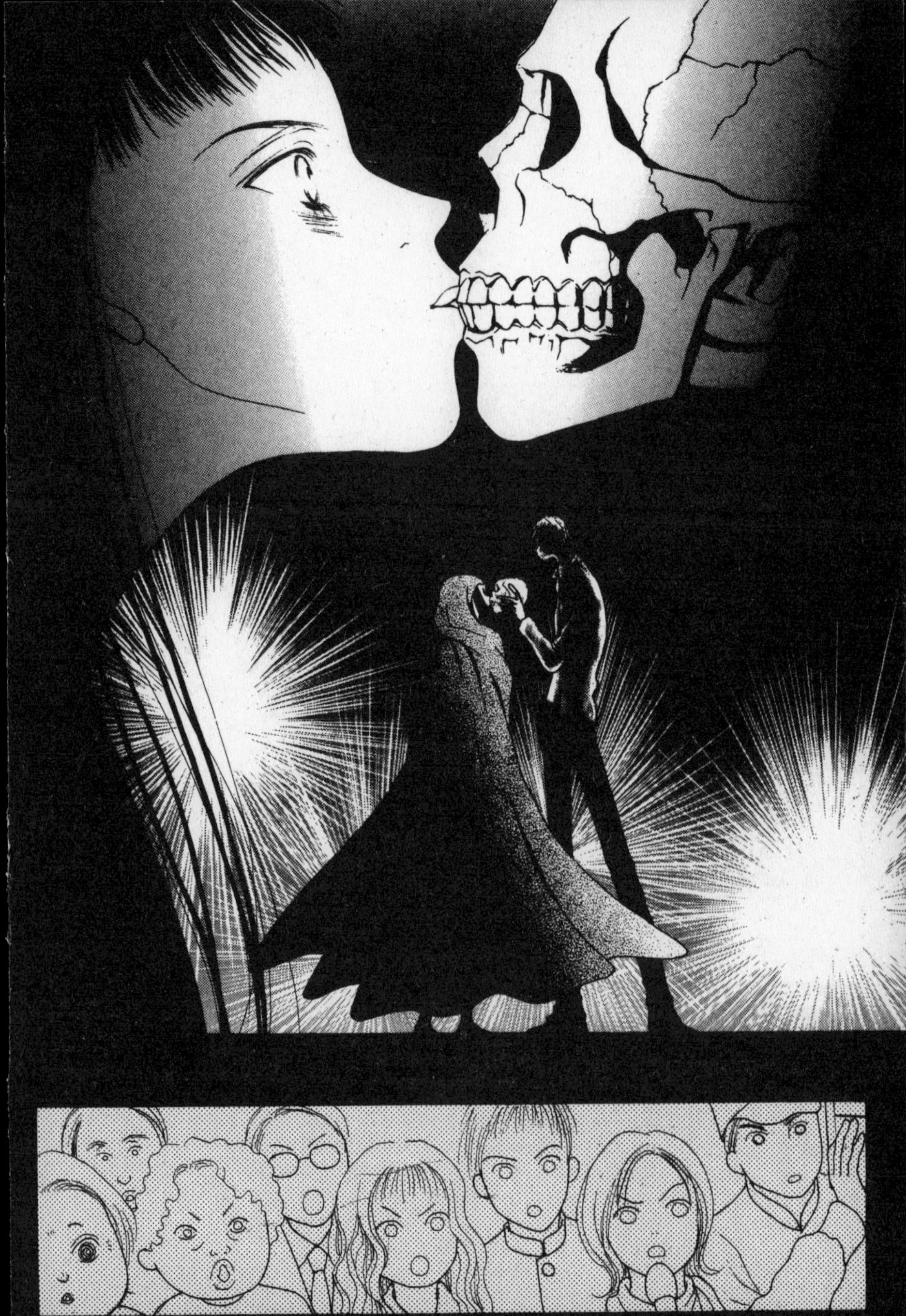

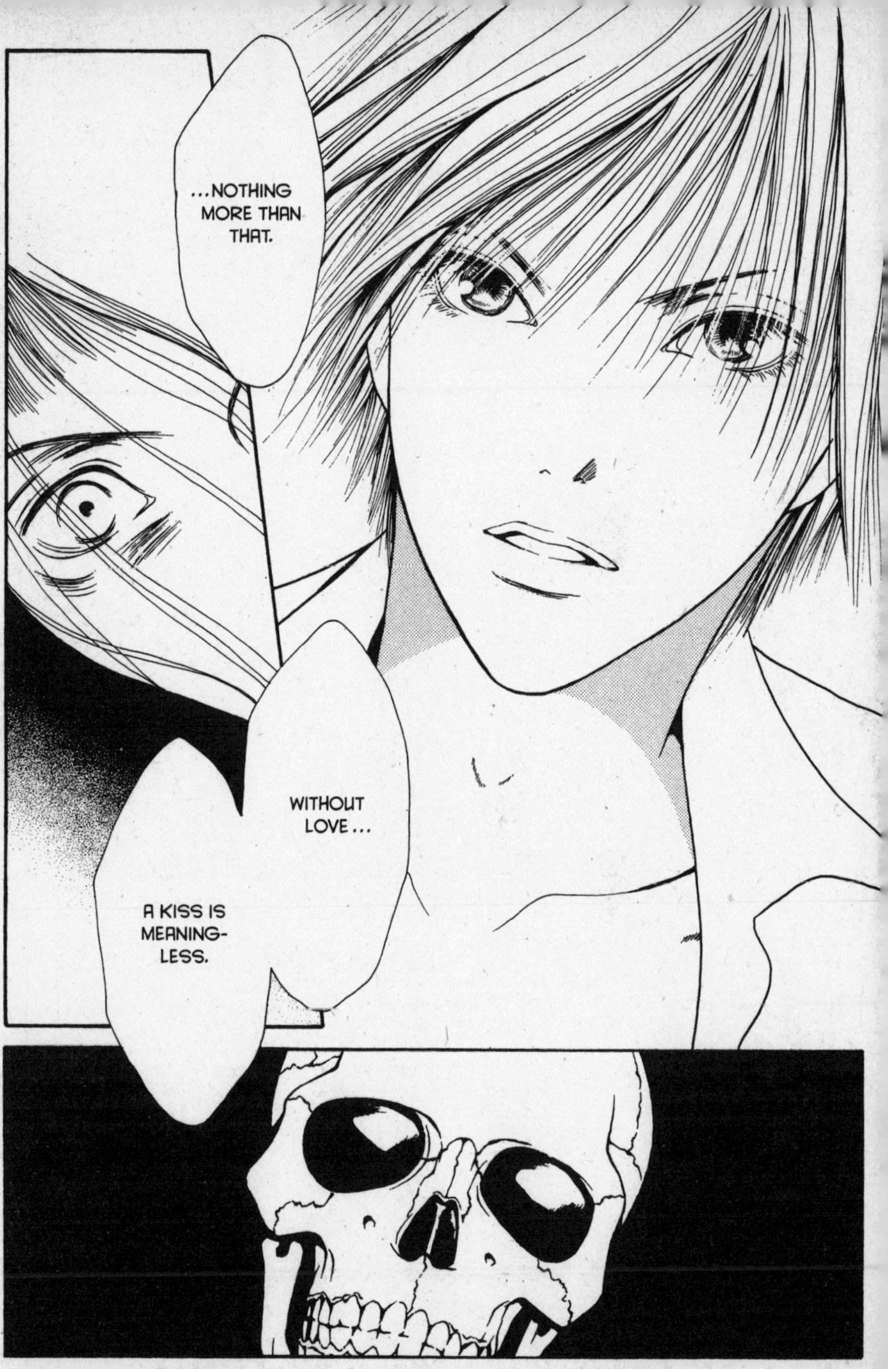
...NOTHING MORE THAN THAT.
WITHOUT LOVE...
A KISS IS MEANING-LESS.

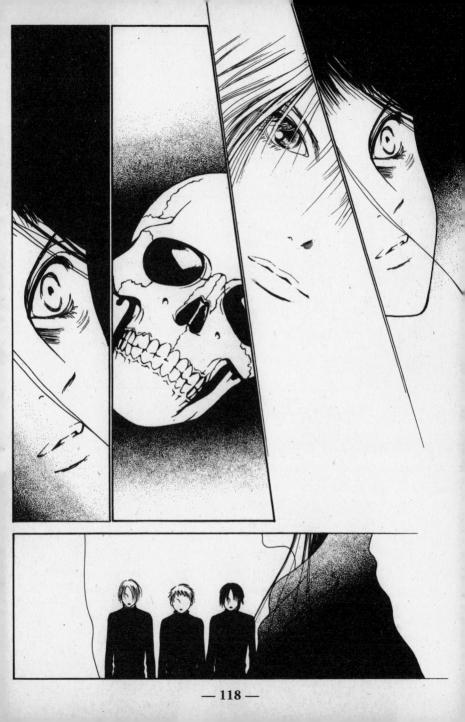

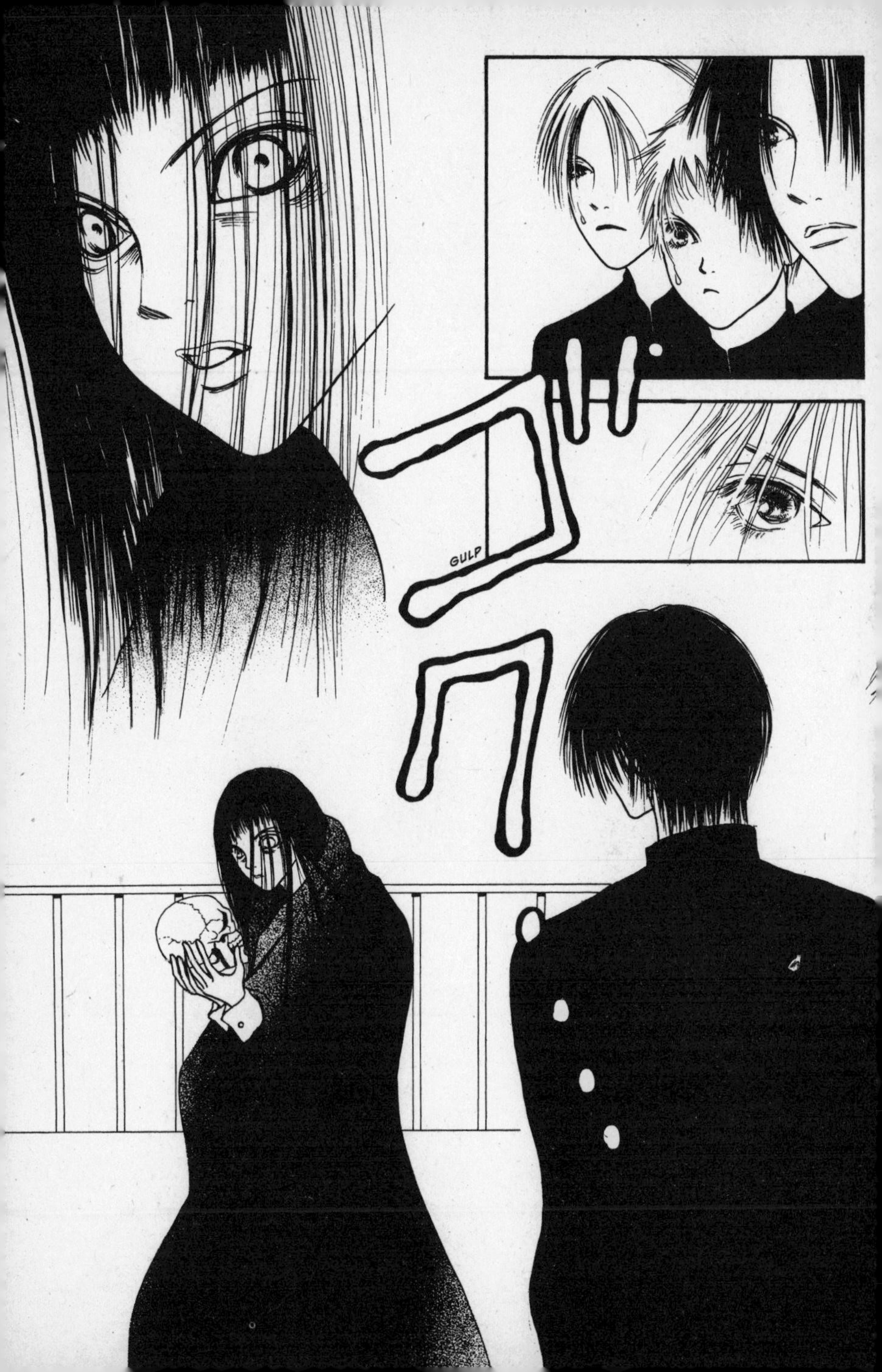
GULP

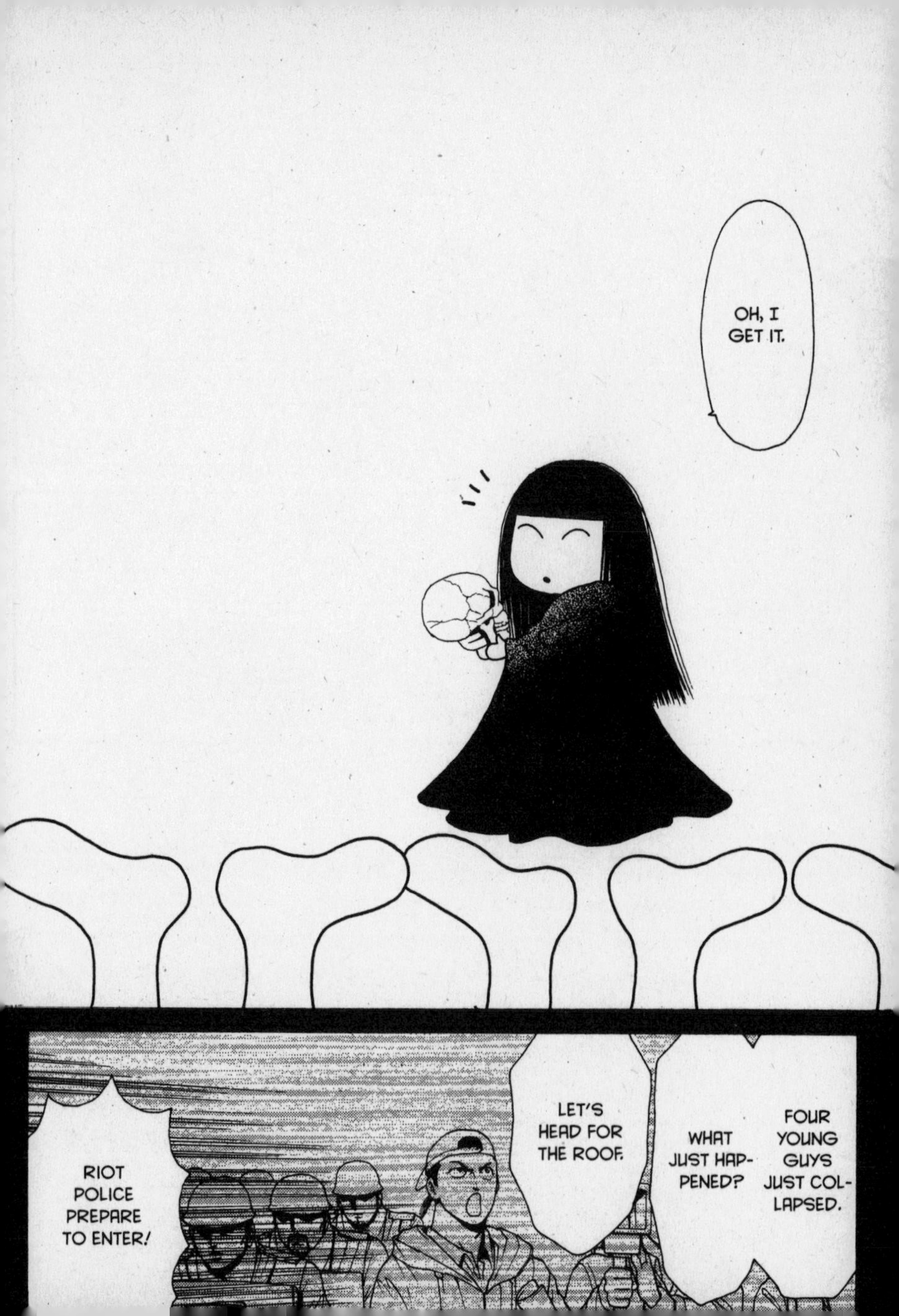
OH, I GET IT.
FOUR YOUNG GUYS JUST COL-LAPSED.
WHAT JUST HAP-PENED?
LET'S HEAD FOR THE ROOF.
RIOT POLICE PREPARE TO ENTER!

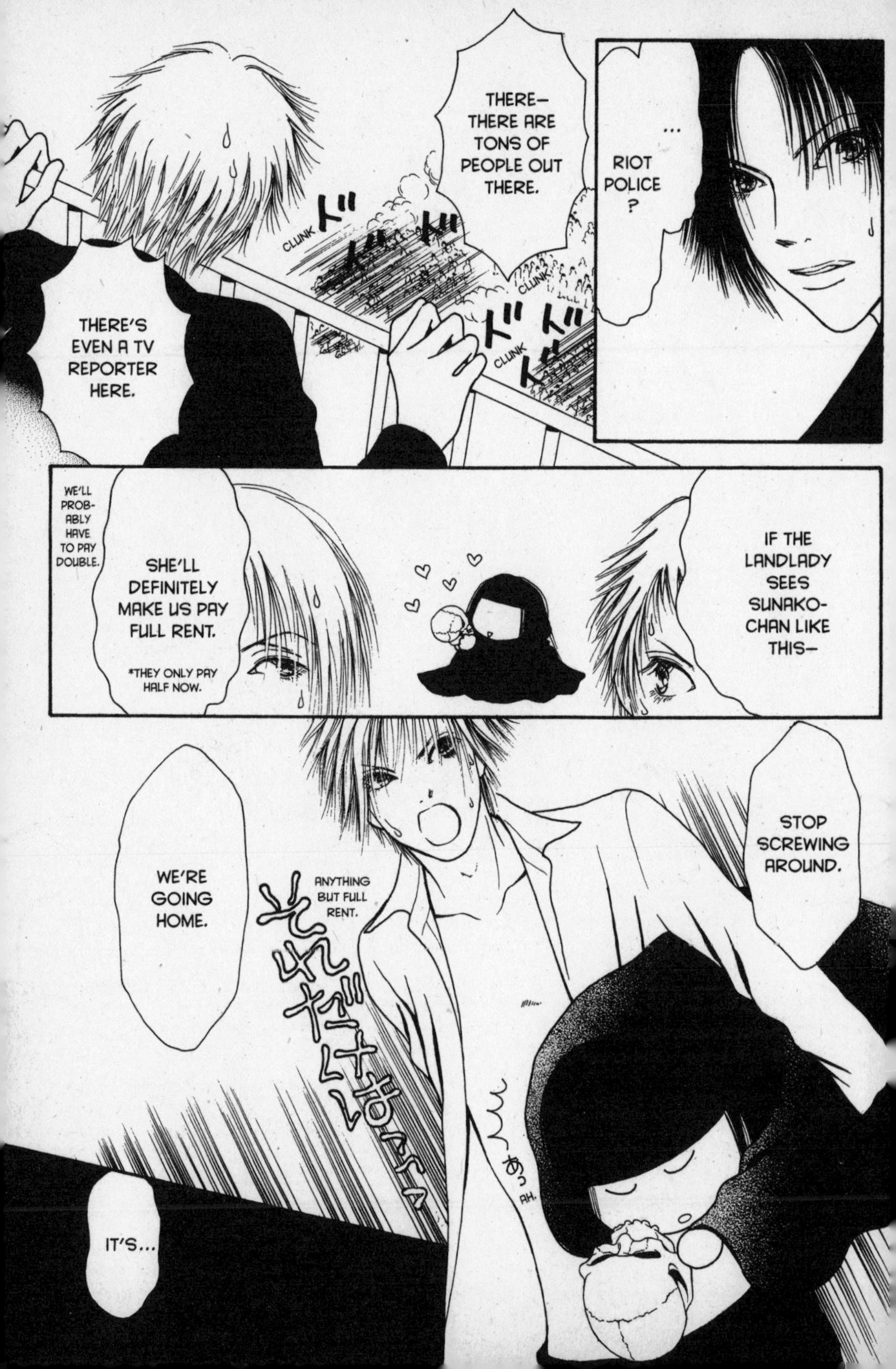
...
RIOT POLICE?
THERE— THERE ARE TONS OF PEOPLE OUT THERE.
CLUNK
CLUNK
CLUNK
THERE'S EVEN A TV REPORTER HERE.
IF THE LANDLADY SEES SUNAKO-CHAN LIKE THIS—
SHE'LL DEFINITELY MAKE US PAY FULL RENT.
*THEY ONLY PAY HALF NOW.
WE'LL PROBABLY HAVE TO PAY DOUBLE.
STOP SCREWING AROUND.
WE'RE GOING HOME.
ANYTHING BUT FULL RENT.
AH.
IT'S...

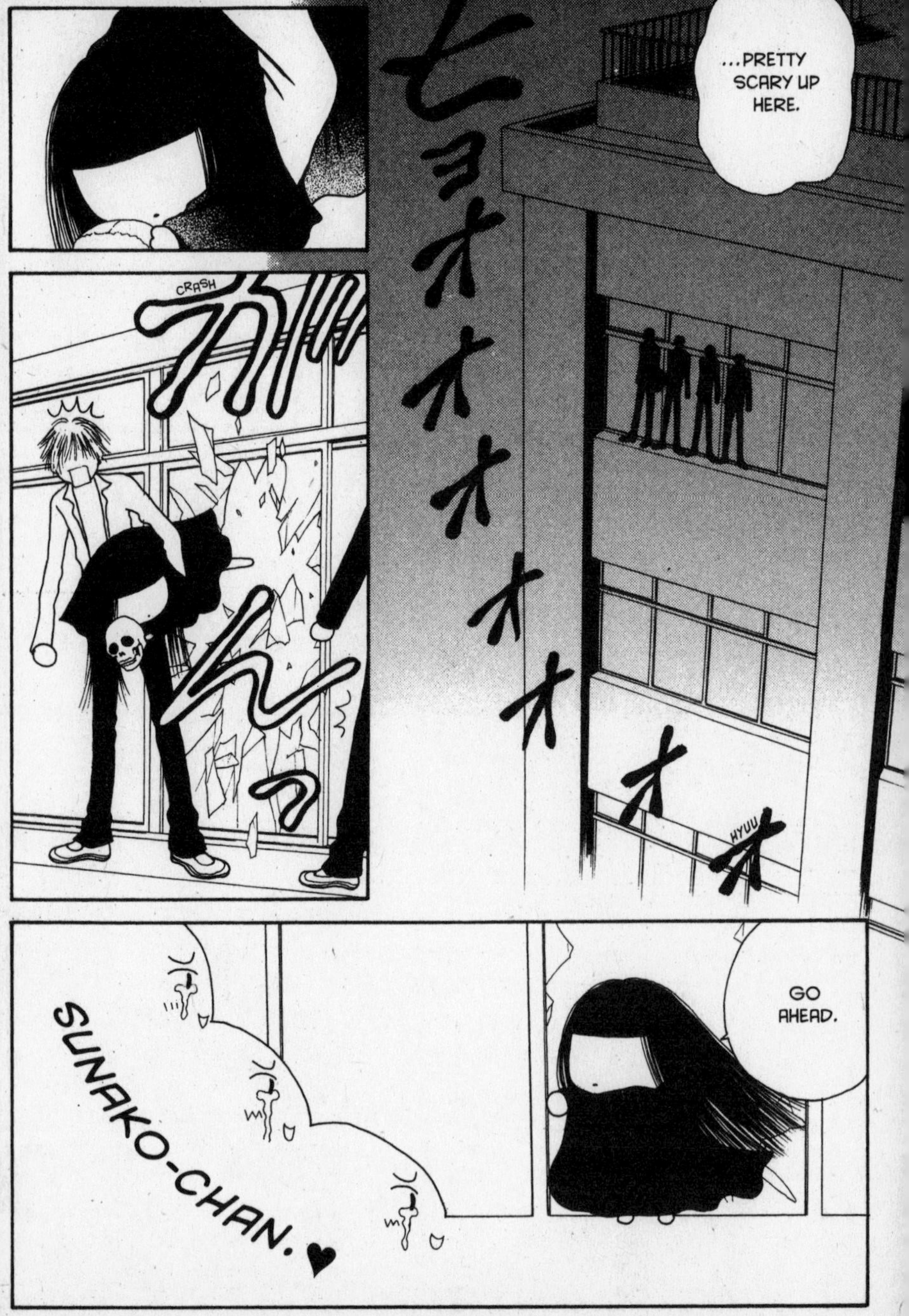
...PRETTY SCARY UP HERE.
HYUU
CRASH
GO AHEAD.
SUNAKO-CHAN. ♥

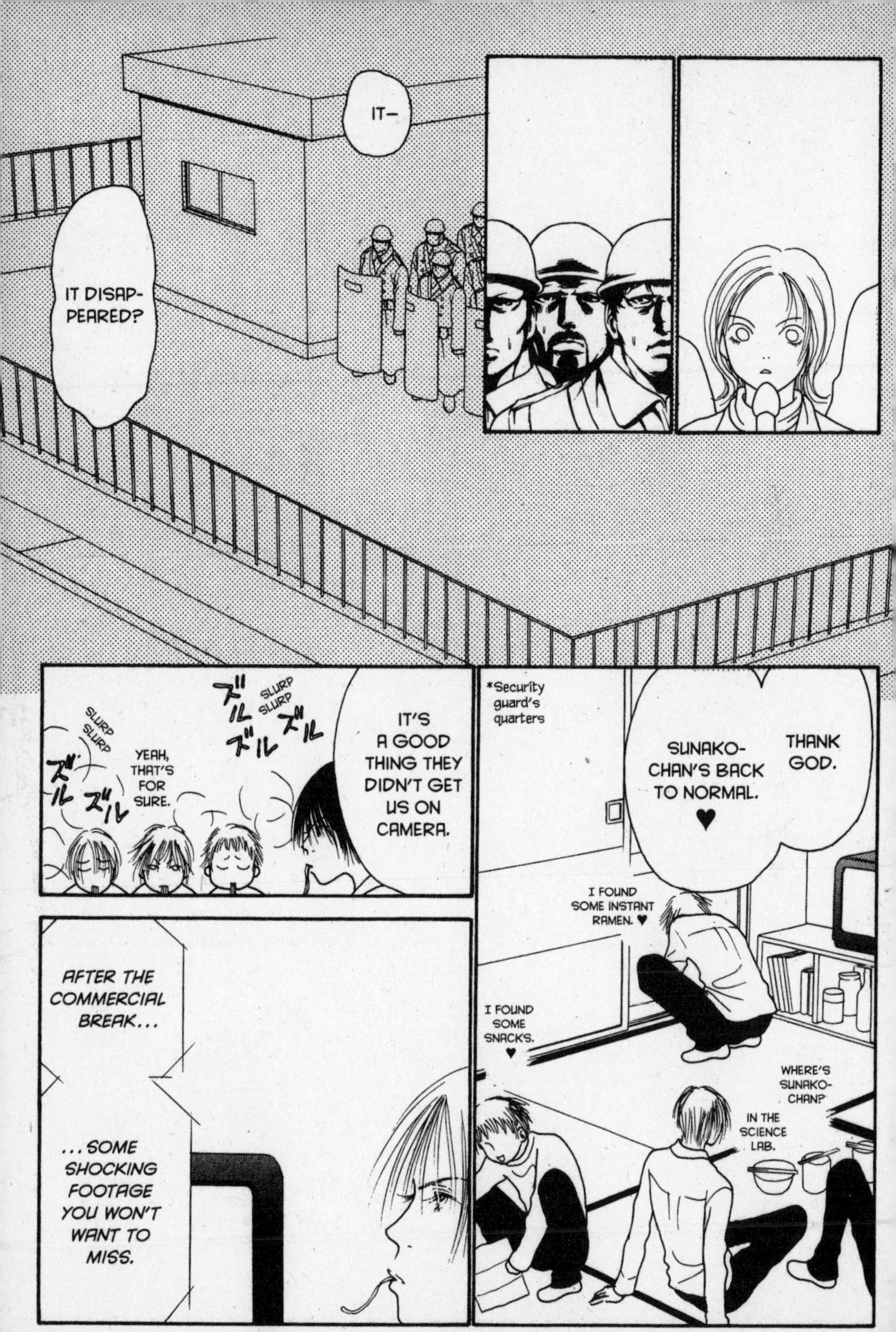
IT—
IT DISAPPEARED?
THANK GOD.
SUNAKO-CHAN'S BACK TO NORMAL. ♥
*Security guard's quarters
I FOUND SOME INSTANT RAMEN. ♥
I FOUND SOME SNACKS. ♥
WHERE'S SUNAKO-CHAN?
IN THE SCIENCE LAB.
IT'S A GOOD THING THEY DIDN'T GET US ON CAMERA.
ズルズルズル SLURP SLURP
YEAH, THAT'S FOR SURE.
ズルズル SLURP SLURP
AFTER THE COMMERCIAL BREAK...
...SOME SHOCKING FOOTAGE YOU WON'T WANT TO MISS.

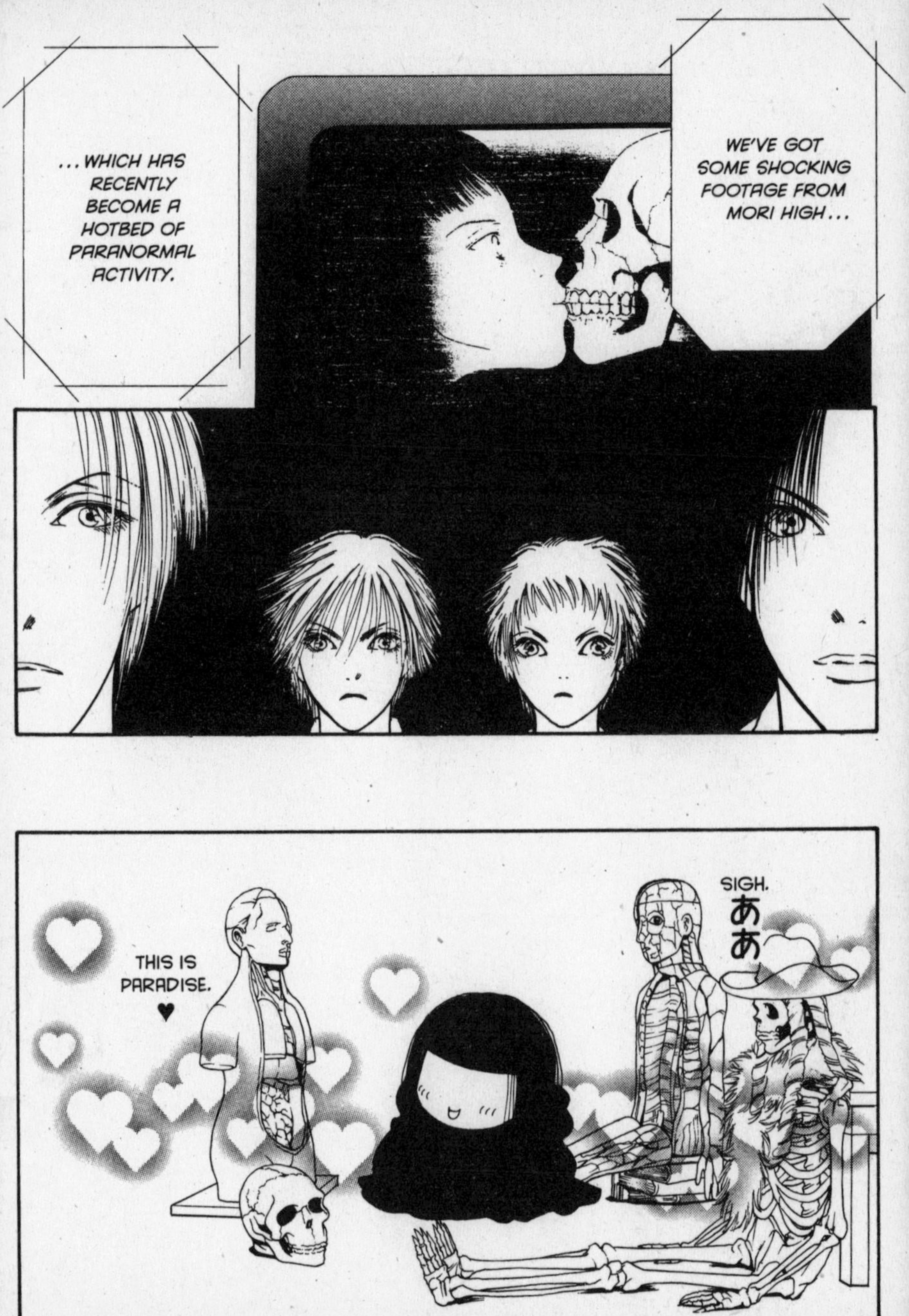
WE'VE GOT SOME SHOCKING FOOTAGE FROM MORI HIGH...
...WHICH HAS RECENTLY BECOME A HOTBED OF PARANORMAL ACTIVITY.
SIGH.
ああ
THIS IS PARADISE. ♥

Chapter 13
Beautiful Party People

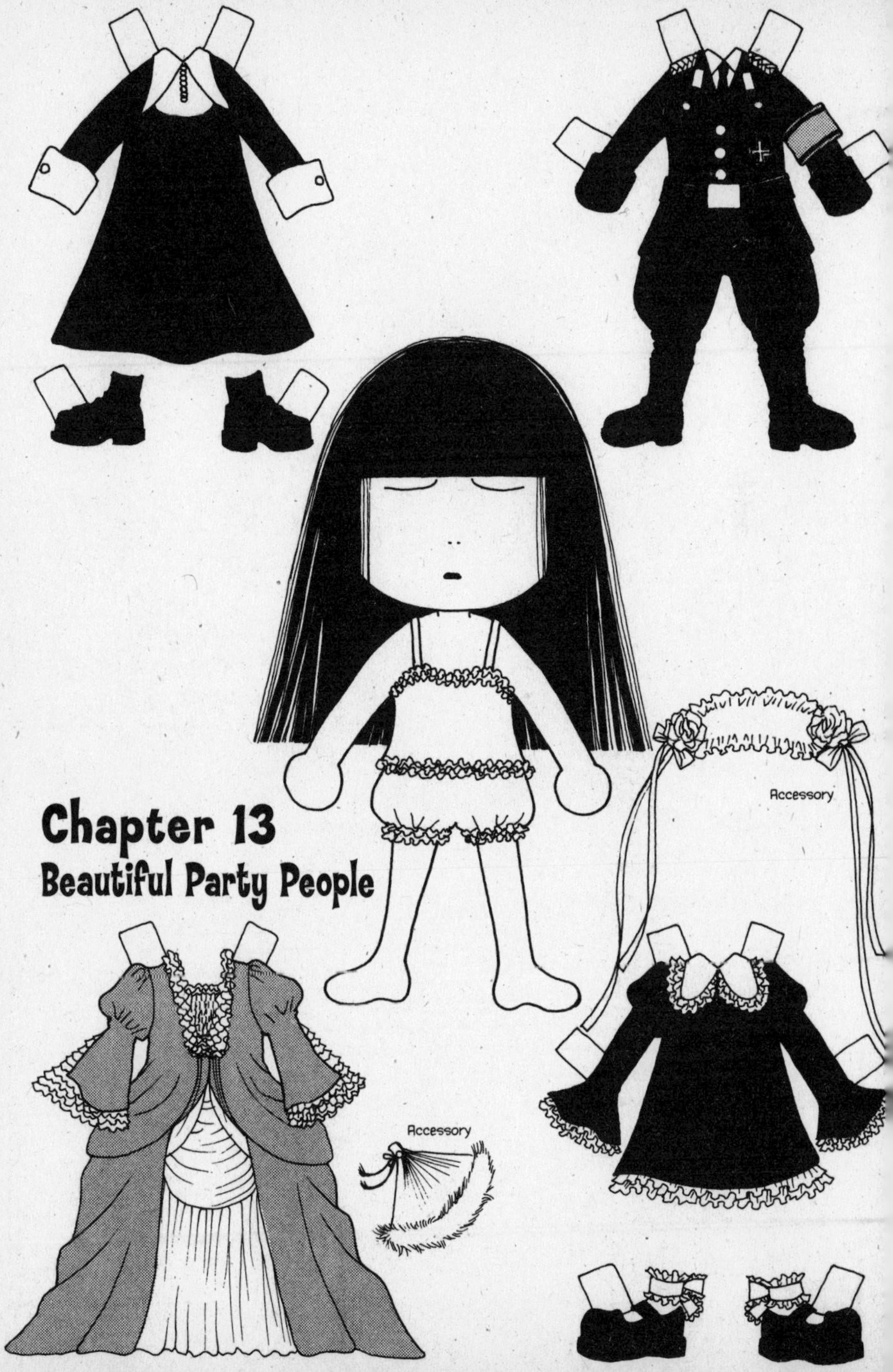
Accessory
Accessory

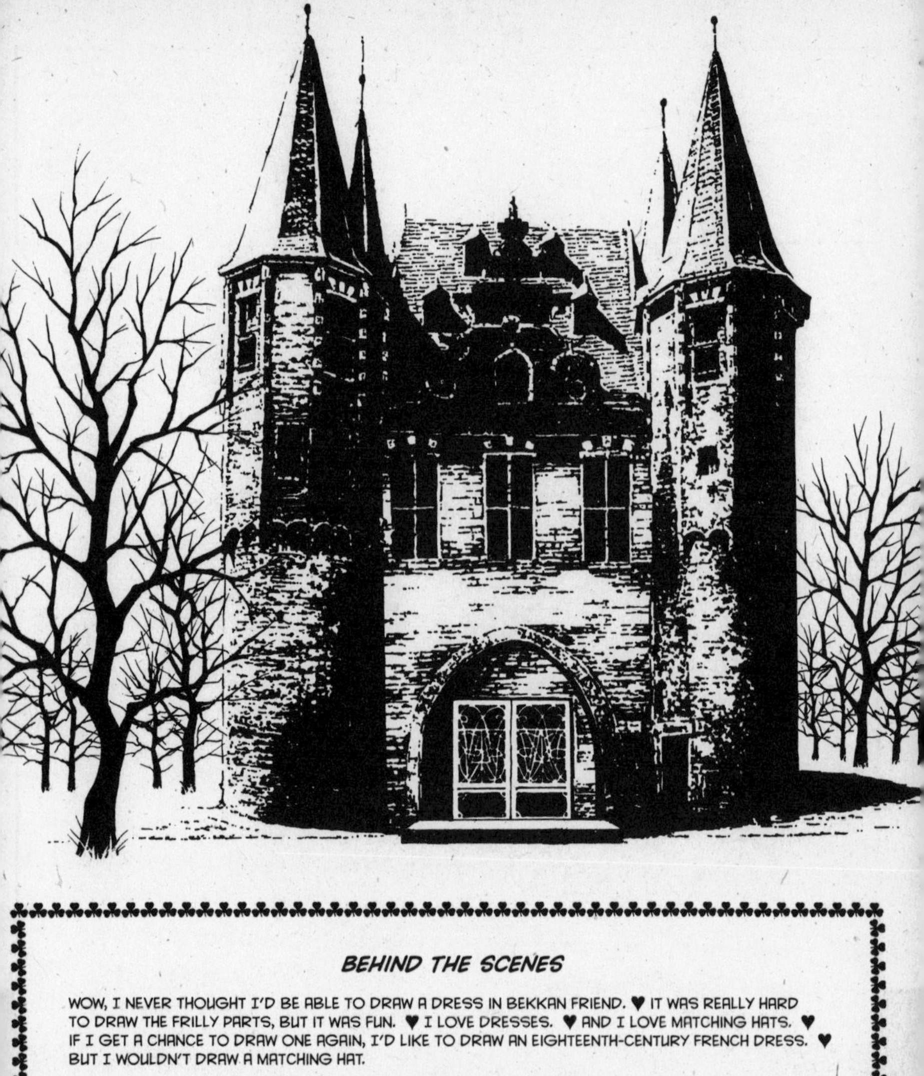

BEHIND THE SCENES

WOW, I NEVER THOUGHT I'D BE ABLE TO DRAW A DRESS IN BEKKAN FRIEND. ♥ IT WAS REALLY HARD TO DRAW THE FRILLY PARTS, BUT IT WAS FUN. ♥ I LOVE DRESSES. ♥ AND I LOVE MATCHING HATS. ♥ IF I GET A CHANCE TO DRAW ONE AGAIN, I'D LIKE TO DRAW AN EIGHTEENTH-CENTURY FRENCH DRESS. ♥ BUT I WOULDN'T DRAW A MATCHING HAT.

ON THE DAY OF MY DEADLINE, MACHIKO SAKURAI ARRANGED FOR ME TO GO OUT WITH MY FAVORITE MANGA ARTIST. SO I HAD TO FINISH MY WORK AS FAST AS I COULD. (OF COURSE, I GOT A LOT OF HELP.)

I WENT OUT WITH MIZUHO AIMOTO, FUYUMI SORYO AND SATORU HIURA! I WAS SO EXCITED.

WE HAD A GREAT TIME. ♥ I WAS SO HAPPY. ♥ I'M SUCH A HUGE FAN. ♥ ON THAT DAY, ♥ I WAS REALLY GLAD TO BE A MANGA ARTIST. ♥

THANKS EVERYBODY. ♥

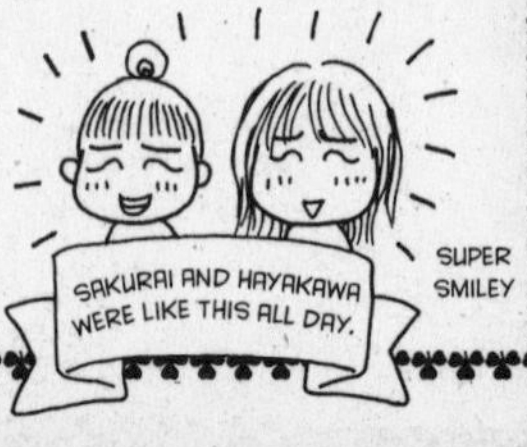
SUPER SMILEY
SAKURAI AND HAYAKAWA WERE LIKE THIS ALL DAY.

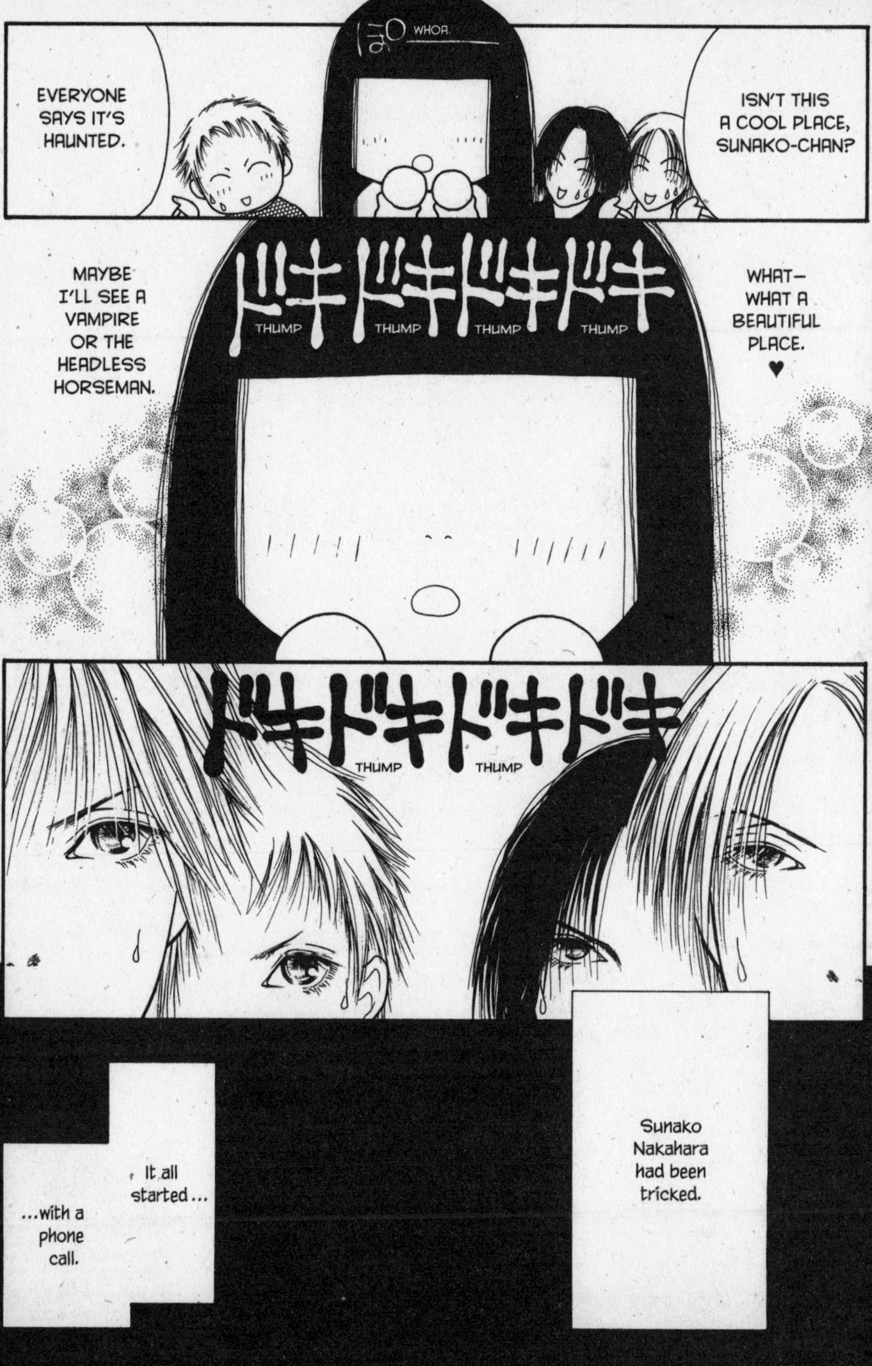
ISN'T THIS A COOL PLACE, SUNAKO-CHAN?
ほぉ
WHOA.
EVERYONE SAYS IT'S HAUNTED.
ドキドキドキドキ
THUMP THUMP THUMP THUMP
WHAT— WHAT A BEAUTIFUL PLACE. ♥
MAYBE I'LL SEE A VAMPIRE OR THE HEADLESS HORSEMAN.
ドキドキドキドキ
THUMP THUMP
Sunako Nakahara had been tricked.
It all started...
...with a phone call.

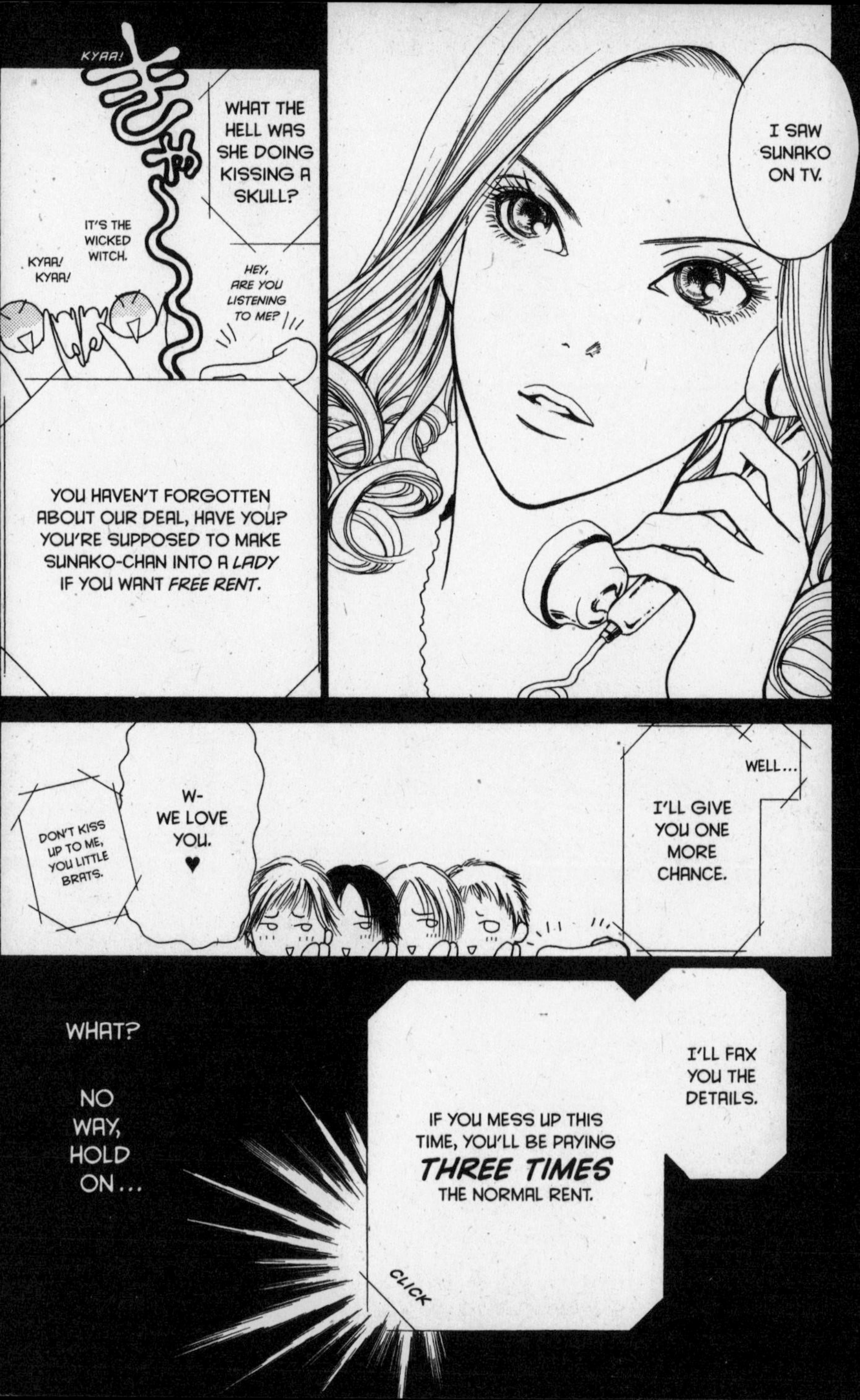
I SAW SUNAKO ON TV.
KYAA!
WHAT THE HELL WAS SHE DOING KISSING A SKULL?
IT'S THE WICKED WITCH.
KYAA! KYAA!
HEY, ARE YOU LISTENING TO ME?
YOU HAVEN'T FORGOTTEN ABOUT OUR DEAL, HAVE YOU? YOU'RE SUPPOSED TO MAKE SUNAKO-CHAN INTO A *LADY* IF YOU WANT *FREE RENT*.
WELL...
I'LL GIVE YOU ONE MORE CHANCE.
W- WE LOVE YOU. ♥
DON'T KISS UP TO ME, YOU LITTLE BRATS.
I'LL FAX YOU THE DETAILS.
IF YOU MESS UP THIS TIME, YOU'LL BE PAYING ***THREE TIMES*** THE NORMAL RENT.
CLICK
WHAT?
NO WAY, HOLD ON...

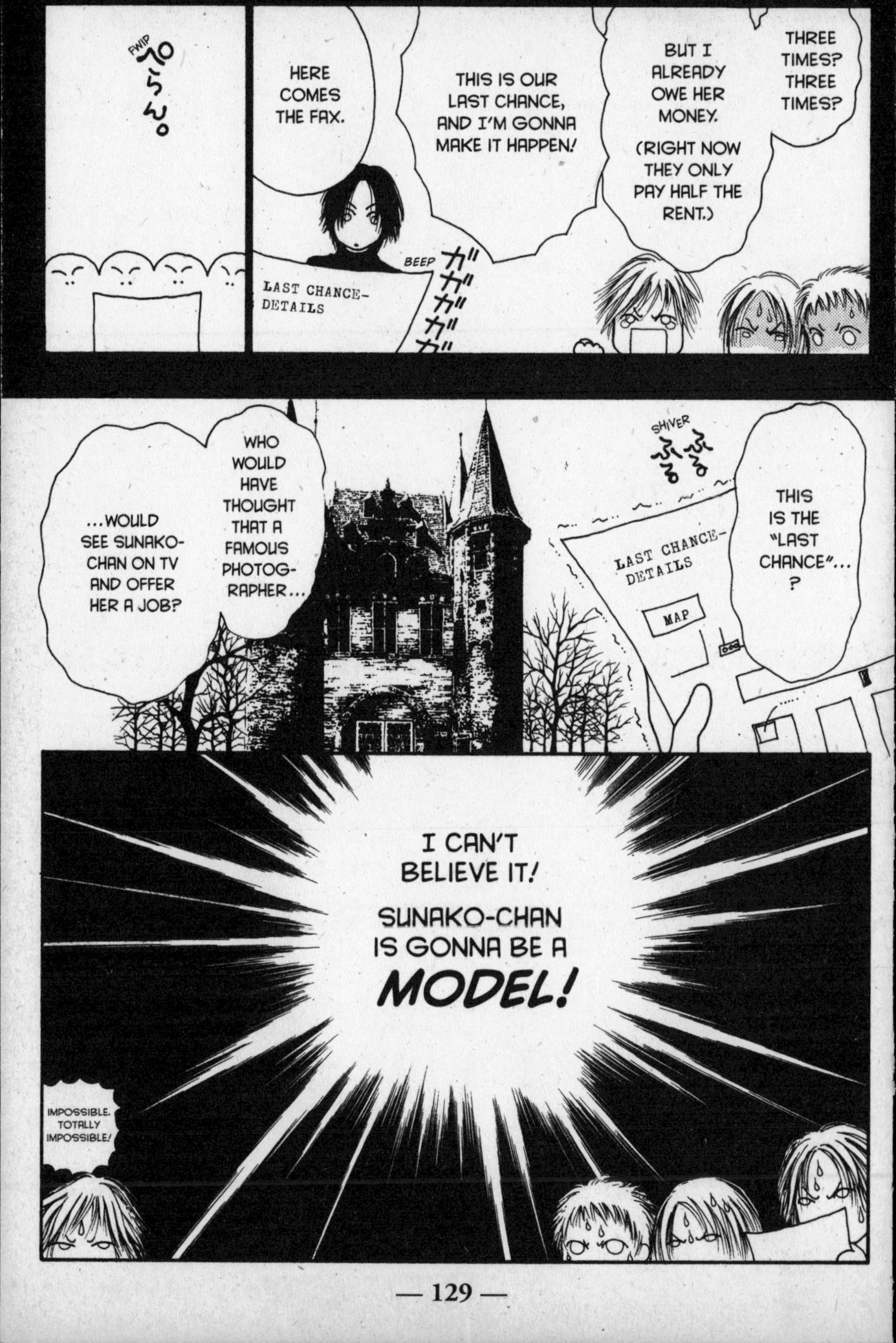
THREE TIMES? THREE TIMES?
BUT I ALREADY OWE HER MONEY.
(RIGHT NOW THEY ONLY PAY HALF THE RENT.)
THIS IS OUR LAST CHANCE, AND I'M GONNA MAKE IT HAPPEN!
HERE COMES THE FAX.
BEEP
ガガガガガ
LAST CHANCE-DETAILS
FWIP
ぺらん。
THIS IS THE "LAST CHANCE"...?
SHIVER
LAST CHANCE-DETAILS
MAP
WHO WOULD HAVE THOUGHT THAT A FAMOUS PHOTOGRAPHER...
...WOULD SEE SUNAKO-CHAN ON TV AND OFFER HER A JOB?
I CAN'T BELIEVE IT!
SUNAKO-CHAN IS GONNA BE A MODEL!
IMPOSSIBLE. TOTALLY IMPOSSIBLE!

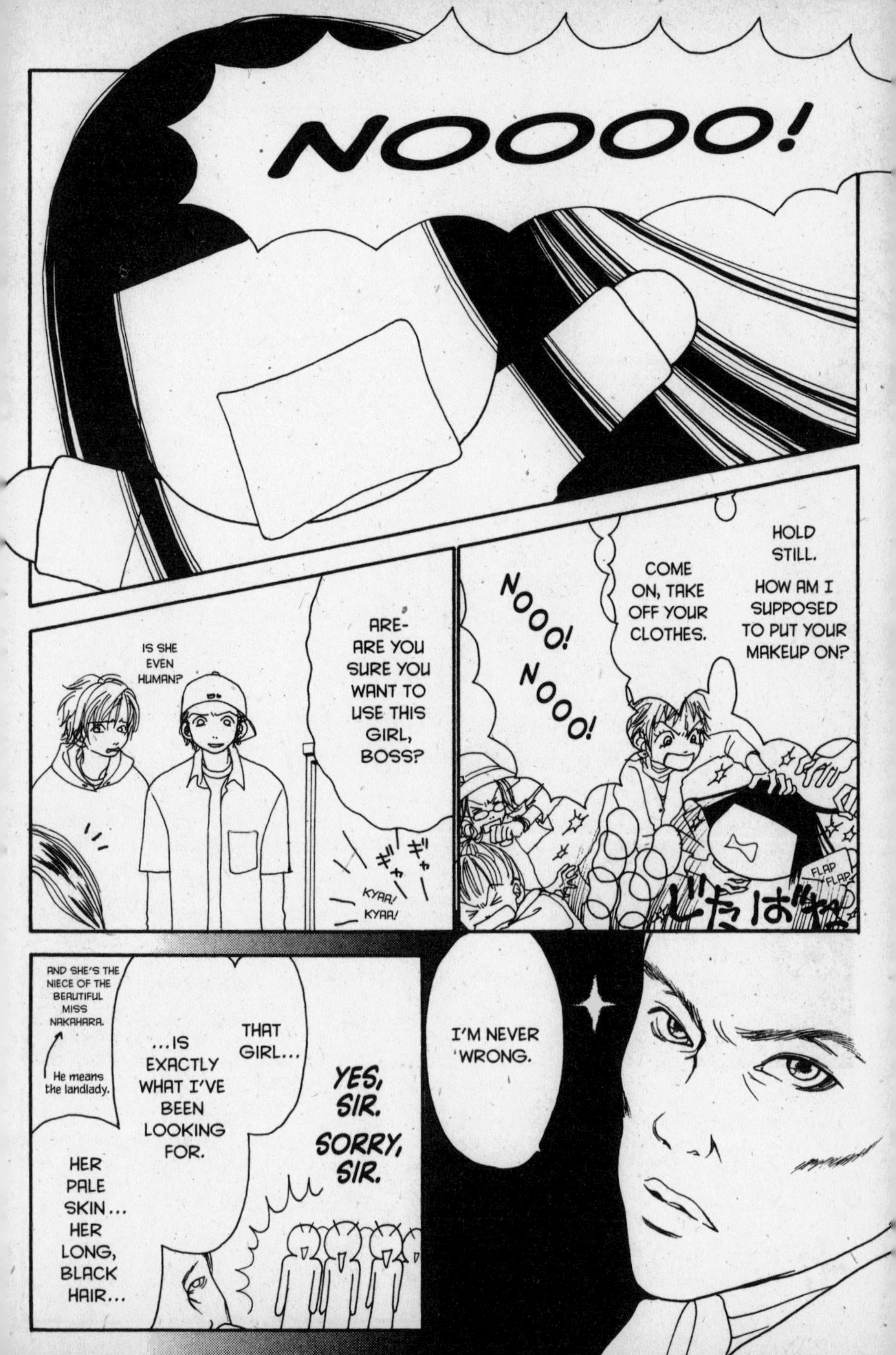
NOOOO!
HOLD STILL.
HOW AM I SUPPOSED TO PUT YOUR MAKEUP ON?
COME ON, TAKE OFF YOUR CLOTHES.
NOOO! NOOO!
FLAP FLAP
じたばた
ARE- ARE YOU SURE YOU WANT TO USE THIS GIRL, BOSS?
IS SHE EVEN HUMAN?
ギャーギャー
KYAA! KYAA!
I'M NEVER 'WRONG.
YES, SIR. SORRY, SIR.
THAT GIRL...
...IS EXACTLY WHAT I'VE BEEN LOOKING FOR.
HER PALE SKIN... HER LONG, BLACK HAIR...
AND SHE'S THE NIECE OF THE BEAUTIFUL MISS NAKAHARA.
He means the landlady.

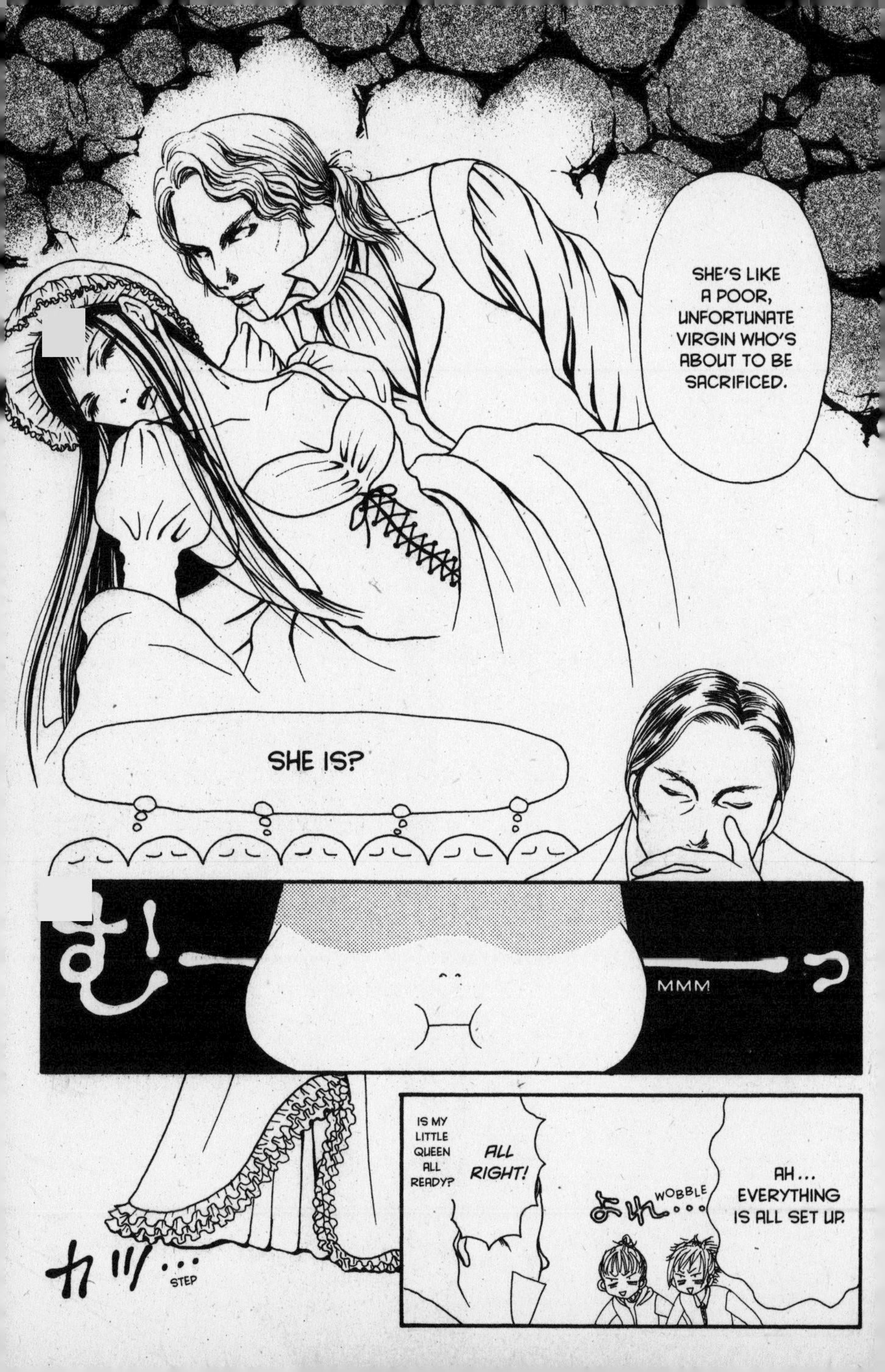
SHE'S LIKE A POOR, UNFORTUNATE VIRGIN WHO'S ABOUT TO BE SACRIFICED.
SHE IS?
MMM
AH... EVERYTHING IS ALL SET UP.
IS MY LITTLE QUEEN ALL READY?
ALL RIGHT!
WOBBLE...
STEP

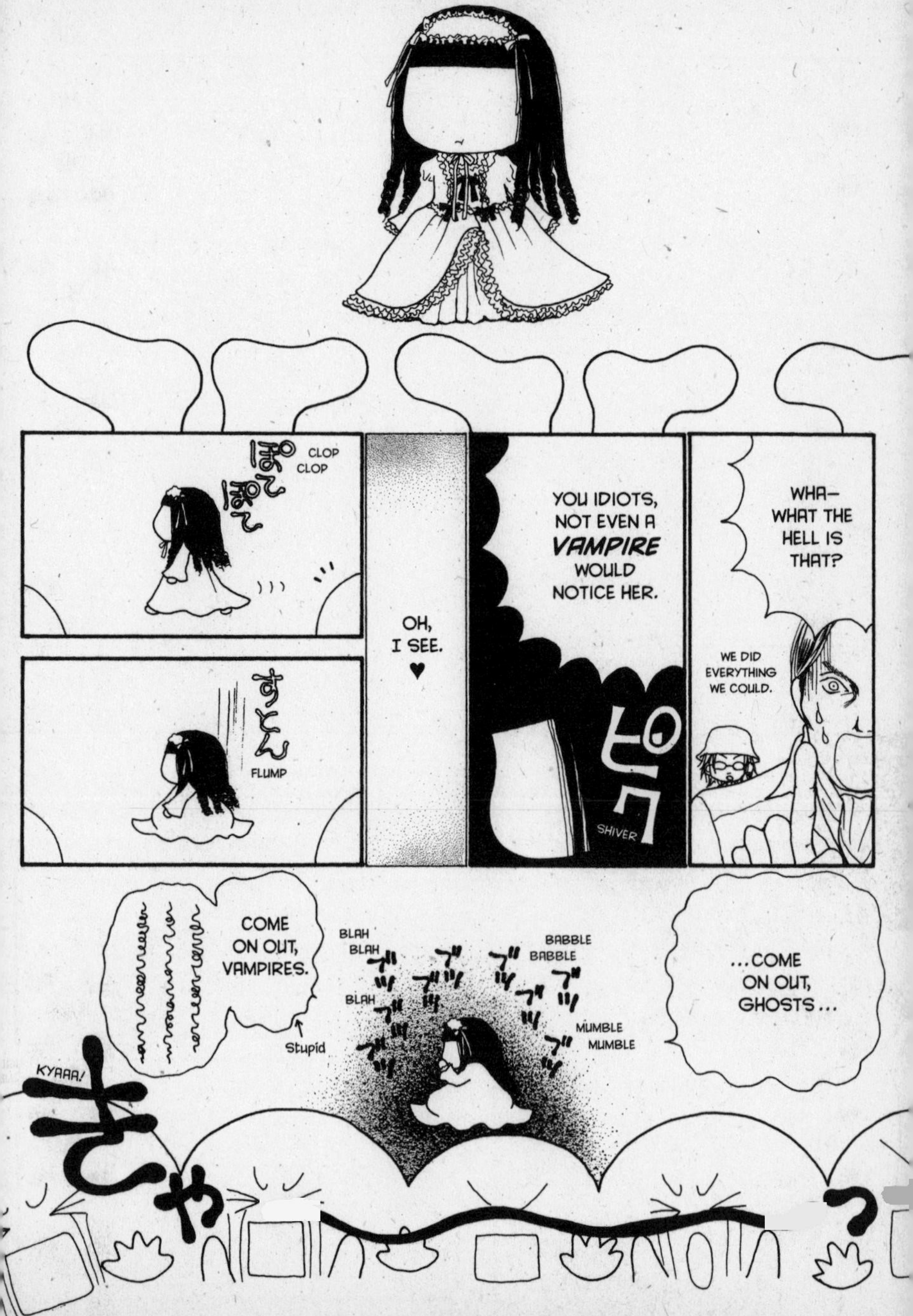
WHA– WHAT THE HELL IS THAT?
WE DID EVERYTHING WE COULD.
YOU IDIOTS, NOT EVEN A *VAMPIRE* WOULD NOTICE HER.
SHIVER
OH, I SEE. ♥
CLOP CLOP
FLUMP
...COME ON OUT, GHOSTS...
BABBLE BABBLE
MUMBLE MUMBLE
BLAH BLAH
BLAH
COME ON OUT, VAMPIRES.
Stupid
KYAAA!

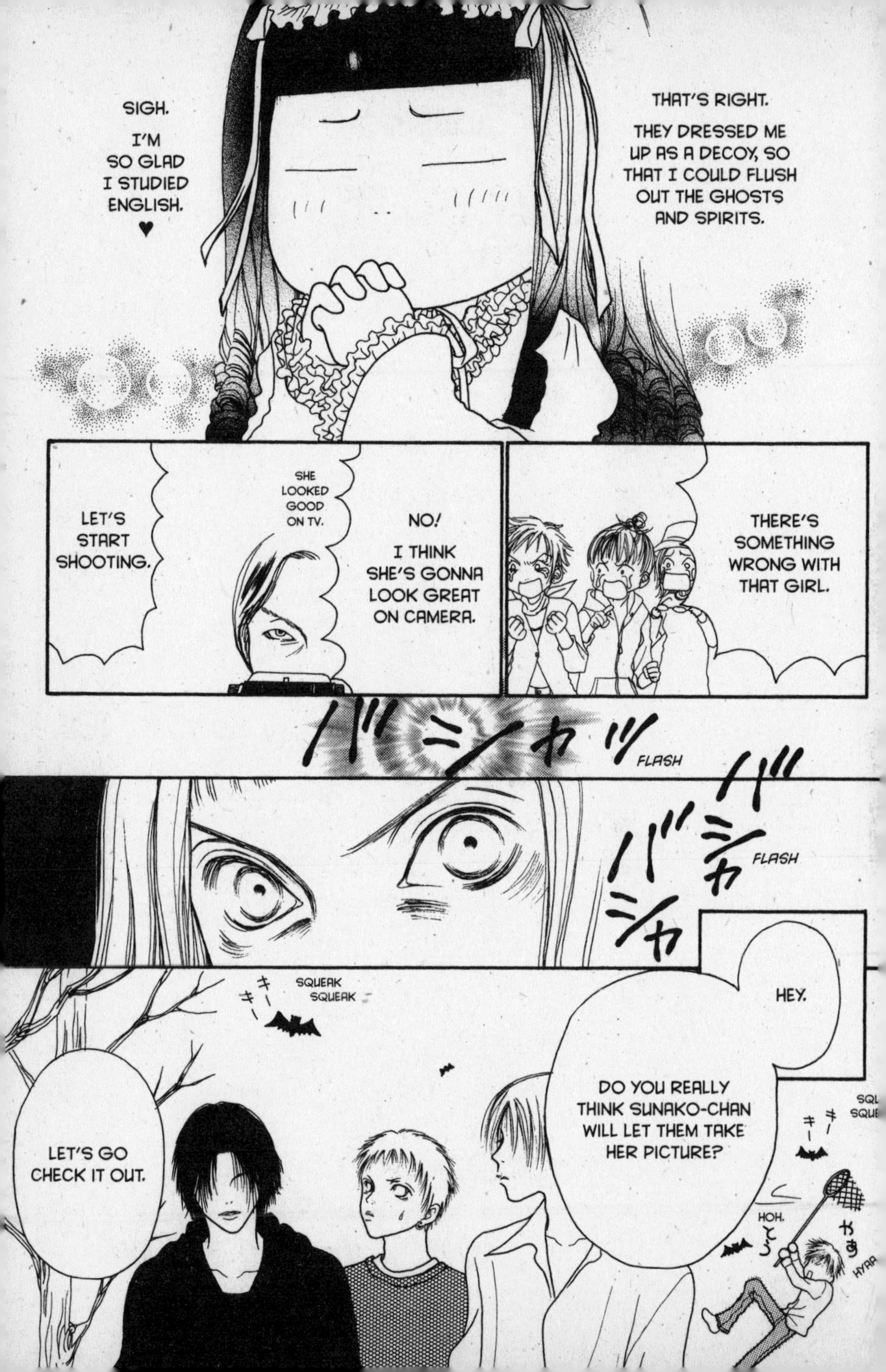
THAT'S RIGHT.
THEY DRESSED ME UP AS A DECOY, SO THAT I COULD FLUSH OUT THE GHOSTS AND SPIRITS.
SIGH.
I'M SO GLAD I STUDIED ENGLISH. ♥
THERE'S SOMETHING WRONG WITH THAT GIRL.
NO!
I THINK SHE'S GONNA LOOK GREAT ON CAMERA.
SHE LOOKED GOOD ON TV.
LET'S START SHOOTING.
バシャッ
FLASH
バシャバシャ
FLASH
HEY.
DO YOU REALLY THINK SUNAKO-CHAN WILL LET THEM TAKE HER PICTURE?
HOH.
HYAA
キーキー
SQUEAK SQUEAK
LET'S GO CHECK IT OUT.

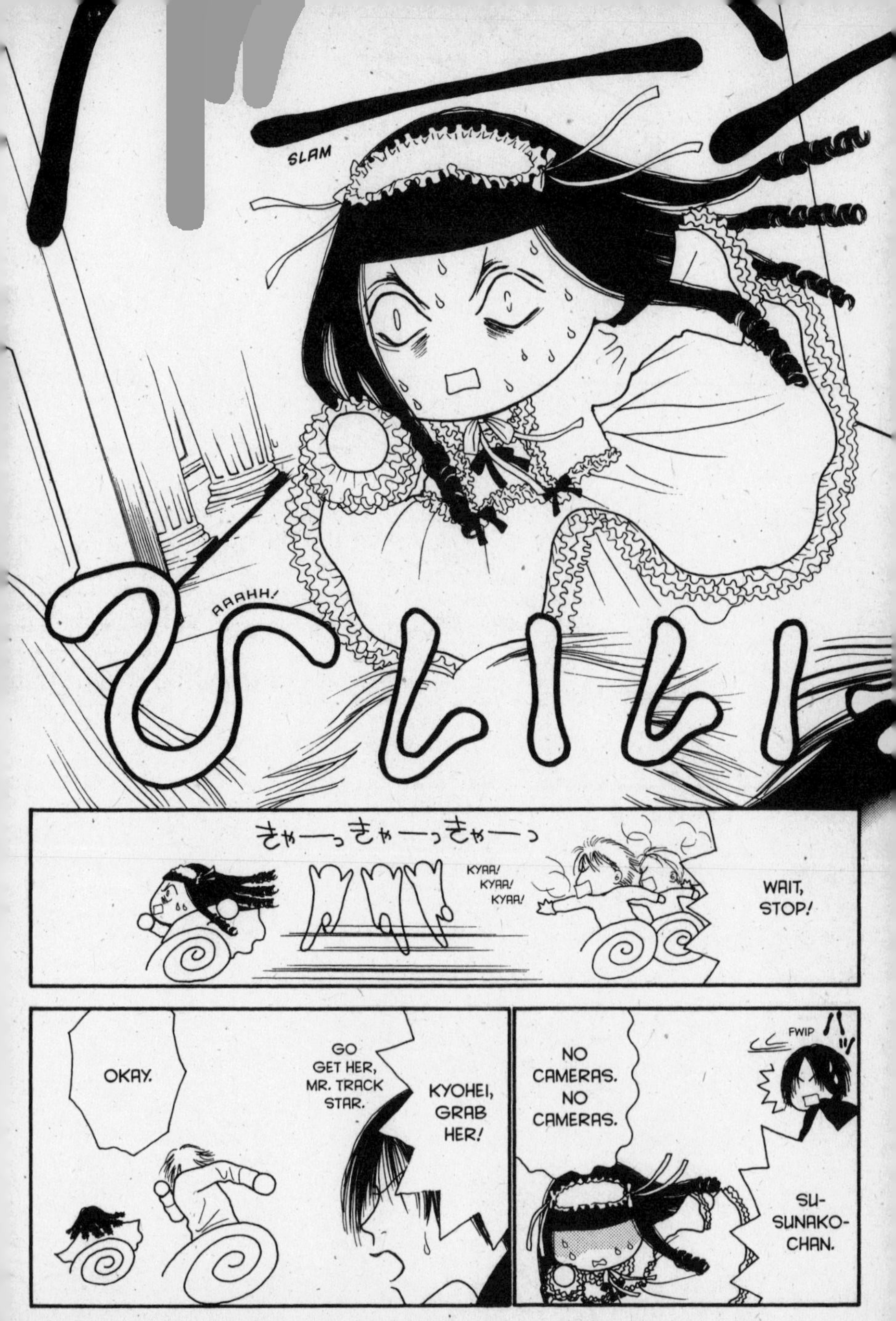
SLAM
AAAHH!
WAIT, STOP!
KYAA! KYAA! KYAA!
きゃーっきゃーっきゃーっ
パッ
FWIP
SU- SUNAKO- CHAN.
NO CAMERAS. NO CAMERAS.
KYOHEI, GRAB HER!
GO GET HER, MR. TRACK STAR.
OKAY.

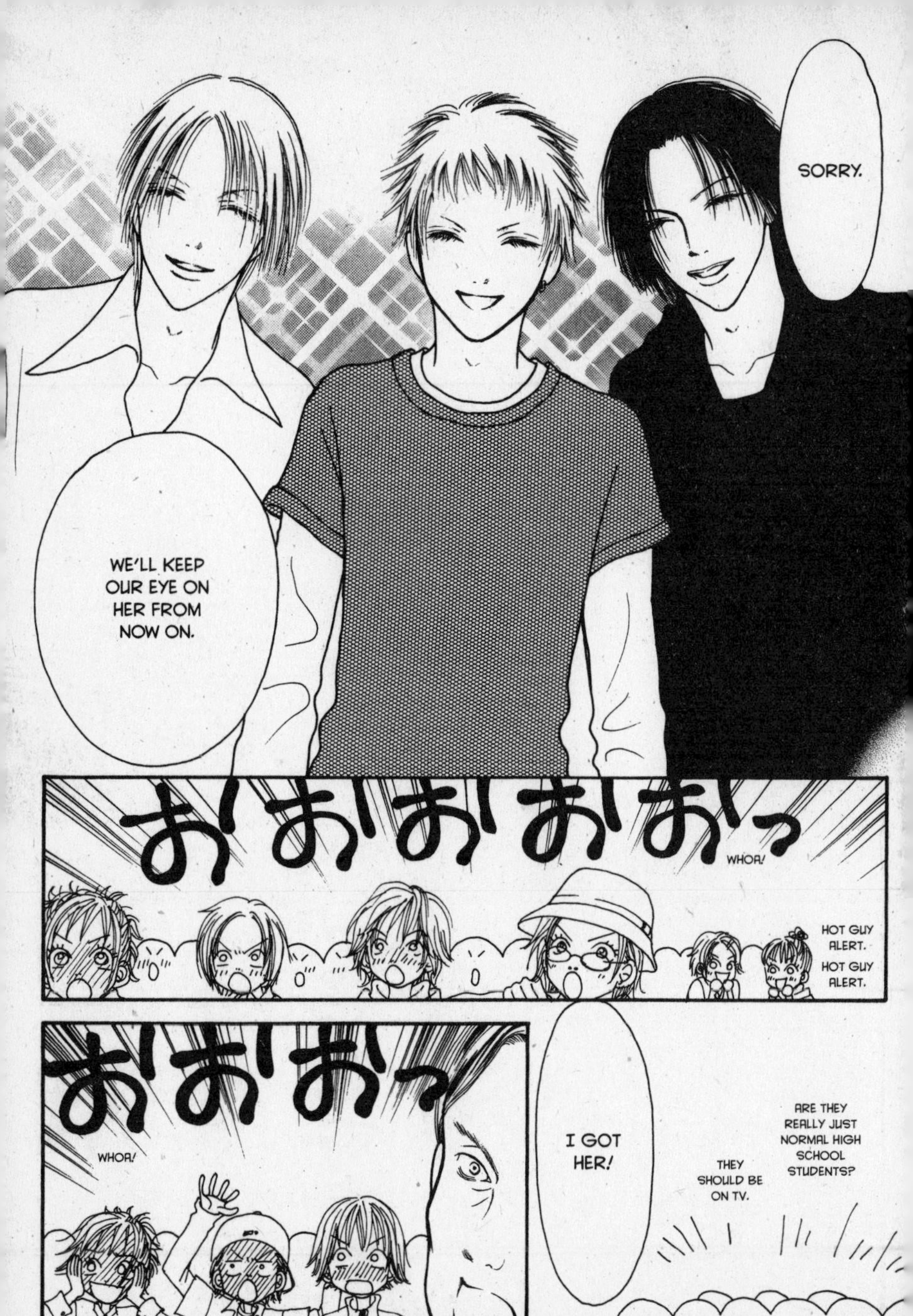
SORRY.
WE'LL KEEP OUR EYE ON HER FROM NOW ON.
お!お!お!お!おっ
WHOA!
HOT GUY ALERT.
HOT GUY ALERT.
ARE THEY REALLY JUST NORMAL HIGH SCHOOL STUDENTS?
THEY SHOULD BE ON TV.
I GOT HER!
お!お!おっ
WHOA!

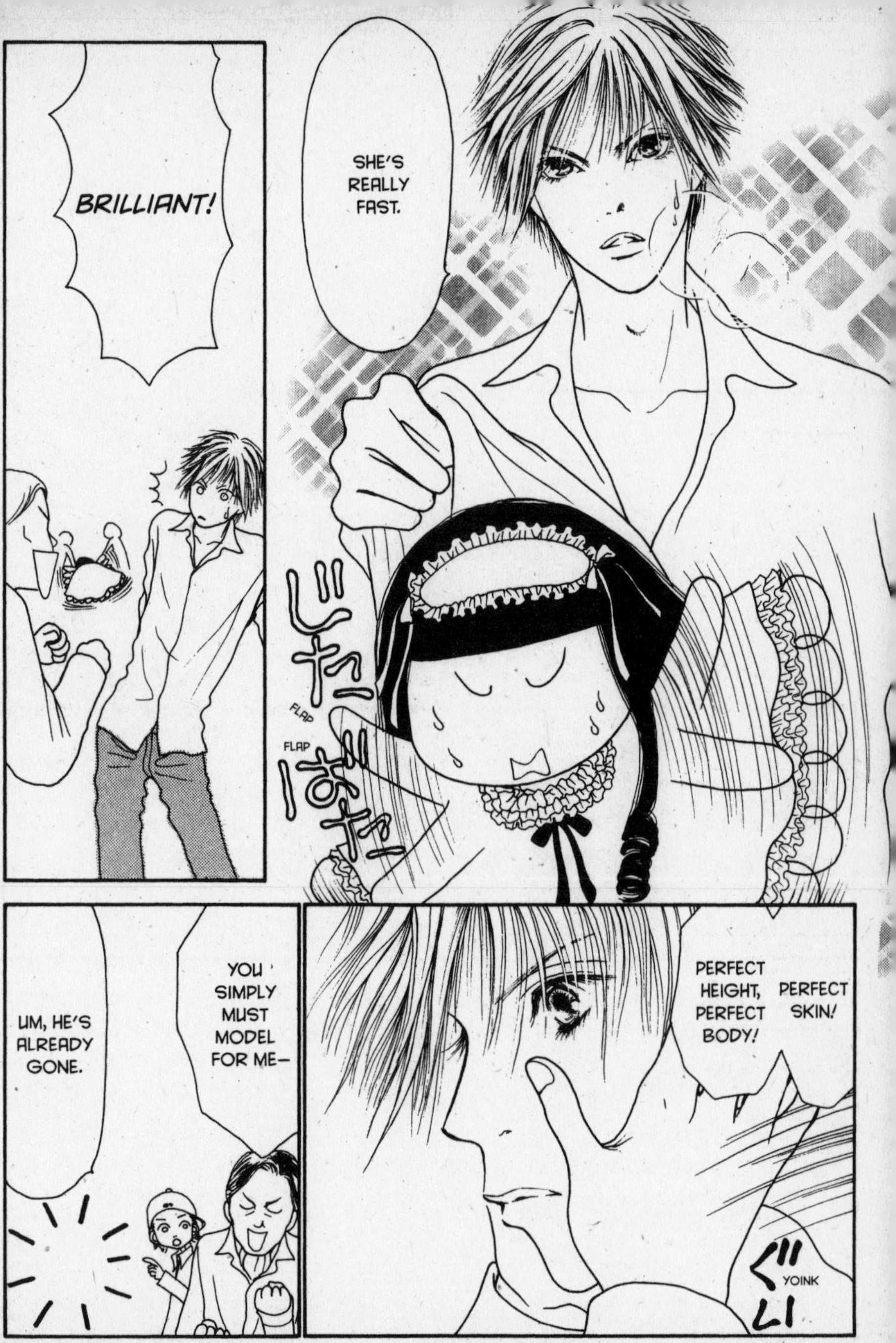
SHE'S REALLY FAST.
FLAP
FLAP
BRILLIANT!
PERFECT SKIN!
PERFECT HEIGHT, PERFECT BODY!
YOINK
YOU SIMPLY MUST MODEL FOR ME—
UM, HE'S ALREADY GONE.

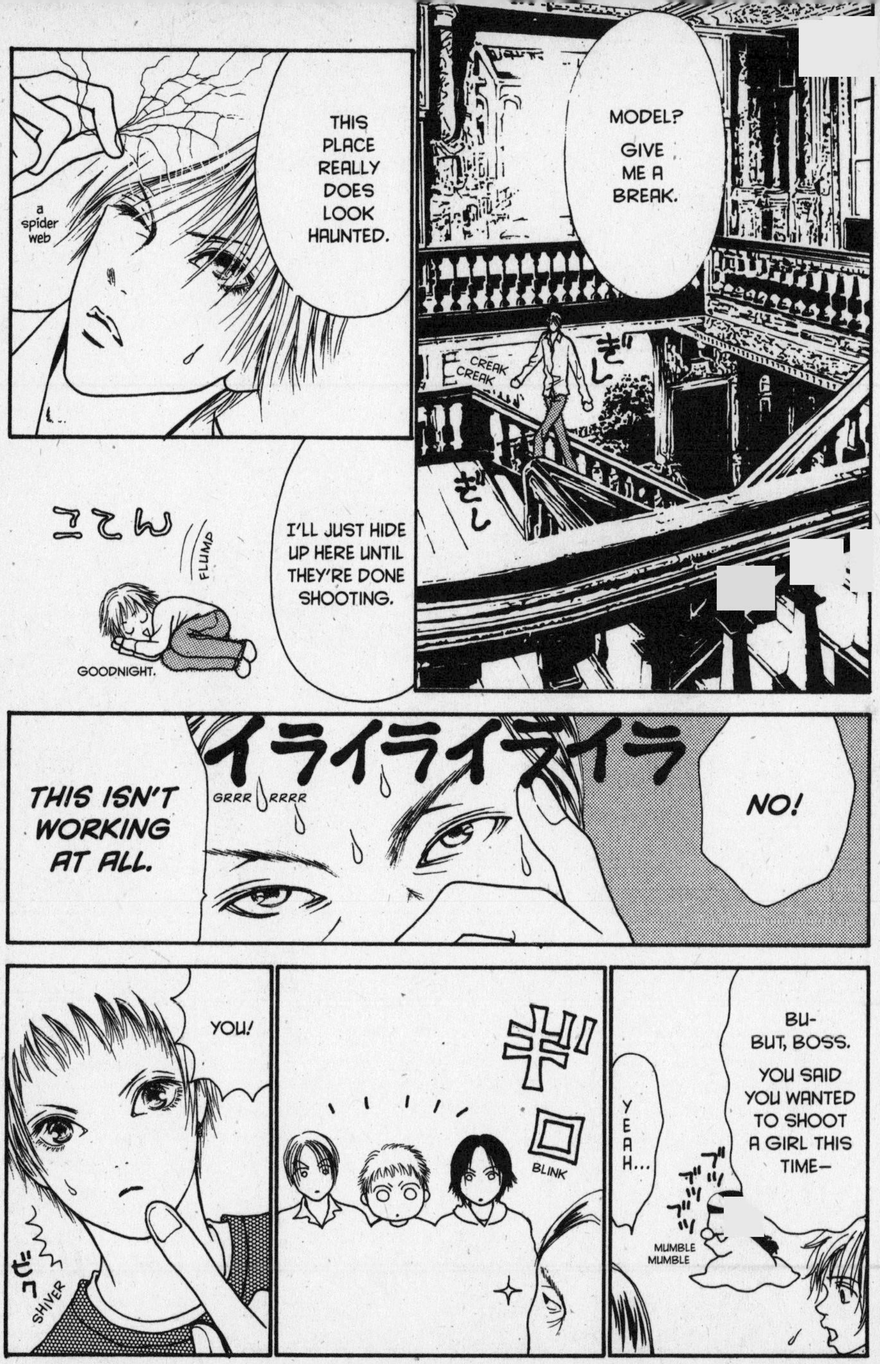
MODEL? GIVE ME A BREAK.
CREAK CREAK
ぎし
ぎし
THIS PLACE REALLY DOES LOOK HAUNTED.
a spider web
I'LL JUST HIDE UP HERE UNTIL THEY'RE DONE SHOOTING.
こてん
FLUMP
GOODNIGHT.
NO!
イライライライラ
GRRR RRRR
THIS ISN'T WORKING AT ALL.
BU- BUT, BOSS. YOU SAID YOU WANTED TO SHOOT A GIRL THIS TIME—
YEAH...
ブツブツブツ
MUMBLE MUMBLE
ギロ
BLINK
YOU!
ビク
SHIVER

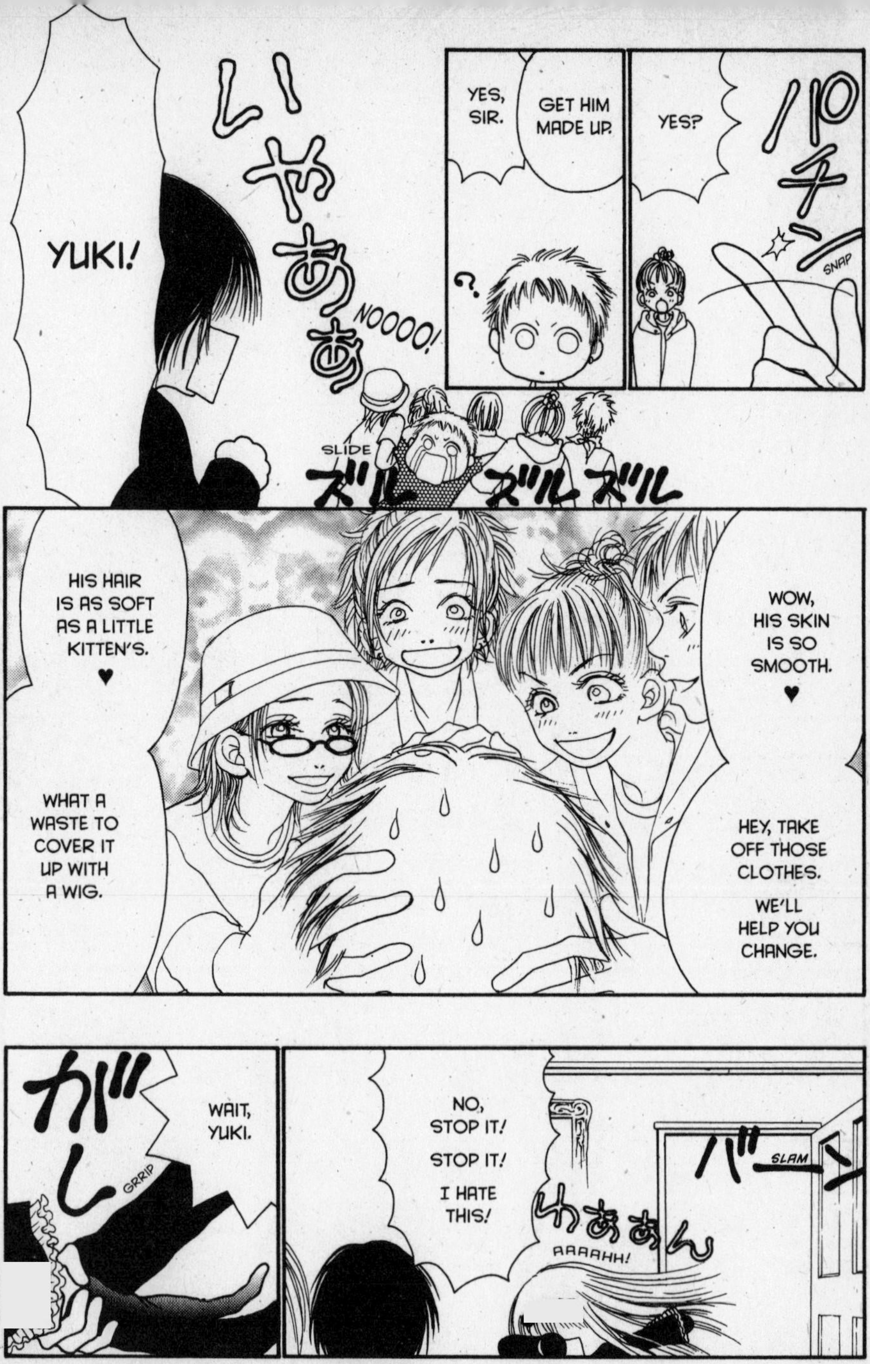
YES?
SNAP
GET HIM MADE UP.
YES, SIR.
NOOOO!
YUKI!
SLIDE
WOW, HIS SKIN IS SO SMOOTH. ♥
HEY, TAKE OFF THOSE CLOTHES.
WE'LL HELP YOU CHANGE.
HIS HAIR IS AS SOFT AS A LITTLE KITTEN'S. ♥
WHAT A WASTE TO COVER IT UP WITH A WIG.
SLAM
NO, STOP IT!
STOP IT!
I HATE THIS!
AAAAHH!
WAIT, YUKI.
GRRIP

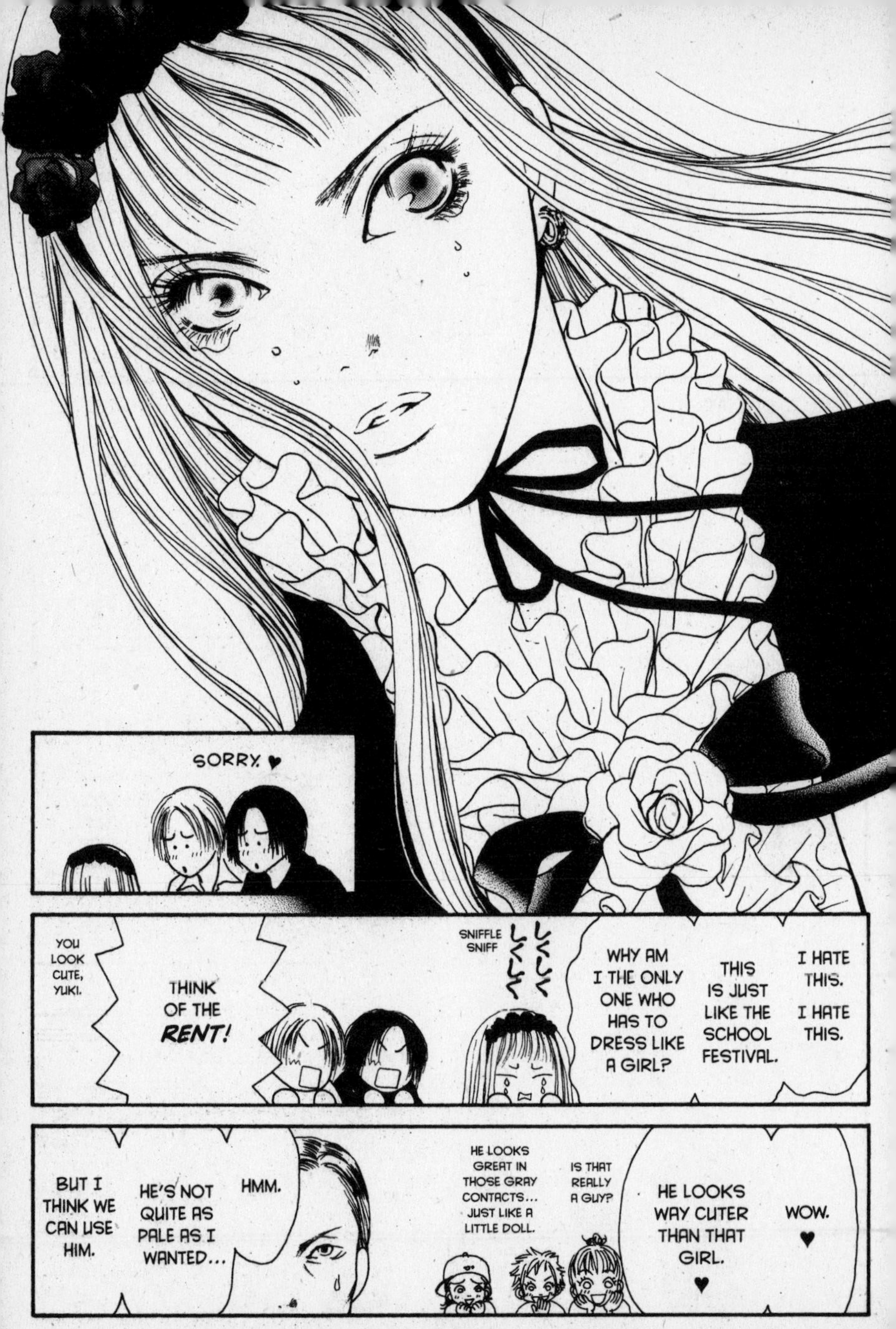
SORRY. ♥
I HATE THIS. I HATE THIS.
THIS IS JUST LIKE THE SCHOOL FESTIVAL.
WHY AM I THE ONLY ONE WHO HAS TO DRESS LIKE A GIRL?
しくしく しくしく
SNIFFLE SNIFF
THINK OF THE RENT!
YOU LOOK CUTE, YUKI.
WOW. ♥
HE LOOKS WAY CUTER THAN THAT GIRL. ♥
IS THAT REALLY A GUY?
HE LOOKS GREAT IN THOSE GRAY CONTACTS... JUST LIKE A LITTLE DOLL.
HMM.
HE'S NOT QUITE AS PALE AS I WANTED...
BUT I THINK WE CAN USE HIM.

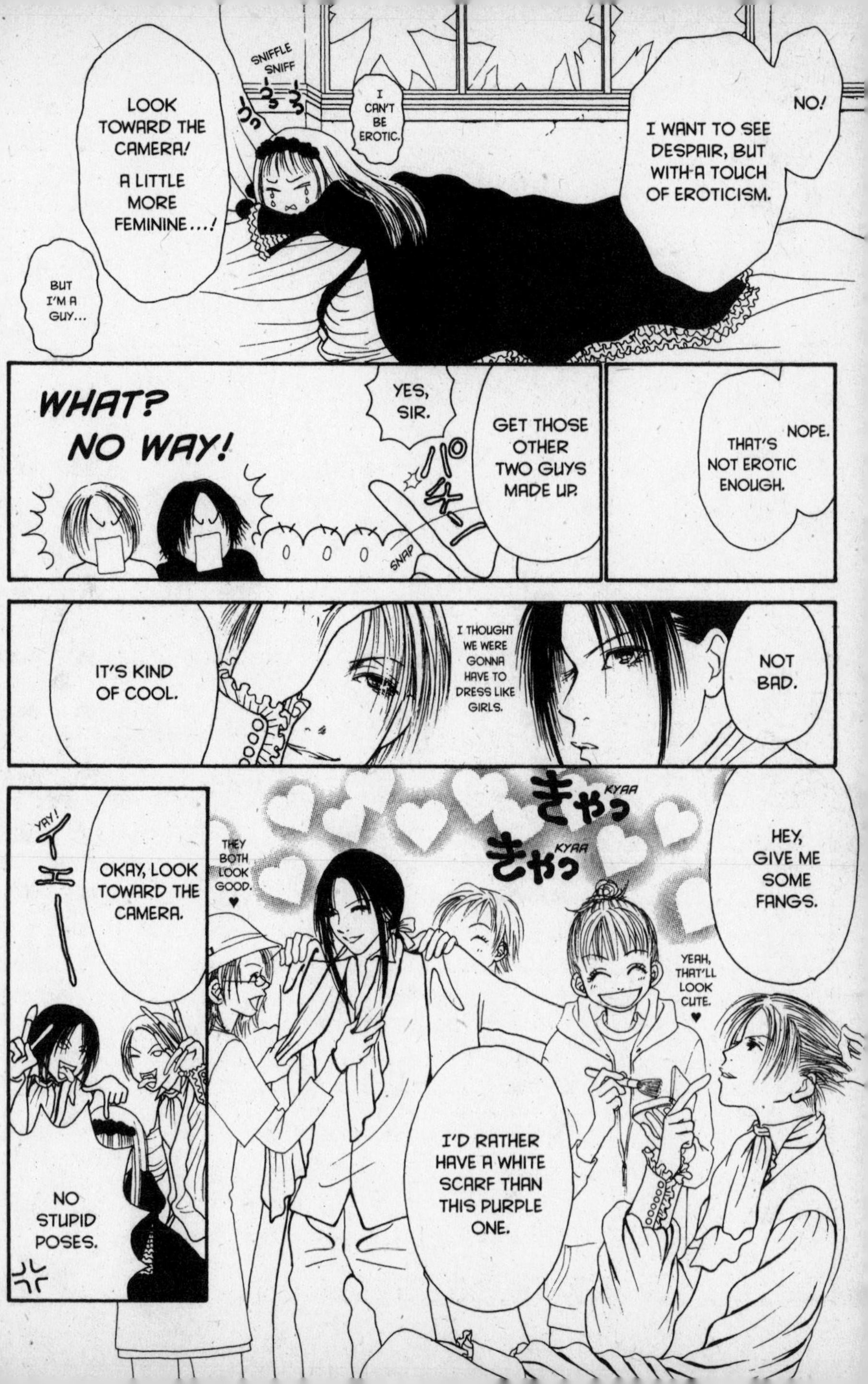
NO!
I WANT TO SEE DESPAIR, BUT WITH A TOUCH OF EROTICISM.
SNIFFLE SNIFF
I CAN'T BE EROTIC.
LOOK TOWARD THE CAMERA!
A LITTLE MORE FEMININE...!
BUT I'M A GUY...
NOPE.
THAT'S NOT EROTIC ENOUGH.
GET THOSE OTHER TWO GUYS MADE UP.
YES, SIR.
SNAP
WHAT? NO WAY!
NOT BAD.
I THOUGHT WE WERE GONNA HAVE TO DRESS LIKE GIRLS.
IT'S KIND OF COOL.
HEY, GIVE ME SOME FANGS.
YEAH, THAT'LL LOOK CUTE. ♥
きゃっ KYAA
きゃっ KYAA
I'D RATHER HAVE A WHITE SCARF THAN THIS PURPLE ONE.
THEY BOTH LOOK GOOD. ♥
OKAY, LOOK TOWARD THE CAMERA.
YAY!
NO STUPID POSES.

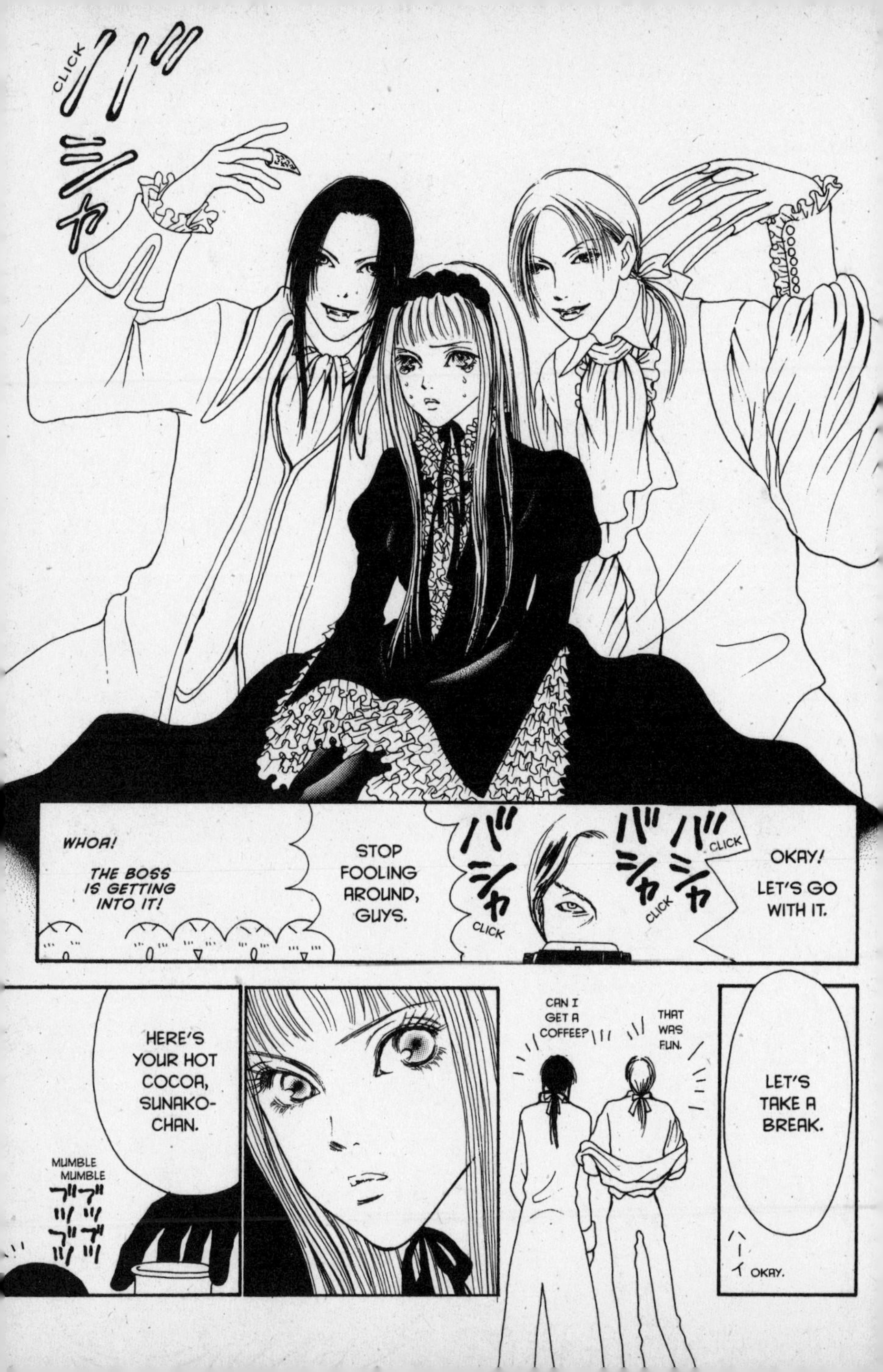
CLICK
バシャ
OKAY! LET'S GO WITH IT.
バシャ バシャ
CLICK
CLICK
バシャ
CLICK
STOP FOOLING AROUND, GUYS.
WHOA! THE BOSS IS GETTING INTO IT!
LET'S TAKE A BREAK.
ハーイ OKAY.
THAT WAS FUN.
CAN I GET A COFFEE?
HERE'S YOUR HOT COCOA, SUNAKO-CHAN.
MUMBLE MUMBLE
ブツブツ ブツブツ

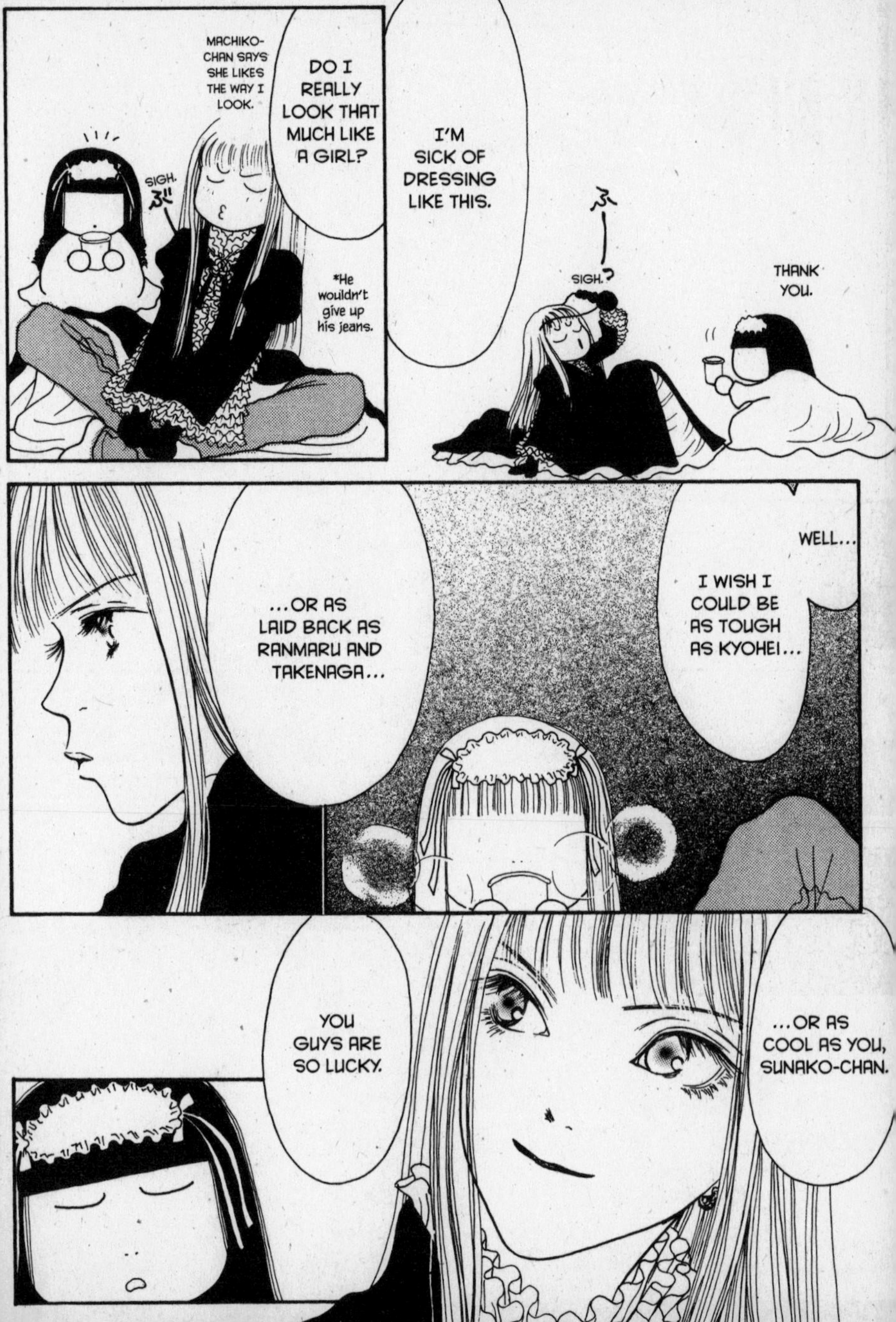

THANK YOU.
SIGH.
ふー
I'M SICK OF DRESSING LIKE THIS.
DO I REALLY LOOK THAT MUCH LIKE A GIRL?
MACHIKO-CHAN SAYS SHE LIKES THE WAY I LOOK.
SIGH.
ぶ
*He wouldn't give up his jeans.
WELL...
I WISH I COULD BE AS TOUGH AS KYOHEI...
...OR AS LAID BACK AS RANMARU AND TAKENAGA...
...OR AS COOL AS YOU, SUNAKO-CHAN.
YOU GUYS ARE SO LUCKY.

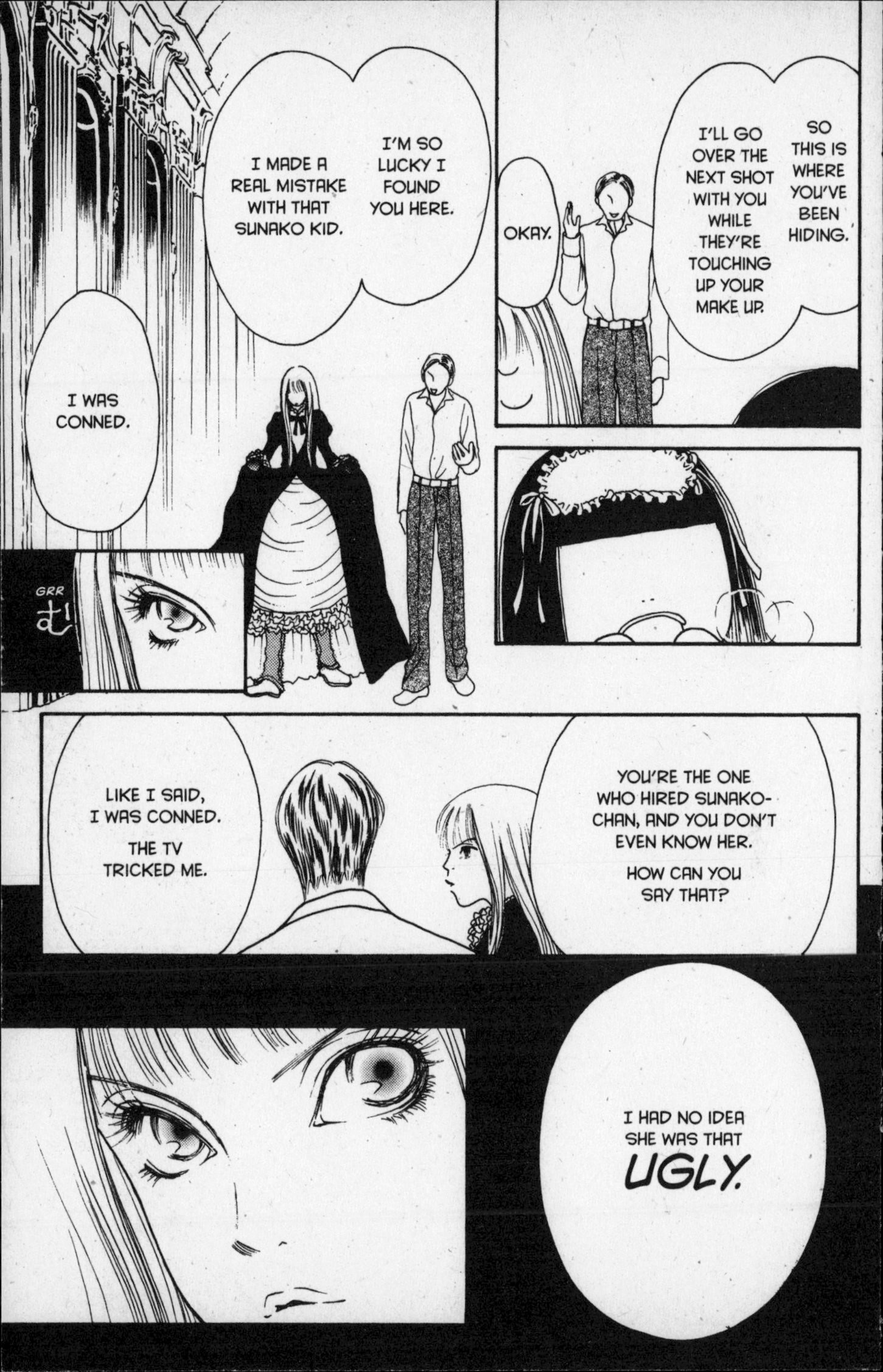
SO THIS IS WHERE YOU'VE BEEN HIDING.
I'LL GO OVER THE NEXT SHOT WITH YOU WHILE THEY'RE TOUCHING UP YOUR MAKE UP.
OKAY.
I'M SO LUCKY I FOUND YOU HERE.
I MADE A REAL MISTAKE WITH THAT SUNAKO KID.
I WAS CONNED.
GRR
YOU'RE THE ONE WHO HIRED SUNAKO-CHAN, AND YOU DON'T EVEN KNOW HER.
HOW CAN YOU SAY THAT?
LIKE I SAID, I WAS CONNED.
THE TV TRICKED ME.
I HAD NO IDEA SHE WAS THAT UGLY.

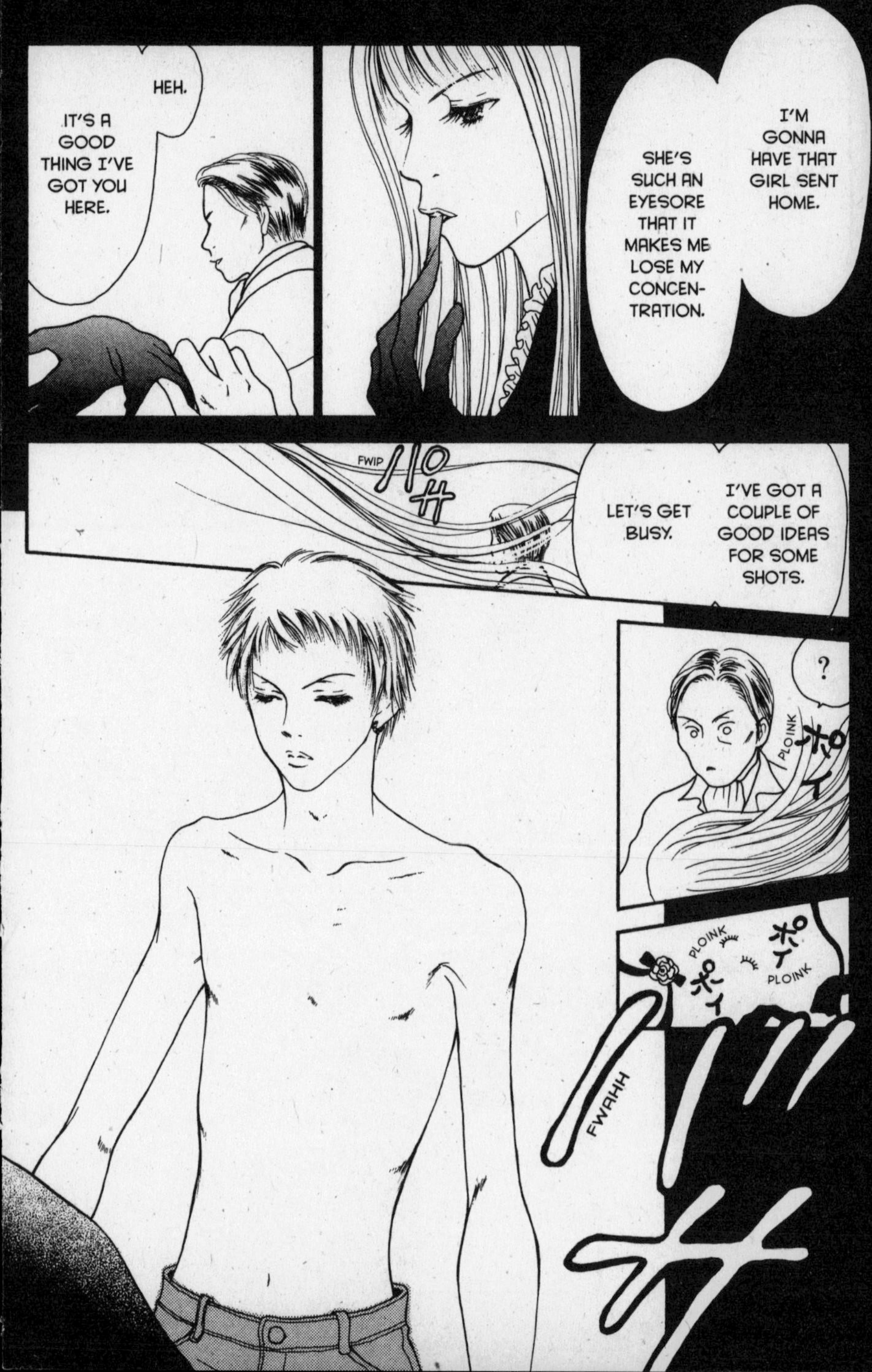
I'M GONNA HAVE THAT GIRL SENT HOME.
SHE'S SUCH AN EYESORE THAT IT MAKES ME LOSE MY CONCEN-TRATION.
HEH.
IT'S A GOOD THING I'VE GOT YOU HERE.
I'VE GOT A COUPLE OF GOOD IDEAS FOR SOME SHOTS.
LET'S GET BUSY.
FWIP
?
PLOINK
PLOINK
PLOINK
FWAHH

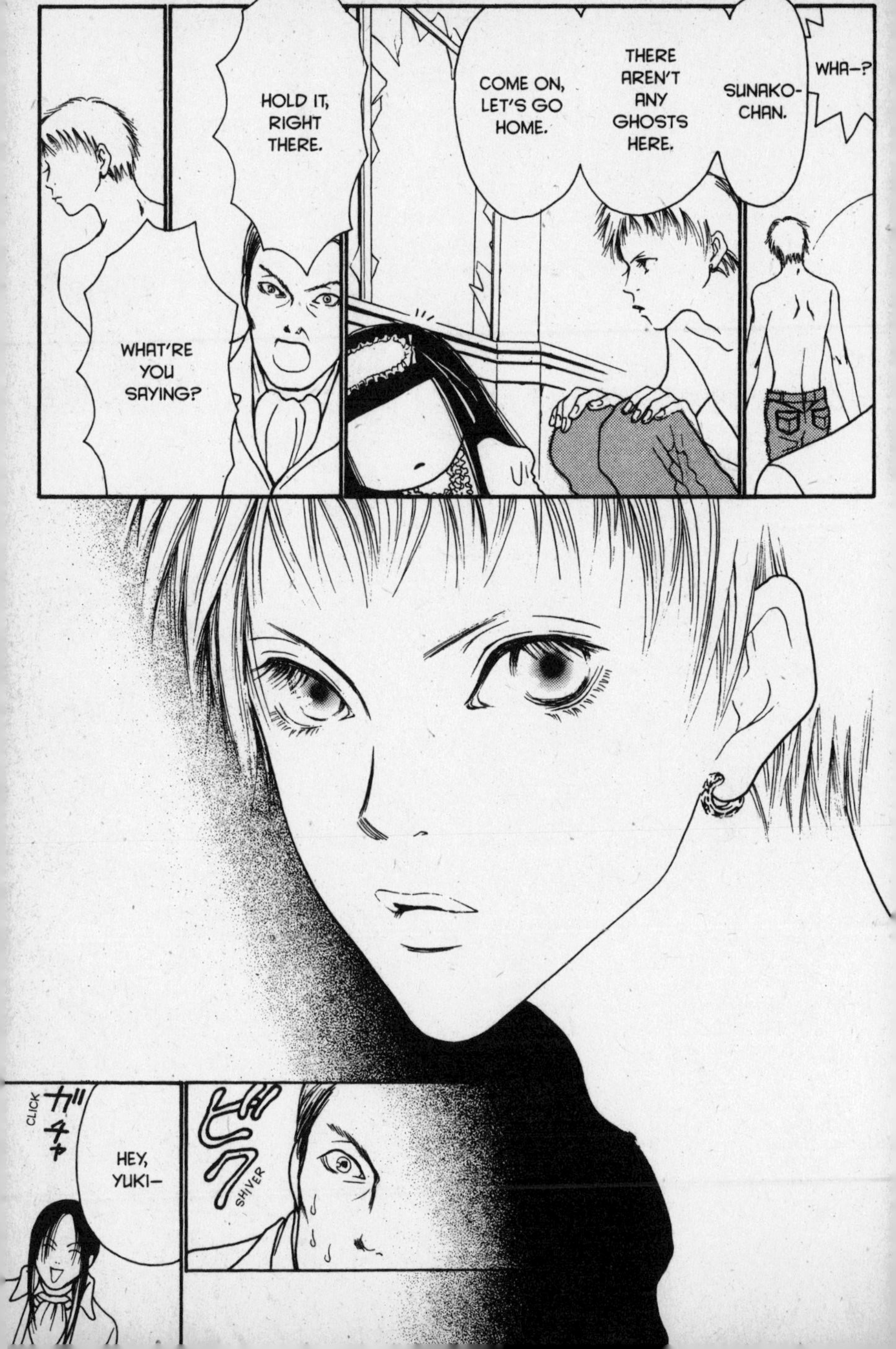
WHA—?
SUNAKO-CHAN.
THERE AREN'T ANY GHOSTS HERE.
COME ON, LET'S GO HOME.
HOLD IT, RIGHT THERE.
WHAT'RE YOU SAYING?
SHIVER
CLICK
HEY, YUKI—

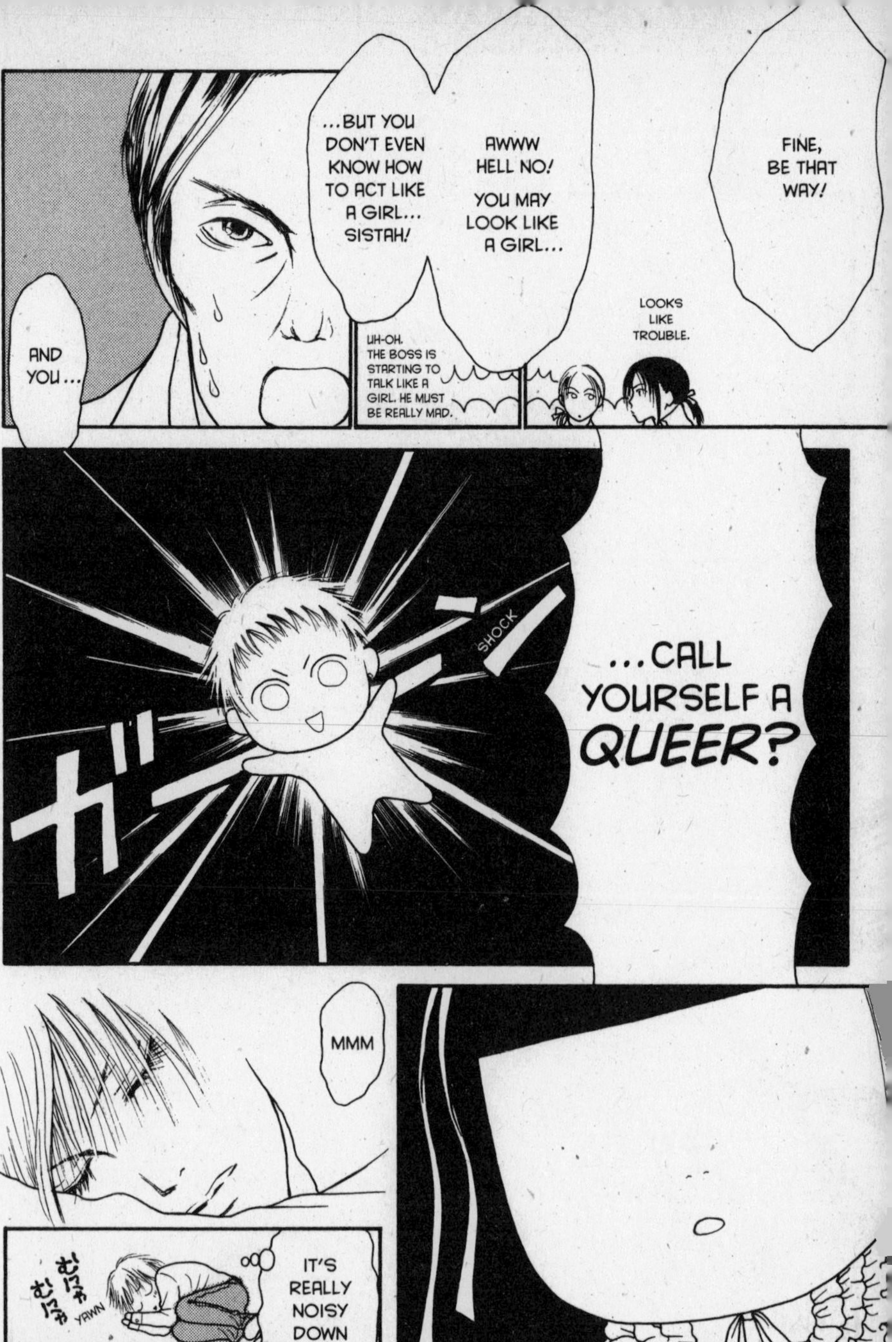
FINE, BE THAT WAY!
LOOKS LIKE TROUBLE.
UH-OH. THE BOSS IS STARTING TO TALK LIKE A GIRL. HE MUST BE REALLY MAD.
AWWW HELL NO!
YOU MAY LOOK LIKE A GIRL...
...BUT YOU DON'T EVEN KNOW HOW TO ACT LIKE A GIRL... SISTAH!
AND YOU...
...CALL YOURSELF A *QUEER?*
SHOCK
MMM
IT'S REALLY NOISY DOWN BELOW.
むにゃ むにゃ
YAWN

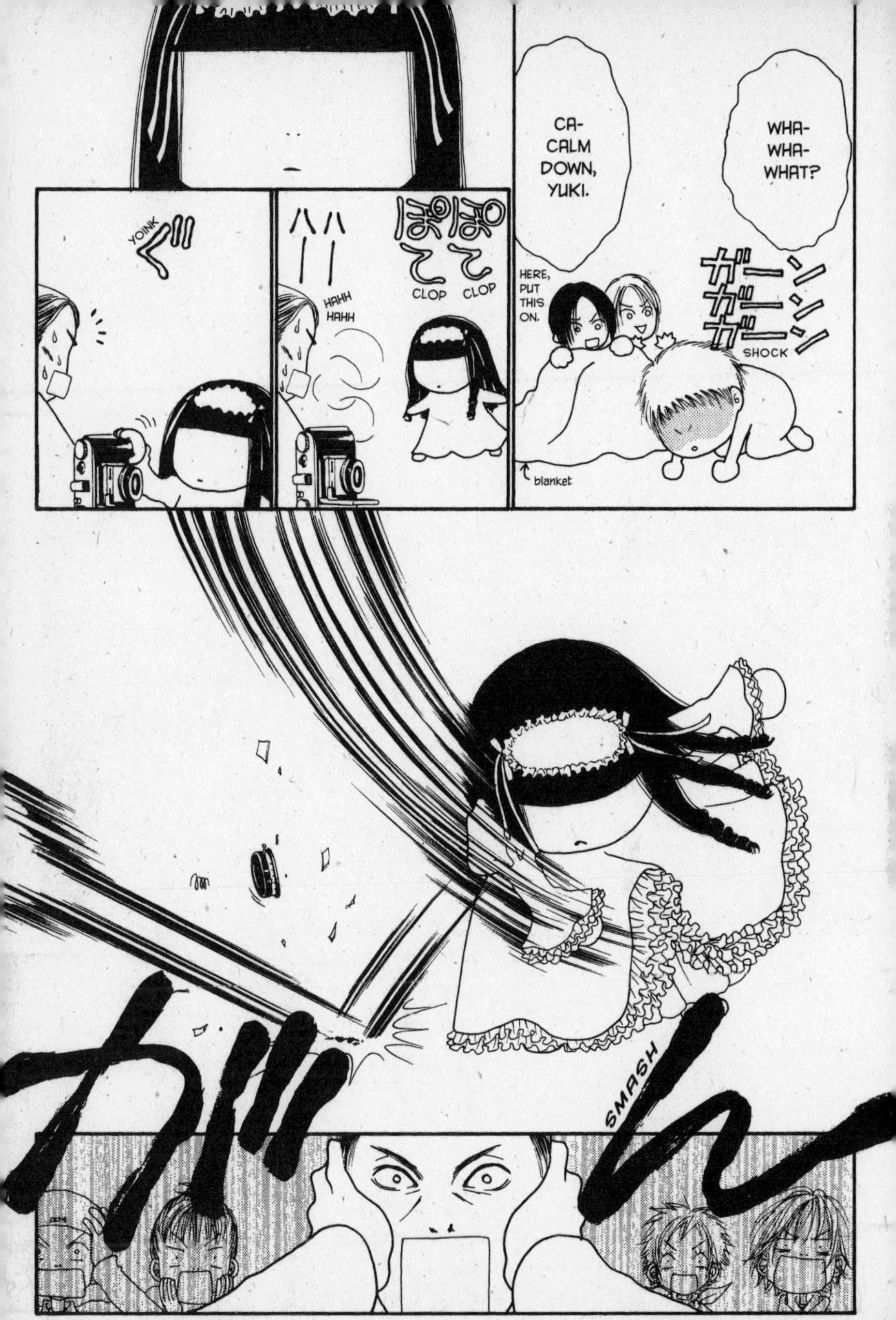
WHA-WHA-WHAT?
ガーンガーンガーン
SHOCK
CA-CALM DOWN, YUKI.
HERE, PUT THIS ON.
blanket
ぽてぽて
CLOP CLOP
HAHH HAHH
YOINK
SMASH

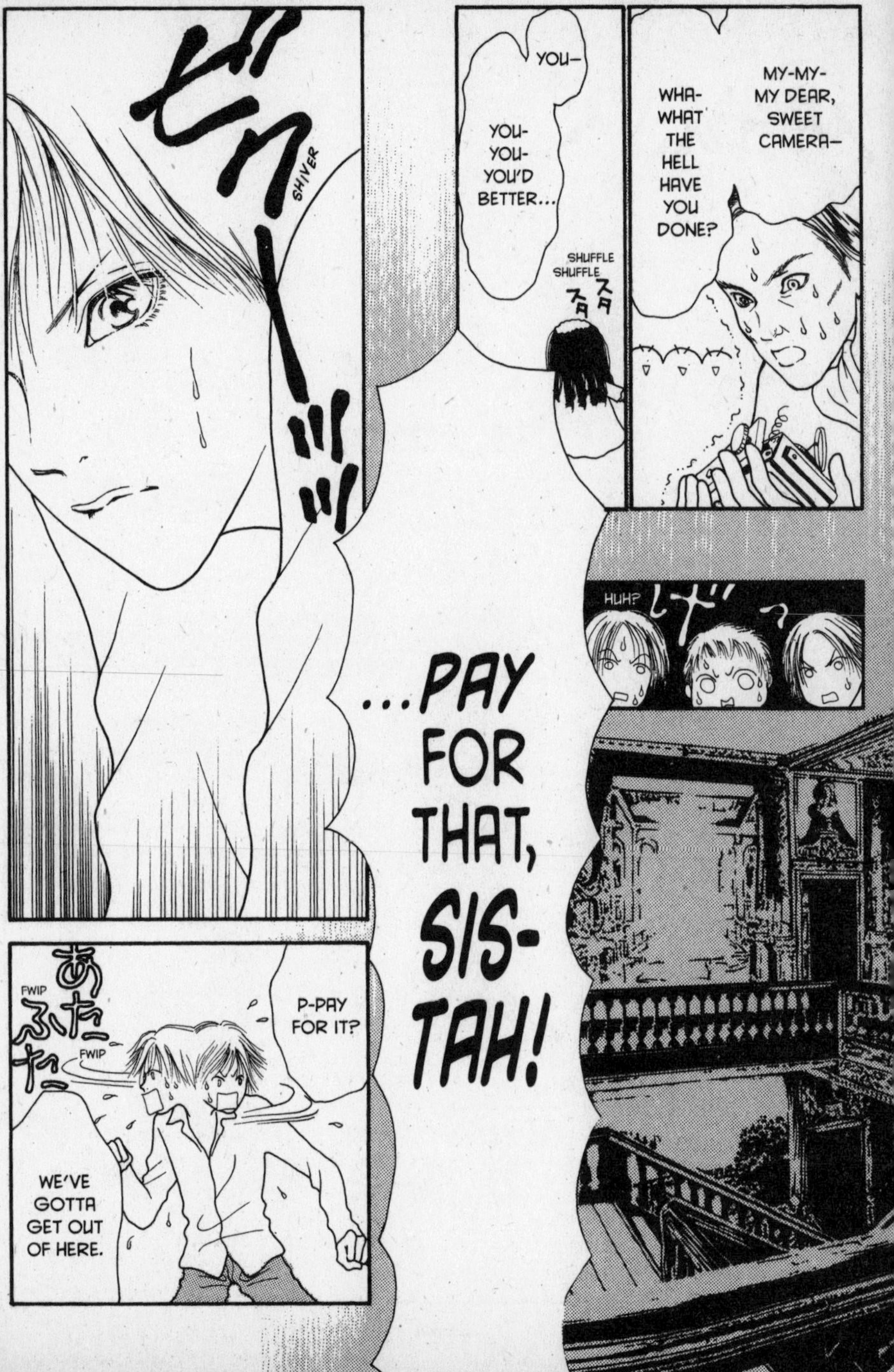

MY-MY-MY DEAR, SWEET CAMERA—
WHA-WHAT THE HELL HAVE YOU DONE?
YOU—
YOU-YOU-YOU'D BETTER...
SHUFFLE SHUFFLE
SHIVER
HUH?
...PAY FOR THAT, SIS-TAH!
P-PAY FOR IT?
FWIP
FWIP
WE'VE GOTTA GET OUT OF HERE.

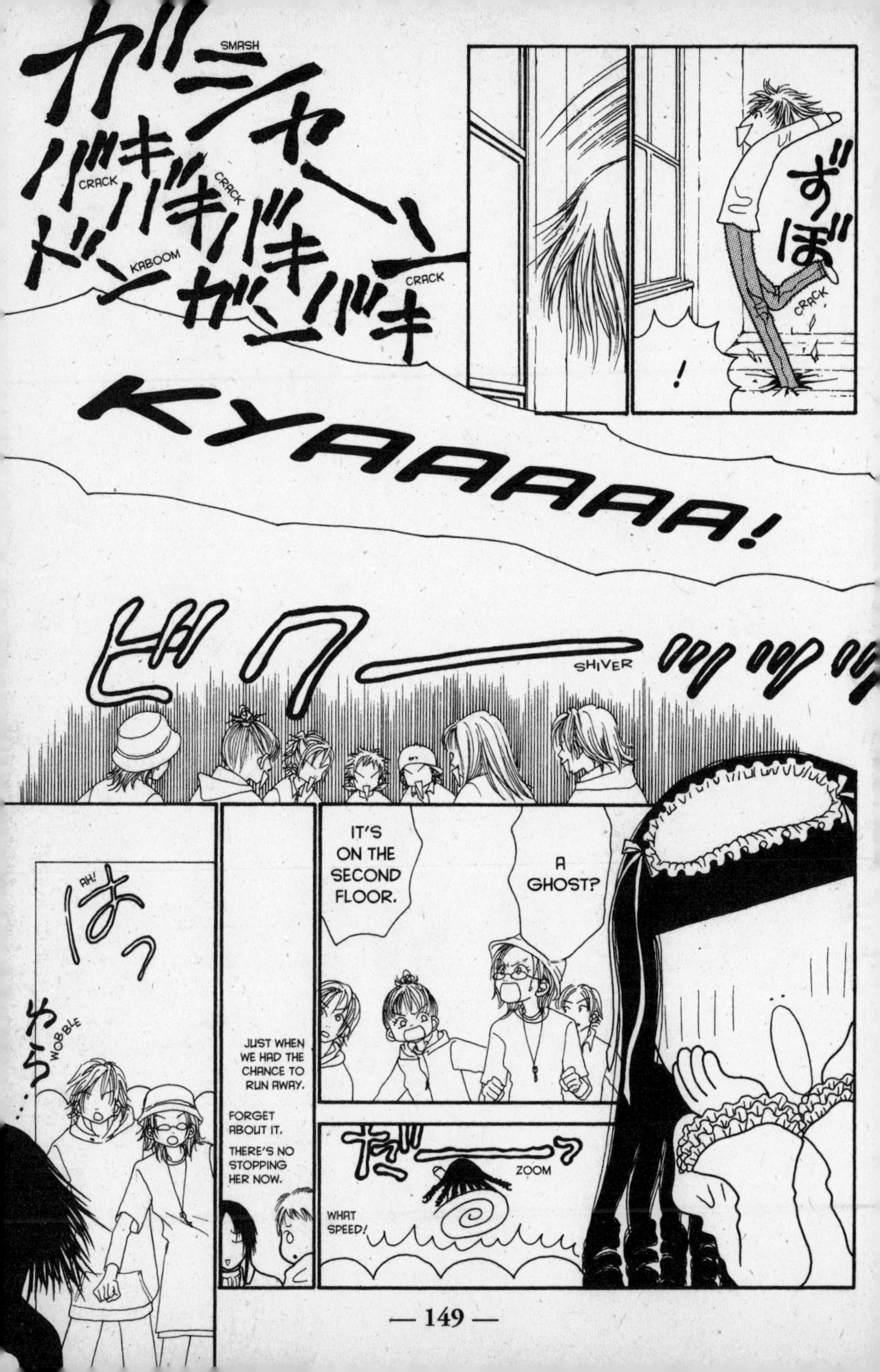

CRACK
!
SMASH
CRACK
CRACK
CRACK
KABOOM
KYAAAAAA!
SHIVER
A GHOST?
IT'S ON THE SECOND FLOOR.
ZOOM
WHAT SPEED!
JUST WHEN WE HAD THE CHANCE TO RUN AWAY.
FORGET ABOUT IT.
THERE'S NO STOPPING HER NOW.
AH!
WOBBLE

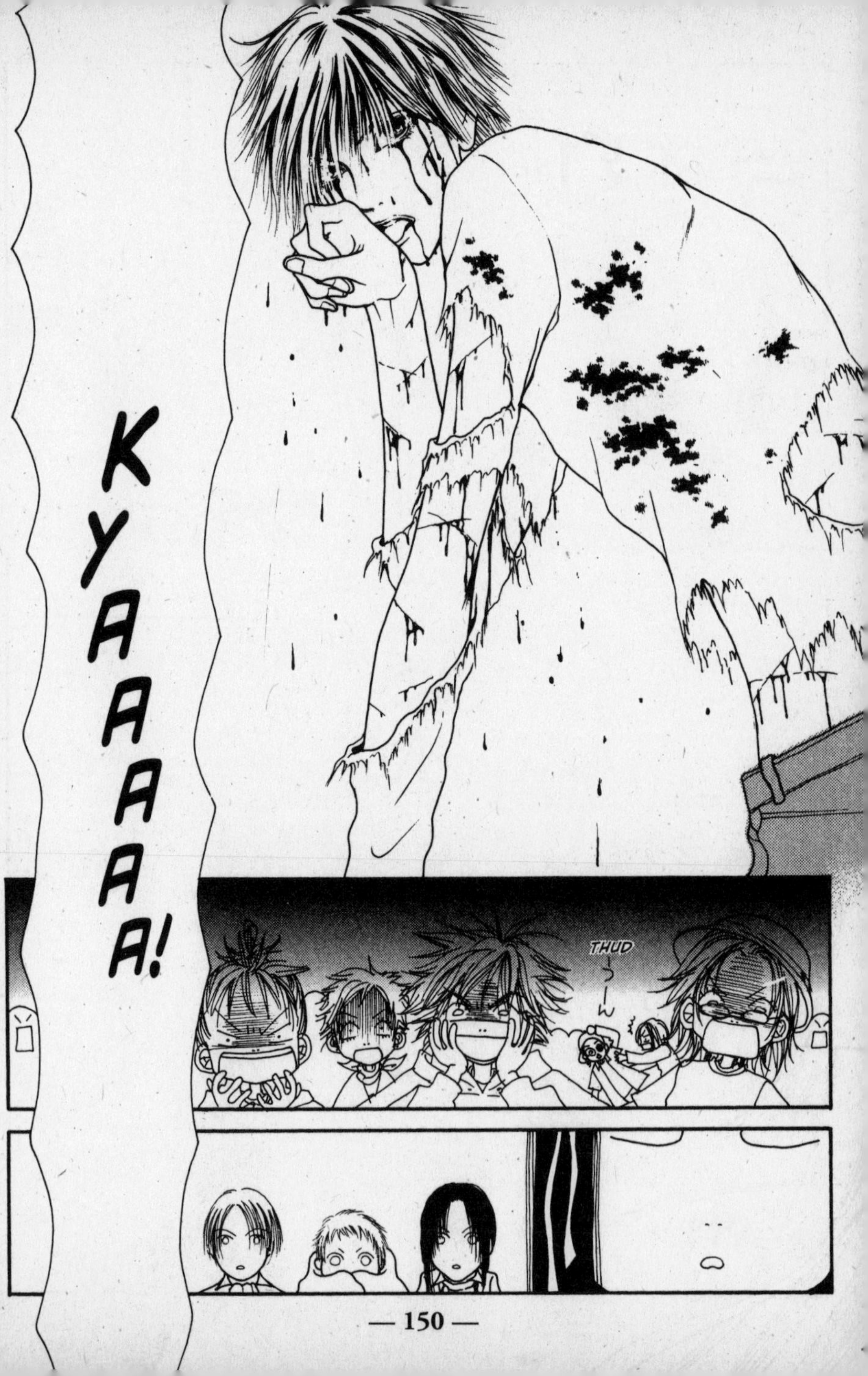
KYAAAAAA!
THUD

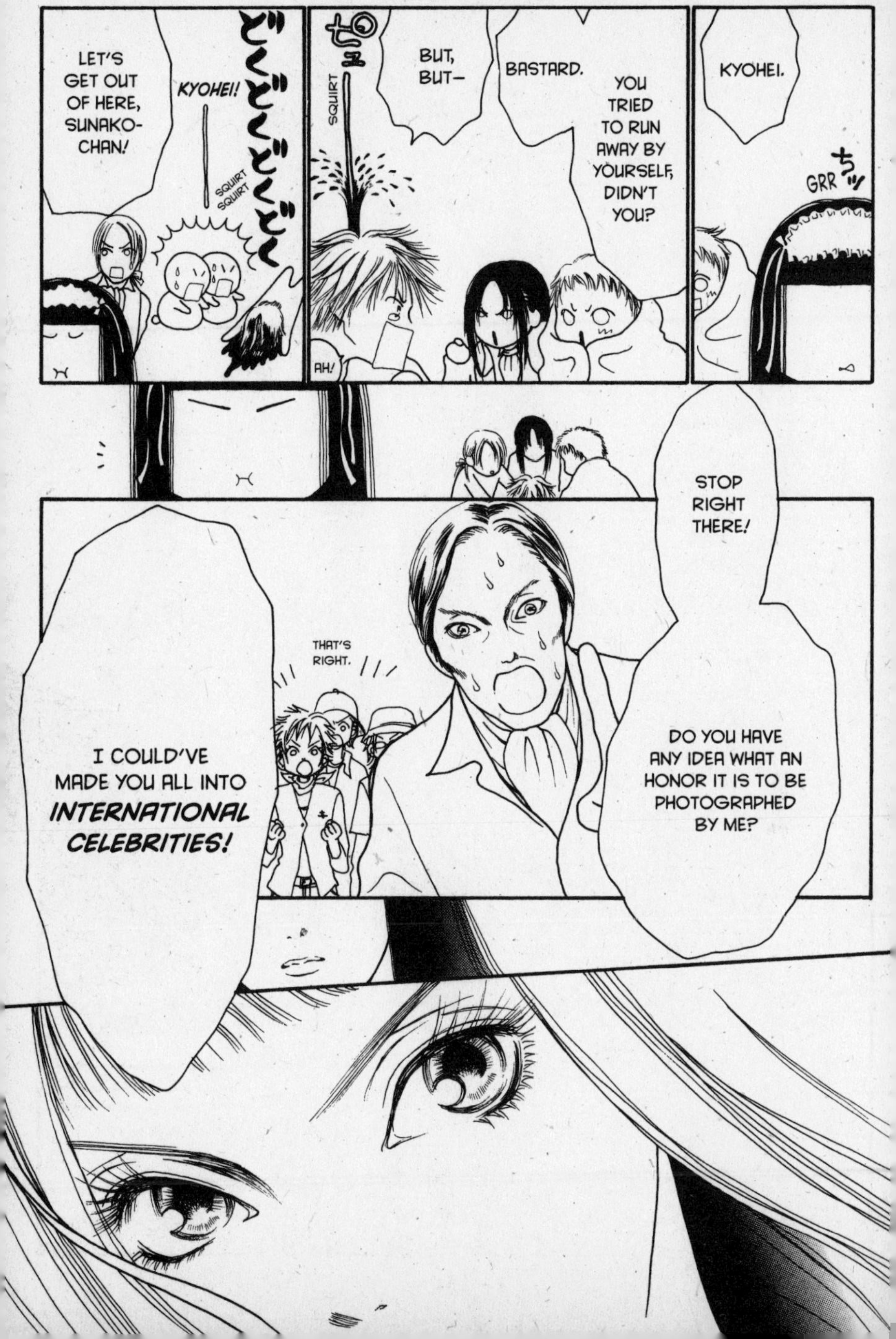
KYOHEI.
GRR
ちッ
BASTARD.
YOU TRIED TO RUN AWAY BY YOURSELF, DIDN'T YOU?
BUT, BUT—
ぴュ
SQUIRT
AH!
KYOHEI!
どくどくどくどく
SQUIRT SQUIRT
LET'S GET OUT OF HERE, SUNAKO-CHAN!
STOP RIGHT THERE!
DO YOU HAVE ANY IDEA WHAT AN HONOR IT IS TO BE PHOTOGRAPHED BY ME?
THAT'S RIGHT.
I COULD'VE MADE YOU ALL INTO *INTERNATIONAL CELEBRITIES!*

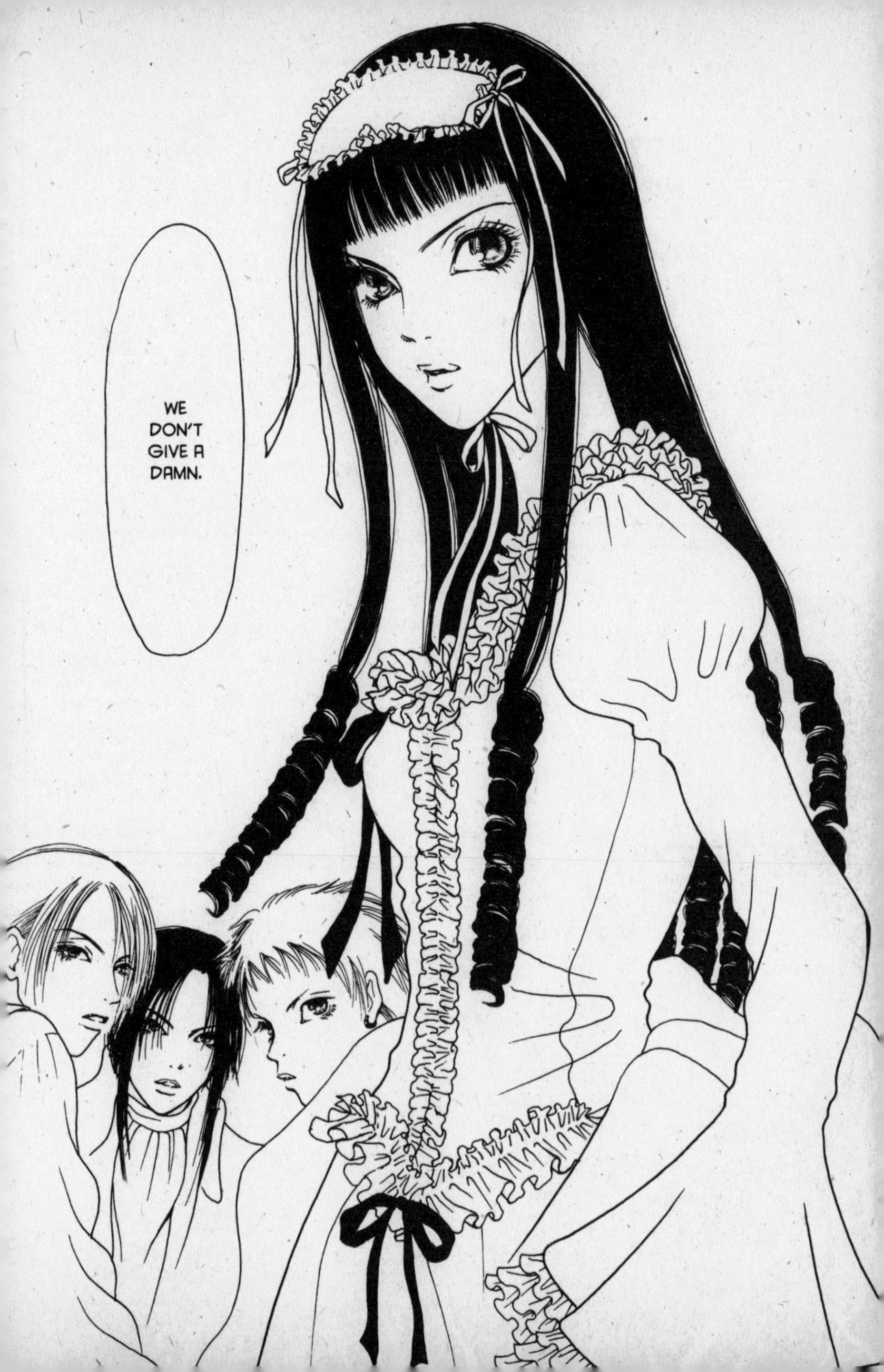
WE DON'T GIVE A DAMN.

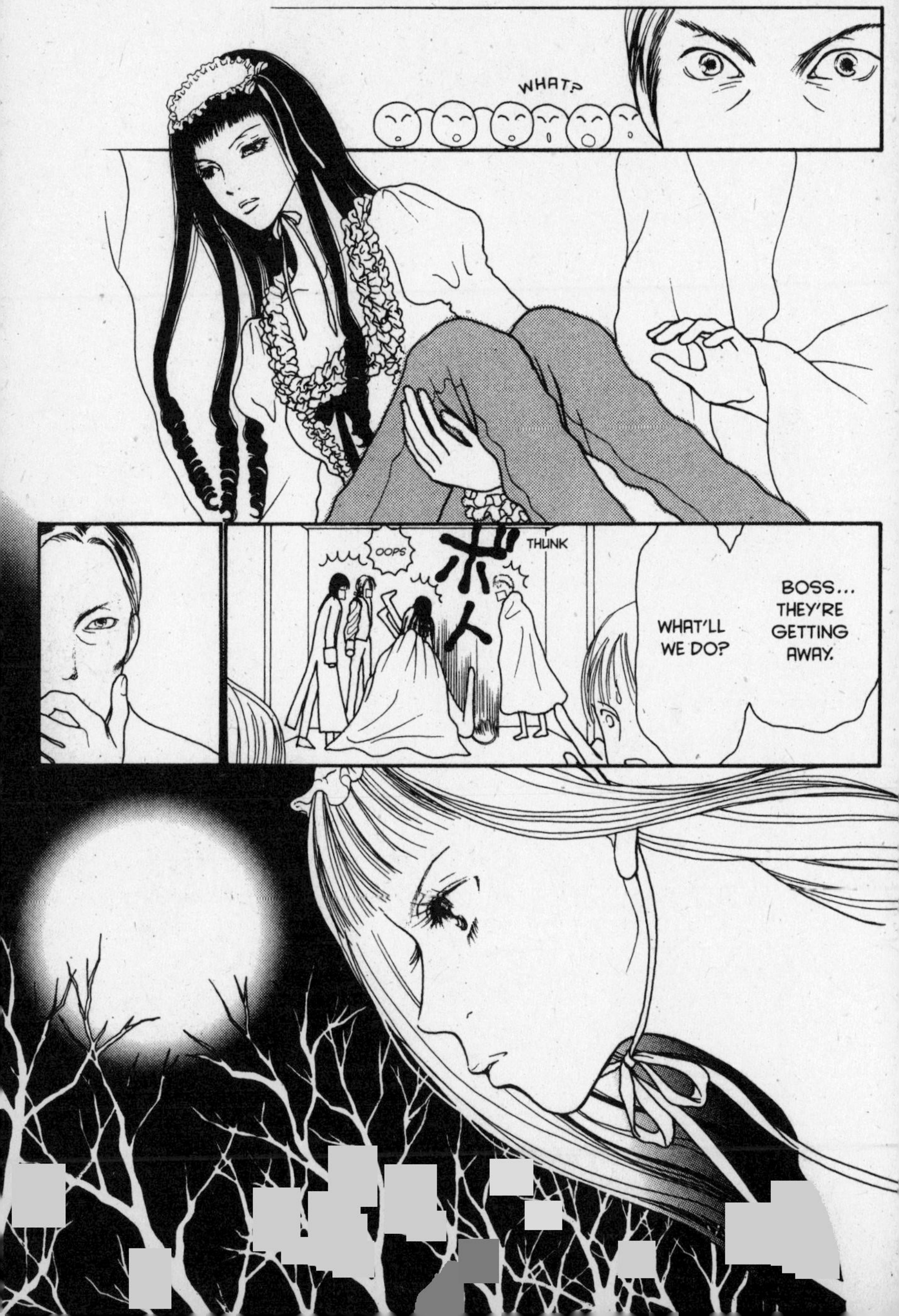
WHAT?
BOSS... THEY'RE GETTING AWAY.
WHAT'LL WE DO?
THUNK
OOPS

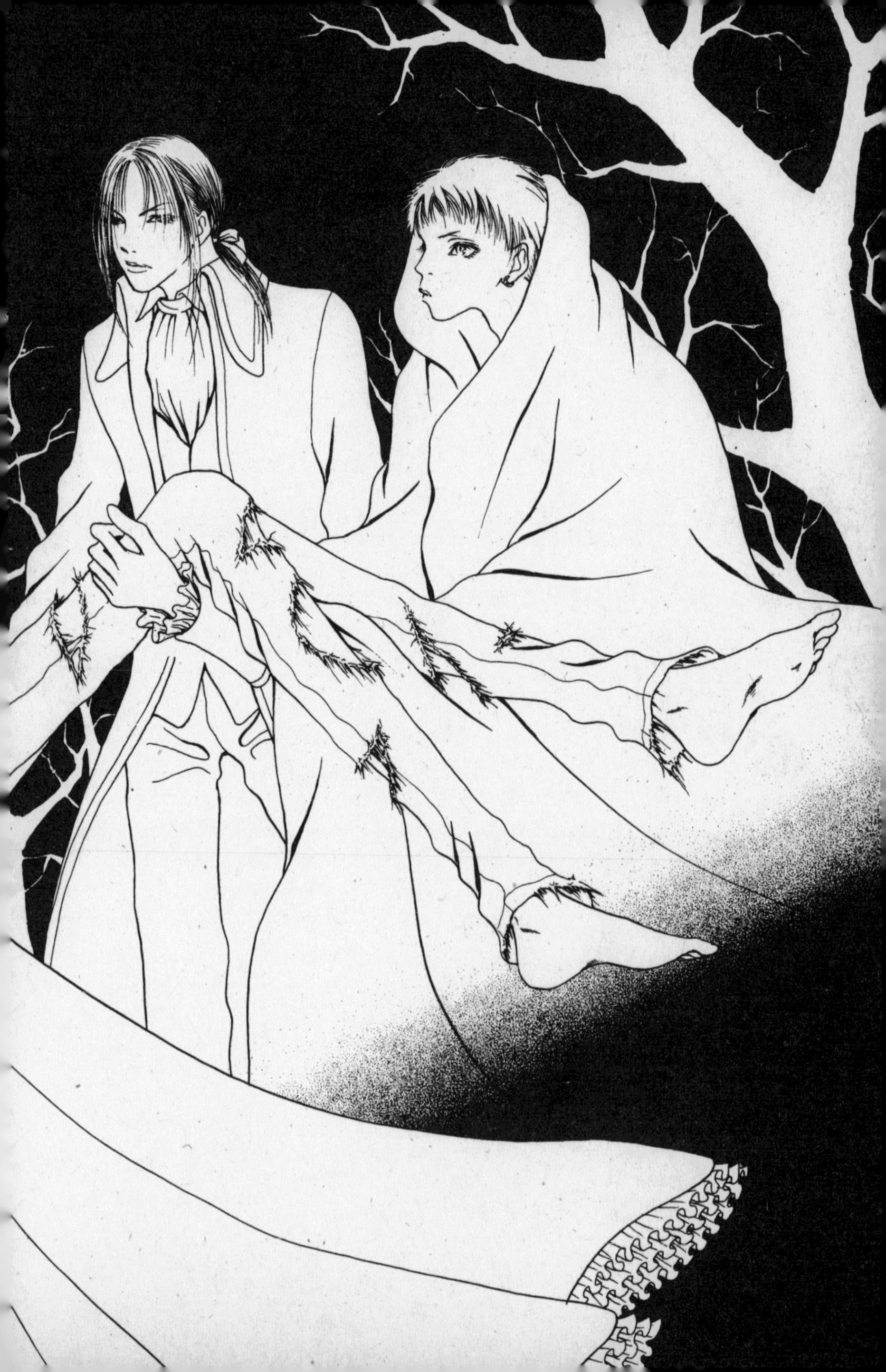

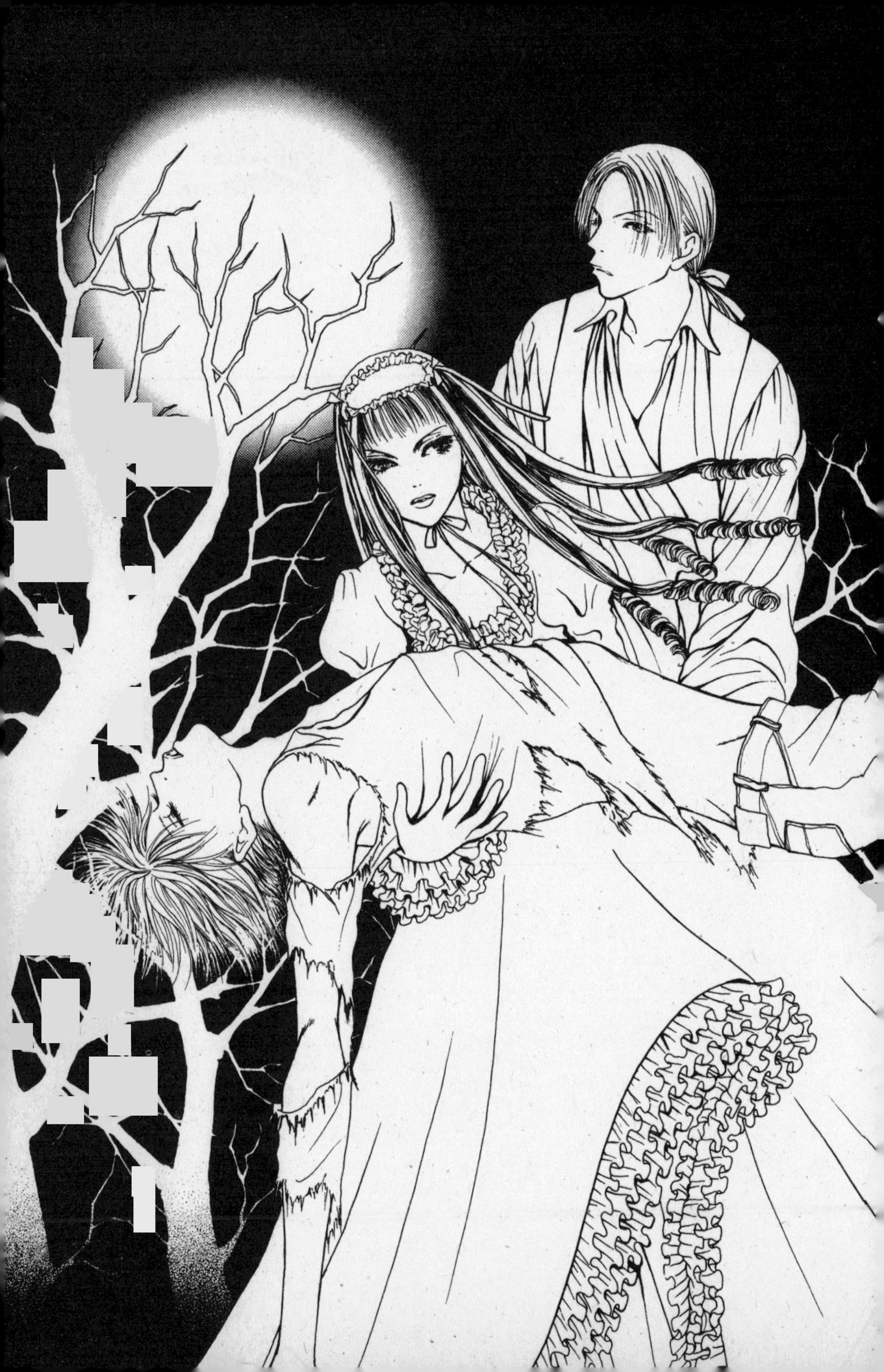

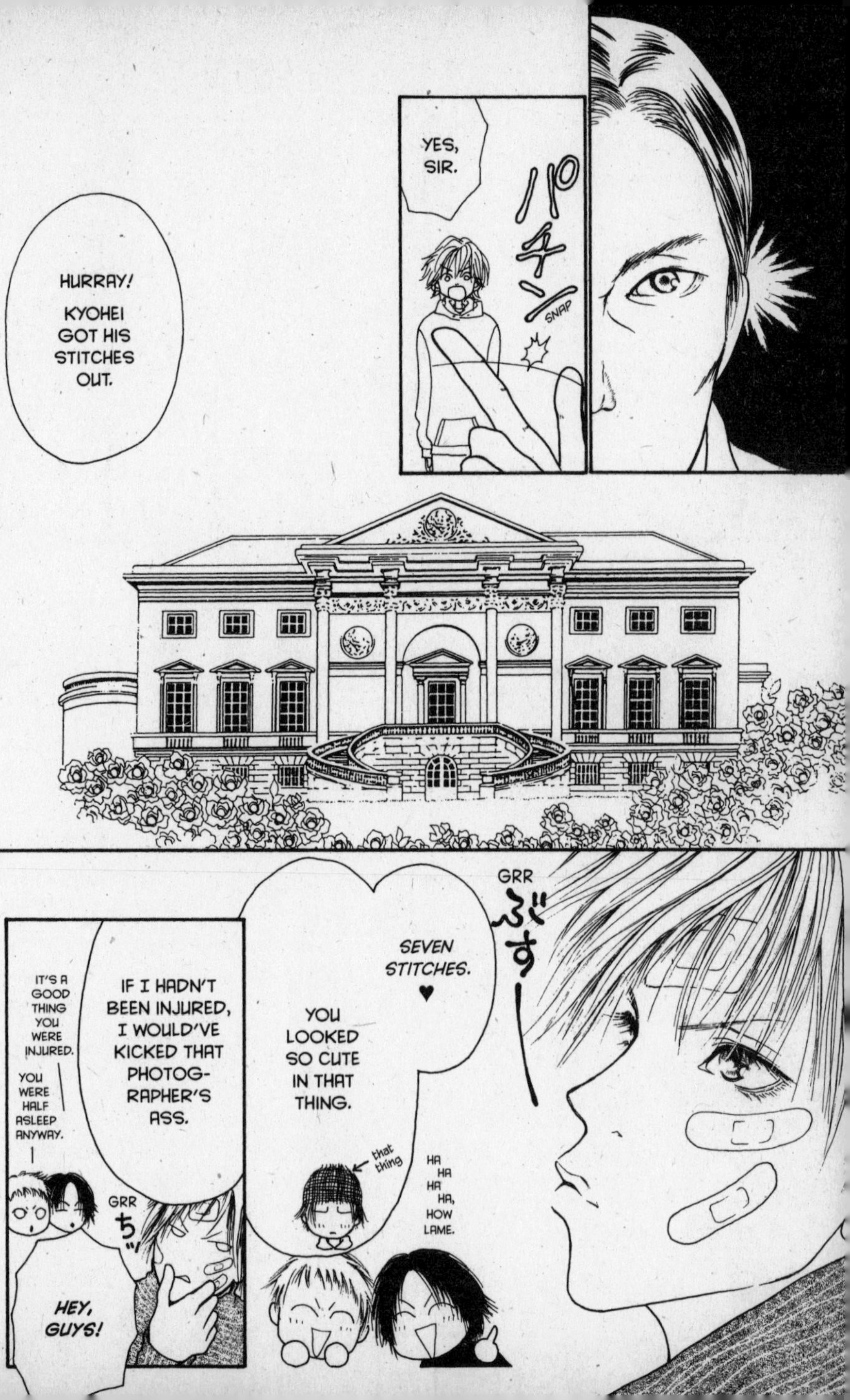
YES, SIR.
パチン
SNAP
HURRAY! KYOHEI GOT HIS STITCHES OUT.
GRR
ぶすー
SEVEN STITCHES. ♥
YOU LOOKED SO CUTE IN THAT THING.
that thing
HA HA HA HA, HOW LAME.
IF I HADN'T BEEN INJURED, I WOULD'VE KICKED THAT PHOTOG-RAPHER'S ASS.
IT'S A GOOD THING YOU WERE INJURED.
YOU WERE HALF ASLEEP ANYWAY.
GRR
ちッ
HEY, GUYS!

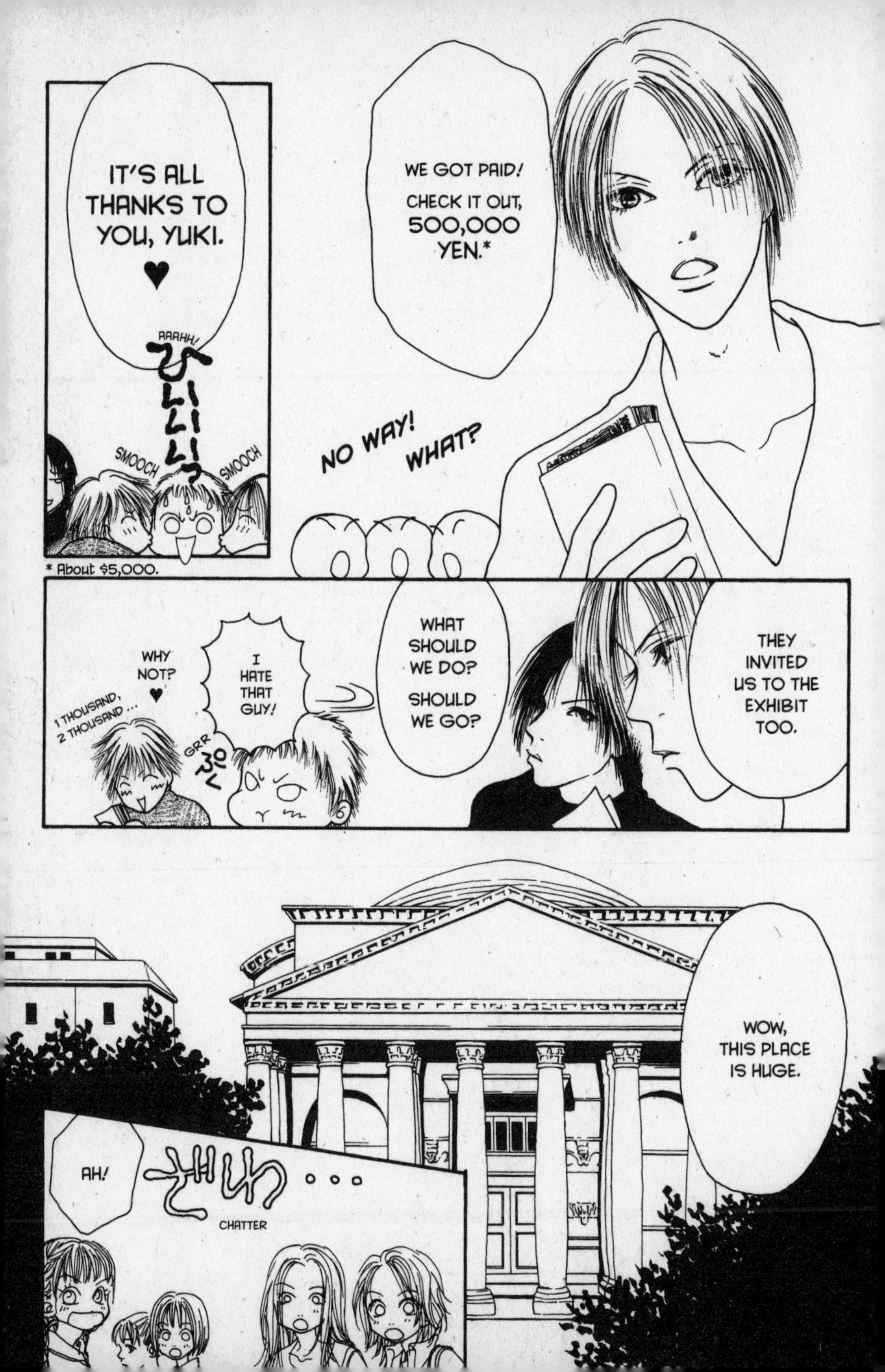
WE GOT PAID! CHECK IT OUT, 500,000 YEN.*
WHAT?
NO WAY!
IT'S ALL THANKS TO YOU, YUKI. ♥
AAAHH!
SMOOCH
SMOOCH
THEY INVITED US TO THE EXHIBIT TOO.
WHAT SHOULD WE DO? SHOULD WE GO?
I HATE THAT GUY!
GRR
WHY NOT? ♥
1 THOUSAND, 2 THOUSAND ...
WOW, THIS PLACE IS HUGE.
CHATTER
AH!

* About $5,000.

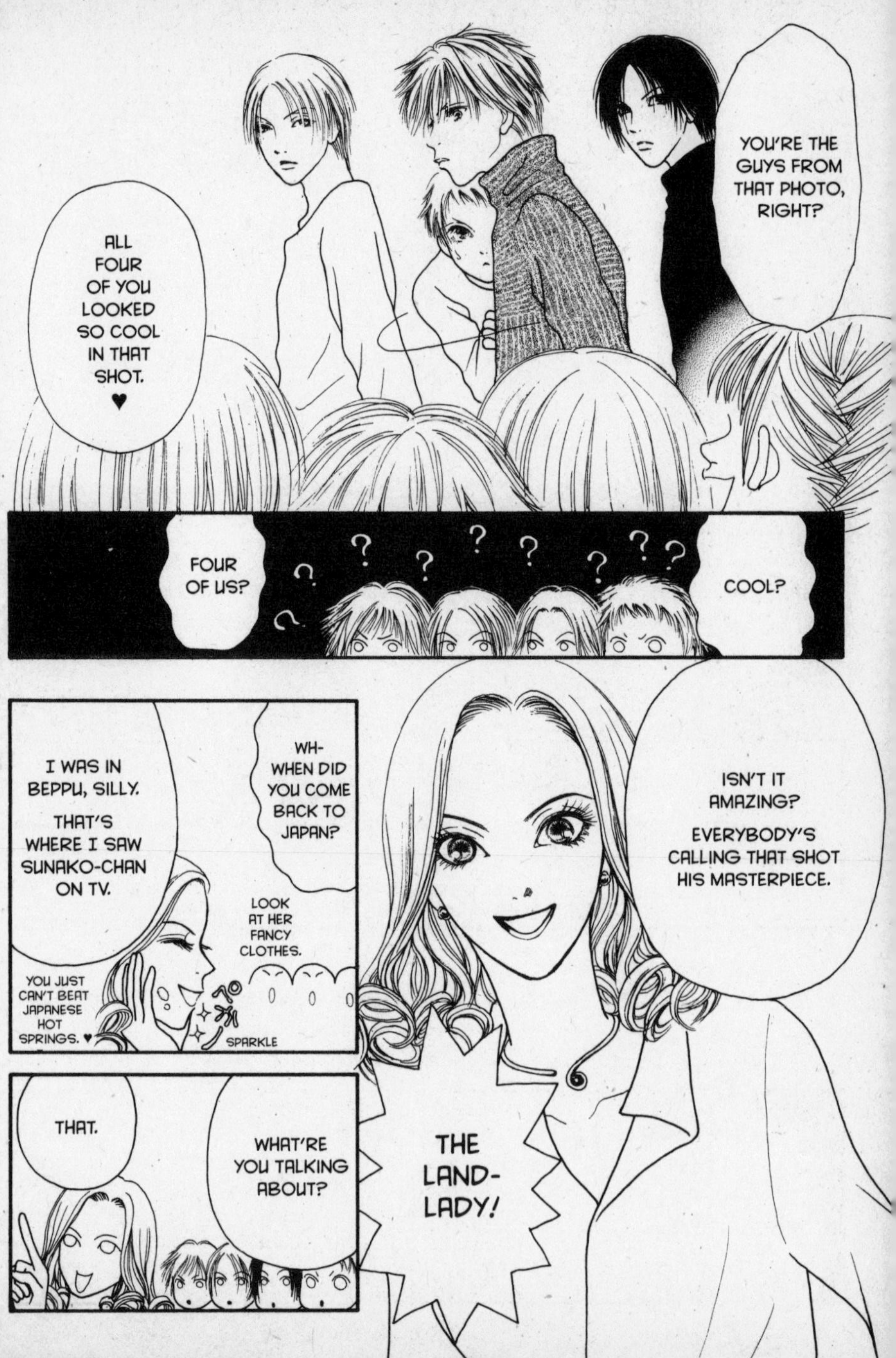
YOU'RE THE GUYS FROM THAT PHOTO, RIGHT?
ALL FOUR OF YOU LOOKED SO COOL IN THAT SHOT. ♥
COOL?
FOUR OF US?
ISN'T IT AMAZING? EVERYBODY'S CALLING THAT SHOT HIS MASTERPIECE.
THE LAND-LADY!
WH- WHEN DID YOU COME BACK TO JAPAN?
LOOK AT HER FANCY CLOTHES.
I WAS IN BEPPU, SILLY. THAT'S WHERE I SAW SUNAKO-CHAN ON TV.
YOU JUST CAN'T BEAT JAPANESE HOT SPRINGS. ♥
SPARKLE
WHAT'RE YOU TALKING ABOUT?
THAT.

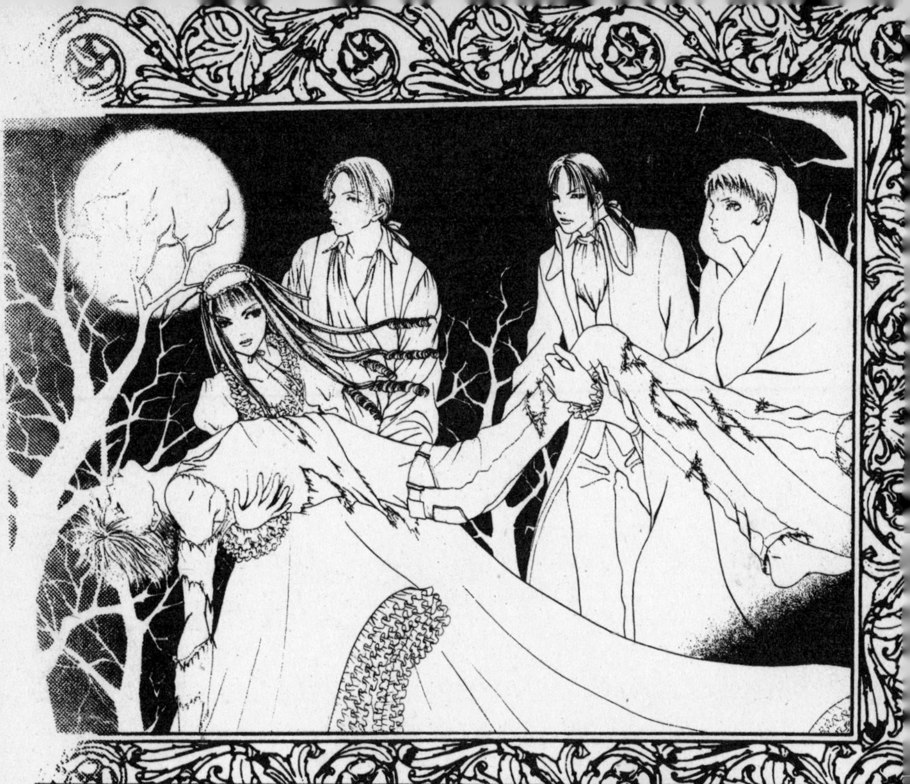

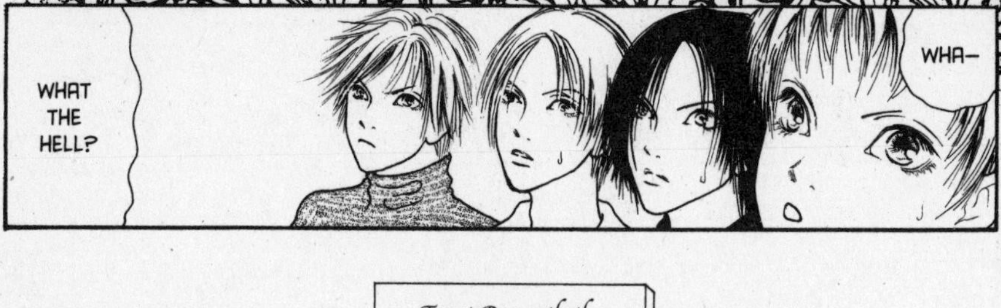
WHA-
WHAT THE HELL?

Feast Beneath the Moonlight

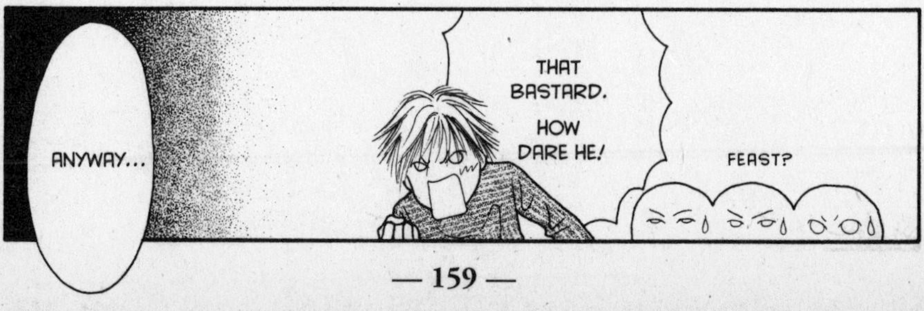
FEAST?
THAT BASTARD.
HOW DARE HE!
ANYWAY...

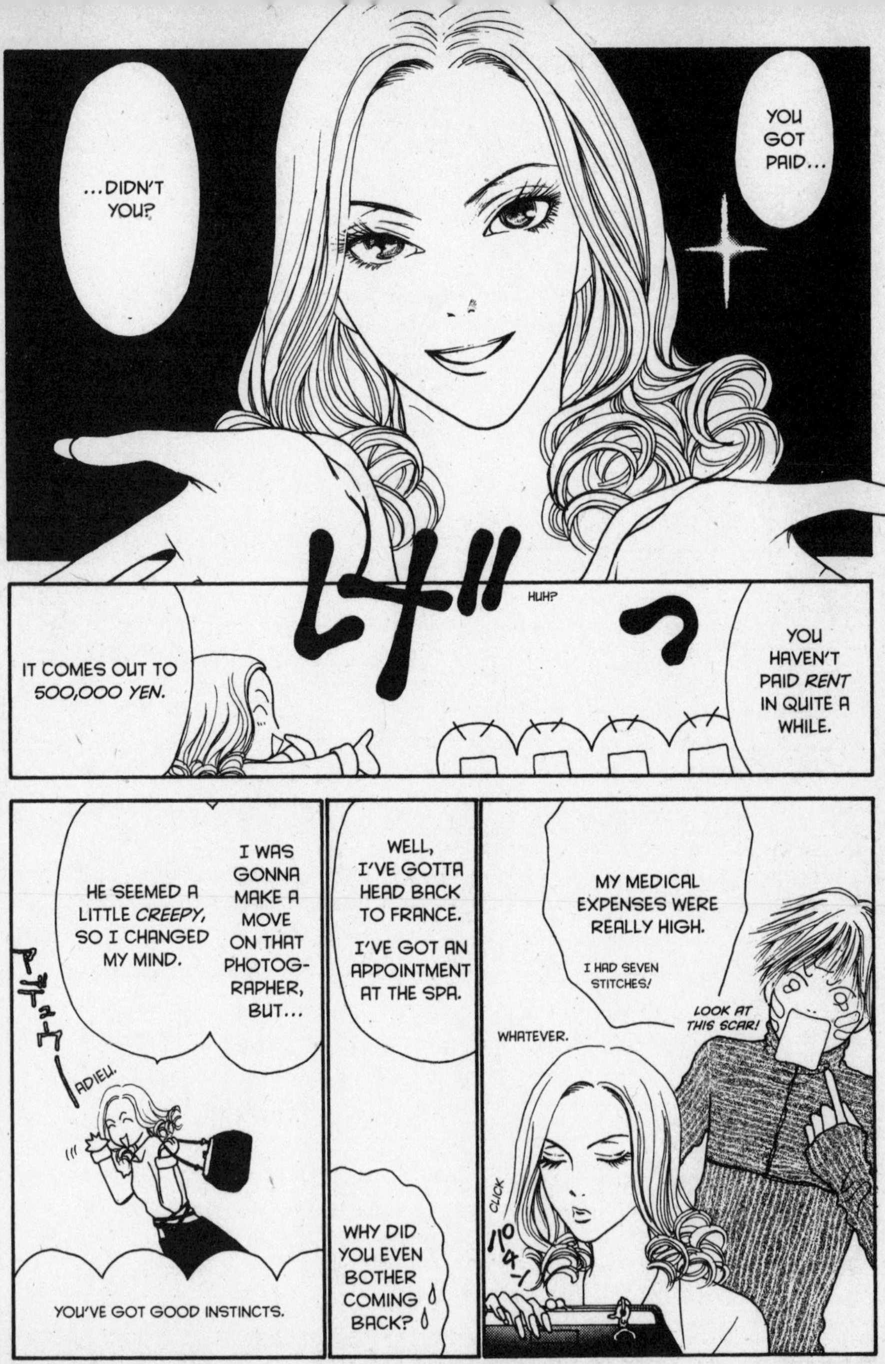

YOU GOT PAID...
...DIDN'T YOU?
YOU HAVEN'T PAID *RENT* IN QUITE A WHILE.
HUH?
IT COMES OUT TO *500,000 YEN.*
MY MEDICAL EXPENSES WERE REALLY HIGH.
I HAD SEVEN STITCHES!
LOOK AT THIS SCAR!
WHATEVER.
CLICK
WELL, I'VE GOTTA HEAD BACK TO FRANCE.
I'VE GOT AN APPOINTMENT AT THE SPA.
WHY DID YOU EVEN BOTHER COMING BACK?
I WAS GONNA MAKE A MOVE ON THAT PHOTOG-RAPHER, BUT...
HE SEEMED A LITTLE *CREEPY,* SO I CHANGED MY MIND.
ADIEU.
YOU'VE GOT GOOD INSTINCTS.

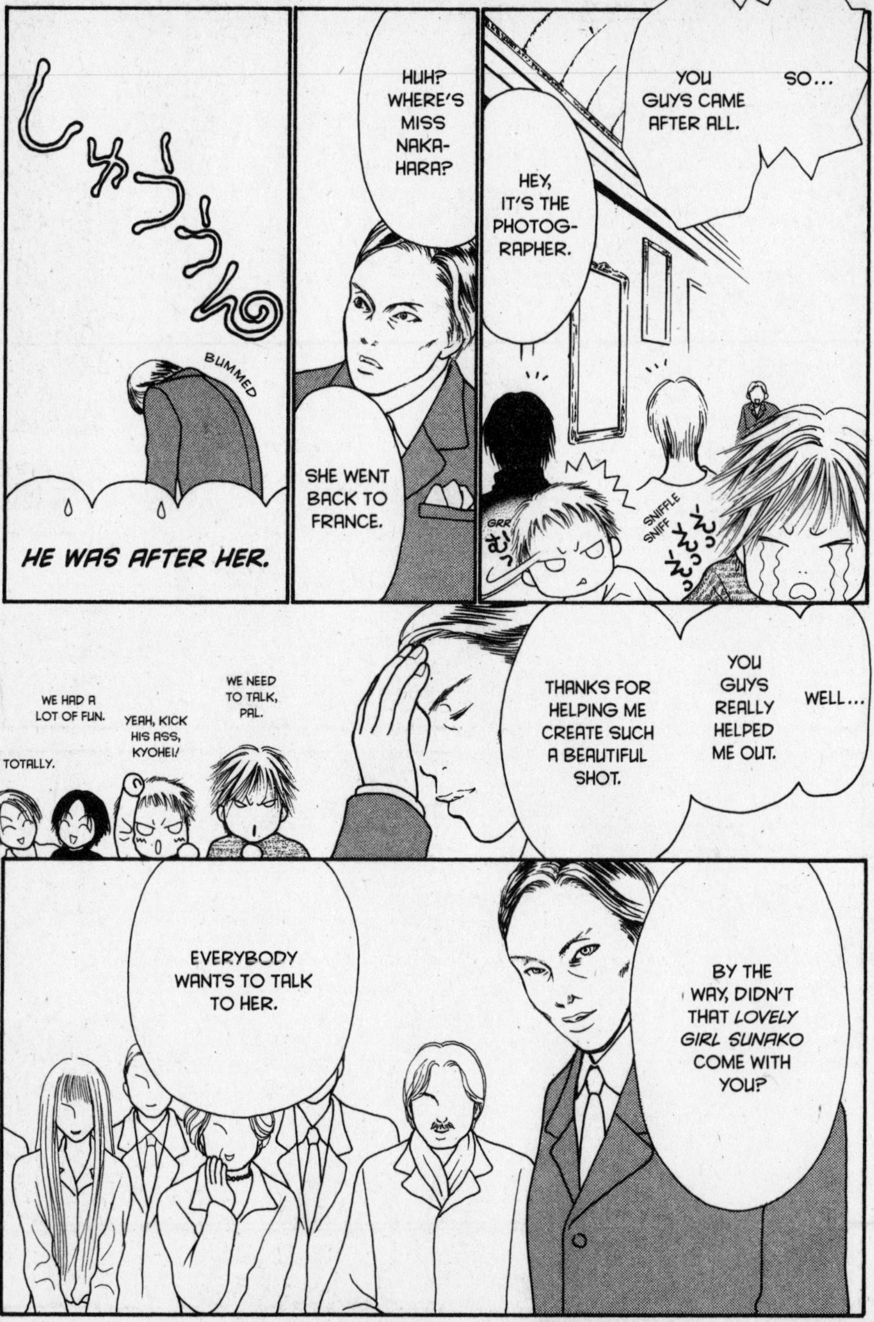
SO...
YOU GUYS CAME AFTER ALL.
HEY, IT'S THE PHOTOGRAPHER.
SNIFFLE SNIFF
えっえっえっ
GRR
むっ
HUH? WHERE'S MISS NAKA-HARA?
SHE WENT BACK TO FRANCE.
しゅううん
BUMMED
HE WAS AFTER HER.
WELL...
YOU GUYS REALLY HELPED ME OUT.
THANKS FOR HELPING ME CREATE SUCH A BEAUTIFUL SHOT.
WE NEED TO TALK, PAL.
YEAH, KICK HIS ASS, KYOHEI!
WE HAD A LOT OF FUN.
TOTALLY.
BY THE WAY, DIDN'T THAT *LOVELY GIRL SUNAKO* COME WITH YOU?
EVERYBODY WANTS TO TALK TO HER.

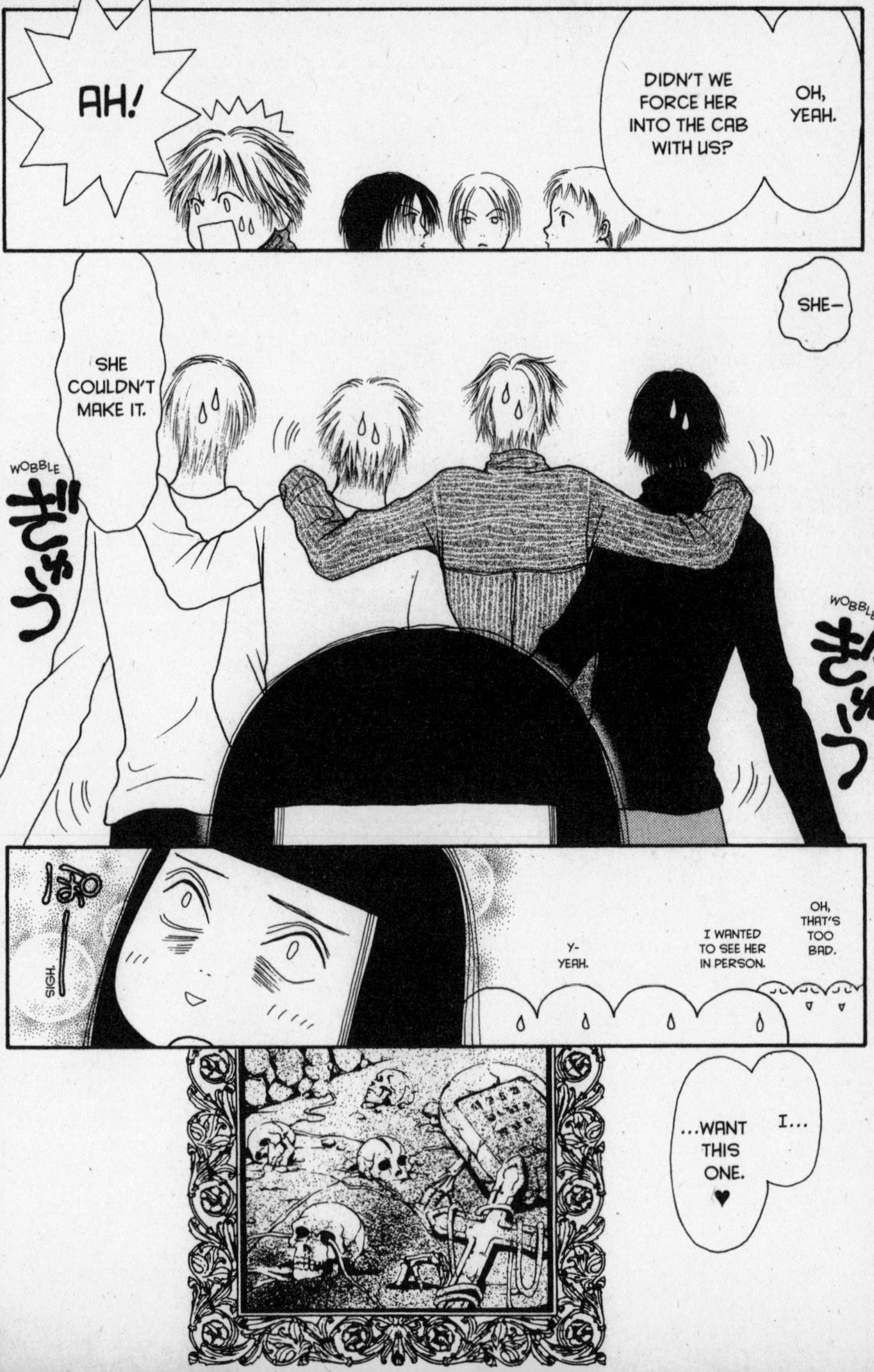
OH, YEAH.
DIDN'T WE FORCE HER INTO THE CAB WITH US?
AH!
SHE—
WOBBLE ぎゅう
SHE COULDN'T MAKE IT.
WOBBLE ぎゅう
OH, THAT'S TOO BAD.
I WANTED TO SEE HER IN PERSON.
Y-YEAH.
SIGH.
I...
...WANT THIS ONE. ♥

Chapter 14
I Am Number One!

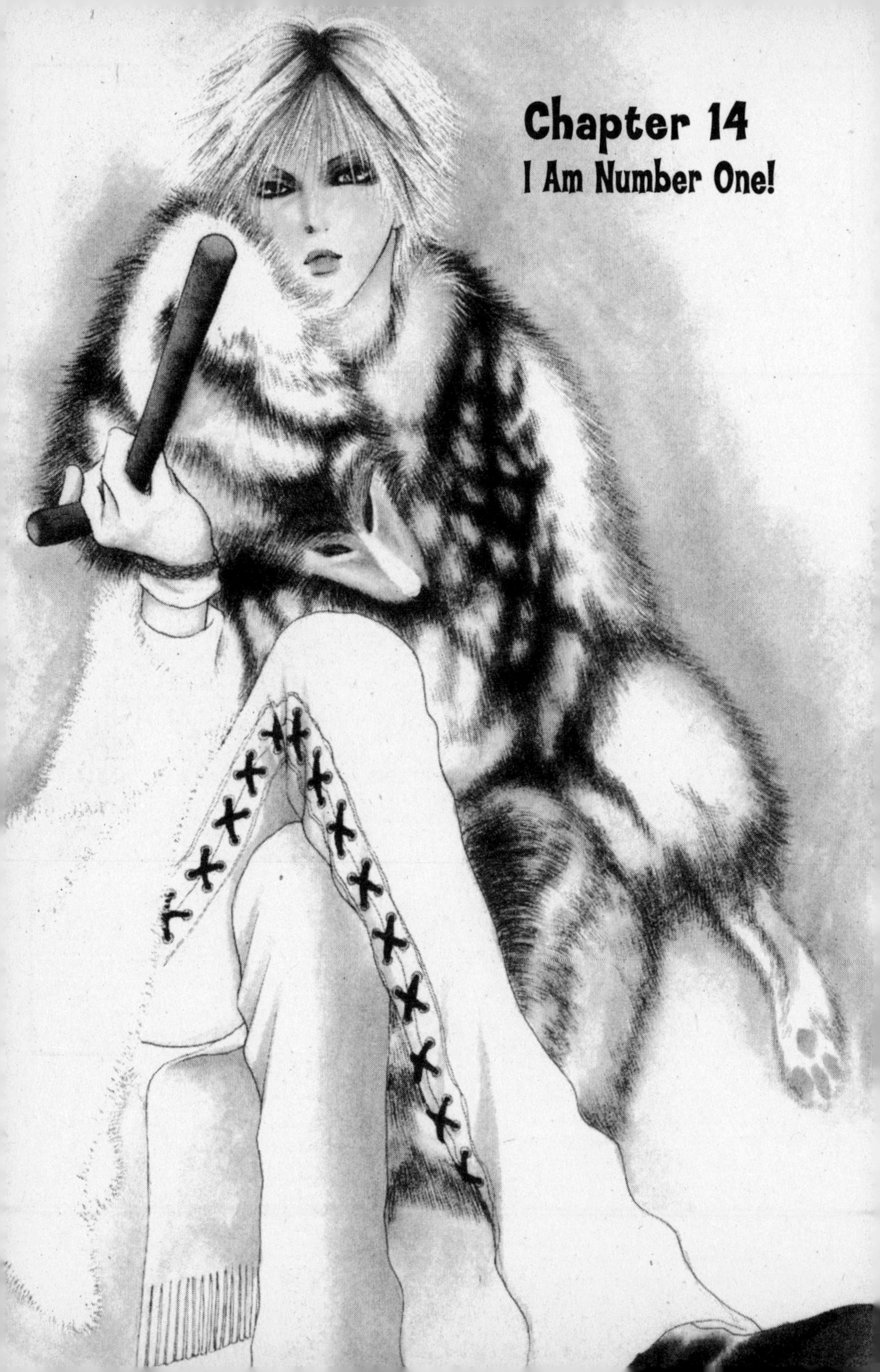

THANK YOU FOR BUYING KODANSHA COMICS.

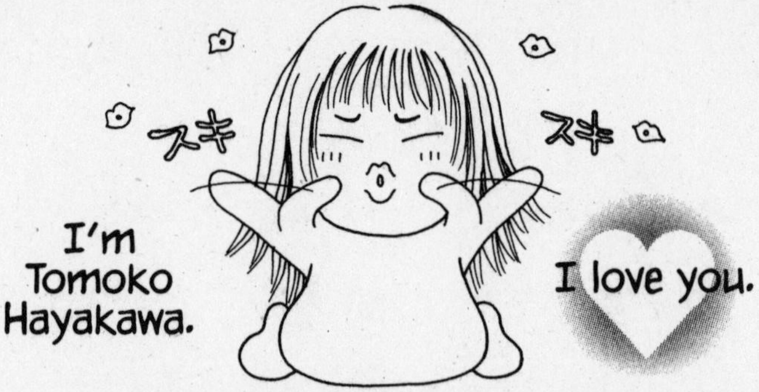

スキ
スキ
I'm Tomoko Hayakawa.
I love you.

THANKS TO EVERYBODY WHO WROTE ME. ♥

I KNOW, I KNOW, IT'S TAKING WAY TOO LONG FOR ME TO REPLY, BUT... PLEASE BE PATIENT.

THANKS TO EVERYBODY WHO SENT ME CLIPPINGS OF KIYOHARU-SAMA. ♥ ***I TREASURE THEM ALL.*** ♥

SOME OF YOU SENT ME CLIPPINGS AND WROTE, "SORRY IF YOU ALREADY HAVE THIS ONE." BUT PLEASE DON'T WORRY, SERIOUSLY, I CAN NEVER HAVE TOO MANY. I LIKE OLDER CLIPPINGS TOO. ♥

THANKS TO EVERYBODY WHO SENT ME **THE NIGHTMARE BEFORE CHRISTMAS** ***STUFF.*** ♥

I PUT ALL THAT STUFF NEXT TO MY FIGURINES. ♥ I HAVE SIX FIGURINES. I LOVE JACK. ♥ I HAVE THREE FIGURINES OF JACK DRESSED AS SANTA, AND I HAVE TWO SALLY FIGURINES. INCLUDING THE SALLYS, I ACTUALLY HAVE EIGHT FIGURINES.

IN BOOK 2, I SAID I WISH YOU ALL WOULD COMPARE THE FOUR GUYS TO BOY BANDS OR CELEBRITIES OR MOVIE STARS. I WAS REALLY HAPPY THAT SO MANY OF YOU TOLD ME WHO YOU THOUGHT THEY WERE BASED ON. A LOT OF YOU MENTIONED THE NAMES OF SOME REALLY HOT GUYS THAT I LIKE, SUCH AS YUUKI OBARA-KUN AND KUBOZUKA-KUN. I WAS KIND OF SURPRISED. (EVEN THOUGH SOME OF THEM DIDN'T EVEN LOOK LIKE MY CHARACTERS.) . . . BUT PEOPLE ARE STILL COMPARING "YUKINOJO" TO THE BASSIST OF A "CERTAIN" POPULAR BAND.

OH, YEAH. ONE OF MY FRIENDS TOLD ME ABOUT THIS WEBPAGE WHERE SOME FANS OF A "CERTAIN" BAND POSTED AN ANGRY MESSAGE SAYING, "WHEN SHE SAYS YUKI IS BASED ON A GUY FROM A 'CERTAIN' POPULAR BAND, SHE'D BETTER NOT BE TALKING ABOUT OUR FAVORITE BAND." I WAS SHOCKED. I SAID THEY WERE REALLY "POPULAR." WHAT'S THEIR PROBLEM?

I'VE SAID THIS BEFORE, BUT THEY'RE NOT MODELED ON ANYONE FAMOUS. I MADE THEM UP. I'M SORRY TO HAVE TO BE THE ONE TO DESTROY YOUR DREAMS.

LATELY, I'VE BEEN GETTING A LOT OF COSPLAY PICTURES IN THE MAIL, AND IT MAKES ME REALLY HAPPY. (BUT THERE WEREN'T ANY OF KIYOHARU. I GUESS GIRLS CAN'T DRESS AS KIYOHARU.) I'VE BEEN LUCKY TO GET LETTERS FROM A LOT OF MUSIC FANS, EVEN THOUGH I'M JUST WRITING A REGULAR MANGA ABOUT SCHOOL KIDS.

I'M ALSO REALLY HAPPY TO GET PICTURES OF ALL YOU GOTHS OUT THERE. ♥ I HARDLY EVER WEAR IT, BUT I LOVE GOTH FASHION. HOORAY FOR ALL THE GOTH GIRLS. ♥

I WAS AMAZED THAT SOME OF YOU GUESSED THAT I'M A GAULTIER FAN. YOU'RE RIGHT.

* OF COURSE, I LOVE ALL THE LETTERS I GET FROM EVERYONE.

YOUR LETTERS ARE THE SOURCE OF MY STRENGTH. THANK YOU SO MUCH. ♥

KNOCK
コン
KNOCK
コン
SUNAKO-CHAN.
MAKE US SOME DINNER–
CLICK
ガチャ

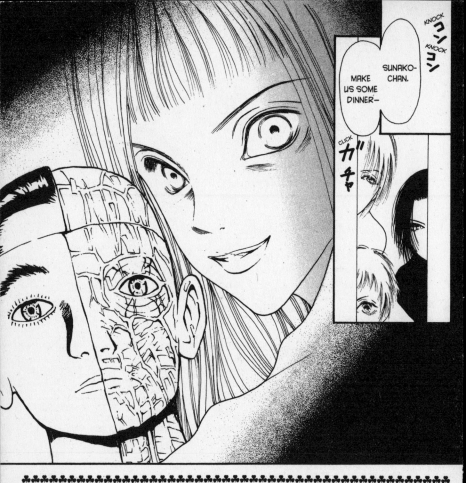

BEHIND THE SCENES

I BARELY FINISHED THIS STORY ON TIME. I JUST COULDN'T GET THE STORYBOARDS RIGHT. (AS ALWAYS.) WHEN I START INKING, MY CARPAL TUNNEL ACTS UP... I'M A MESS. I WAS PLANNING ON DRAWING THE BOSS MYSELF, BUT I ENDED UP HAVING SOMEONE ELSE DO IT. (A REAL GENIUS DID IT.) I REALLY WANTED TO MAKE HIM A '70S STYLE MOBSTER, BUT THE GENIUS WAS BETTER AT DRAWING '80S STYLE MOBSTERS. (BUT HE'S A '70S STYLE MOBSTER ON THE INSIDE.)

BY THE WAY, KYOHEI IS LOSING WAY TOO MUCH BLOOD. HE'S GOTTEN ALL BLOODY TWICE IN A ROW. IF THIS WEREN'T MANGA, HE'D BE DEAD BY NOW.

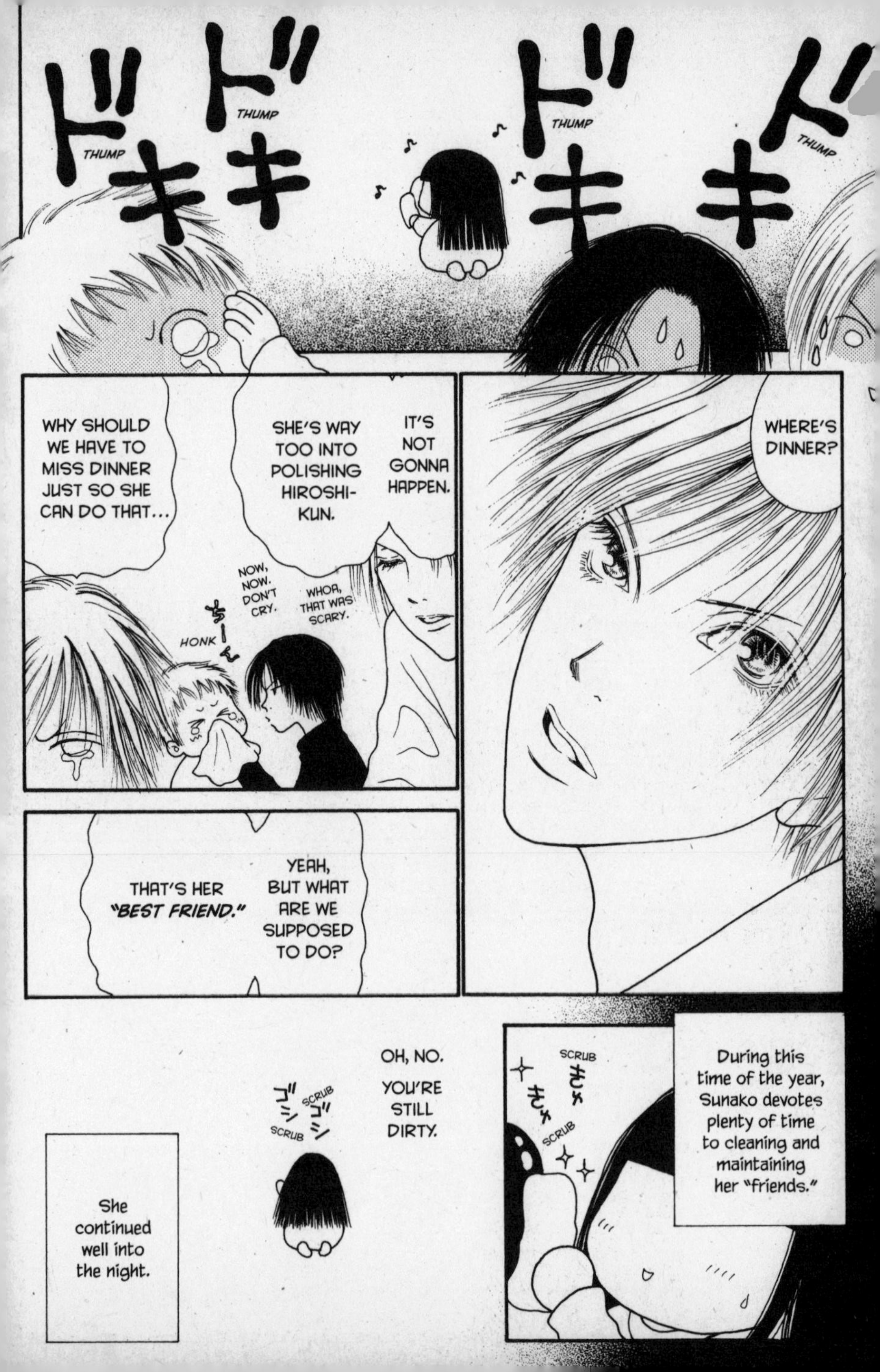
ドキドキ
THUMP
THUMP
ドキドキ
THUMP
THUMP
WHERE'S DINNER?
IT'S NOT GONNA HAPPEN.
SHE'S WAY TOO INTO POLISHING HIROSHI-KUN.
WHY SHOULD WE HAVE TO MISS DINNER JUST SO SHE CAN DO THAT…
WHOA, THAT WAS SCARY.
NOW, NOW. DON'T CRY.
HONK
YEAH, BUT WHAT ARE WE SUPPOSED TO DO?
THAT'S HER *"BEST FRIEND."*
During this time of the year, Sunako devotes plenty of time to cleaning and maintaining her "friends."
SCRUB
SCRUB
OH, NO.
YOU'RE STILL DIRTY.
ゴシゴシ
SCRUB
SCRUB
She continued well into the night.

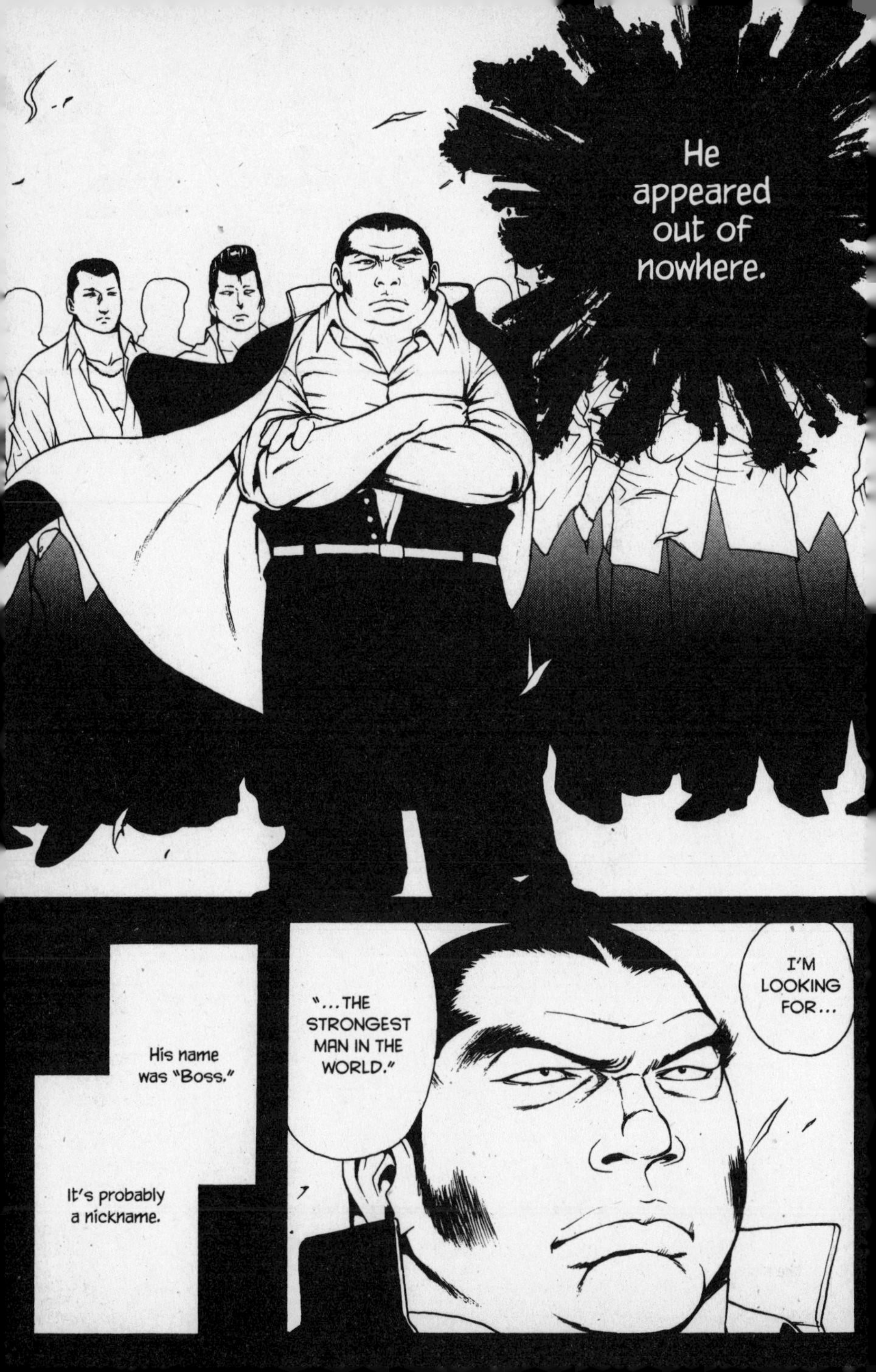
He appeared out of nowhere.
I'M LOOKING FOR...
"...THE STRONGEST MAN IN THE WORLD."
His name was "Boss."
It's probably a nickname.

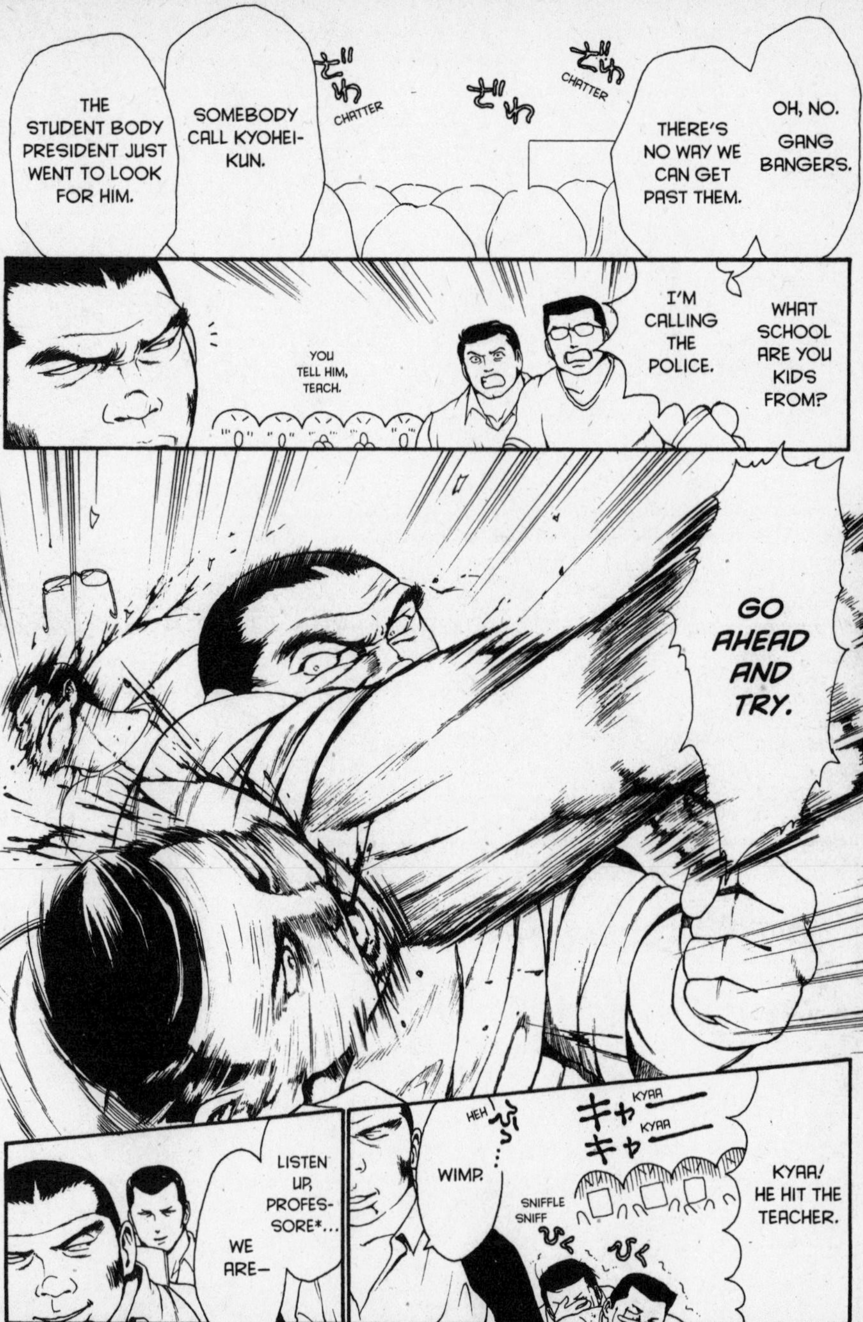
OH, NO.
GANG BANGERS.
THERE'S NO WAY WE CAN GET PAST THEM.
CHATTER
CHATTER
SOMEBODY CALL KYOHEI-KUN.
THE STUDENT BODY PRESIDENT JUST WENT TO LOOK FOR HIM.
WHAT SCHOOL ARE YOU KIDS FROM?
I'M CALLING THE POLICE.
YOU TELL HIM, TEACH.
GO AHEAD AND TRY.
KYAA! HE HIT THE TEACHER.
KYAA
KYAA
HEH
WIMP.
SNIFFLE
SNIFF
LISTEN UP, PROFES-SORE*...
WE ARE—

*The Boss speaks his own language.

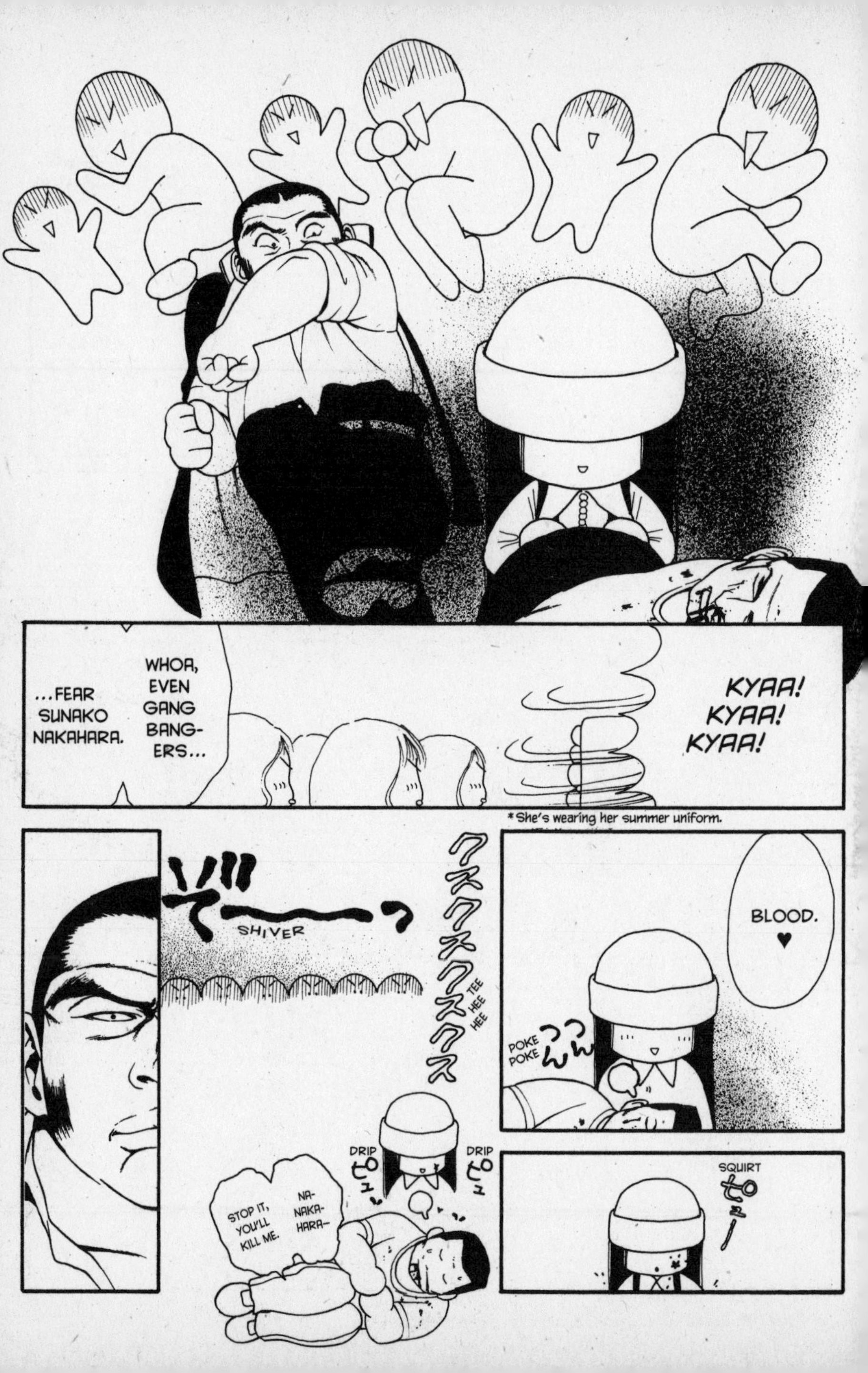
KYAA! KYAA! KYAA!
WHOA, EVEN GANG BANG- ERS...
...FEAR SUNAKO NAKAHARA.
* She's wearing her summer uniform.
BLOOD. ♥
POKE POKE つんつん
SQUIRT ぴゅー
クスクスクスクス TEE HEE HEE
DRIP ぴュ
DRIP ぴュ
NA- NAKA- HARA—
STOP IT, YOU'LL KILL ME.
ゾ
ぞーっ SHIVER

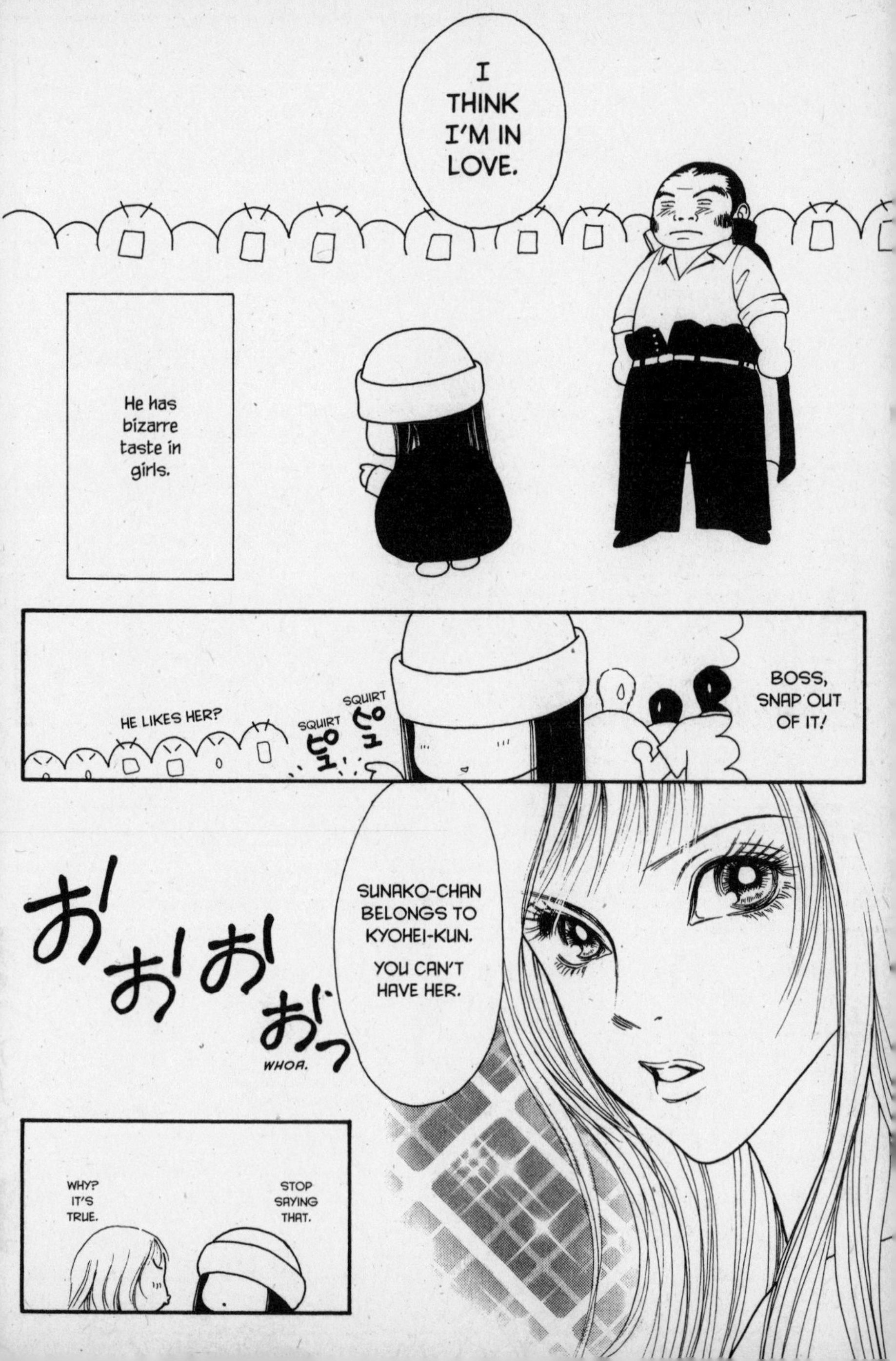
I THINK I'M IN LOVE.
He has bizarre taste in girls.
BOSS, SNAP OUT OF IT!
ピュ
SQUIRT
ピュ
SQUIRT
HE LIKES HER?
SUNAKO-CHAN BELONGS TO KYOHEI-KUN.
YOU CAN'T HAVE HER.
おおおおっ
WHOA.
STOP SAYING THAT.
WHY? IT'S TRUE.

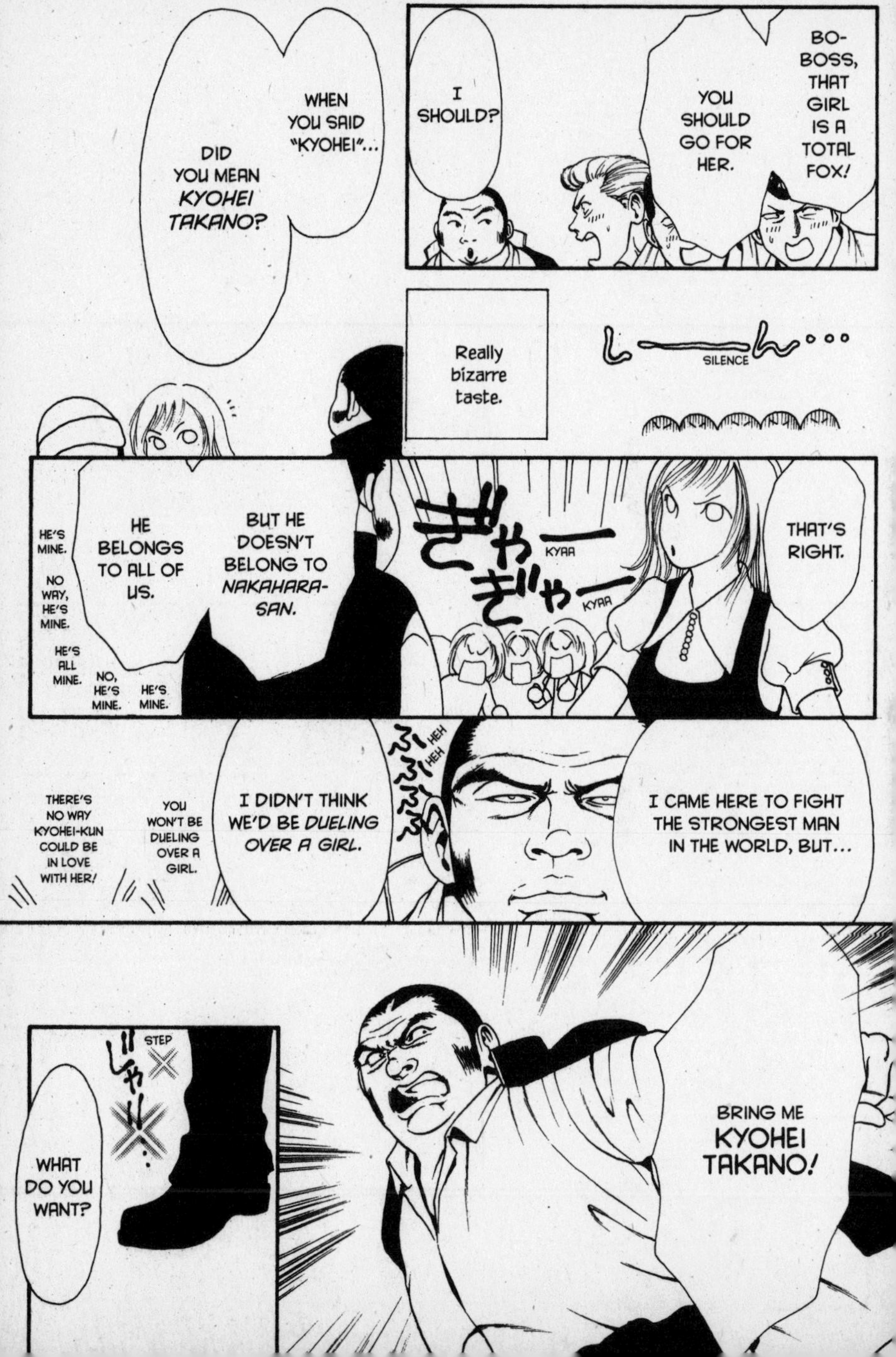
BO-BOSS, THAT GIRL IS A TOTAL FOX!
YOU SHOULD GO FOR HER.
I SHOULD?
WHEN YOU SAID "KYOHEI"...
DID YOU MEAN KYOHEI TAKANO?
しーーん… SILENCE
Really bizarre taste.
THAT'S RIGHT.
ぎゃー KYAA
ぎゃー KYAA
BUT HE DOESN'T BELONG TO NAKAHARA-SAN.
HE BELONGS TO ALL OF US.
HE'S MINE.
NO WAY, HE'S MINE.
HE'S ALL MINE.
NO, HE'S MINE.
HE'S MINE.
I CAME HERE TO FIGHT THE STRONGEST MAN IN THE WORLD, BUT...
ふふふふ HEH HEH
I DIDN'T THINK WE'D BE DUELING OVER A GIRL.
YOU WON'T BE DUELING OVER A GIRL.
THERE'S NO WAY KYOHEI-KUN COULD BE IN LOVE WITH HER!
BRING ME KYOHEI TAKANO!
じゃり… STEP
WHAT DO YOU WANT?

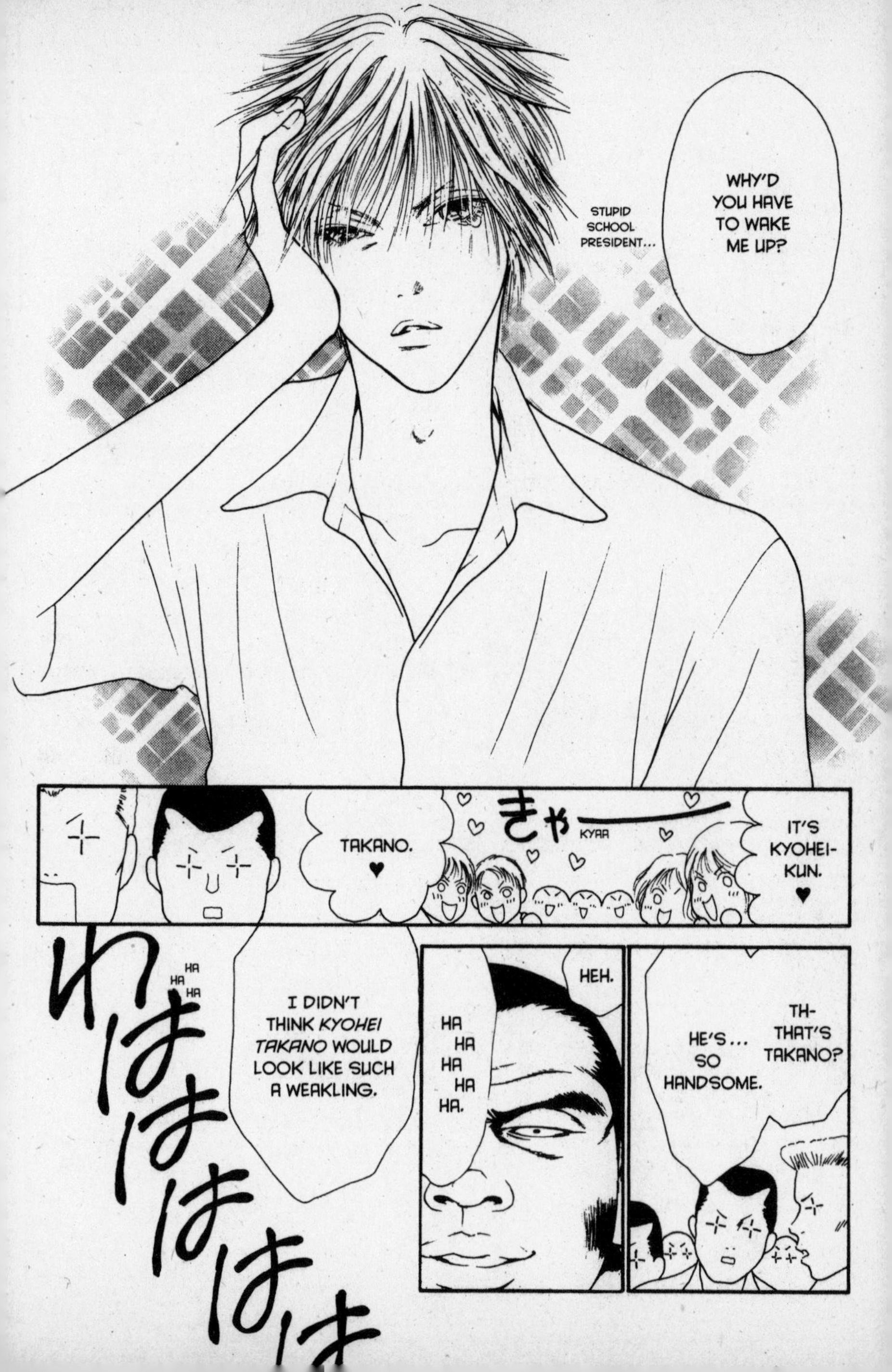
WHY'D YOU HAVE TO WAKE ME UP?
STUPID SCHOOL PRESIDENT...
IT'S KYOHEI-KUN. ♥
きゃー
KYAA
TAKANO. ♥
TH-THAT'S TAKANO?
HE'S... SO HANDSOME.
HEH.
HA HA HA HA HA.
I DIDN'T THINK *KYOHEI TAKANO* WOULD LOOK LIKE SUCH A WEAKLING.
わはははは
HA HA HA

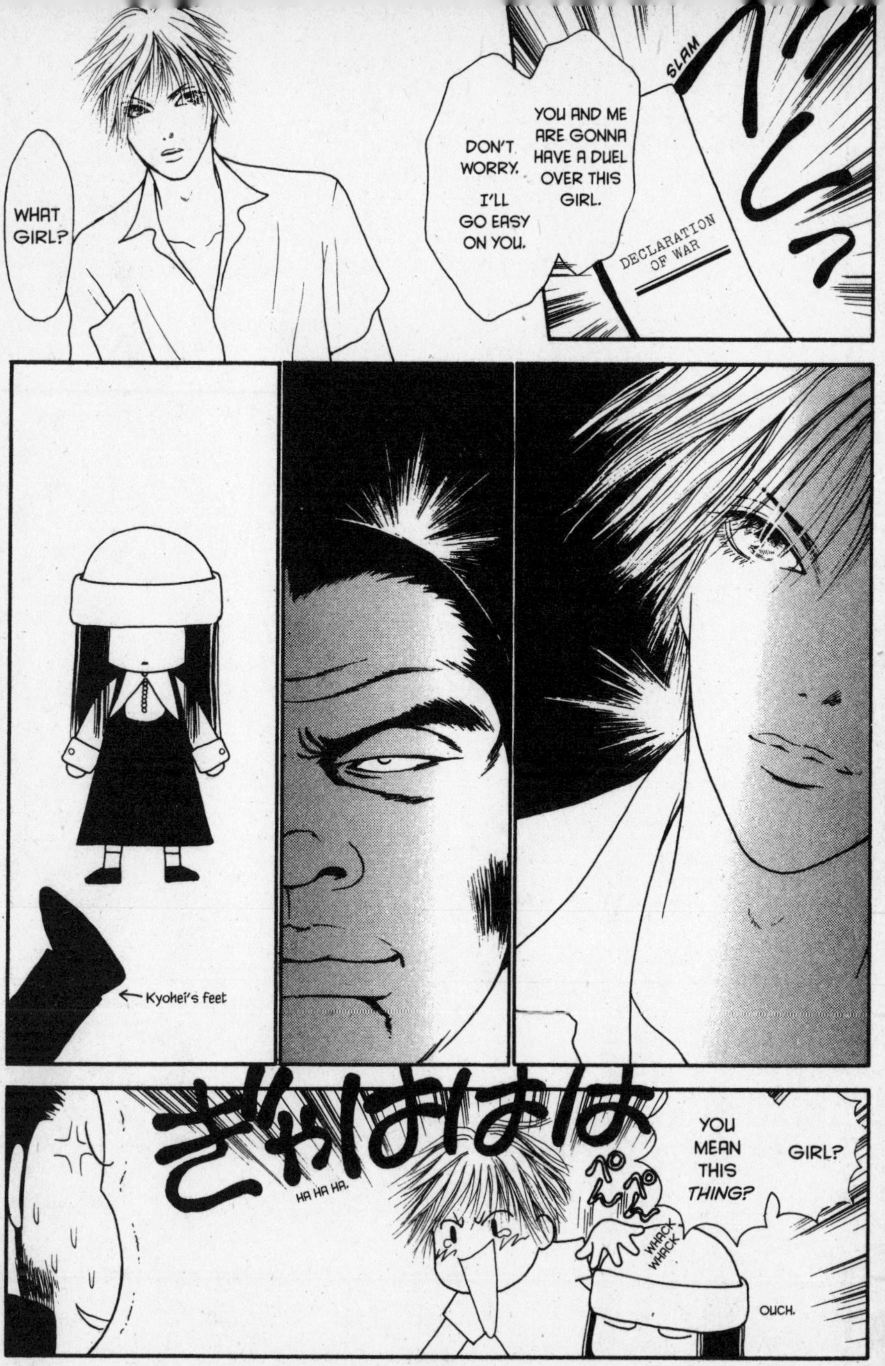
SLAM
DECLARATION OF WAR
YOU AND ME ARE GONNA HAVE A DUEL OVER THIS GIRL.
DON'T WORRY. I'LL GO EASY ON YOU.
WHAT GIRL?
Kyohei's feet
GIRL?
YOU MEAN THIS *THING*?
きゃははは
HA HA HA.
WHACK WHACK
OUCH.

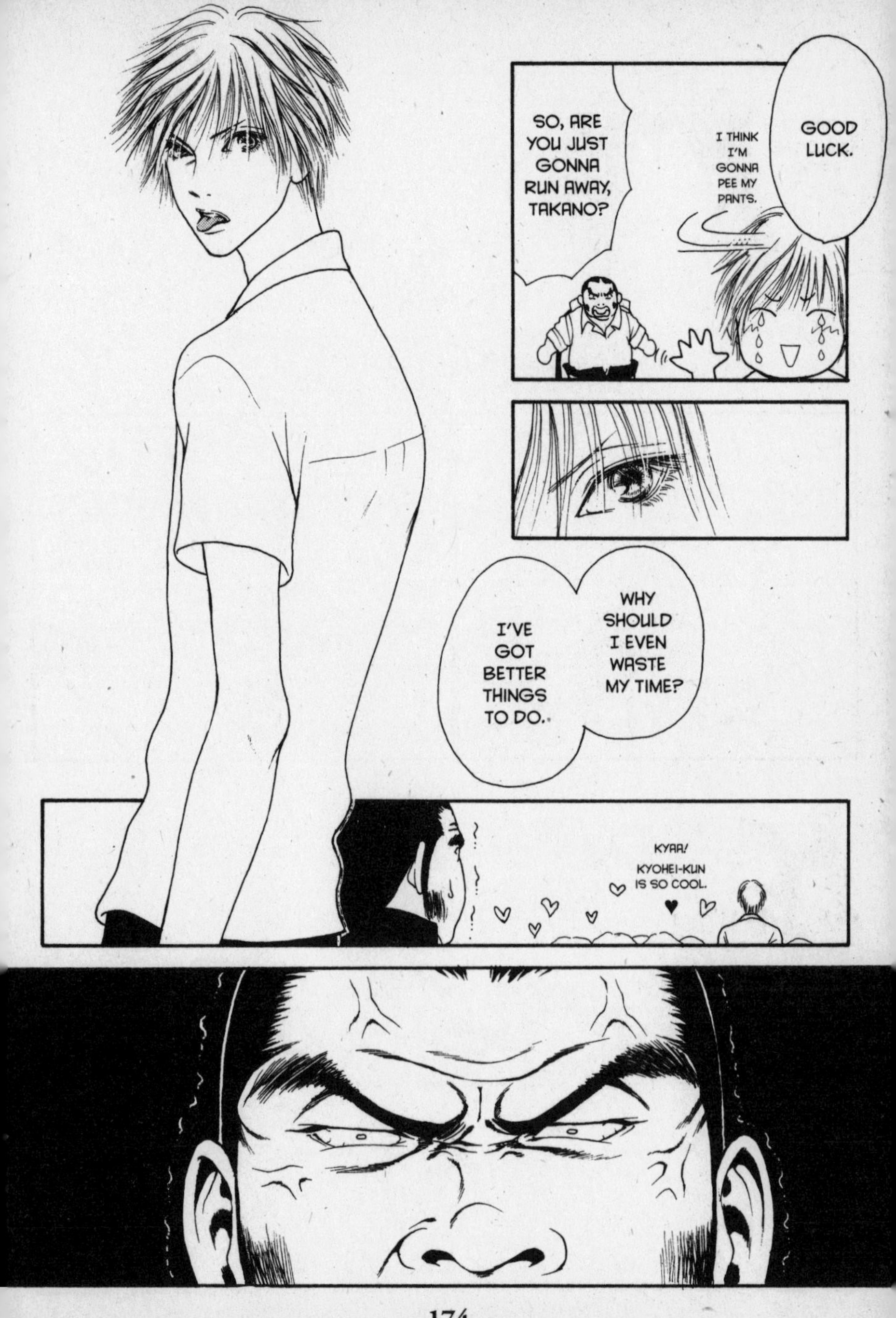
GOOD LUCK.
I THINK I'M GONNA PEE MY PANTS.
SO, ARE YOU JUST GONNA RUN AWAY, TAKANO?
WHY SHOULD I EVEN WASTE MY TIME?
I'VE GOT BETTER THINGS TO DO.
KYAA! KYOHEI-KUN IS SO COOL.

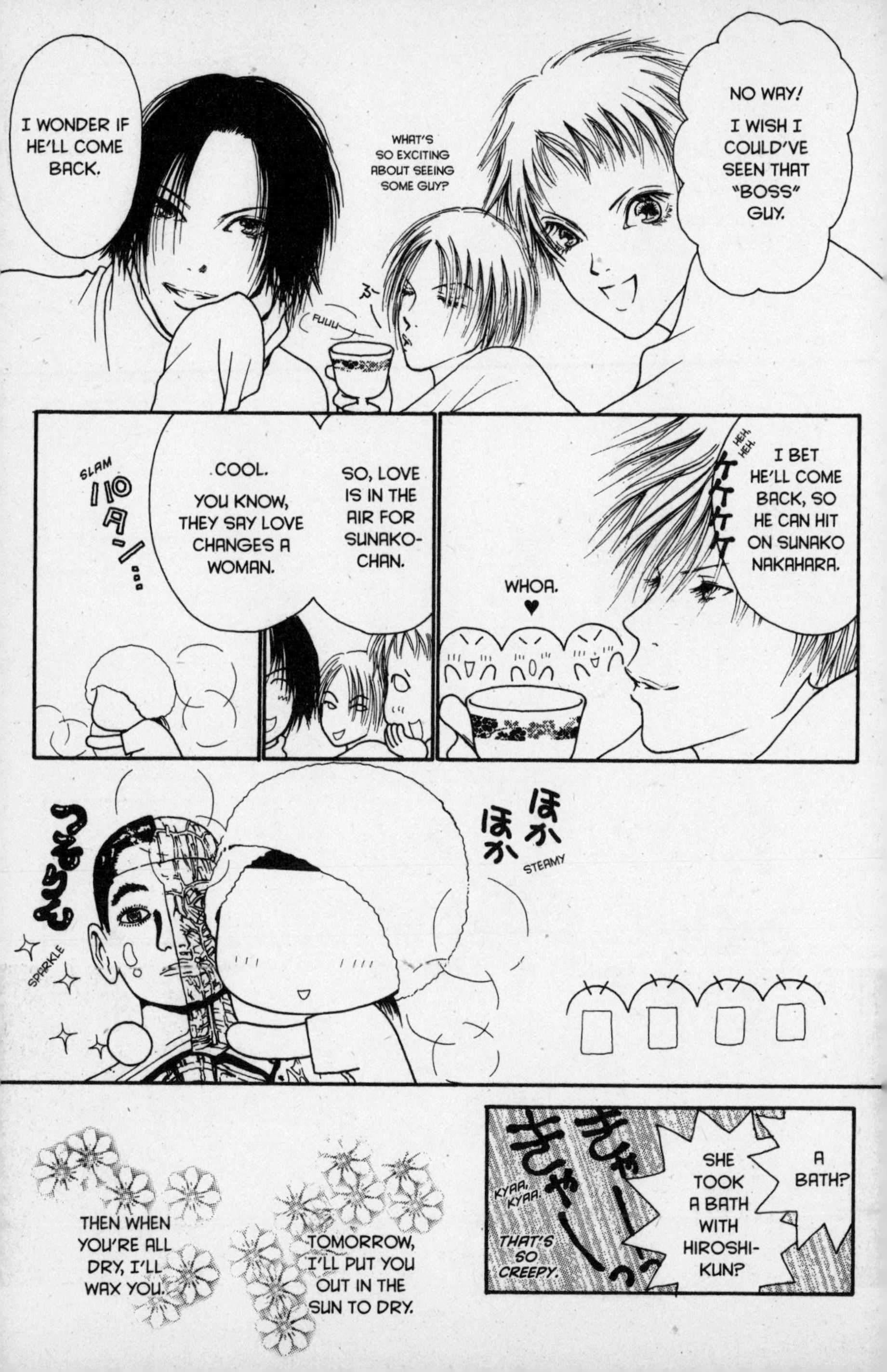
NO WAY! I WISH I COULD'VE SEEN THAT "BOSS" GUY.
WHAT'S SO EXCITING ABOUT SEEING SOME GUY?
FUUU
I WONDER IF HE'LL COME BACK.
HEH, HEH.
I BET HE'LL COME BACK, SO HE CAN HIT ON SUNAKO NAKAHARA.
WHOA. ♥
SO, LOVE IS IN THE AIR FOR SUNAKO-CHAN.
COOL. YOU KNOW, THEY SAY LOVE CHANGES A WOMAN.
SLAM
ほかほか
STEAMY
SPARKLE
A BATH?
SHE TOOK A BATH WITH HIROSHI-KUN?
KYAA, KYAA.
THAT'S SO CREEPY.
TOMORROW, I'LL PUT YOU OUT IN THE SUN TO DRY.
THEN WHEN YOU'RE ALL DRY, I'LL WAX YOU.

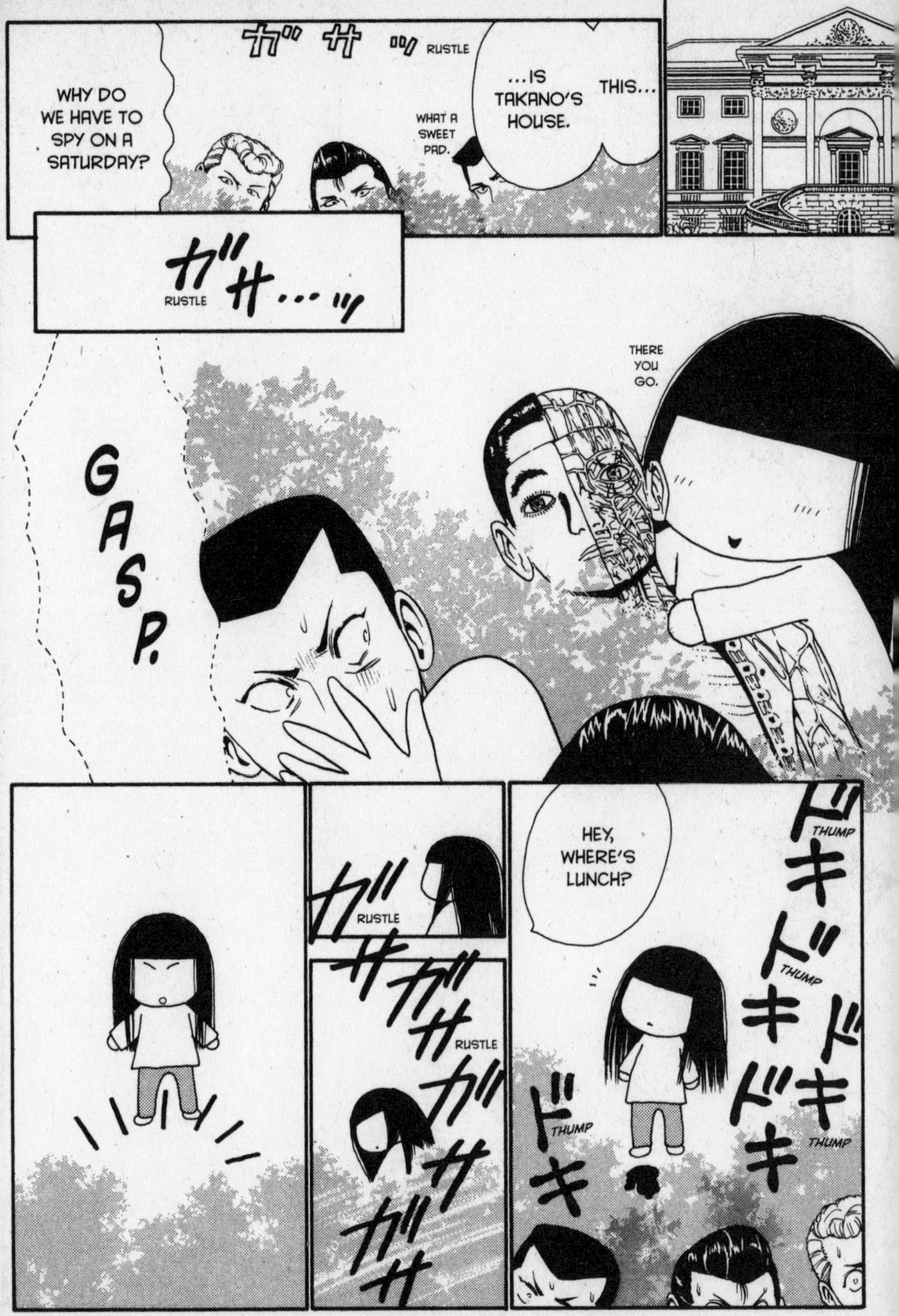
THIS...
...IS TAKANO'S HOUSE.
ガサッ
RUSTLE
WHAT A SWEET PAD.
WHY DO WE HAVE TO SPY ON A SATURDAY?
ガサ…ッ
RUSTLE
THERE YOU GO.
GASP.
ドキドキ
THUMP
THUMP
ドキドキ
THUMP
THUMP
ドキ
HEY, WHERE'S LUNCH?
ガ
RUSTLE
サガサ
RUSTLE
ガサガサ

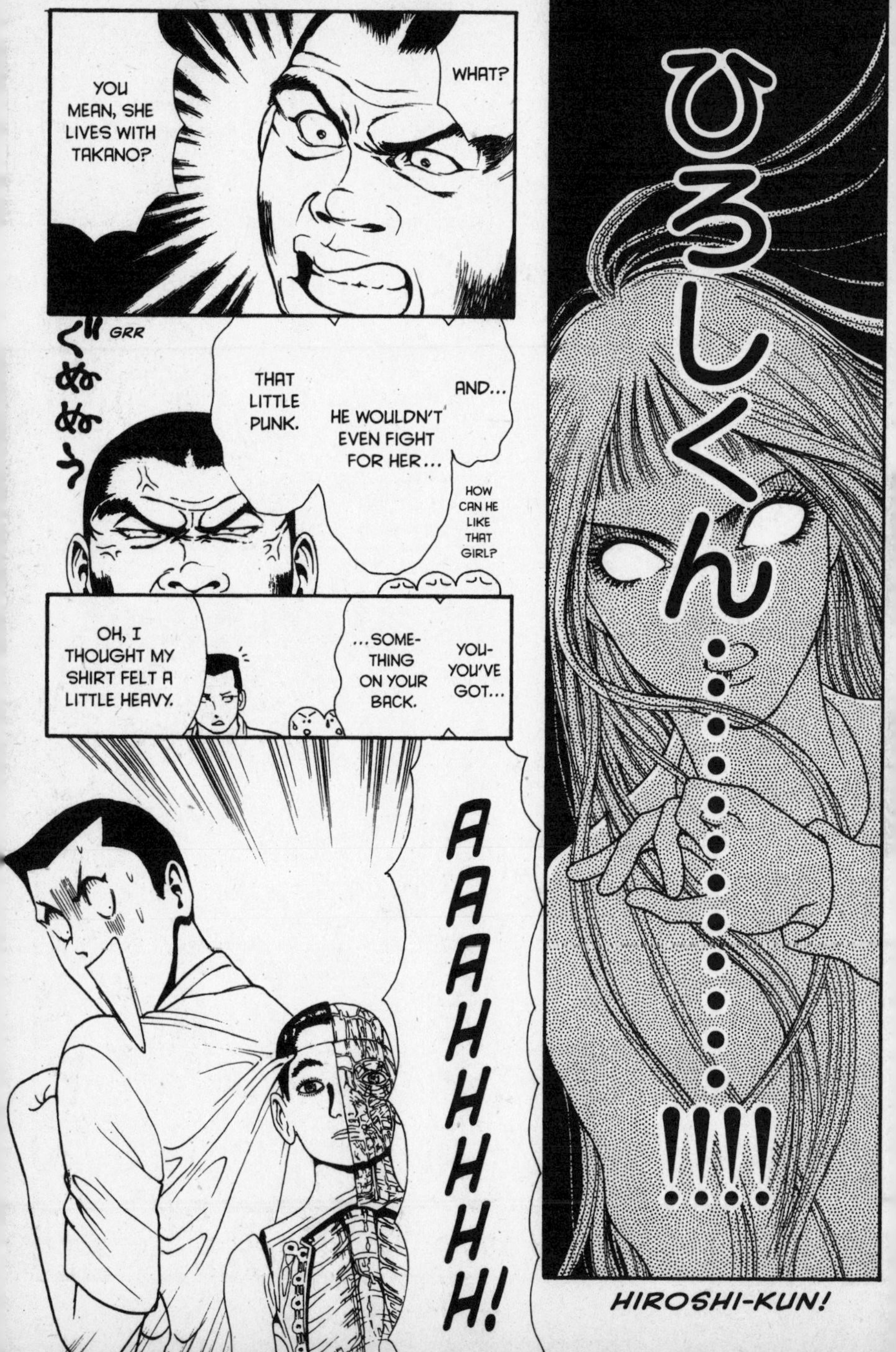
ひろしくん……!!!!
HIROSHI-KUN!
WHAT?
YOU MEAN, SHE LIVES WITH TAKANO?
AND... HE WOULDN'T EVEN FIGHT FOR HER...
THAT LITTLE PUNK.
HOW CAN HE LIKE THAT GIRL?
ぐぬぬぬっ
GRR
YOU-YOU'VE GOT...
...SOME-THING ON YOUR BACK.
OH, I THOUGHT MY SHIRT FELT A LITTLE HEAVY.
AAAHHHHHH!

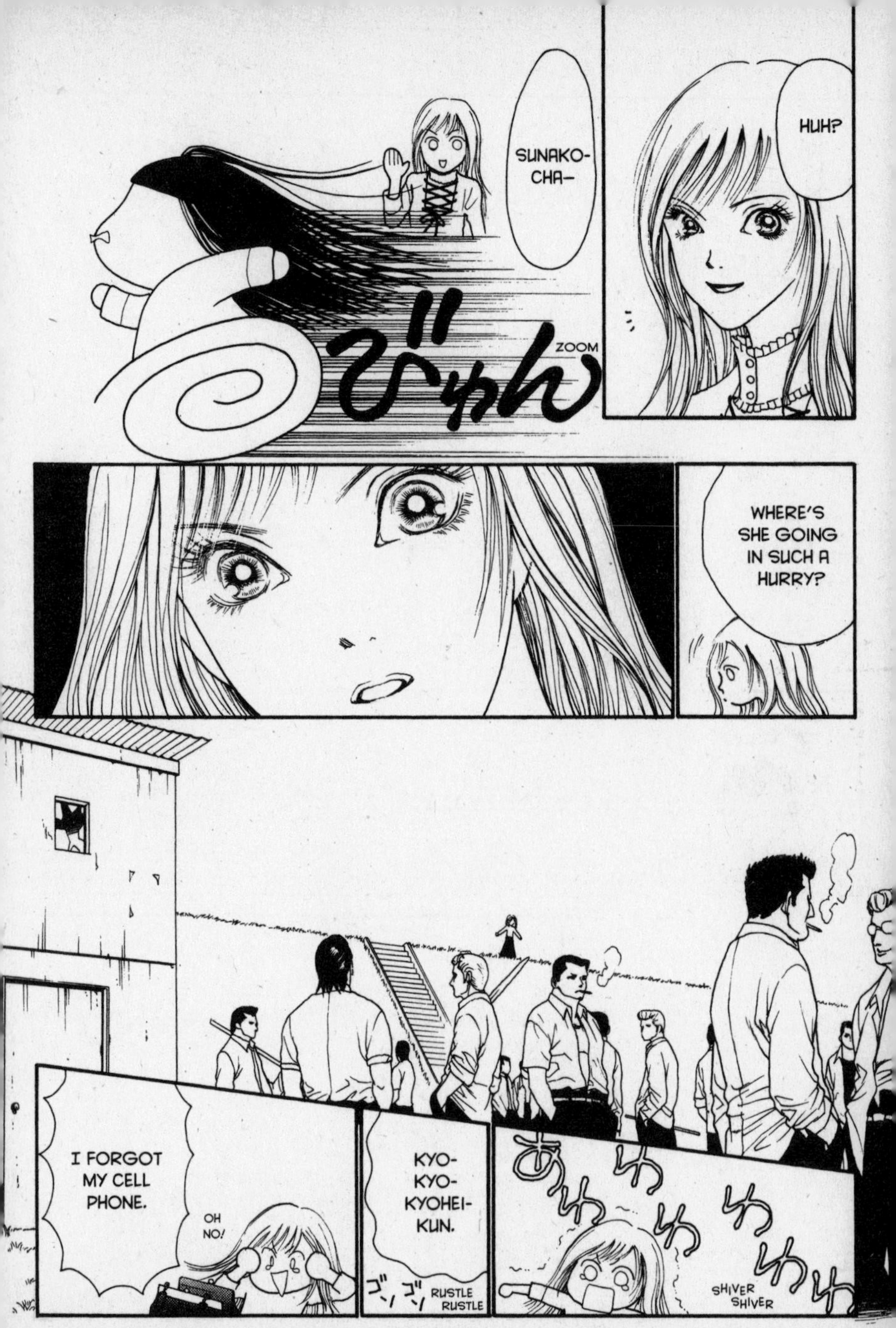
HUH?
SUNAKO-CHA-
びゅん
ZOOM
WHERE'S SHE GOING IN SUCH A HURRY?
SHIVER SHIVER
KYO-KYO-KYOHEI-KUN.
ゴソゴソ
RUSTLE RUSTLE
I FORGOT MY CELL PHONE.
OH NO!

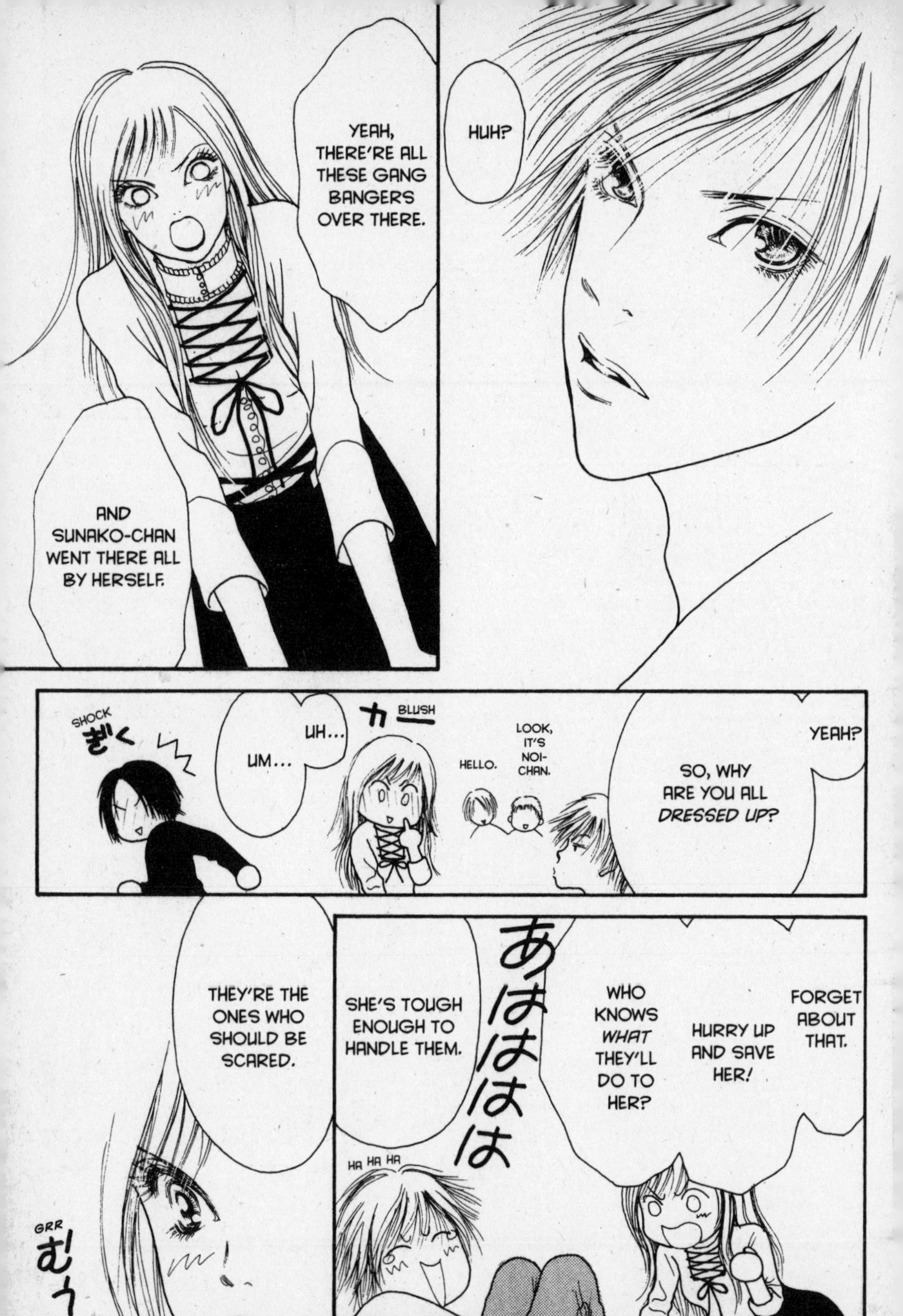
HUH?
YEAH, THERE'RE ALL THESE GANG BANGERS OVER THERE.
AND SUNAKO-CHAN WENT THERE ALL BY HERSELF.
YEAH?
SO, WHY ARE YOU ALL *DRESSED UP*?
LOOK, IT'S NOI-CHAN.
HELLO.
BLUSH
カー
UH...
UM...
SHOCK
ぎく
FORGET ABOUT THAT.
HURRY UP AND SAVE HER!
WHO KNOWS *WHAT* THEY'LL DO TO HER?
あははは
HA HA HA
SHE'S TOUGH ENOUGH TO HANDLE THEM.
THEY'RE THE ONES WHO SHOULD BE SCARED.
GRR
むぅ

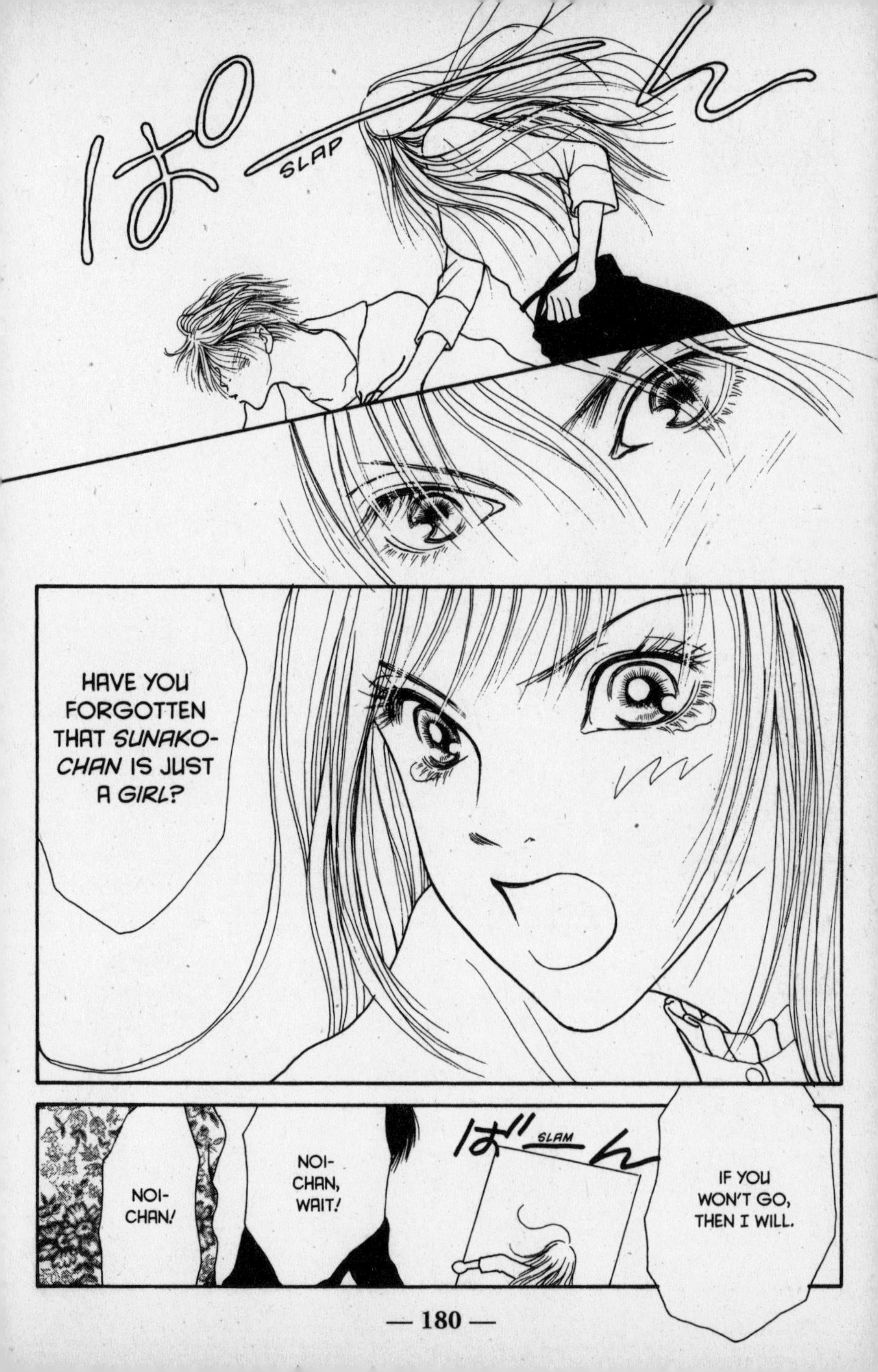
ぱん
SLAP
HAVE YOU FORGOTTEN THAT *SUNAKO-CHAN* IS JUST A *GIRL*?
IF YOU WON'T GO, THEN I WILL.
ばーん
SLAM
NOI-CHAN, WAIT!
NOI-CHAN!

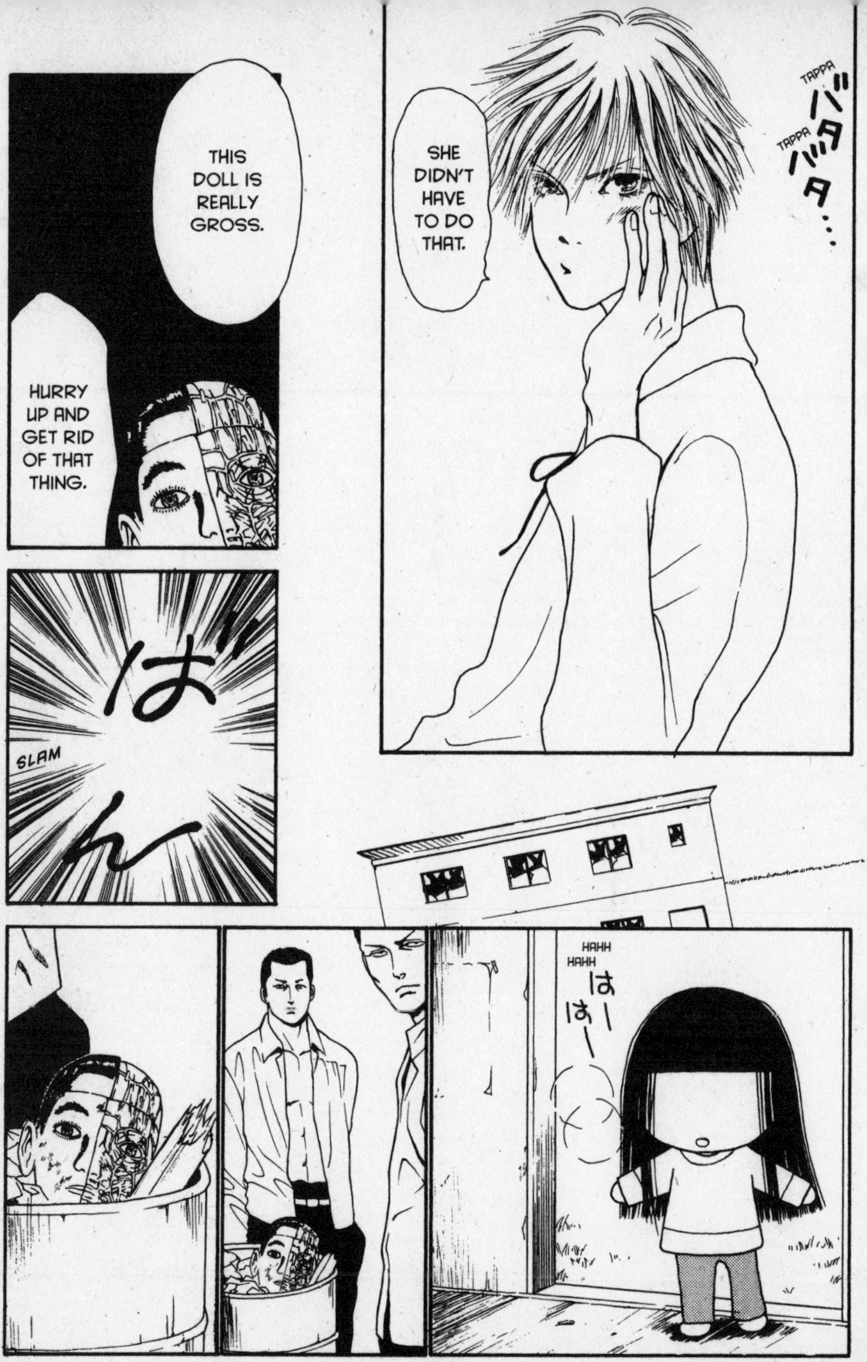
TAPPA
バタ
TAPPA
バタ…
SHE DIDN'T HAVE TO DO THAT.
THIS DOLL IS REALLY GROSS.
HURRY UP AND GET RID OF THAT THING.
ばん
SLAM
HAHH HAHH
はーはー

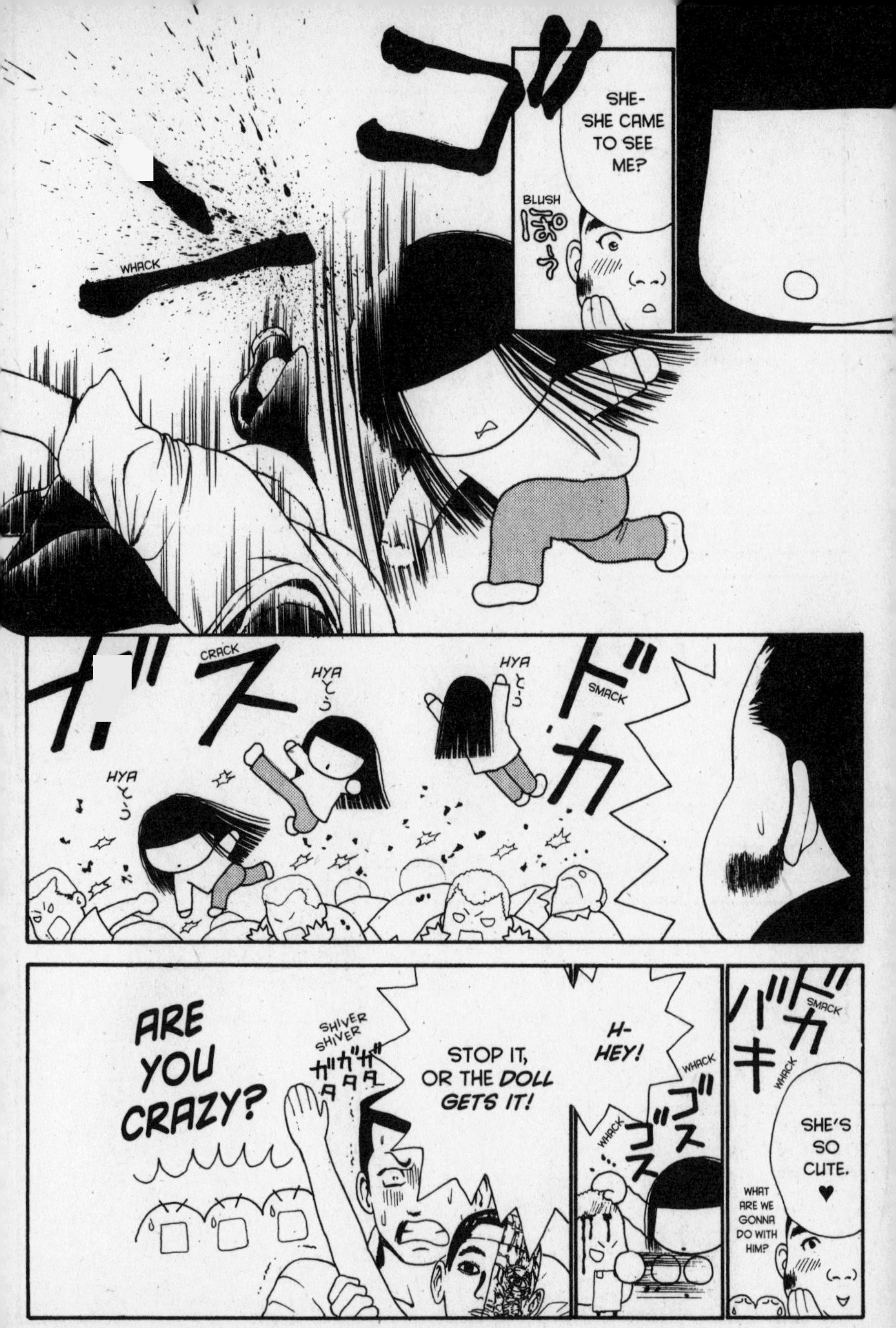
SHE- SHE CAME TO SEE ME?
BLUSH
ぽっ
WHACK
SMACK
ドカ
HYA
とう
HYA
とう
HYA
とう
CRACK
SMACK
ドカ
バキ
WHACK
SHE'S SO CUTE. ♥
WHAT ARE WE GONNA DO WITH HIM?
H- HEY!
WHACK
WHACK
ゴス
ゴス
STOP IT, OR THE *DOLL GETS IT!*
SHIVER SHIVER
ガタガタ
ARE YOU CRAZY?

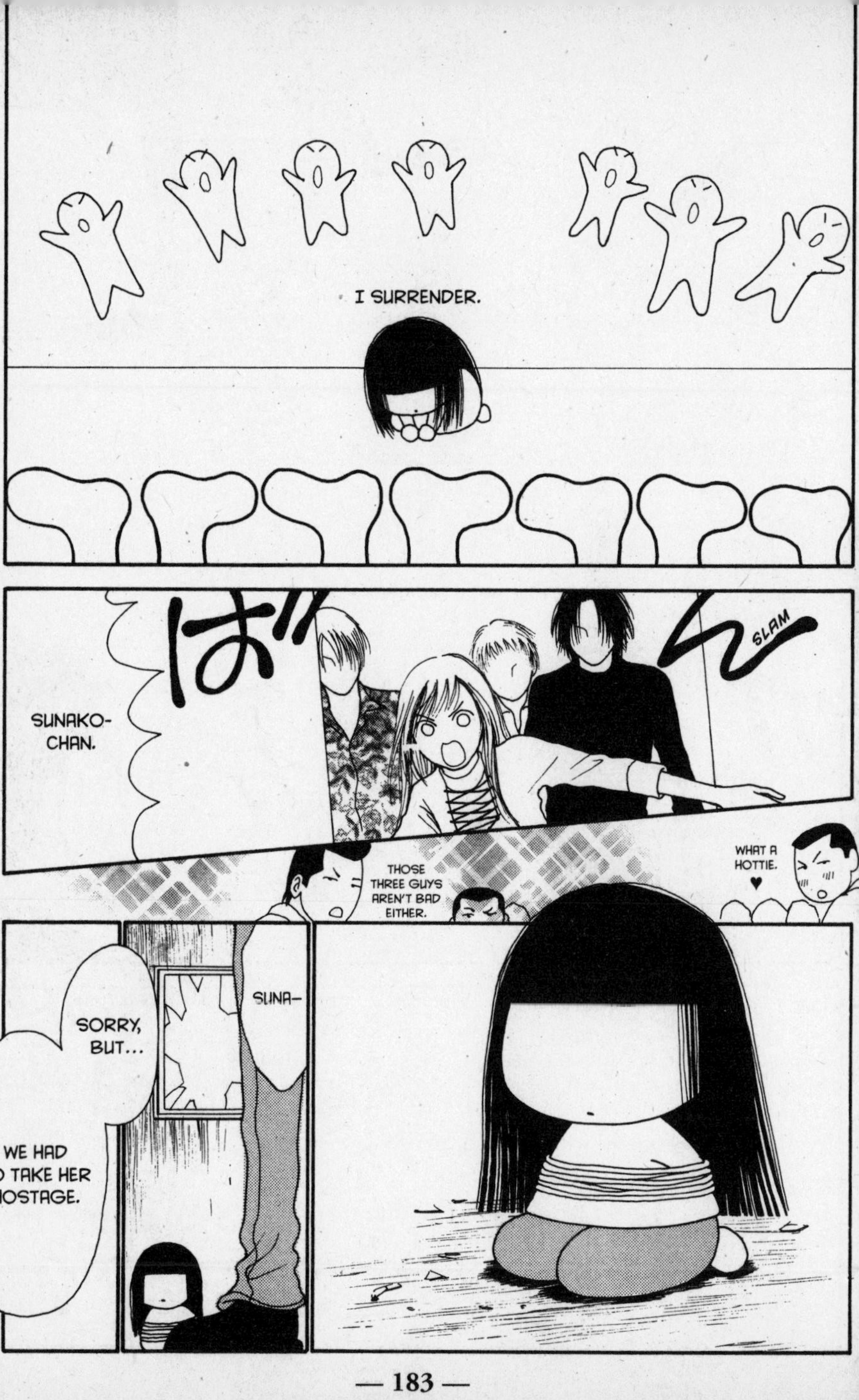
I SURRENDER.
SLAM
SUNAKO-CHAN.
WHAT A HOTTIE. ♥
THOSE THREE GUYS AREN'T BAD EITHER.
SUNA-
SORRY, BUT...
WE HAD TO TAKE HER HOSTAGE.

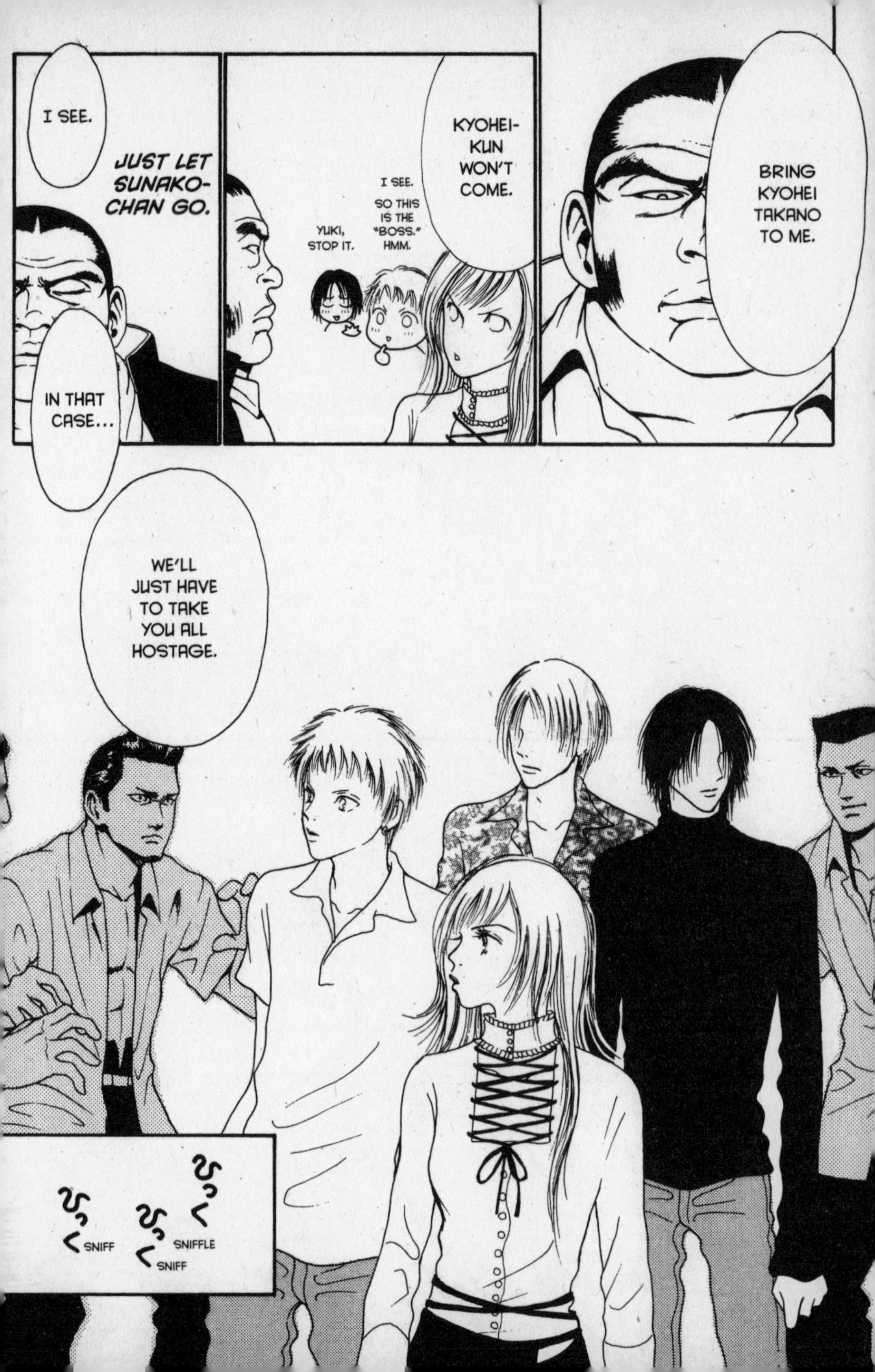
BRING KYOHEI TAKANO TO ME.
KYOHEI-KUN WON'T COME.
I SEE. SO THIS IS THE "BOSS." HMM.
YUKI, STOP IT.
I SEE.
JUST LET SUNAKO-CHAN GO.
IN THAT CASE...
WE'LL JUST HAVE TO TAKE YOU ALL HOSTAGE.
ひっく SNIFFLE
ひっく SNIFF
ひっく SNIFF

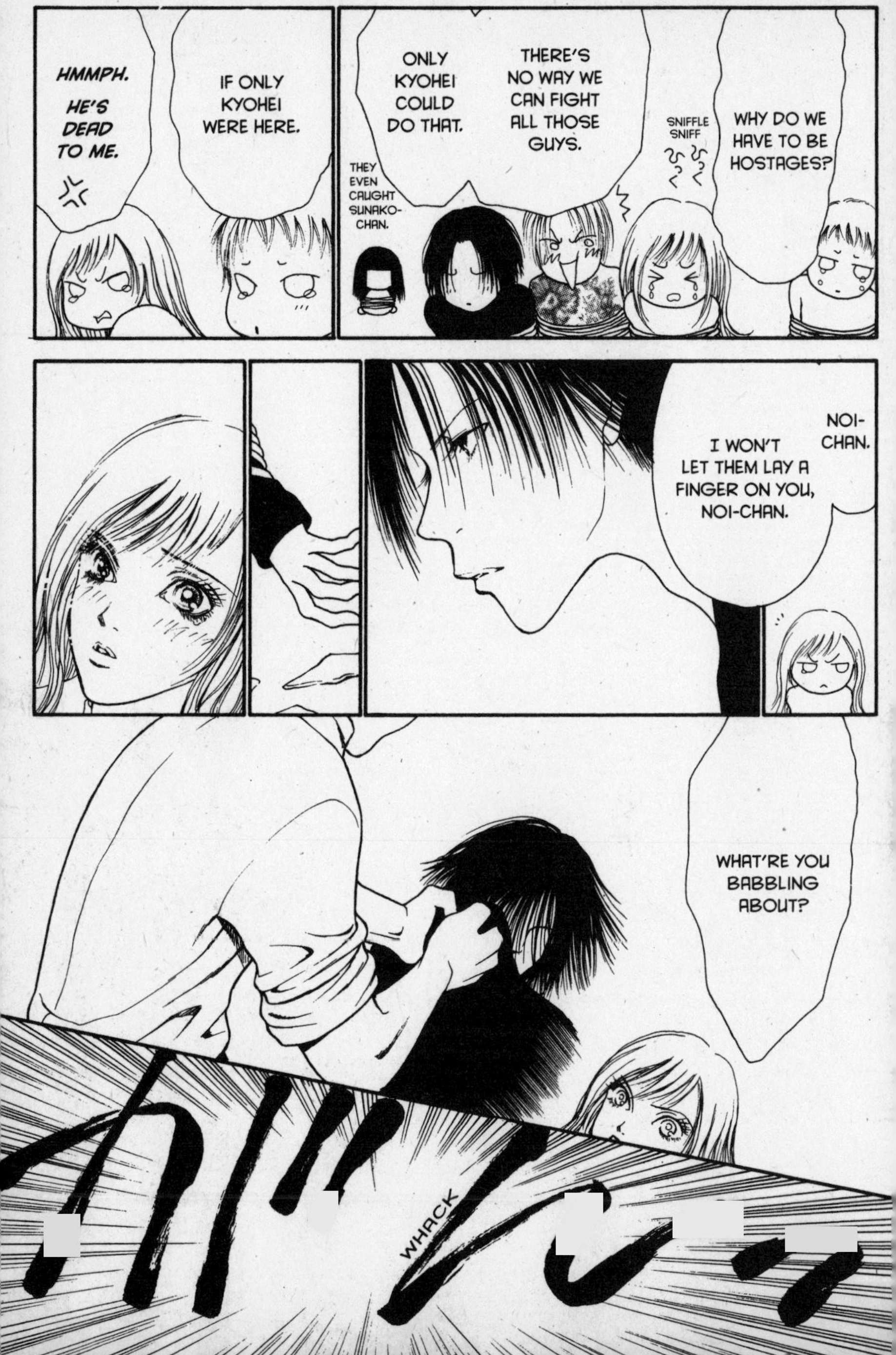
WHY DO WE HAVE TO BE HOSTAGES?
SNIFFLE SNIFF
THERE'S NO WAY WE CAN FIGHT ALL THOSE GUYS.
ONLY KYOHEI COULD DO THAT.
THEY EVEN CAUGHT SUNAKO-CHAN.
IF ONLY KYOHEI WERE HERE.
HMMPH. HE'S DEAD TO ME.
NOI-CHAN.
I WON'T LET THEM LAY A FINGER ON YOU, NOI-CHAN.
WHAT'RE YOU BABBLING ABOUT?
WHACK

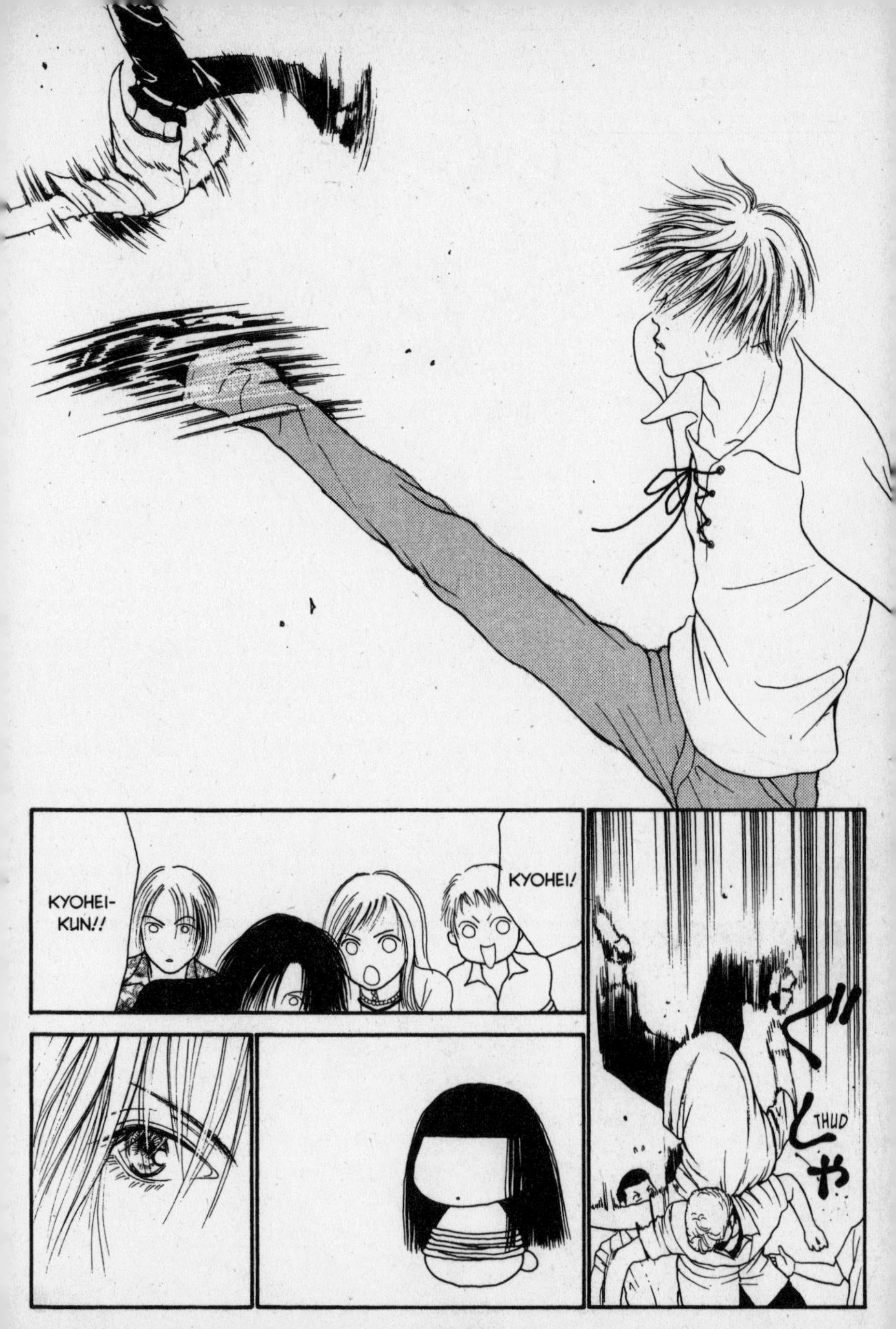
ぐしゃ
THUD
KYOHEI!
KYOHEI-KUN!!

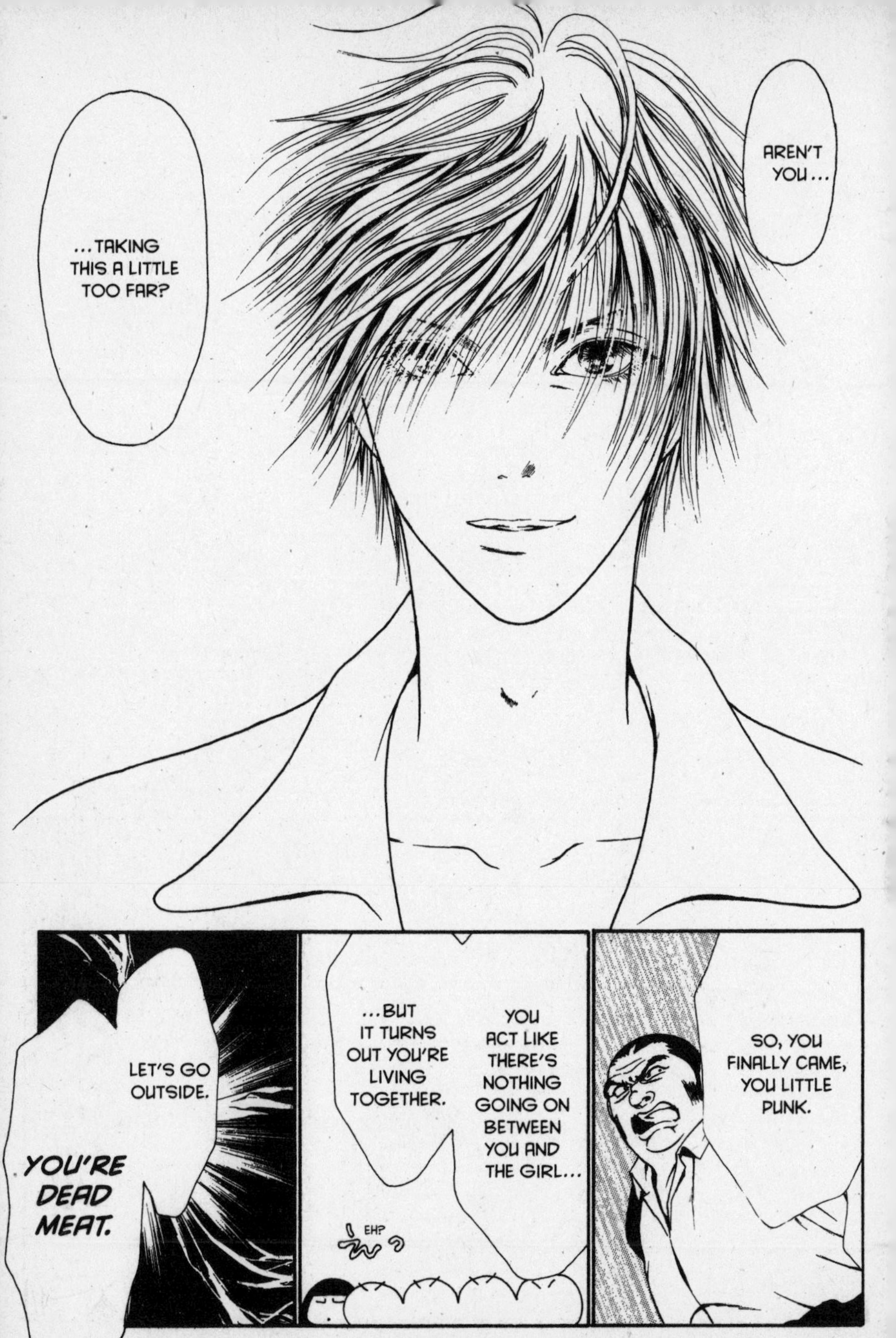
AREN'T YOU...
...TAKING THIS A LITTLE TOO FAR?
SO, YOU FINALLY CAME, YOU LITTLE PUNK.
YOU ACT LIKE THERE'S NOTHING GOING ON BETWEEN YOU AND THE GIRL...
...BUT IT TURNS OUT YOU'RE LIVING TOGETHER.
EH?
LET'S GO OUTSIDE.
YOU'RE DEAD MEAT.

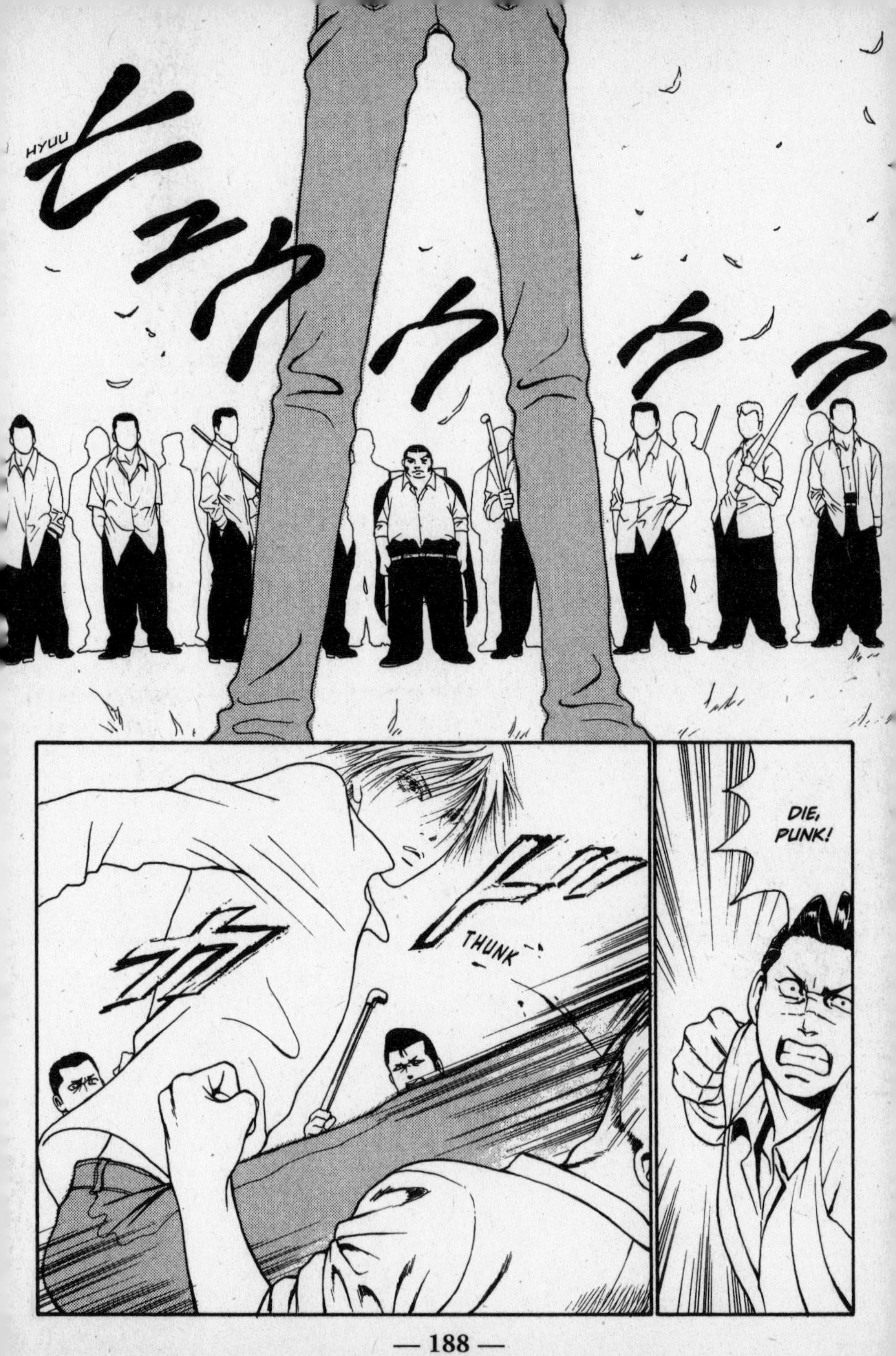
HYUU
DIE, PUNK!
THUNK

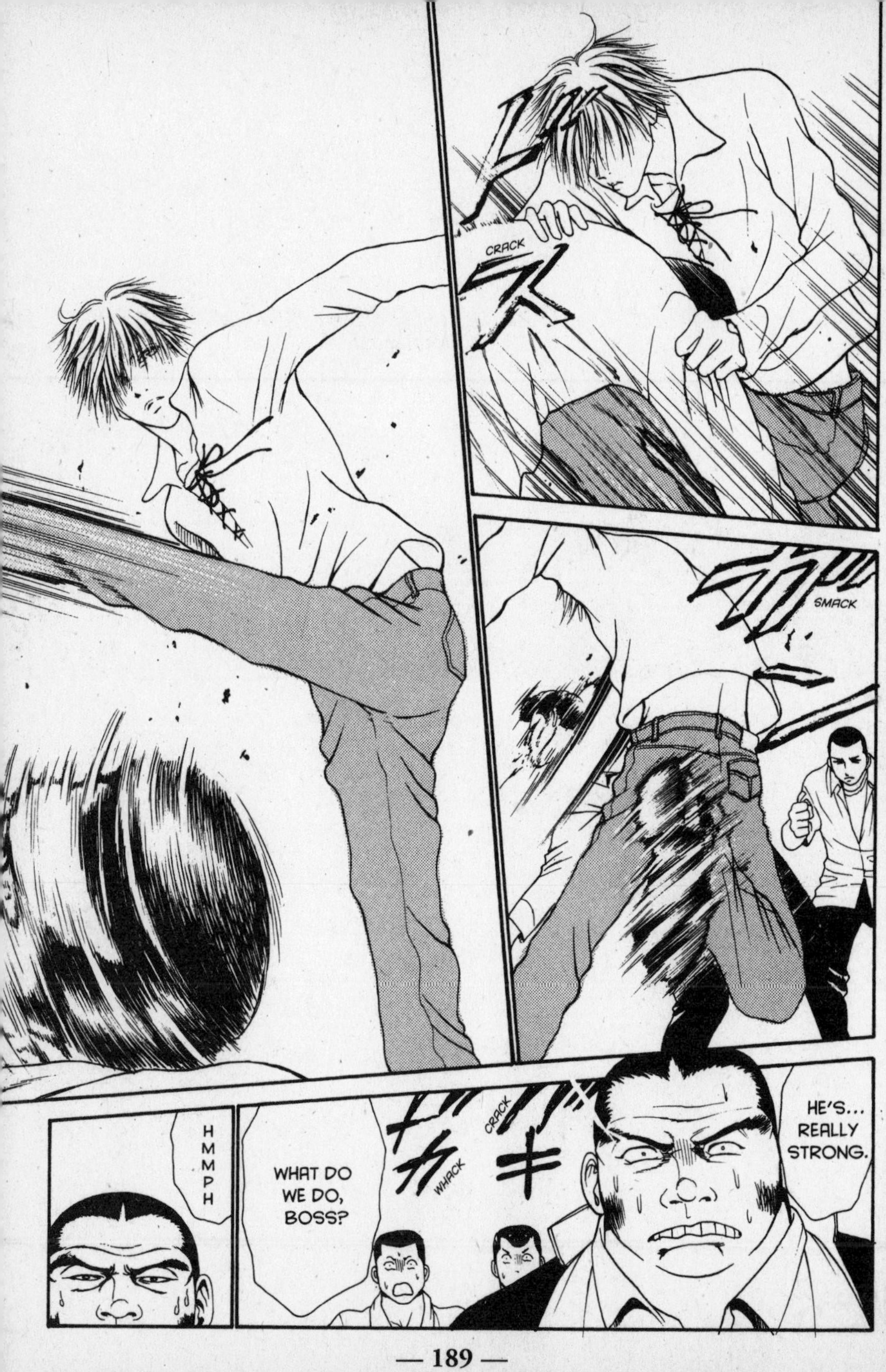
CRACK
SMACK
HE'S... REALLY STRONG.
CRACK
WHACK
WHAT DO WE DO, BOSS?
HMMPH

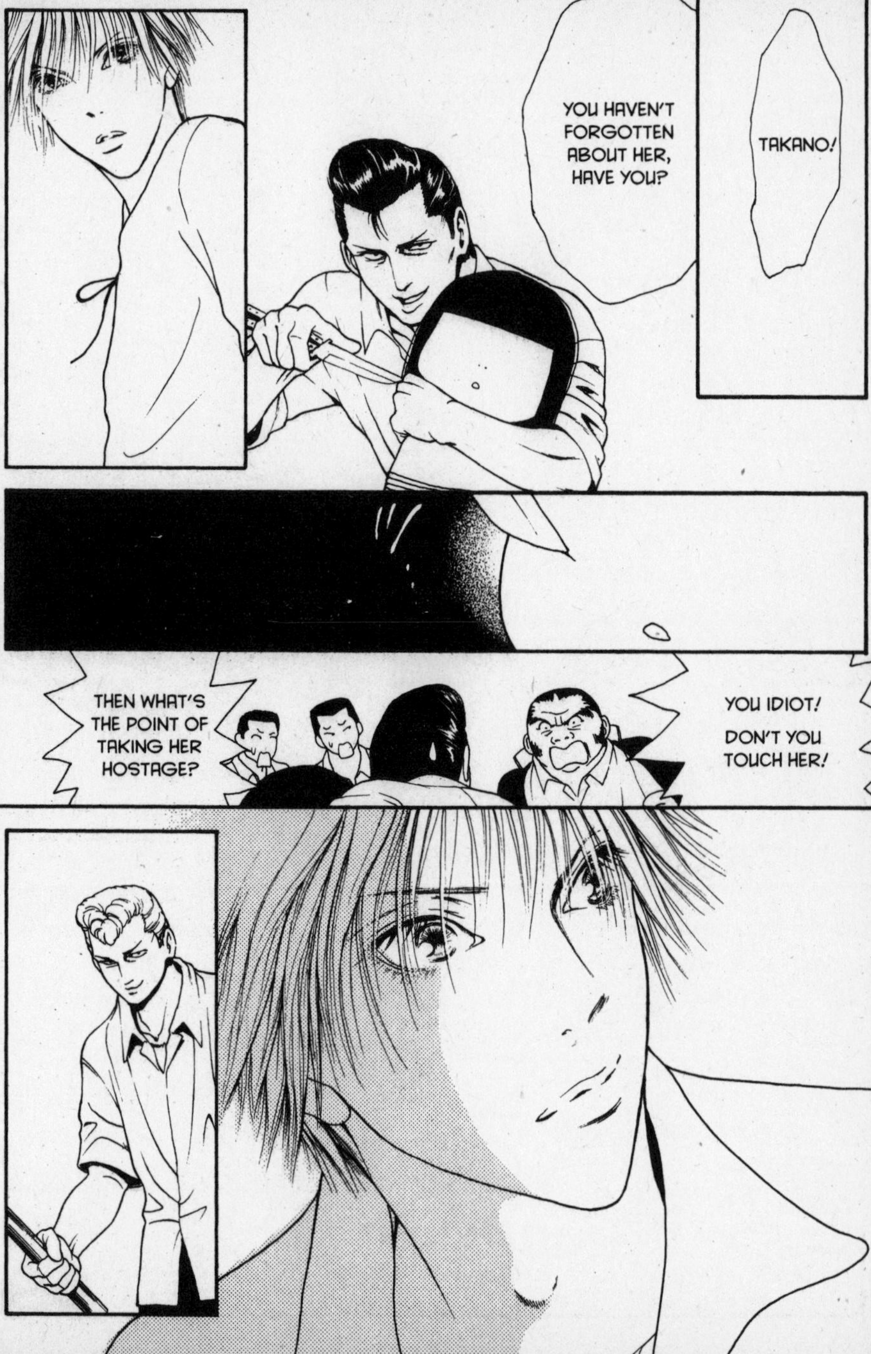
TAKANO!
YOU HAVEN'T FORGOTTEN ABOUT HER, HAVE YOU?
YOU IDIOT!
DON'T YOU TOUCH HER!
THEN WHAT'S THE POINT OF TAKING HER HOSTAGE?

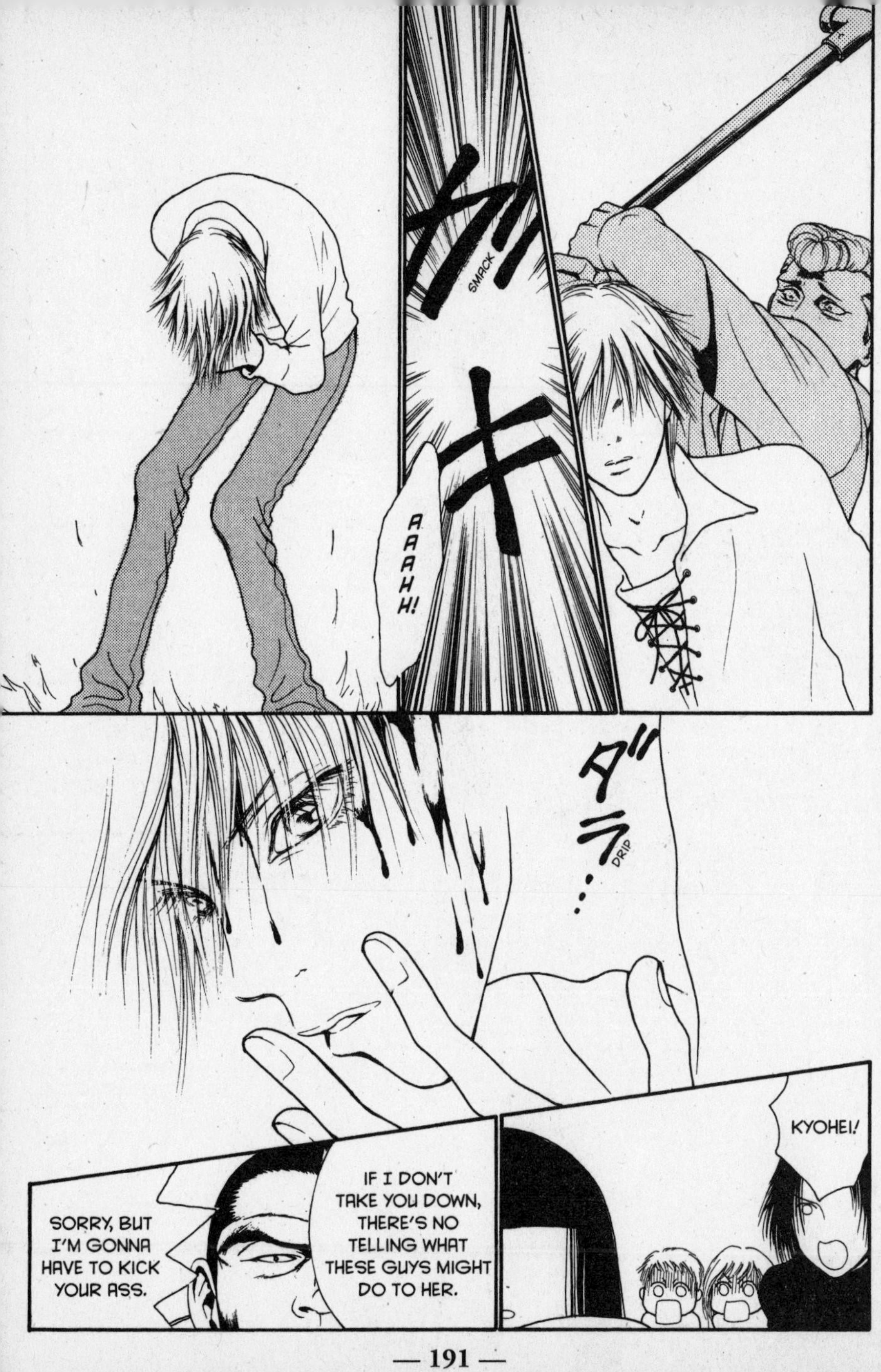
SMACK
AAAAH!
DRIP
KYOHEI!
IF I DON'T TAKE YOU DOWN, THERE'S NO TELLING WHAT THESE GUYS MIGHT DO TO HER.
SORRY, BUT I'M GONNA HAVE TO KICK YOUR ASS.

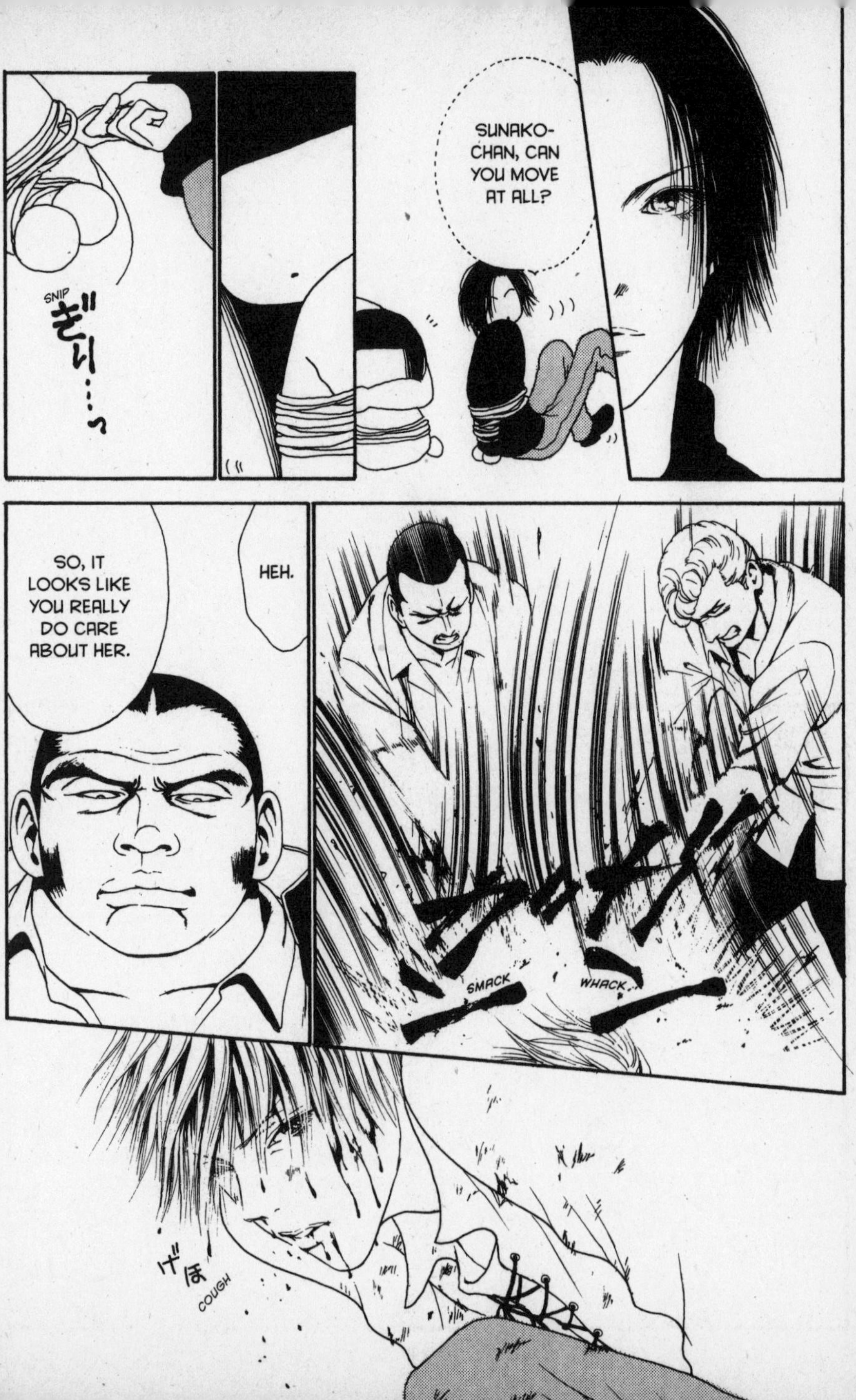

SUNAKO-CHAN, CAN YOU MOVE AT ALL?
SNIP
ぎり…
SMACK
WHACK
HEH.
SO, IT LOOKS LIKE YOU REALLY DO CARE ABOUT HER.
げほ
COUGH

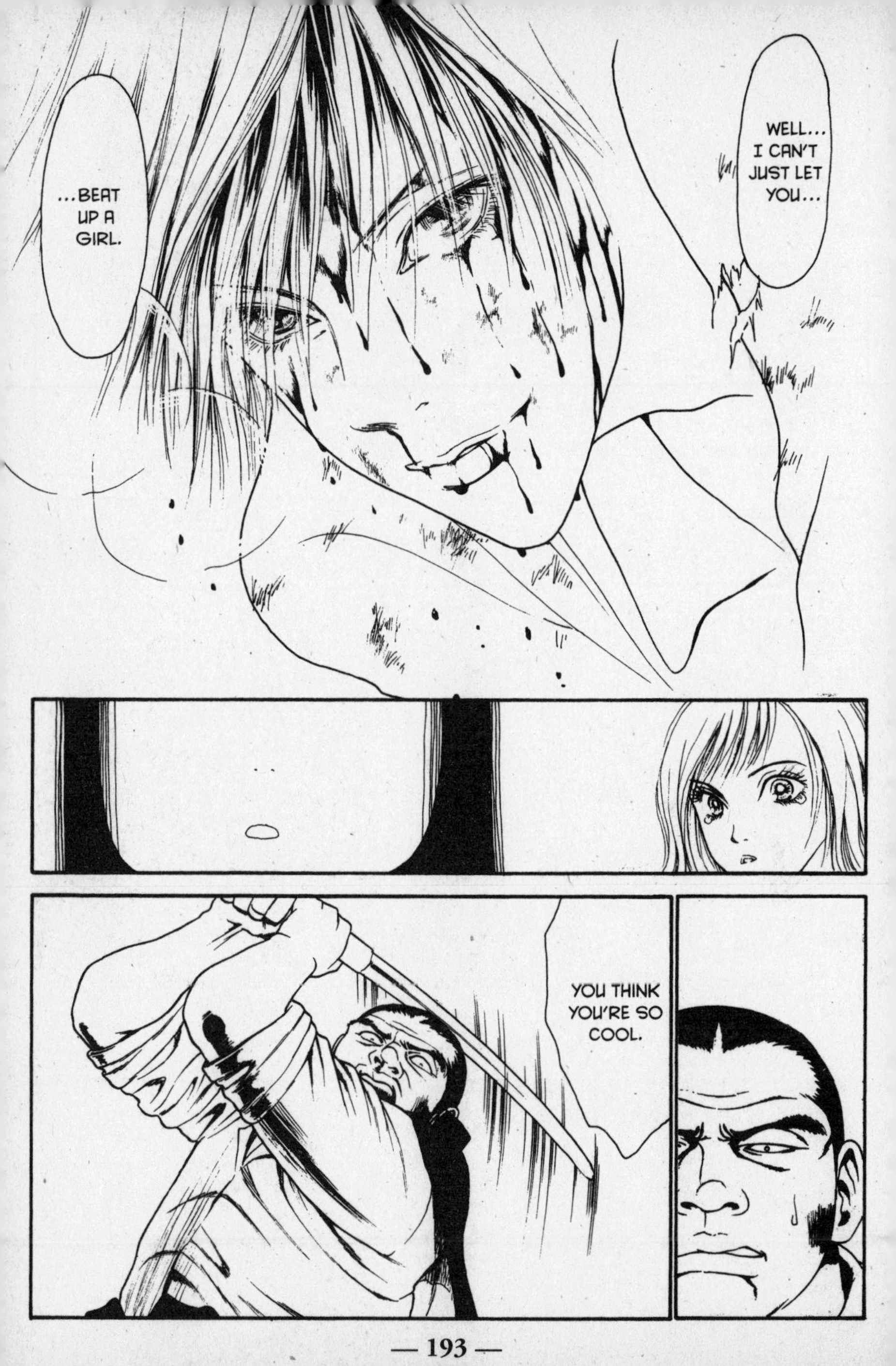
WELL... I CAN'T JUST LET YOU...
...BEAT UP A GIRL.
YOU THINK YOU'RE SO COOL.

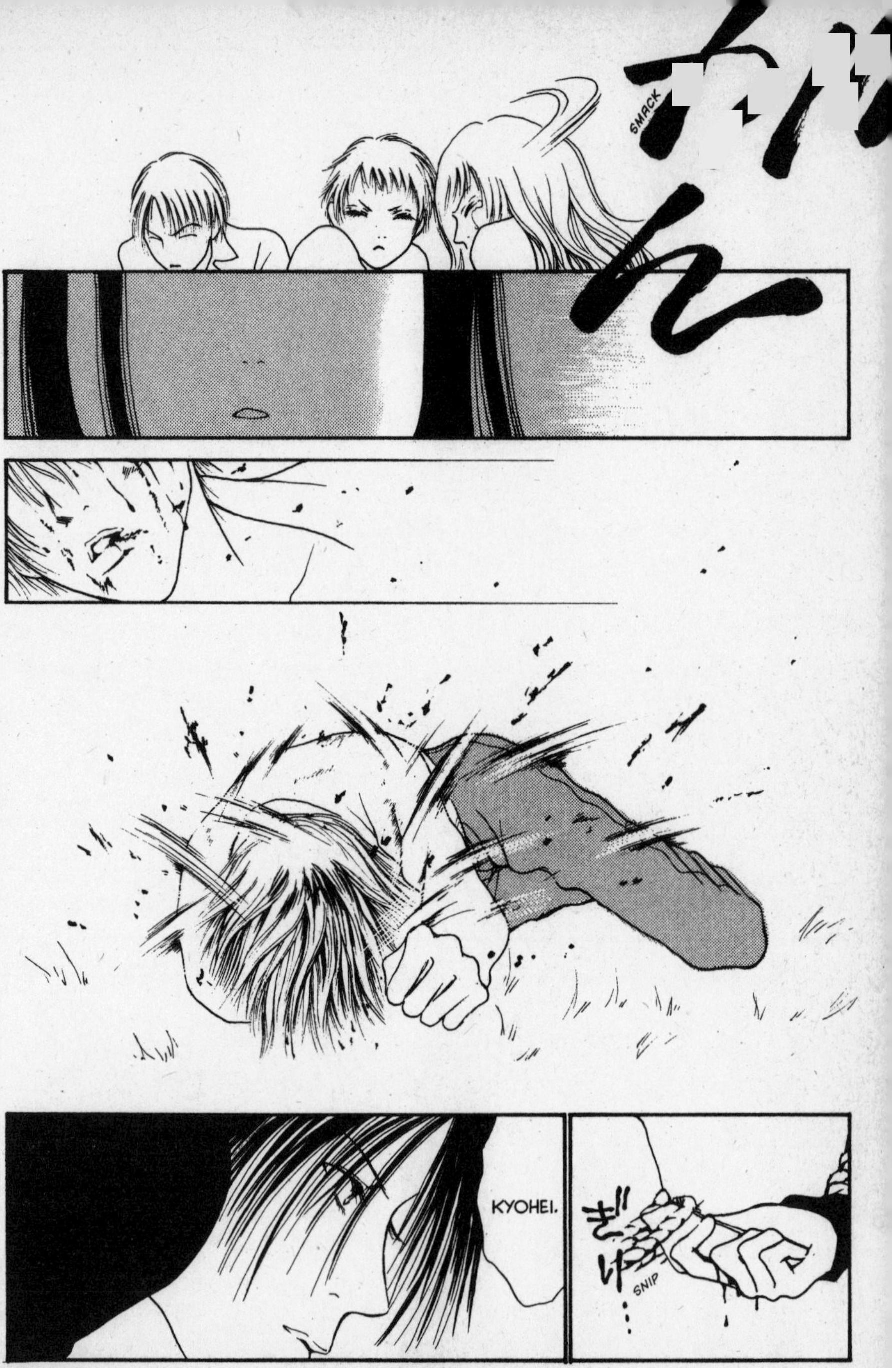
SMACK
SNIP
KYOHEI.

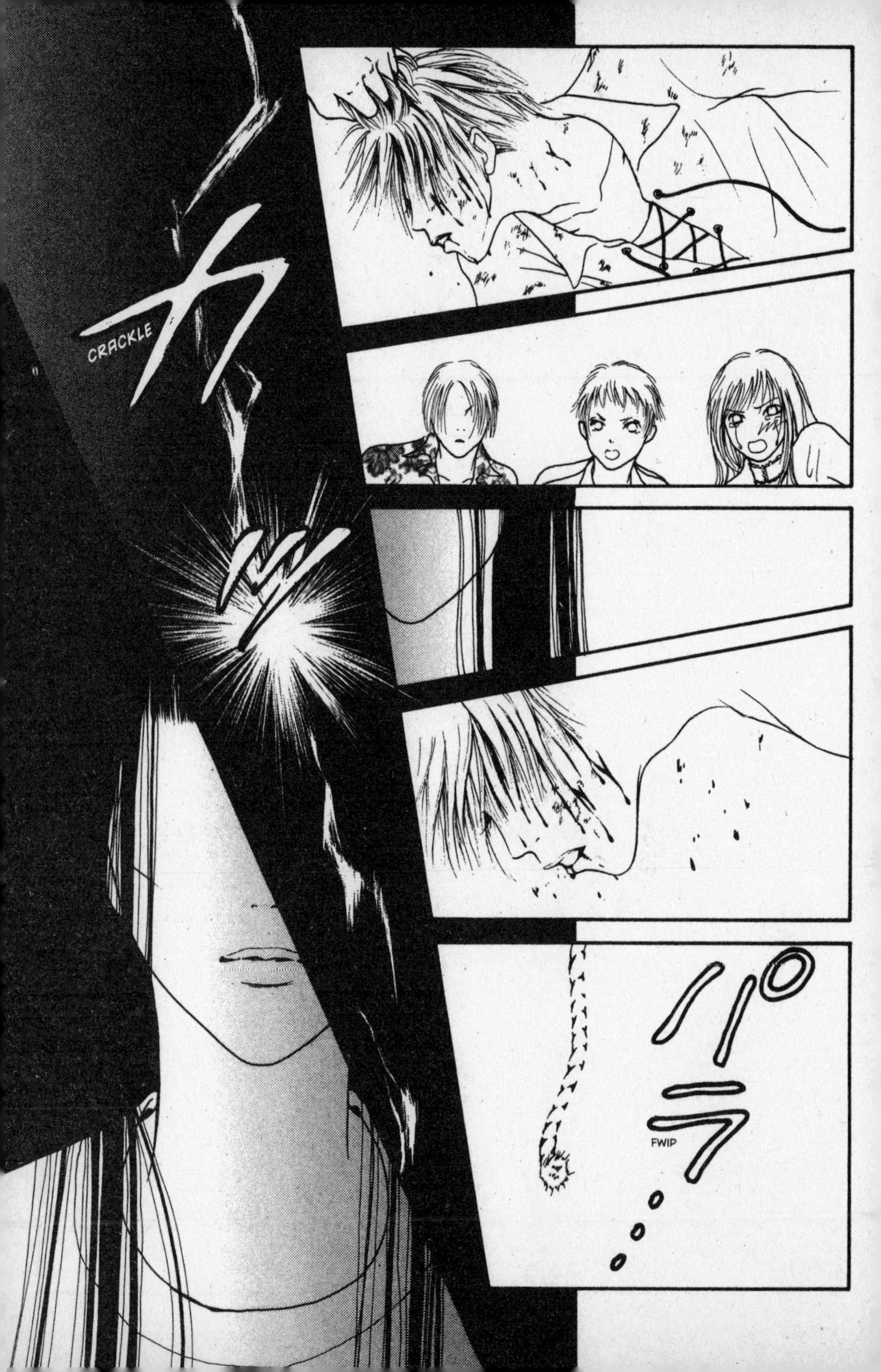
CRACKLE
FWIP

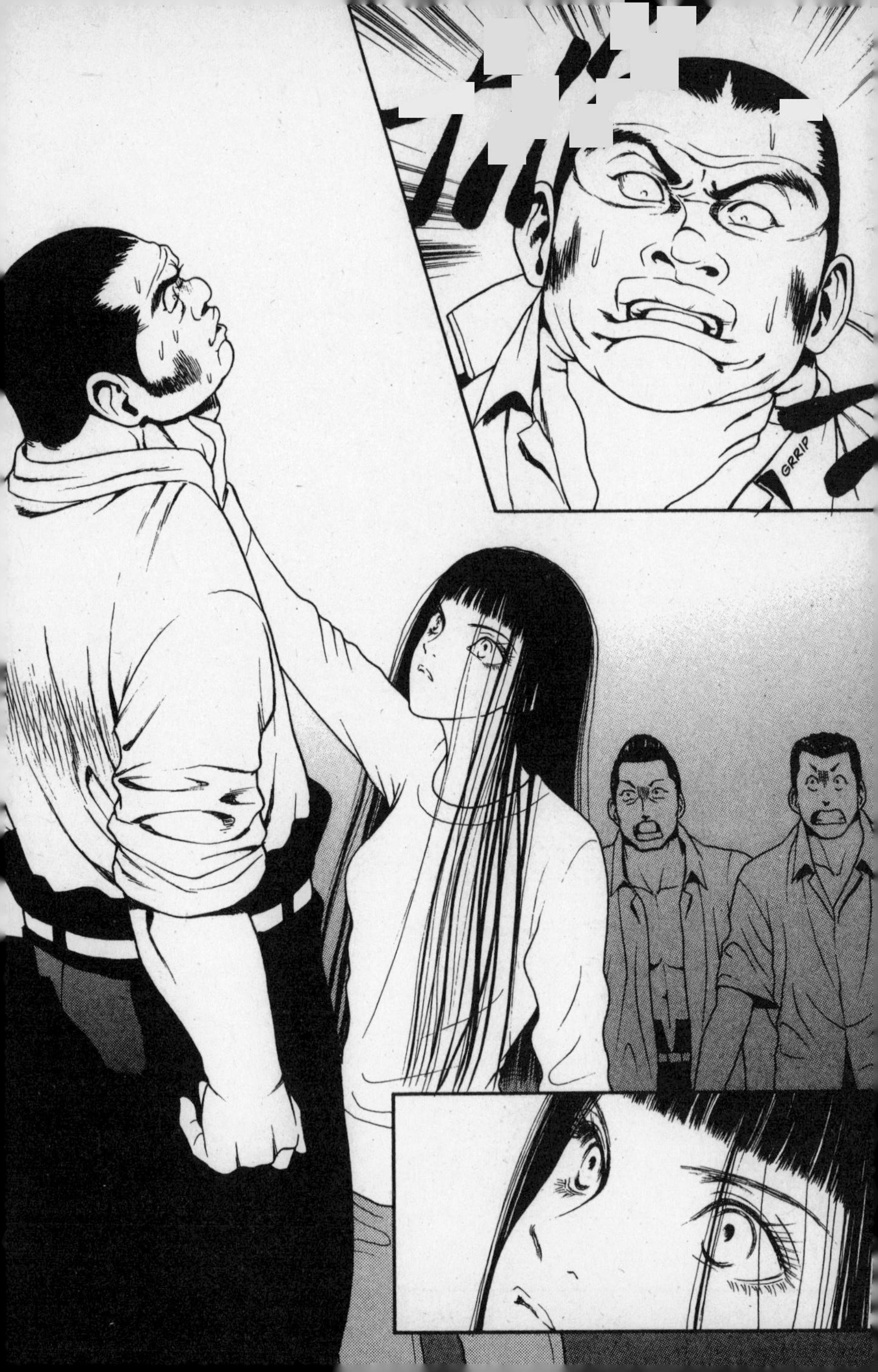
GRRIP

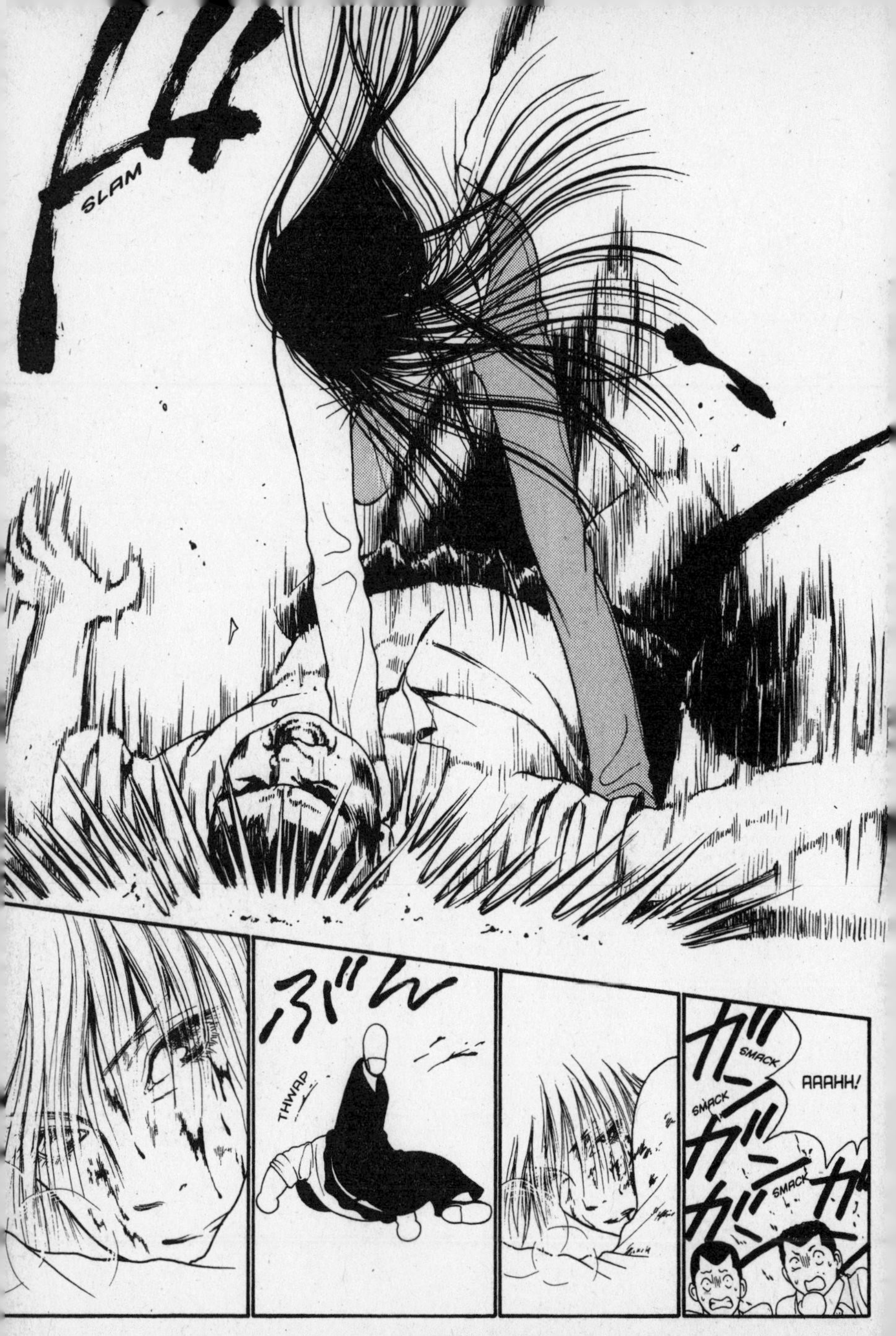
SLAM
AAAHH!
SMACK
SMACK
SMACK
ぶん
THWAP

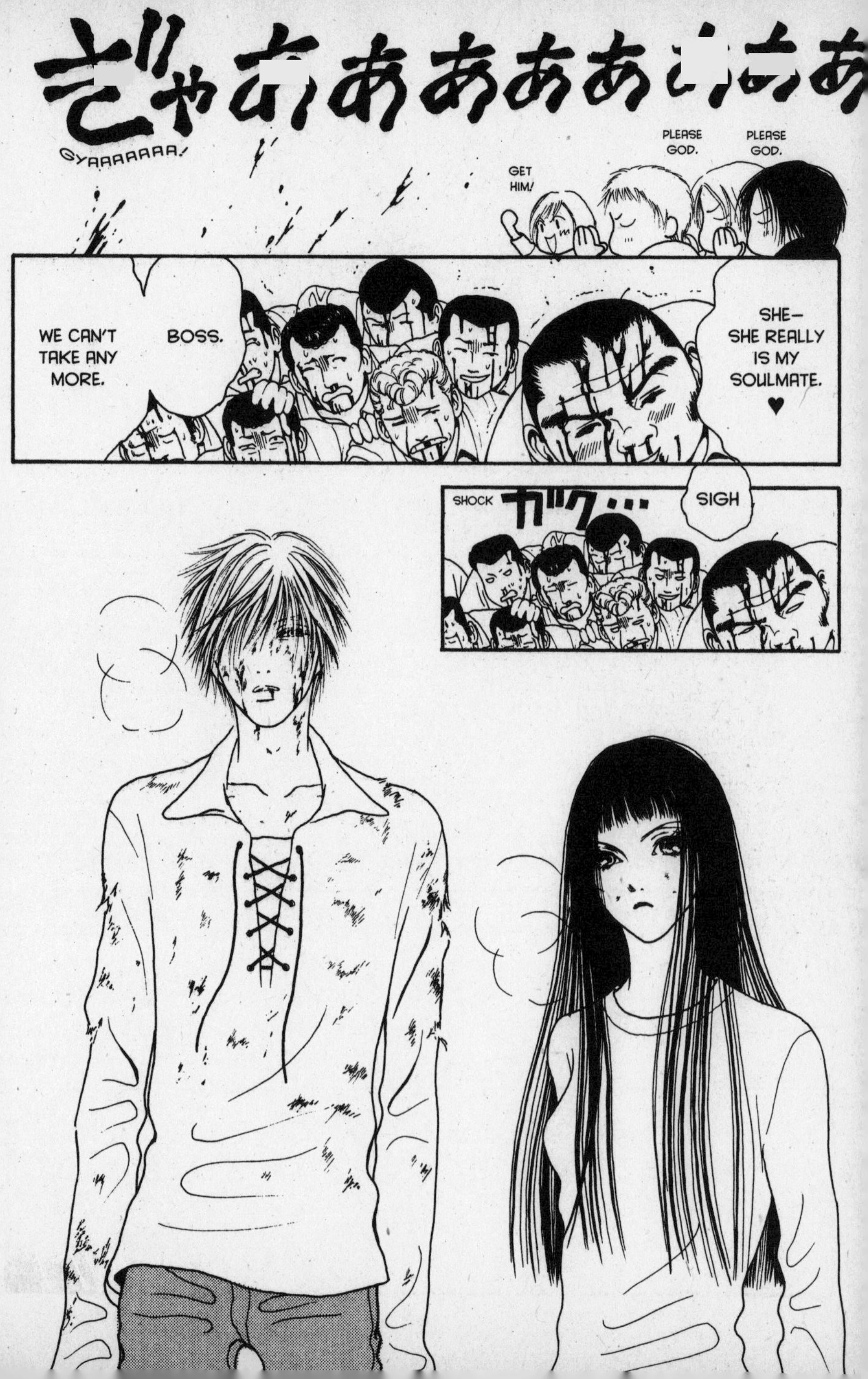
GYAAAAAAA!
PLEASE GOD.
PLEASE GOD.
GET HIM!
SHE— SHE REALLY IS MY SOULMATE. ♥
BOSS.
WE CAN'T TAKE ANY MORE.
SIGH
ガク…
SHOCK

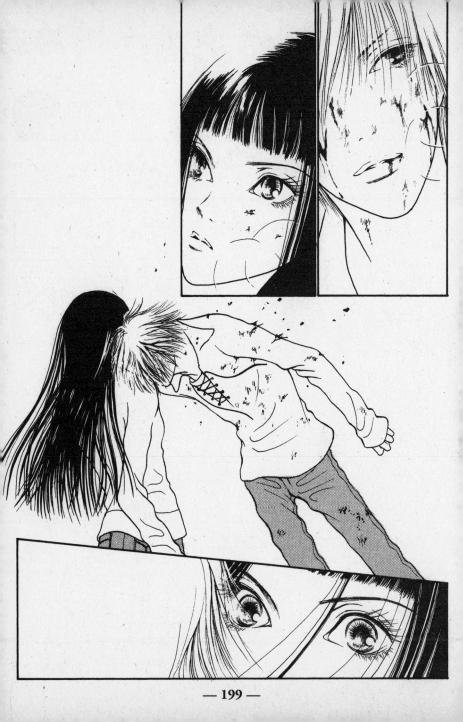

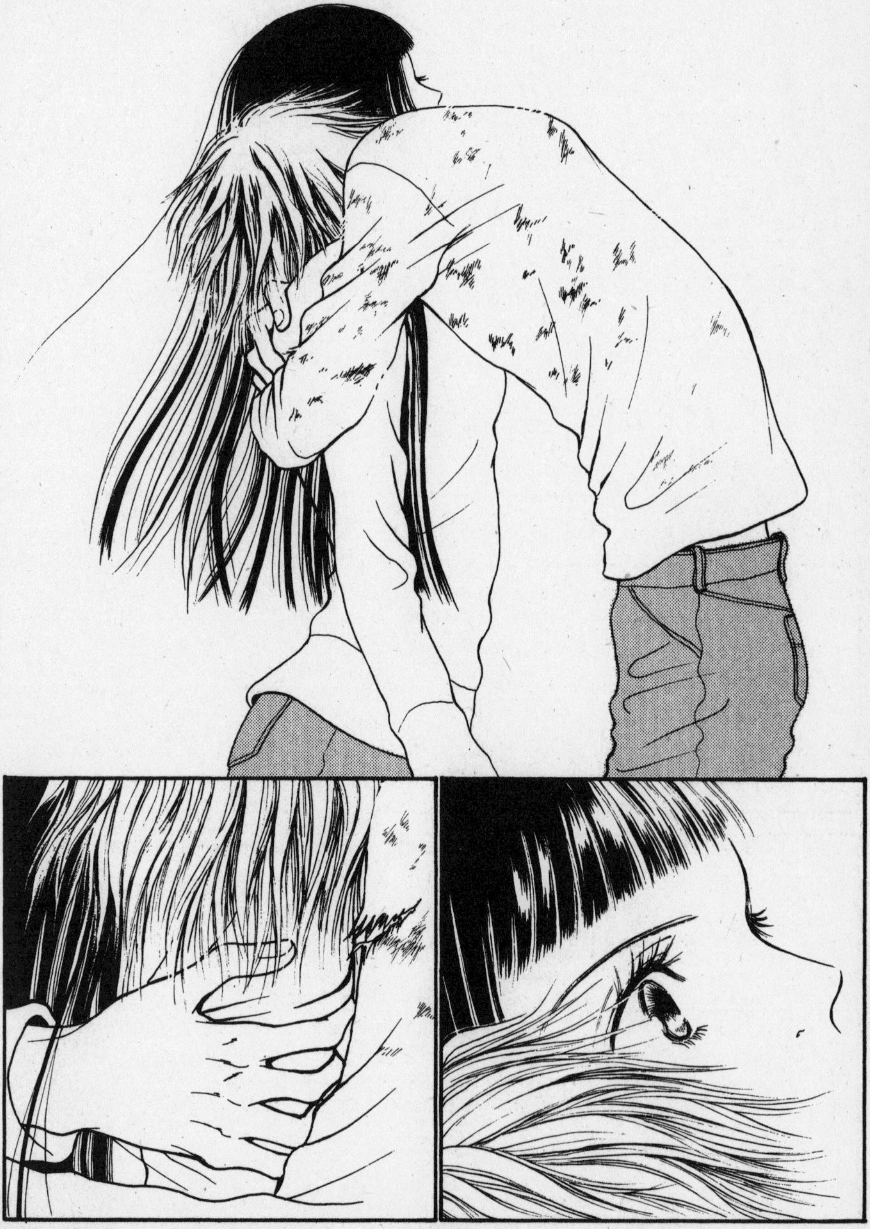

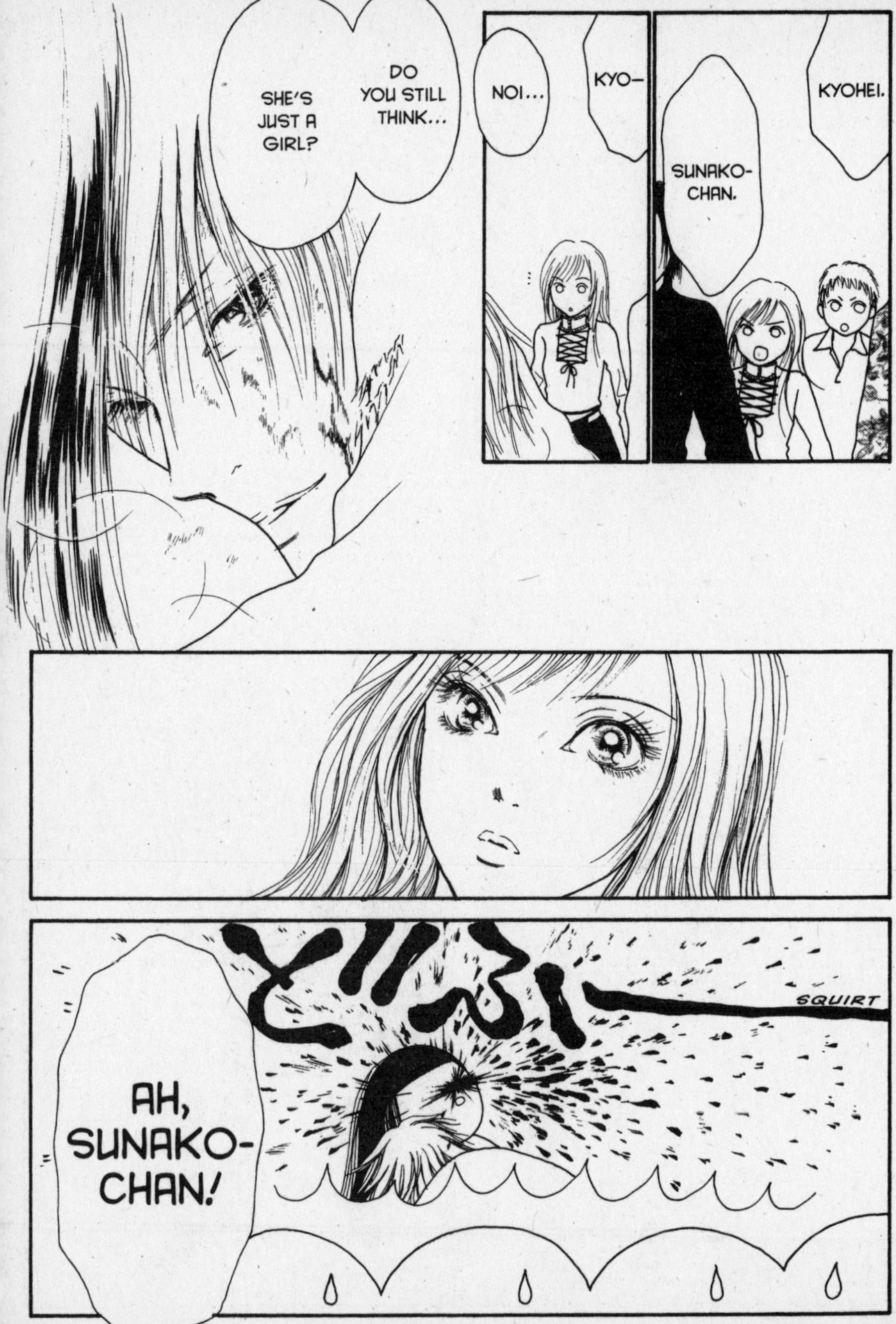
KYOHEI.
SUNAKO-CHAN.
KYO—
NOI...
DO YOU STILL THINK...
SHE'S JUST A GIRL?
SQUIRT
AH, SUNAKO-CHAN!

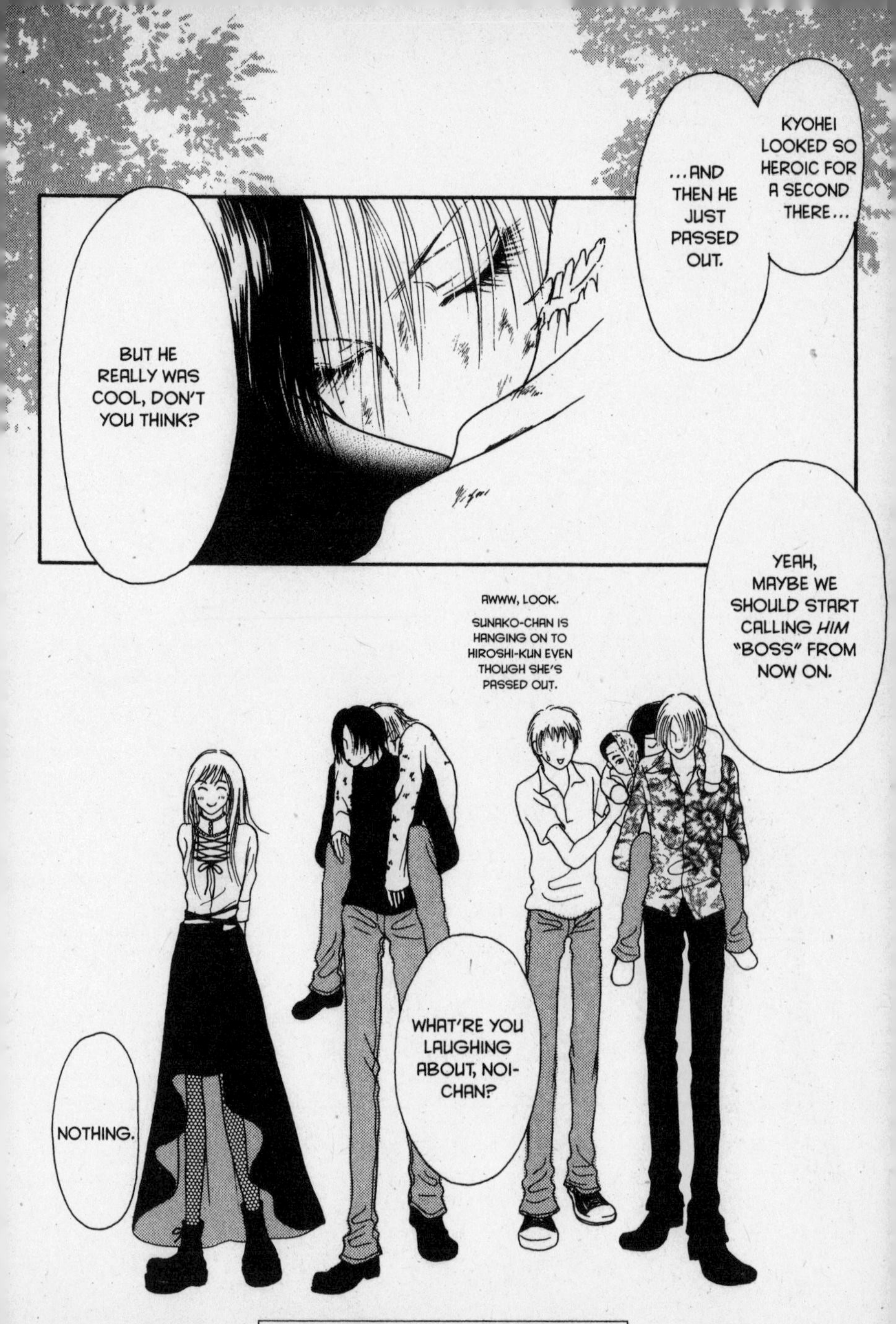
KYOHEI LOOKED SO HEROIC FOR A SECOND THERE...
...AND THEN HE JUST PASSED OUT.
BUT HE REALLY WAS COOL, DON'T YOU THINK?
YEAH, MAYBE WE SHOULD START CALLING *HIM* "BOSS" FROM NOW ON.
AWWW, LOOK.
SUNAKO-CHAN IS HANGING ON TO HIROSHI-KUN EVEN THOUGH SHE'S PASSED OUT.
WHAT'RE YOU LAUGHING ABOUT, NOI-CHAN?
NOTHING.

TO BE CONTINUED IN WALLFLOWER BOOK 4

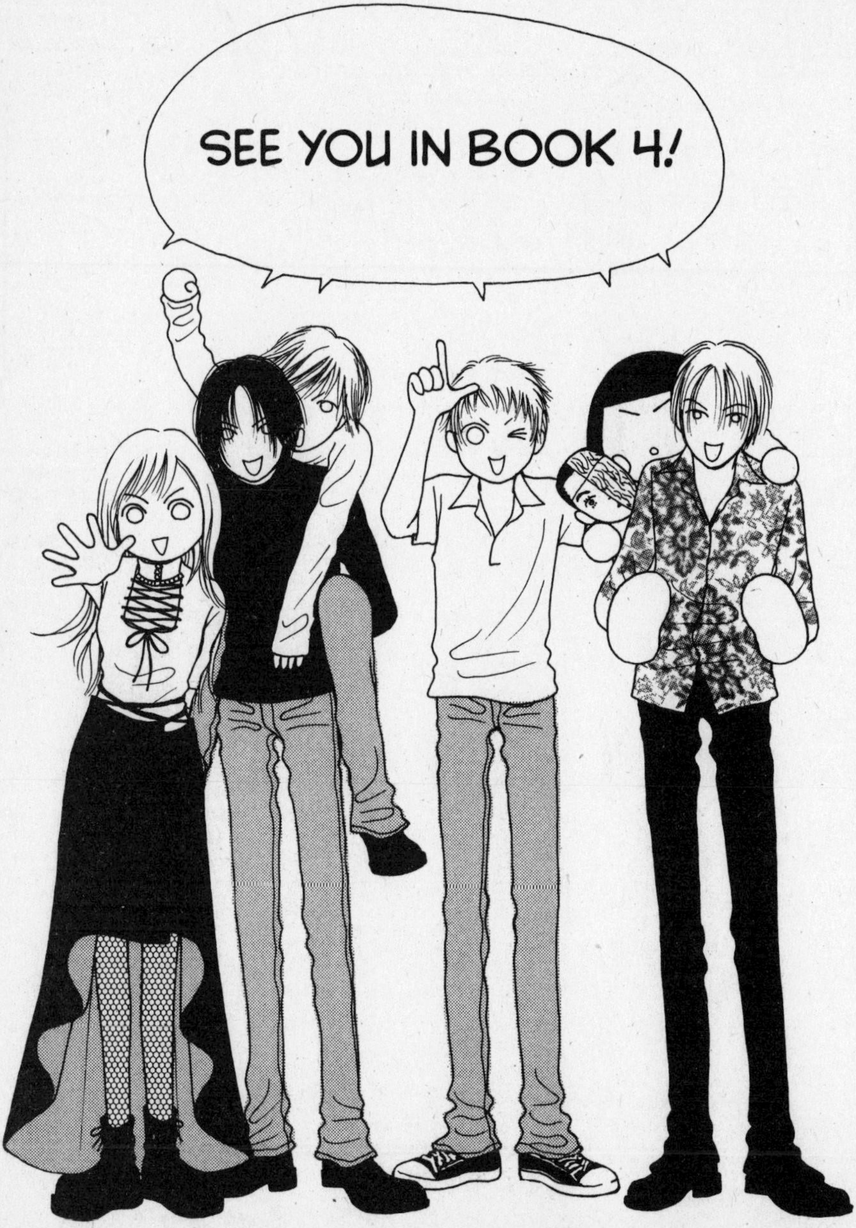
SEE YOU IN BOOK 4!

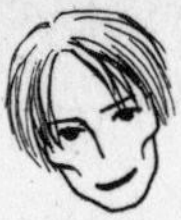

HANA-CHAN LOOKS A LITTLE BIT LIKE TAKAMIZAWA.

A WORD ABOUT "THE GENIUS HANA-CHAN" WHO IS ALWAYS HELPING ME...

HE REALLY DRAWS AMAZING PICTURES. HE DRAWS DRAGONS, THE BUILDINGS IN THE BACKGROUND, SKULLS, GUTS AND EVEN THE "BOSS." HE TRULY IS AMAZING.

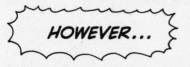

HOWEVER...

(HE DRAWS MANGA FOR A MEN'S MAGAZINE. HE'S NOT WORKING RIGHT NOW, SO HE'S HELPING ME OUT. OH, AND I KNOW "HANA-CHAN" SOUNDS LIKE A GIRL'S NAME, BUT HE'S ACTUALLY A GUY.)

HE'S A REAL TROUBLEMAKER. YOU WOULDN'T **BELIEVE** THE THINGS HE DOES.

FIRST OF ALL, WHEN I ASK HIM TO GO TO THE STORE FOR ME, HE ALMOST NEVER BRINGS ME WHAT I ASKED FOR.

THAT'S NOT REALLY A BIG DEAL. IT'S NOTHING COMPARED TO THIS...

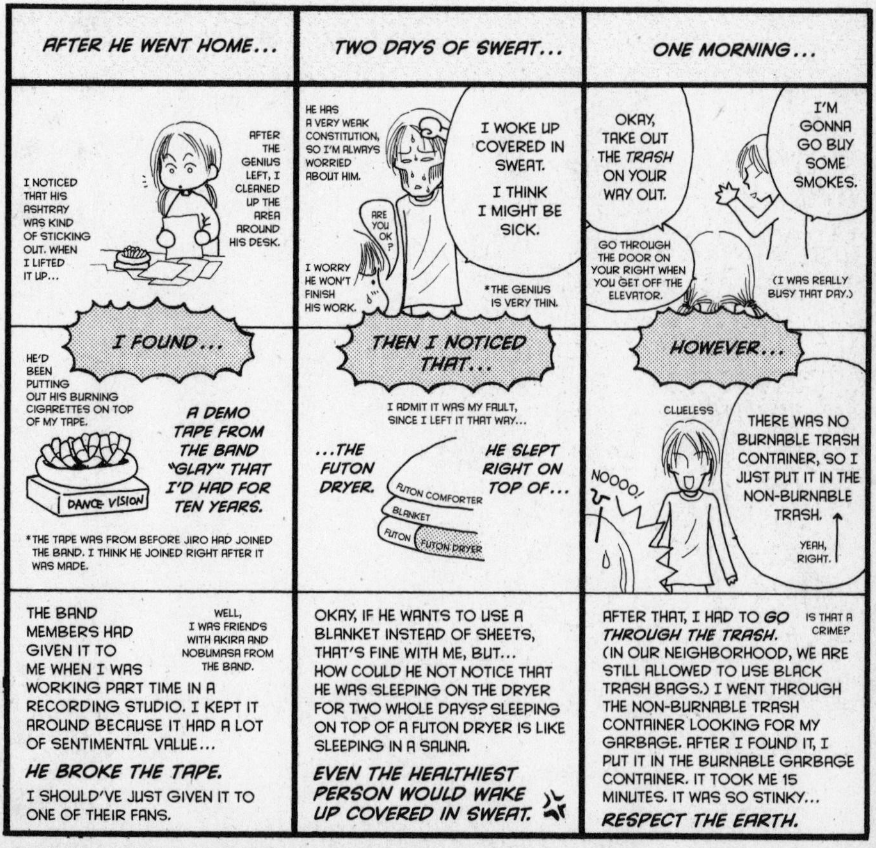

ONE MORNING...
I'M GONNA GO BUY SOME SMOKES.
OKAY, TAKE OUT THE TRASH ON YOUR WAY OUT.
GO THROUGH THE DOOR ON YOUR RIGHT WHEN YOU GET OFF THE ELEVATOR.
(I WAS REALLY BUSY THAT DAY.)
HOWEVER...
THERE WAS NO BURNABLE TRASH CONTAINER, SO I JUST PUT IT IN THE NON-BURNABLE TRASH.
YEAH, RIGHT.
CLUELESS
NOOOO!
AFTER THAT, I HAD TO GO THROUGH THE TRASH.
IS THAT A CRIME?
(IN OUR NEIGHBORHOOD, WE ARE STILL ALLOWED TO USE BLACK TRASH BAGS.) I WENT THROUGH THE NON-BURNABLE TRASH CONTAINER LOOKING FOR MY GARBAGE. AFTER I FOUND IT, I PUT IT IN THE BURNABLE GARBAGE CONTAINER. IT TOOK ME 15 MINUTES. IT WAS SO STINKY...
RESPECT THE EARTH.
TWO DAYS OF SWEAT...
I WOKE UP COVERED IN SWEAT.
I THINK I MIGHT BE SICK.
HE HAS A VERY WEAK CONSTITUTION, SO I'M ALWAYS WORRIED ABOUT HIM.
ARE YOU OK?
I WORRY HE WON'T FINISH HIS WORK.
*THE GENIUS IS VERY THIN.
THEN I NOTICED THAT...
I ADMIT IT WAS MY FAULT, SINCE I LEFT IT THAT WAY...
HE SLEPT RIGHT ON TOP OF...
...THE FUTON DRYER.
FUTON COMFORTER
BLANKET
FUTON
FUTON DRYER
OKAY, IF HE WANTS TO USE A BLANKET INSTEAD OF SHEETS, THAT'S FINE WITH ME, BUT... HOW COULD HE NOT NOTICE THAT HE WAS SLEEPING ON THE DRYER FOR TWO WHOLE DAYS? SLEEPING ON TOP OF A FUTON DRYER IS LIKE SLEEPING IN A SAUNA.
EVEN THE HEALTHIEST PERSON WOULD WAKE UP COVERED IN SWEAT.
AFTER HE WENT HOME...
AFTER THE GENIUS LEFT, I CLEANED UP THE AREA AROUND HIS DESK.
I NOTICED THAT HIS ASHTRAY WAS KIND OF STICKING OUT. WHEN I LIFTED IT UP...
I FOUND...
A DEMO TAPE FROM THE BAND "GLAY" THAT I'D HAD FOR TEN YEARS.
HE'D BEEN PUTTING OUT HIS BURNING CIGARETTES ON TOP OF MY TAPE.
DANCE VISION
*THE TAPE WAS FROM BEFORE JIRO HAD JOINED THE BAND. I THINK HE JOINED RIGHT AFTER IT WAS MADE.
WELL, I WAS FRIENDS WITH AKIRA AND NOBUMASA FROM THE BAND.
THE BAND MEMBERS HAD GIVEN IT TO ME WHEN I WAS WORKING PART TIME IN A RECORDING STUDIO. I KEPT IT AROUND BECAUSE IT HAD A LOT OF SENTIMENTAL VALUE...
HE BROKE THE TAPE.
I SHOULD'VE JUST GIVEN IT TO ONE OF THEIR FANS.

*I DON'T KNOW ANY OF THE CURRENT MEMBERS OF "GLAY."

BUT HE PUTS UP WITH ME EVEN THOUGH I'M REALLY MOODY. HE'S A REALLY GREAT GUY, AND HIS GIRLFRIEND IS CUTE TOO.

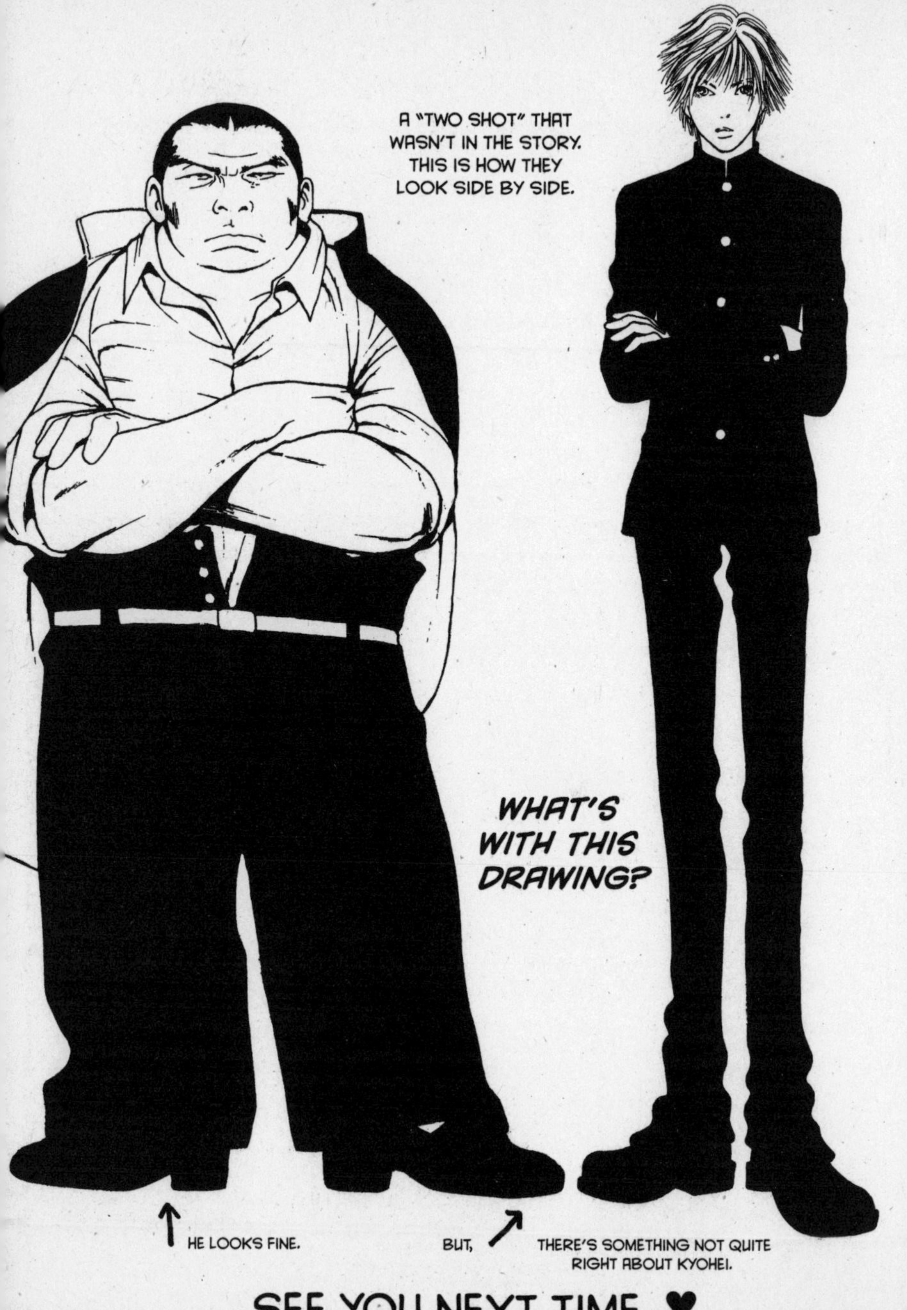
A "TWO SHOT" THAT WASN'T IN THE STORY. THIS IS HOW THEY LOOK SIDE BY SIDE.
WHAT'S WITH THIS DRAWING?
HE LOOKS FINE.
BUT,
THERE'S SOMETHING NOT QUITE RIGHT ABOUT KYOHEI.
SEE YOU NEXT TIME. ♥

About the Creator

Tomoko Hayakawa was born on March 4.

Since her debut as a manga creator, Tomoko Hayakawa has worked on many shojo titles with the theme of romantic love—only to realize that she could write about other subjects as well. She decided to pack her newest story with the things she likes most, which led to her current, enormously popular series, *The Wallflower*.

Her favorite things are: Tim Burton's *The Nightmare Before Christmas*, Jean-Paul Gaultier, and samurai dramas on TV. Her hobbies are collecting items with skull designs and watching *bishonen* (beautiful boys). Her dream is to build a mansion like the one that the Addams family lives in. Her favorite pastime is to lie around at home with her cat, Ten (whose full name is Tennosuke).

Her zodiac sign is Pisces, and her blood group is AB.

Honorifics

Throughout the Del Rey Manga books, you will find Japanese honorifics left intact in the translations. For those not familiar with how the Japanese use honorifics, and more important, how they differ from American honorifics, we present this brief overview.

Politeness has always been a critical facet of Japanese culture. Ever since the feudal era, when Japan was a highly stratified society, use of honorifics—which can be defined as polite speech that indicates relationship or status—has played an essential role in the Japanese language. When addressing someone in Japanese, an honorific usually takes the form of a suffix attached to one's name (example: "Asuna-san"), or as a title at the end of one's name or in place of the name itself (example: "Negi-sensei," or simply "Sensei!").

Honorifics can be expressions of respect or endearment. In the context of manga and anime, honorifics give insight into the nature of the relationship between characters. Many translations into English leave out these important honorifics, and therefore distort the "feel" of the original Japanese. Because Japanese honorifics contain nuances that English honorifics lack, it is our policy at Del Rey not to translate them. Here, instead, is a guide to some of the honorifics you may encounter in Del Rey Manga.

-san: This is the most common honorific, and is equivalent to Mr., Miss, Ms., Mrs., etc. It is the all-purpose honorific and can be used in any situation where politeness is required.

-sama: This is one level higher than "-san" and it is used to confer great respect.

-dono: This comes from the word "tono," which means "lord." It is an even higher level than "-sama," and confers utmost respect.

-kun: This suffix is used at the end of boys' names to express familiarity or endearment. It is also sometimes used by men among friends, or when addressing someone younger or of a lower station.

-chan: This is used to express endearment, mostly toward girls. It is also used for little boys, pets, and even among lovers. It gives a sense of childish cuteness.

Bozu: This is an informal way to refer to a boy, similar to the English term "kid" or "squirt."

Sempai: This title suggests that the addressee is one's "senior" in a group or organization. It is most often used in a school setting, where underclassmen refer to their upperclassmen as "sempai." It can also be used in the workplace, such as when a newer employee addresses an employee who has seniority in the company.

Kohai: This is the opposite of "sempai," and is used toward underclassmen in school or newcomers in the workplace. It connotes that the addressee is of lower station.

Sensei: Literally meaning "one who has come before," this title is used for teachers, doctors, or masters of any profession or art.

[blank]: Usually forgotten in these lists, but perhaps the most significant difference between Japanese and English. The lack of honorific means that the speaker has permission to address the person in a very intimate way. Usually, only family, spouses, or very close friends have this kind of permission. Known as *yobisute*, it can be gratifying when someone who has earned the intimacy starts to call one by one's name without an honorific. But when that intimacy hasn't been earned, it can be very insulting.

Translation Notes

Japanese is a tricky language for most Westerners, and translation is often more art than science. For your edification and reading pleasure, here are notes on some of the places where we could have gone in a different direction in our translation of the work, or where a Japanese cultural reference is used.

The Yukata, page 43

A yukata is a special casual kimono often worn at resorts.

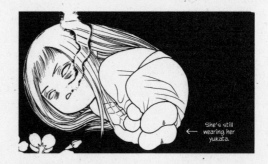

She's still wearing her yukata.

Kato-Chan and Kuroyume, page 46

(*See* "Behind the Scenes.") Kato-Chan is a comedian who sometimes wears funny, black-rimmed glasses. Kuroyume is a band.

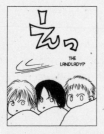

THE LANDLADY?

Obasan, page 48

This is similar to the predicament that occurs in Book 1. Ranmaru is actually saying "Obasan?" or "Landlady?", and the guys are saying "Huh?" It's been tweaked so that it sounds less awkward in English.

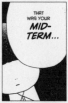

THAT WAS YOUR MID-TERM...

Chuukan Test, page 50

In panel 4, the teacher actually says, "That was your chuukan test." Chuukan means mid-term, but chuu means kiss. When Sunako hears the word chuu, she is reminded of Kyohei's kiss.

Chuu Chuu, page 64

The mice are actually saying "Chuu chuu," which sounds like a mouse noise but also means kiss. It's similar to the "Chuukan test" joke above.

KISSY, KISSY.
YOINK ぴょこ

WHO CARES IF SHE SUCKS AT MATH.
SHE'S GOOD AT SO MANY OTHER THINGS.
EVERYTHING EXCEPT FOR MATH.
I PREFER COOKING JAPANESE FOOD.

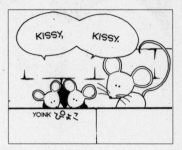

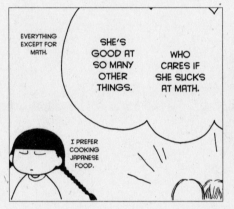

Western food, page 81

Fried shrimp and deep fried foods in general are considered Western foods in Japan. Sunako actually says "I am not good at cooking western style food."

The Answer Sheet, page 82

In Japanese classes, students do their work on a separate problem sheet and only hand in the answer sheet.

SU-SUNAKO-CHAN.
YOU WROTE YOUR WORK DOWN ON THE PROBLEM SHEET, RIGHT?
LET ME SEE IT.

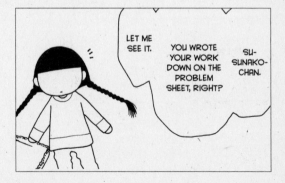

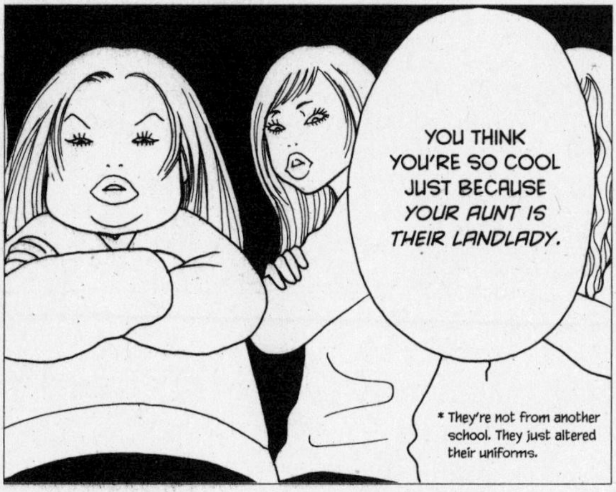
YOU THINK YOU'RE SO COOL JUST BECAUSE YOUR AUNT IS THEIR LANDLADY.
* They're not from another school. They just altered their uniforms.

School Uniforms, page 93

In Japan, each school has its own uniform. Some kids alter their uniforms by shortening their skirts.

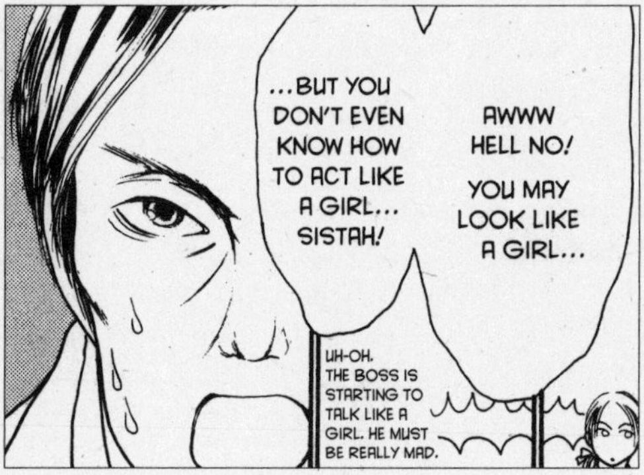
AWWW HELL NO!
YOU MAY LOOK LIKE A GIRL...
...BUT YOU DON'T EVEN KNOW HOW TO ACT LIKE A GIRL... SISTAH!
UH-OH. THE BOSS IS STARTING TO TALK LIKE A GIRL. HE MUST BE REALLY MAD.

The Boss, page 146

The Boss, although male, is using feminine Japanese phrases that suggest he is either gay or just acting very feminine.

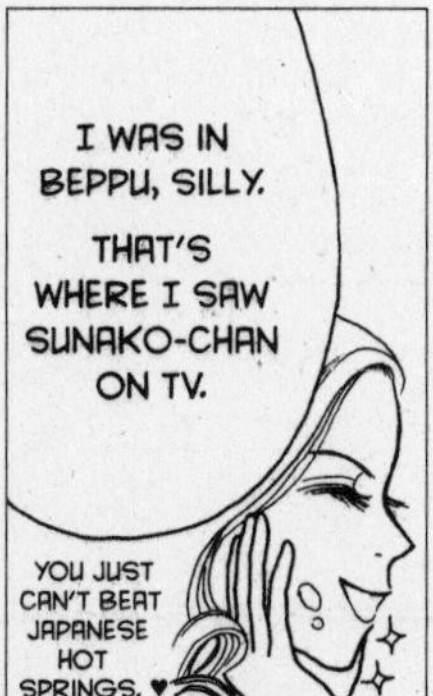
I WAS IN BEPPU, SILLY.
THAT'S WHERE I SAW SUNAKO-CHAN ON TV.
YOU JUST CAN'T BEAT JAPANESE HOT SPRINGS. ♥

Beppu, page 158

Beppu is a famous hot springs resort in southern Japan.

Jean Paul Gaultier, page 164

(See note of thanks from Tomoko Hayakawa.) Jean Paul Gaultier is a designer.

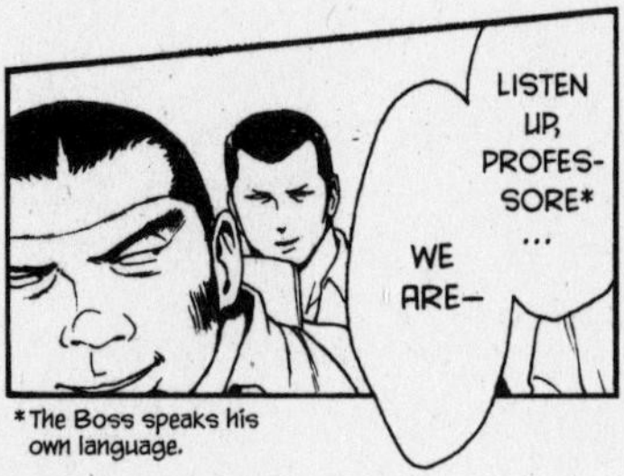
LISTEN UP, PROFES-SORE* ...
WE ARE—
*The Boss speaks his own language.

Senkou, page 168

The Boss actually says, "Senkou," which is an old '80s Japanese slang term for "Teacher." It's so old that it sounds funny.

Gekimabu, page 171

The gangster actually says that Noi is "gekimabu." This comes from the word "mabui," which was a slang term for "beautiful" from the '80s.

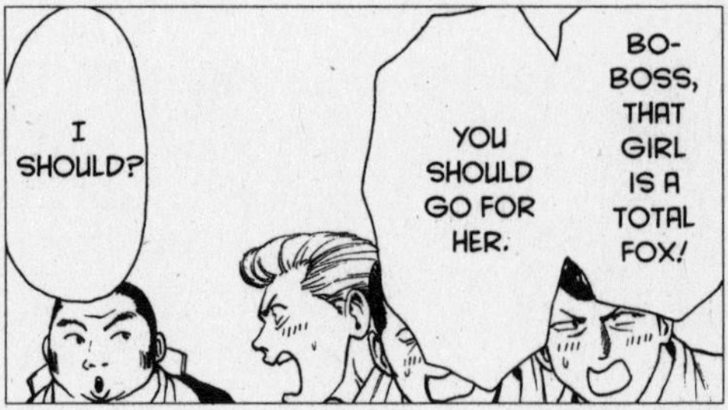
BO-BOSS, THAT GIRL IS A TOTAL FOX!
YOU SHOULD GO FOR HER.
I SHOULD?

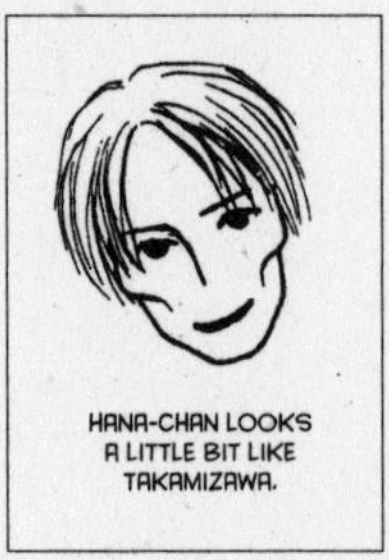
HANA-CHAN LOOKS A LITTLE BIT LIKE TAKAMIZAWA.

Takamizawa, page 204

Takamizawa is a musician from the band "The Alfee."

HOWEVER...
CLUELESS
THERE WAS NO BURNABLE TRASH CONTAINER, SO I JUST PUT IT IN THE NON-BURNABLE TRASH.
YEAH, RIGHT.
NOOOO!
AFTER THAT, I HAD TO GO THROUGH THE TRASH.
IS THAT A CRIME?
(IN OUR NEIGHBORHOOD, WE ARE STILL ALLOWED TO USE BLACK TRASH BAGS.) I WENT THROUGH THE NON-BURNABLE TRASH CONTAINER LOOKING FOR MY GARBAGE. AFTER I FOUND IT, I PUT IT IN THE BURNABLE GARBAGE CONTAINER. IT TOOK ME 15 MINUTES. IT WAS SO STINKY...
RESPECT THE EARTH.

To Burn or not to Burn, page 204

In Japan, garbage must be separated into burnable and non-burnable garbage.

Garbage Bags, page 204

The use of black garbage bags is forbidden in many parts of Japan. Clear garbage bags are used instead.

Preview of Volume 4

We're pleased to present you a preview from Volume 4. This volume will be available in English on June 28, 2005, but for now you'll have to make do with Japanese!

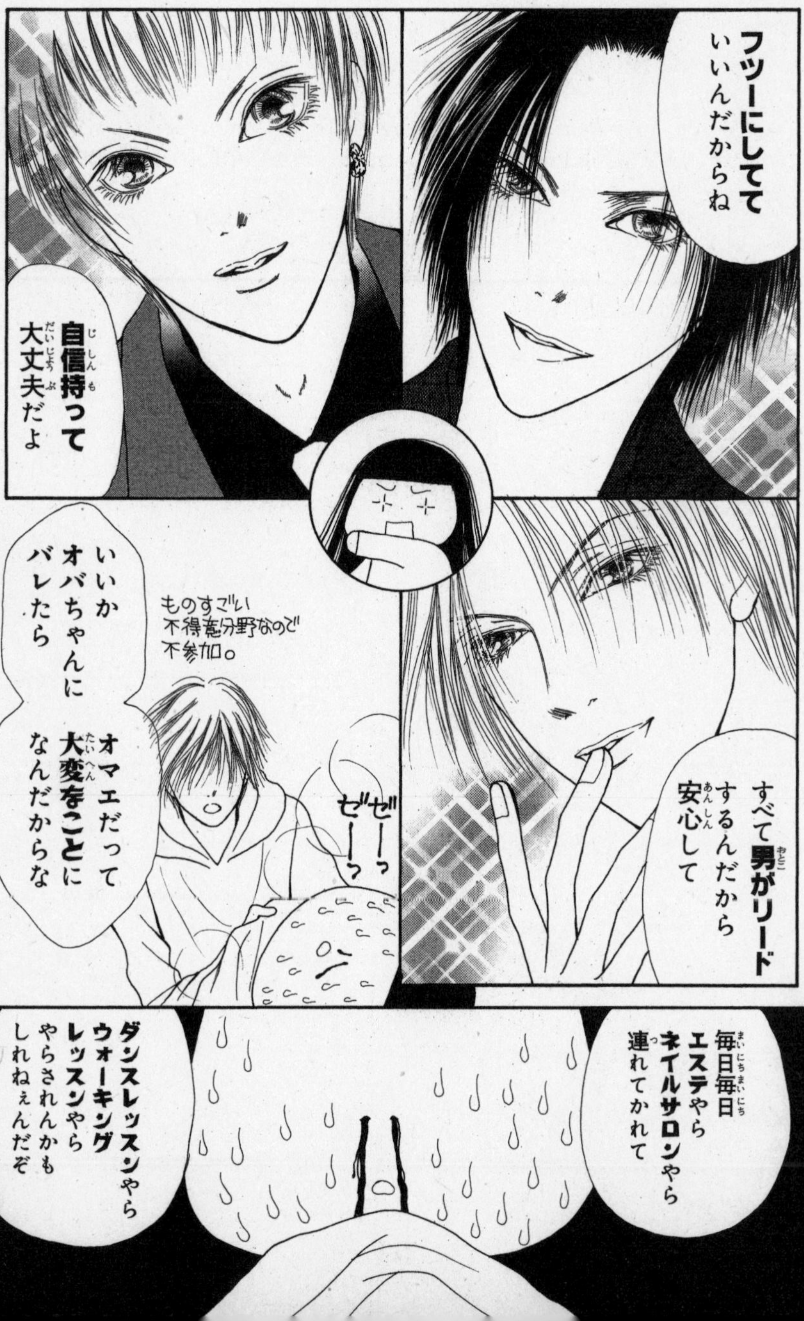
フツーにしてて いいんだからね
自信持って 大丈夫だよ
すべて男がリード するんだから 安心して
いいか オバちゃんに バレたら オマエだって 大変なことに なんだからな
ものすごい 不得意分野なので 不参加。
ぜーっ ぜーっ
毎日毎日 エステやら ネイルサロンやら 連れてかれて
ダンスレッスンやら ウォーキング レッスンやら やらされんかも しれねぇんだぞ

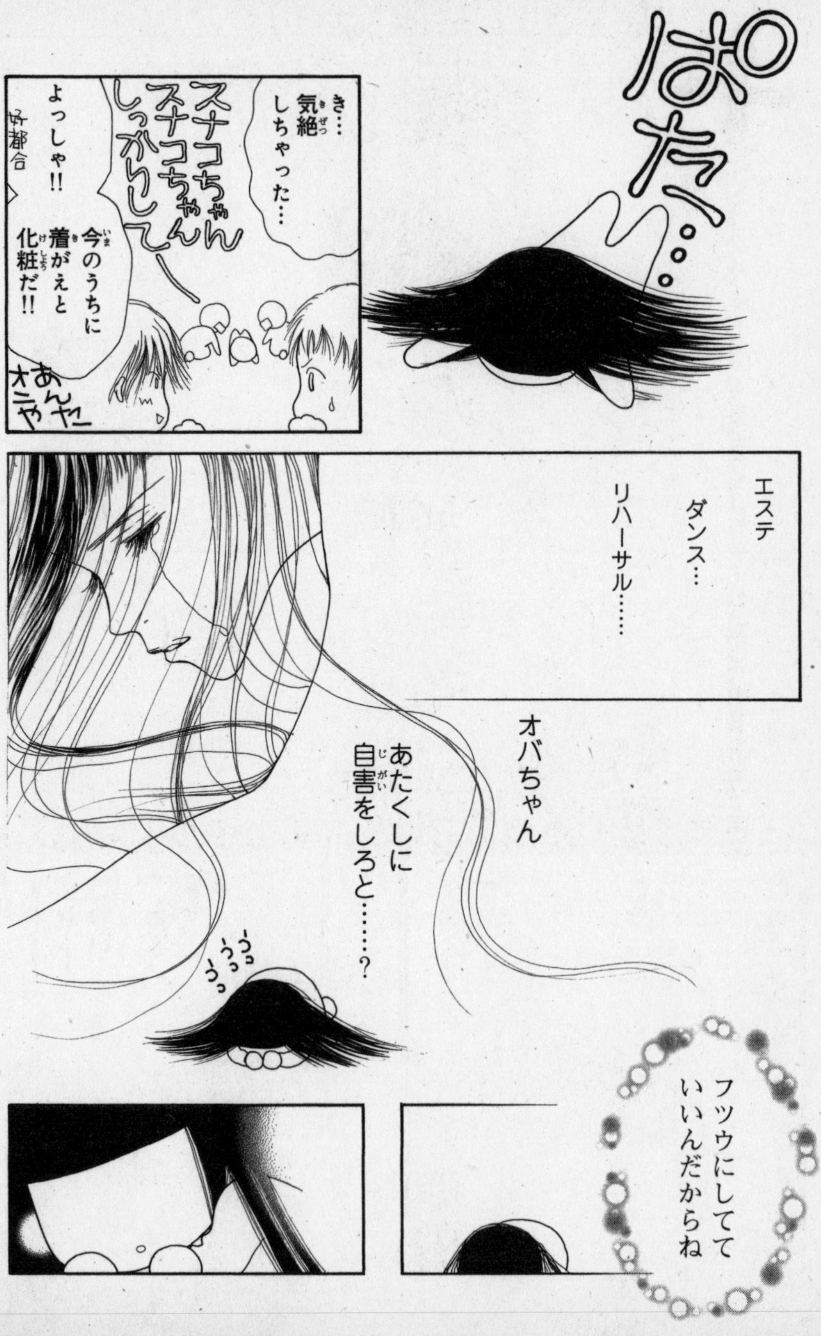
ぱた～ん…
き…気絶しちゃった…
スナコちゃんスナコちゃんしっかりして～
よっしゃ!! 今のうちに着がえと化粧だ!!
好都合
エステ
ダンス…
リハーサル……
オバちゃん
あたくしに自害をしろと……?
うっうっうっ
フツウにしてていいんだからね

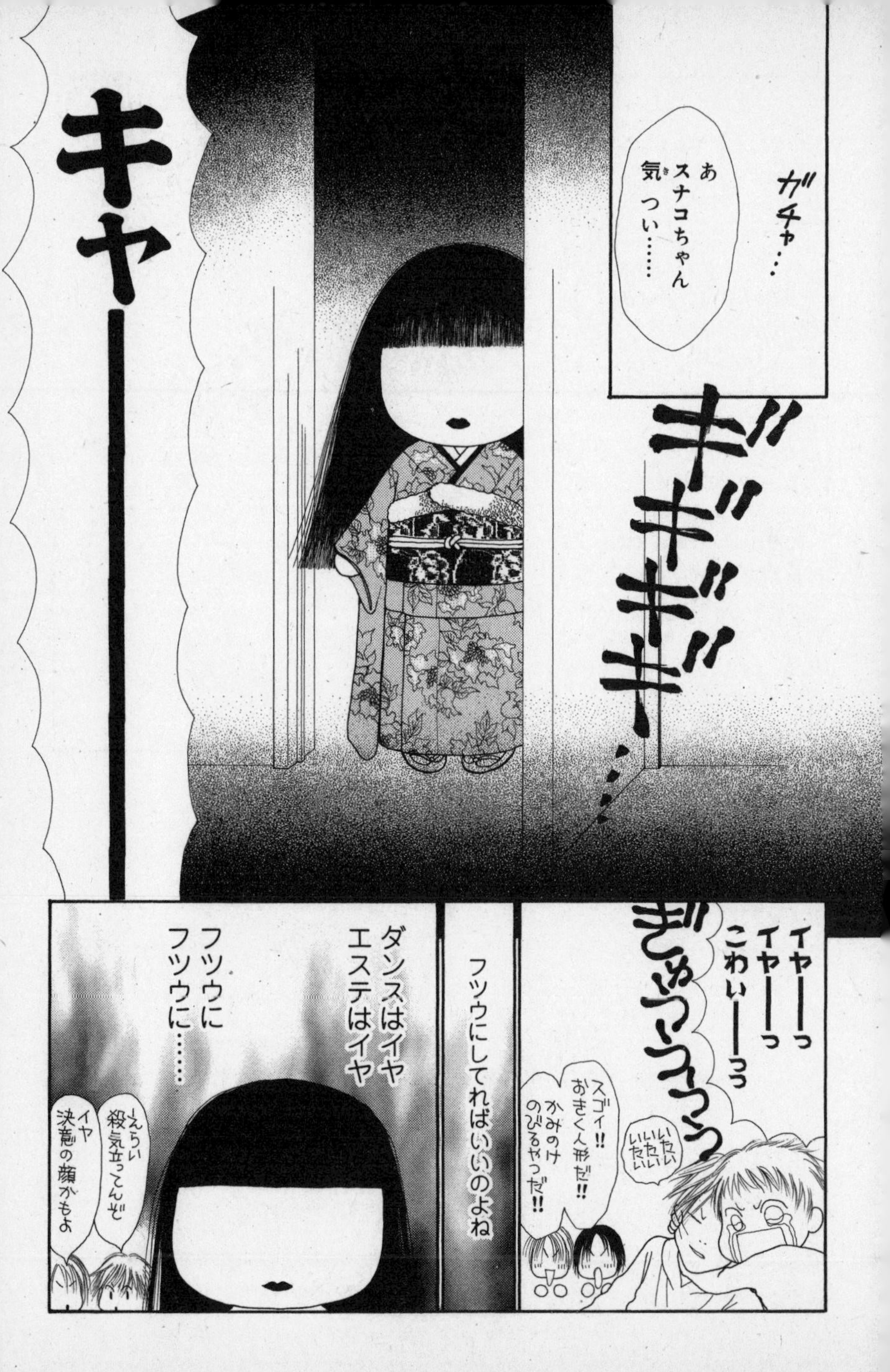
ガチャ…
あ
スナコちゃん
気つい……
ギギギギ…
キャー
ぎゅうううう
イヤーっ
イヤーっ
こわいーっっ
いたい
いたい
いたい
スゴイ!!
おきく人形だ!!
かみのけのびるやつだ!!
フツウにしてればいいのよね
ダンスはイヤ
エステはイヤ
フツウに
フツウに……
えらい殺気立ってんぞ
イヤ
決意の顔かもよ

Guru Guru Pon-Chan

VOLUME 1

BY SATOMI IKEZAWA

1
Guru Guru Pon-Chan
SATOMI IKEZAWA Creator of *Othello!*

Ages 13+

Ponta is a normal Labrador retriever puppy, the Koizumi family's pet. Full of energy, she is always up to some kind of trouble. However, when Grandpa Koizumi, a passionate amateur inventor, creates the "Guru Guru Bone," which empowers animals with human speech, Ponta turns into a human girl!

Surprised but undaunted, Ponta ventures out of the house and meets Mirai Iwaki, the most popular boy at school. Saved by Mirai from a speeding car, Ponta reverts to her normal puppy self. Yet much has changed for Ponta during her short adventure as a human. Her heart throbs and her face flushes when she thinks of Mirai now. She is in love! Using the power of the "Guru Guru Bone," Ponta switches back and forth from dog to human, but can she win Mirai's love?

WINNER OF THE KODANSHA MANGA OF THE YEAR AWARD!

Includes special extras after the story!

VOLUME 1: On sale July 26, 2005

DEL REY

For more information and to sign up for Del Rey's manga e-newsletter, visit www.delreymanga.com

VOLUME 3

BY SATOMI IKEZAWA

Timid Yaya is the victim of every bully in school, but she has a secret kept even from herself: She has another personality named Nana, who is all too willing to kick butt. While nice-guy guitarist Moriyama begins a tentative romance with Yaya, the constant appearances of brash Nana reveal the truth about his would-be girlfriend. And soon Moriyama's charismatic professional-musician friend Shôhei takes too much of an interest in Nana's killer singing voice...and body! Can Nana resist the very man Yaya has idealized all her life?!

VOLUME 3: On sale March 29, 2005 • VOLUME 4: On sale June 28, 2005

For more information and to sign up for Del Rey's manga e-newsletter, visit www.delreymanga.com

TOMARE!

止まれ

[STOP!]

You're going the wrong way!

Manga is a completely different type of reading experience.

To start at the *beginning*, go to the *end*!

That's right! Authentic manga is read the traditional Japanese way—from right to left. Exactly the *opposite* of how American books are read. It's easy to follow: Just go to the other end of the book, and read each page—and each panel—from right side to left side, starting at the top right. Now you're experiencing manga as it was meant to be!